The Power in Your Hands:

Writing Nonfiction in High School

2nd Edition

D1702618

Companion volume for this course:

The Power in Your Hands: Writing Nonfiction in High School, 2nd Edition, Teacher's Guide

Other Courses by Sharon Watson:

Jump In: A Workbook for Reluctant and Eager Writers (middle school)
Writing Fiction [in High School]: Bringing Your Stories to Life!
Illuminating Literature: When Worlds Collide

E-Books by Sharon Watson

Let's Eat Fifi: Commas, Word Usage, and Other Goofy Essentials of Grammar
What's Your Secret? Middle School Writing Prompts
What Are You Waiting For? High School Writing Prompts
Holiday-Themed Writing Prompts (middle and high school)
Teach Your Students How to Take Notes (junior and senior high)
Unlock the Secrets of Compare-and-Contrast Writing (senior high)

The Power in Your Hands:

Writing Nonfiction in High School

2nd Edition

Sharon Watson

WritingWithSharonWatson.com

The Power in Your Hands: Writing Nonfiction in High School, 2nd Edition

ISBN-13: 978-1519417763
ISBN-10: 1519417764

Companion volume for this course:
The Power in Your Hands: Writing Nonfiction in High School, 2nd Edition, Teacher's Guide

Printed in the United States of America

First printing January 2016

The David and Goliath chart in chapter 17 was previously published in *Unlock the Secrets of Compare-and-Contrast Writing* e-Book.

Some of the material in chapter 18 was previously published in *Writing Fiction [in High School]* by Sharon Watson.

Some of the grammar tutorials in chapter 10 were previously published on http://writingwithsharonwatson.com.

Special thanks to Matt and Tanya for being such great models and to all the wonderful students who contributed their homework to the cause!

Cover photo and internal icon photos © Esther Moulder, www.clickphotography.biz.

Material in examples written by students is for teaching purposes only and is not deemed to be accurate.

WritingWithSharonWatson.com

Dedicated
with deepest gratitude
to the memory of these inspiring teachers:

Pauline Davidson
Dorothy Broadwell
Caesar Struglia

Table of Contents

Part 1: Before You Write

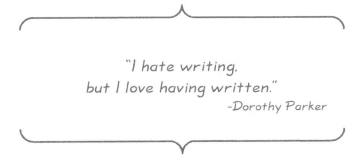

*"I hate writing,
but I love having written."*
-Dorothy Parker

Chapter 1: Thinking & Planning

Lesson 1

Some people say that writing is a mystery, that there are no rules, and that it is all subjective. You may be glad to know that those people are wrong.

Sure, what we *like* about the written word is subjective. Some readers enjoy fantasy or adventure novels while others prefer a thrilling article about last night's ball game or the latest scoop on fashions. But professional and school writing follow definite patterns and guidelines that are objective and measurable. Writers use specific tools to help them create newspaper articles, travel brochures, and riveting biographies. You can, too.

> WARNING: Cheesy analogy ahead. Proceed at your own risk. And bring tortilla chips and maybe some salsa.

Learning to write is like learning to cook. The amateur cook learns to use the kitchen equipment, combine the ingredients, and follow a recipe. In the same way, writers learn how to use their tools (parallelism, the thesaurus, similes, cheesy analogies, the Fog Index, proofreading skills, and so forth); combine ingredients like introductions, topic sentences, various paragraph types, and conclusions; and follow the recipe of specific structures for each type of writing.

When you combine the methods and tools in this course with the skills you will develop from practicing them, you will be unbeatable. Or at least hard to catch up with.

You will learn how to correct your own work, too, using an objective set of criteria. In addition, because of all your practice, you will develop a gut instinct about the quality of your own writing.

Your Writing Self

You may love the objectivity of writing reports; research and facts give you a thrill. Or maybe the challenge of creating an imaginative story excites you, but reports leave you baffled. This is perfectly normal. Not every student is good at every type of writing. It is a rare student that excels in both research papers and storytelling. Those are two separate writing skills and involve varying personalities and different areas of the brain.

Be aware of the conditions that help you write best. Why write early in the morning when you think best late at night?

Many things about writing are hard. Find out what makes writing a chore for you and in what circumstances it becomes easier. Understanding your writing self will help you strengthen your weaknesses and build your strengths.

Find your writing self in the following descriptions. Check all that apply to you:

❑ I like to write only about topics that are interesting to me.

❑ Writing stories is much more fun than writing reports and essays.

❑ I would rather walk across a burning desert at high noon with buzzards circling overhead while I drag a bone-dry water bottle than write anything whatsoever.

❑ It's hard for me to know how to begin and end my essays or reports.

❑ Writing is easier if it is very quiet around me.

❑ Research is interesting.

❑ I have trouble coming up with good ideas.

❑ Late at night is the best time to write.

❑ Writing by hand is pure torture, but writing at the keyboard is a little easier.

❑ It's hard to think of enough points or reasons for my assignments.

❑ When something interesting happens to me, I like to write it down.

❑ I like to try to change someone's mind with my writing.

❑ I have sloppy handwriting and/or bad spelling seils skylls skills.

❑ I can't find enough information to finish a paper.

❑ I write best when I'm with friends or listening to music.

❑ I don't care one way or the other about writing.

❑ The ideas are in my head, but I can't make them come out and sound right on paper.

❑ I make lists and like to take notes; they help me remember sermons and lectures.

❑ I have many ideas for writing, and I keep them in a notebook so I can use them later.
❑ I don't like to research. It's tedious.
❑ If I'm not interested in the topic, I have trouble doing the assignment.
❑ I need a lot of time to think about the assignment before I begin to write.
❑ Finding a topic I'm interested in is hard.
❑ Forget everything else—let me write stories.
❑ I would like to know how to write better.
❑ You gotta be kidding. Checking this box is enough writing for me for one day.
❑ Feeling the pencil or pen on the paper helps me write better.
❑ I like playing with words and finding just the right one.
❑ I don't mind writing essays and reports, but I have trouble writing interesting stories.

Do you identify with any of those statements?

If you do not, please jot in the margin a statement or two about what is true for you about writing.

No matter what your attitude or proficiency, you will learn enough guidelines and tools and read enough examples in this course to help you improve your writing abilities. If you apply what you learn here, you will develop practical writing skills you can use anywhere for the rest of your life.

Lesson 2

The Planning Phase

BE ADVISED: The rest of this chapter may be TOO EASY if you are an **intermediate** or **accomplished** writer! You may already know the material. Hang in there. New stuff is on the way.

Some brief definitions are in order before we proceed . . .

Beginning writer: one who has not had much experience writing for school.
Intermediate writer: one who has written some essays for school but has not had much experience in the different types of writing (persuasion, exposition, description, and narration).
Accomplished writer: one who has written many kinds of essays and reports in high school and is preparing for college and/or professional writing.

Now back to your regularly scheduled lesson.

You wouldn't build a dog house without planning it first. The same is true for writing: Before you write, plan.

And part of planning, for a writer, is the tool of **brainstorming.**

 Brainstorming helps you think. It means writing down ideas in a spontaneous, free-flowing manner, which is an essential tool for any writer. This is not the time to evaluate your ideas or hold them back. Just write them quickly and evaluate them later. Often a silly idea will lead to a usable one.

When your teacher gives you a broad topic, brainstorm. Make a list of ideas you can write about within the topic. If the teacher's topic is ecology, you have dozens of options. You could write about any of the following narrowed-down topics and still be in the general topic of ecology: recycling, the effect of a natural disaster on an area's ecology, toxic waste clean-ups, or a person who had an impact on how we think about conservation. If you have trouble thinking of ideas, ask a friend, classmate, or parent for ideas or go to a book on the subject and read the chapter headings.

Brainstorming can be effective—and more fun—when done with others. Many times you'll glean an idea from a brainstorming session with friends or classmates that you might not have thought of alone.

Try brainstorming with the brightness turned down on your computer screen; that's one weird way to gather ideas without immediately evaluating them. When you're through, turn the brightness back up and ponder your possibilities. And your spelling mistakes.

By now you may have thought of specific topics within the general topic of ecology. Write at least two ideas in the space below. If you get stuck, talk to others or consult a book on the subject for more ideas. Discuss your topics with your teacher. You will not be writing this as a report. This is just for practice—so have fun with it.

Practice 1.1

And the lesson continues . . .

The Trick to Finding a Topic

There is a trick to writing anything: find a topic that interests you. Writing about recycling may bore you to tears, but writing about saving eagles may capture your attention. When you have the chance to choose your topic, find an interesting angle and concentrate on that.

If your topic is chosen for you, hunt around until you find something about that topic that makes you tingle. It could be an electrifying finger-in-the-socket tingle or only a kids' carnival-ride sensation, but search for the thing that moves you. For instance, perhaps you have to write about World War II, but you usually give wars a yawn in history class. It now becomes your job to read about that war in order to find something that warms your blood or fires your imagination. Perhaps acts of heroism inspire you, or you may find that because one side won, your grandparents immigrated to another country. Maybe spy stories, POW (prisoner of war) facts, or stories of the Navajo Code Talkers fascinate you. Search for the interesting angle and follow it.

A bored student often produces a boring paper, and, let me tell you, your teacher already has enough boring papers to read. Let your paper be the one that shines. You just might make the writing experience more fun for yourself, as well.

Practice 1.2

Choose a topic that is too broad or that is of no interest to you. Write it on a clean piece of paper, the back of an envelope, the inside of an old cereal box, whatever. Then brainstorm different facets of that topic narrow it down or to find something of interest in it.

Be spontaneous with your ideas and don't criticize them. Identify something worth writing about in that too-broad or too-boring topic. Discuss your results with your teacher. You will not be writing this for a report; just take your ideas out for a joyride. To use a colorful worksheet on the benefits of bike riding, go to http://writingwithsharonwatson.com/benefits-of-bike-riding-brainstorm-and-organize/ .

"You can't wait for inspiration.
You have to go after it with a club."

- Jack London

Chapter 2: Opinions

Lesson 1

Opinions are the doorway to persuasive writing, so let's stand on the porch for a few moments and talk about your opinions.

In the first chapter, you learned the trick of finding a topic that fires up your brain. The same is true for writing opinions. Choose something about which you have strong feelings, whether positive or negative. Writing is less painful if there is some intensity behind it.

Writing your opinion includes stating what you like—or don't like—and then listing why. Perhaps you like gardening because you can control the herbicides and pesticides applied to the plants, you like grubbing around in the soil, and you enjoy the fresh taste of newly picked garden vegetables. Or maybe you cannot stand gardening because weeding is sweaty and tedious work, you grow more rocks than vegetables, and you don't even like vegetables.

Moving your opinion from a statement to a whole essay requires some finesse. The next sections will show you how to shape your paper.

SMUG ALERT: **Intermediate** and **accomplished** writers will already be familiar with the material in The Structure of an Essay, coming up next. Treat it as a quick review.

The Structure of an Essay

All nonfiction papers follow a certain format. They begin with an introductory paragraph, add *at least* three paragraphs for points or reasons, and end with a paragraph for a conclusion. That's the simple structure for any essay or report. It looks something like this (each rectangle represents a separate paragraph):

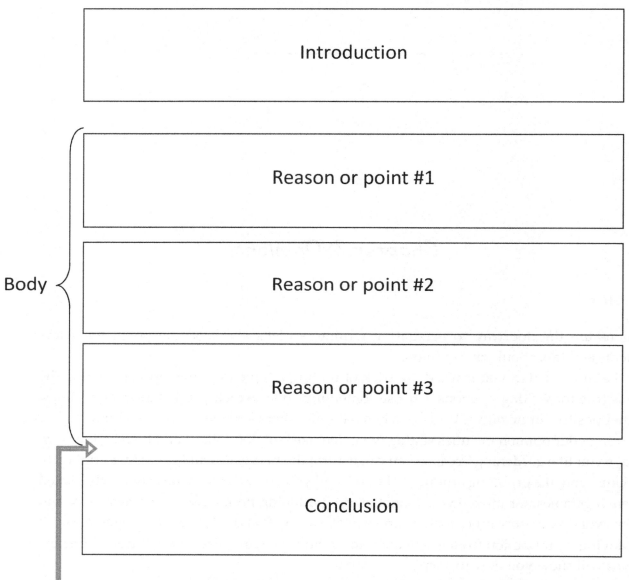

Additional paragraphs are needed here if you have more than three points or if your points are detailed and need more than one paragraph each.

Of course, the first sentence in each paragraph is **indented three to five spaces**. Long reports or an in-depth treatment of a topic may require two or more paragraphs for an introduction. Each paragraph in the body develops only one main point, as stated in the topic sentence (more on topic sentences in chapter 3). For beginning writers, one paragraph = one point. Intermediate or accomplished writers may need more than one paragraph for a point.

> If you find that your essay is one long paragraph, fix it. Go back through your work and make separate paragraphs: one to introduce your topic, one for each point, and one to conclude your topic.

Do you sit around and agonize over that first sentence for your essay? Agonize no more. Begin in the middle—the points or reasons, more commonly known as the **body**. The bulk of your paper is the body, so it makes sense to start there.

What about the thesis statement? Aren't you supposed to develop that before you can write anything?

If you know how to develop and use a thesis statement, go ahead and begin writing the introduction. If you have no idea what a thesis statement is yet, don't worry about it. You will learn soon enough. In the meantime, simply begin writing in the middle—your points— and add an introduction and conclusion that fit your points later.

Practice 2.1

On a separate piece of paper, use one sentence to state your opinion of teens owning credit cards. Write it in sentence form. Then make a list of at least five reasons why you hold this opinion. You may be able to think of plausible reasons for *and* against, but for this practice, please **choose a definite side**.

Lesson 2

Your Toolbox: Point Orders, part 1

Every profession needs tools, even the writing profession. This course includes many useful tools to make you a more knowledgeable and polished writer. You've already learned the brainstorming tool.

Today's tool is **point order**. When you brainstorm, you write ideas as they come to you. That's good. That's how to brainstorm. When it comes to planning the paragraphs, however, you will put your ideas in a rational order, with each reason getting at least one paragraph.

This course discusses six orders. A family of three orders is in this lesson, and the rest are in the next lesson.

The first order is a family or cluster of orders and is often called the **order of importance** or **emphatic order** ("emphatic" because the points are arranged according to their strength or emphasis). In this section, the words *strength*, *urgency*, *importance*, and *compelling* mean the same thing.

Inverted Triangle

A popular way to arrange points based on their importance or strength is the **inverted triangle:**

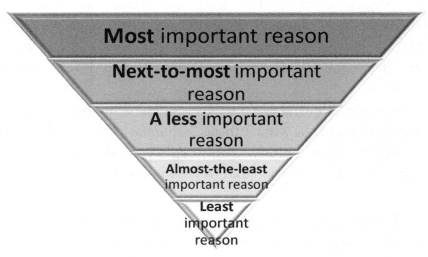

This example has five reasons. Your number of reasons may vary, but the line-up—from **most** compelling to **least** compelling—will remain the same when you use this order.

It would be easy to think that, because you are writing a "least important" reason, it can be wimpy, like overcooked broccoli. Not so. All of your reasons should be sparkling, brilliant, and awe inspiring.

Reporters typically use the above method (and they call it the *inverted triangle*) for two reasons: 1) they need to capture their readers' attention quickly, and 2) they are not in control of their article's final length. The editor can lop off the end of the article, depending on how much space is available on the newspaper page. So the reporter puts the most important information in the beginning of the article and arranges all the other points in descending order of importance. This order will come in handy for some of your own essays or papers, too.

How do you know which points are the most important? Sometimes it will be obvious; their strength will leap out at you. Other times you will decide which ones are the most compelling reasons based on your audience. If you're writing to children about the dangers of drinking too much sugary soda, your point about potential kidney problems will be in the "least compelling" category because children have difficulty grasping the idea of themselves in the future.

Point Orders

Importance or emphatic orders:
- Inverted triangle
- Psychological order
- Climactic order

Chronological order
Spatial order
Effect-size order
Specific-to-general order
General-to-specific order

Psychological Order

The **psychological order** belongs in the importance family (shaped like a strange hourglass):

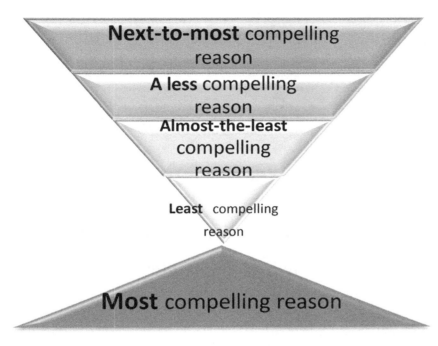

The psychological order takes into account that people often read the first and last reasons and only skim the middle ones.

This order is much like a band or choir concert. It begins with the second-best song the band or choir performs so the audience is wowed by the performers' expertise. At the end, the program delivers the best song, leaving no doubt of the band or choir's superior musical talent. Many professional writers sift through their facts and anecdotes to find one that has the most impact, and they save that for the last point, giving the biggest bang at the end. Readers are left with an indelible image.

Point Orders

Importance or emphatic orders:
- Inverted triangle
- **Psychological order**
- Climactic order

Chronological order
Spatial order
Effect-size order
Specific-to-general order
General-to-specific order

When you write the last and most important point in your essay using the psychological order, include a key phrase that will alert readers of its importance:

✓ But most important . . .
✓ Of greatest consequence . . .
✓ But nothing beats . . .
✓ Ultimately . . .
✓ It is of the utmost importance . . .

Avoid using the psychological order if you have only three reasons; it feels as if the middle drops out of the article, and your strongest reason will be diluted. Use it with four or more reasons or points.

Climactic Order

Another pattern belongs in this order-of-importance family. It's called the **climactic order**:

Least urgent reason

Next-to-least urgent reason

More urgent reason

Next-to-most urgent reason

Most urgent reason

Point Orders
Importance or emphatic orders:
- Inverted triangle
- Psychological order
- **Climactic order**
Chronological order
Spatial order
Effect-size order
Specific-to-general order
General-to-specific order

The climactic order builds from weakest to strongest, "weakest" being a relative term. The key phrases used in the psychological order work well in this one, too, as you work through to your most important reason.

Two other methods of arranging your points are worthy of mention here:

✓ Simplest to most complex
✓ Most familiar to least familiar

Choosing an appropriate order for your points makes the information easier to understand and assimilate. No reader wants to feel dizzy and confused, as though bouncing around in a pinball machine.

Below you'll find an opinion and four points to support it. Put numbers next to each point to indicate **most** important (1) to **least** important (4). Then decide which importance order will be most effective for this topic and write it in the margin.

Opinion: Cell phone usage while driving needs government regulation.

Reasons:

- Distracted drivers cause many accidents.
- Distractions such as talking on a cell phone or texting while driving cause drivers to miss turns or exits or make poor driving decisions.
- Accident fatalities involving cell phone usage are increasing.
- Many drivers are already multitasking. Cell phone usage puts this trend over the top.

Lesson 3

Your Toolbox: Point Orders, part 2

In addition to that great family of importance orders you learned about in your last lesson, you have other useful orders at your disposal.

Today's lesson covers these: chronological, spatial, effect size, specific-to-general, and general-to-specific.

Chronological

The **chronological order** recounts events in the order they occur, through time or history, and can be used to describe a process, like this:

- Long ago or first
- Sometime later or second
- Most recently or third

Point Orders

Importance or emphatic orders:
- Inverted triangle
- Psychological order
- Climactic order

Chronological order
Spatial order
Effect-size order
Specific-to-general order
General-to-specific order

Using the words "first," "second," "third," and so on can also be called the **sequential order**, which is very handy for instructions and process writing.

As for your opinion on why you shouldn't take out the garbage, you could use the chronological order like this:

Long ago: How taking out the garbage ruined my summer
Sometime later: How taking out the garbage ruined my first day at school
Most recently: How taking out the garbage ruined my plans yesterday

That's a silly example, but you get the idea. It tracks something through time. Writers are not limited to three points, as in the above example. The main thing is to move your topic through time, typically from long ago to most recent.

If you use the words *first, second, third,* and so on, it is tempting to slap an *ly* on the end: *firstly, secondly, thirdly, lastly.* But don't. Just stick with the plain ordinal numbers. (**Ord**inal, **ord**er—get it?) The same goes for *most importantly* when writing your last point; skip the *-ly* and write *most important.*

Spatial Order

While the chronological order moves readers through time, the **spatial** (SPAY-shul) **order** moves them through, well, space, as in a location or physical position. For instance, you might organize your points according to the following examples:

Point Orders
Importance or emphatic orders:
- Inverted triangle
- Psychological order
- Climactic order
Chronological order
Spatial order
Effect-size order
Specific-to-general order
General-to-specific order

Top to bottom (how to wash a car)
Bottom to top (how to make a pizza)
Left to right (describing a room)
Outside to inside (describing a person's appearance and then attributes)
East to west (showing the effect of a drought on regions of a nation)

Transitions are important when using the spatial order. "Behind," "to the right," "beneath her hard exterior," and "in the deep South" will give visual clues to readers and keep them tracking with your material.

Effect-size Order

Speaking of tracking with the material, don't wander off yet. Just three more organizational methods to go. Here's the **effect-size order**:

Point Orders
Importance or emphatic orders:
- Inverted triangle
- Psychological order
- Climactic order
Chronological order
Spatial order
Effect-size order
Specific-to-general order
General-to-specific order

Reason 1 affects a **small group** of people or has a small effect.
Reason 2 affects a **larger group** of people or has a larger effect.
Reason 3 affects the **largest number** of people or has the largest effect.

This order could easily be called the pond-ripple order, and here's why: When you drop a pebble (why is it always a pebble and not a cell phone?) into a pond, rings form. The first ring is small. The next ring is larger in diameter and farther from the entry point. The next ring is even larger and farther away, as effects become larger and larger.

Consider these examples of how to use the effect-size order:

"I bought candles from the fundraiser because..."

1—They make my room smell nice. [It affects me.]

2—I can give them away as gifts. [It affects a few other people.]

3—They were manufactured in my town, so I'm supporting the local economy. [It affects a whole community.]

This example happens to use three reasons. You may want to use more.

Note how the impact or the effect grew from small to large, from one person to a whole community. Consider how the effect-size order looks in your opinion of taking out the garbage:

1—How it affects me

2—How it affects my family

3—How it affects my neighborhood

World ® Dryers (manufacturers of hand dryers for public restrooms) uses the effect-size order in reverse when listing reasons for using their hand dryers:

1—Uses fewer trees [The effect is off in the distance somewhere.]

2—Reduces paper waste [The effect is getting closer.]

3—Is more sanitary to use and keeps the facility cleaner [The effect reached me.]

Not through yet. The lesson continues on the next pages.

Specific-to-general Order

This order, **specific to general**, arranges the points on the basis of how specific or how general they are. When writing about the advantages of owning an elephant, you could begin with very specific points and then move to the general ones. In other words, you move from reasons that are concrete or easy to pin down to reasons that are abstract or hard to define, as you'll see in the example here:

Specific

Reason 1: He could help us pick up large branches in the yard after a storm. [specific]

Reason 2: We could balance on his trunk to reach the guttering when we need to clean out the leaves. [specific]

Reason 3: He could be helpful by towing heavy things: the car when it breaks down or the team's float in the parade. [specific]

Reason 4: He could give all the neighbors and us rides. [specific]

Reason 5: We could never lose another tug-of-war game. [specific]

General

Reason 6: He could add to the family's feeling of togetherness as we feed and care for him, making him a family project. [general; you can't touch *togetherness*]

Reason 7: We could feel good about ourselves because we had worked to keep him out of a bleak zoo environment, giving him a home better suited to his needs. [general; *feeling good* is harder to define than *tug of war*]

The first five reasons are easy to pin down because they are concrete. Anyone can understand picking up sticks or pulling a parade float. The last two reasons are harder to visualize. They are abstract—family togetherness and feeling good about oneself.

The specific-to-general method of organizing works well if you are writing about something with which your audience is unfamiliar. Readers will grasp the specific and concrete (the Ford Mustang, hubcaps, and miles per gallon, for example) before moving to the general and abstract things (style, value, and efficiency).

And just when you thought it was safe, you find another order on the next page.

General-to-specific Order

Finally, the last point order! Given the simplicity of the specific-to-general order, why would anyone begin with abstract ideas and move to the concrete? Read this outline, written with the **general-to-specific order**, on the dangers of bingeing and purging to find out why:

Point Orders

Importance or emphatic orders:
- Inverted triangle
- Psychological order
- Climactic order

Chronological order

Spatial order

Effect-size order

Specific-to-general order

General-to-specific order

General

Specific

Reason 1: It keeps young women trapped on the roller coaster of self-gratification and self-denial. [general or abstract; you can't "see" *self-denial*]

Reason 2: Young women become stuck in an adolescent stage, never growing up into curvaceous and healthy womanhood. [general]

Reason 3: Constant vomiting eats away at the esophageal lining and tooth enamel. [specific or concrete]

Reason 4: It puts young women at risk for malnutrition and other dangerous health issues. [specific]

Reason 5: Bingeing and purging may result in death. [specific]

The general-to-specific order begins with general statements (the abstract ones) and finishes with specific, concrete ones. In this case, it gives the writer a chance to put the most important result of bingeing and purging—death—last. This emphasizes it and ends on a reason that is urgent.

Practice 2.3

To review the six point orders you learned about in this lesson and the previous one, write them here—in no particular order. The first order below is really a cluster of three. Then proceed to Practice 2.4.

1. Importance or emphatic order

    •

    •

    •

2.

3.

4.

5.

6.

Practice 2.4   In Practice 2.1, you wrote an opinion of teens owning credit cards and brainstormed reasons in the margin to support that opinion. Now it's time to put those reasons into a logical order. Choose an appropriate order and write its name in the blank. Then rearrange your top five reasons by that order. Explain your rationale to your teacher.

I choose this order: _____

1.

2.

3.

4.

5.

Lesson 4

The Introduction: Hooking Your Reader

When you've written a stellar essay about a topic you feel strongly about, how do you get the reader interested in it?

Professional Tip
You have **one paragraph** in which to capture your reader's attention. That is **less than one minute** of reading time.

Create an interest or curiosity in your topic by hooking your reader in the introduction. In fact, your first sentence or paragraph is called a **hook.**

Later in this lesson you will learn five very specific tools for hooking your reader. For now, though, think about choosing the right words or painting a vivid picture. As a high school writer, you are too old to begin an essay like this:

Horses are my favorite animal.

Instead, you will use well-placed words to indicate to the reader that your favorite animal is the horse:

> Nothing can match the steady rhythm of my horse as he gallops across the meadow. He carries me with him, and I feel the power of his sturdy body as we fly. For a few moments, I am riding a living, breathing magic carpet.

Underline the words in that example that tell the reader that the horse is this student's favorite animal. Notice that the writer tries to pull the reader into the experience instead of simply reporting an opinion. Keep in mind this more mature way of writing when you hit the keyboard.

Avoid telling the reader in the introduction what you eventually are going to tell him in your essay. Giving an audience a heads up may be a good tactic for speeches or sermons, but it bores and insults readers. This introductory paragraph is suitable for elementary school writing:

> I am going to write my opinion on why I like my youth choir. I like it because I love to sing, I enjoy the challenge of learning new and difficult songs, and I have the opportunity to travel to many cities and sing with other choirs.

That paragraph is a yawner. It does not create any interest or curiosity in the reader because it's only a dry list of what will follow in the paper. Younger students may have learned how to write this way; it aided them in organizing their thoughts. But you are too old for that now.

As an older student, you need more mature techniques. This introduction to an opinion is appropriate for high school writing:

> We file onto the dark stage and take our positions on the risers, trying to ignore the buzz from the audience on the other side of the curtain as we quietly hum our first measures over and over. The girl next to me hums her lines, too, and she throws me off. I clear my throat, unlock my knees, and wish I could look at my music just one more time. Beyond the curtain, I hear the director's shoes squeak across the stage as the audience quiets itself. Now the curtain is lifting. The audience is clapping. Above the noise, I try to hear the note from the pitch pipe. The baton moves. I take a deep breath. I wouldn't miss this concert for the world.

This scenario successfully uses descriptions to show the writer's love of the choir, and it creates some excitement and anticipation.

Here are five practical tools for beginning your **introductory paragraph** (or **introduction**). They're arranged below in a stunning display of palindromic beauty:

Q - An intriguing **question**
S - A thought-provoking **statement**
F - A shocking, tantalizing, or to-the-point **fact**
S - An engaging **story**
Q - A clever **quotation**

Choose one to begin each of your essays. Read the following examples of the above tools. Real students wrote some of them:

Question: Do *you* know the latest technological advance that affects you most?

Statement: Many parents today are raising pirates. [Written by a student on pirating songs from the Internet.]

Fact: Fifty children are diagnosed with autism every day, according to the Autism Society of America, and boys are affected more often than girls.

Story: Ben and Jodi have a teenage daughter who stays out too late partying and always comes home drunk. They feel that the only way to keep Mackenzie safe is to host the parties and take away the car keys belonging to her friends. Mackenzie agrees and often invites her friends over for a night of fun. Unfortunately, Mackenzie's family is not unusual.

Quotation: "If I had known how hard it would be to quit smoking, I never would have started," says Jodi Heffernan, a ninth-grader at Central High.

Practice 2.5   Earlier, you wrote your opinion of teens owning credit cards. Beside each tool, write a first sentence or two that is calculated to capture the interest of the reader. Invent a fact or make up a quotation if you need to (something you won't do in a real paper!). Then put a mark next to the tool you like the best for the topic of credit cards.

Question:

Statement:

Fact:

Story:

Quotation:

Now that you have practiced writing your own sentences, it is time to evaluate other students' sentences. Firstly—oops! *First*—label them according to which QSFSQ tool they used. Then give each hook a grade based on how much interest or curiosity it creates (even if you don't yet know what the topic is). Then read the introductory paragraph that follows.

Practice 2.6:
Do they make
the grade?

1. One of the most urgent problems in modern society is the growing shortage of petroleum.

2. Like a viper, he waits for his next victim to criticize.

3. You walk into a restaurant and smell the wonderful aroma of secondhand smoke, not the scent of steaks cooking.

4. Do you like to cook?

5. If I was hoping for a dull, tedious interview with George, I was going to be very disappointed.

6. How many car accidents are caused by intersections?

7. We cannot let them steal it all!

8. When he was three, he developed an ear infection that, undetected, resulted in a 75 percent hearing loss.

9. The art of annoyance is almost utterly lost in its true form, but in its pure, unsaturated form, it is a beauty to behold.

10. A volley of bullets ripped the air, colliding with the blue-coated men across the field.

Here's an introductory paragraph about recycling. It begins with a quotation that creates some curiosity for the topic. What grade would you give this paragraph? Write it in the margin.

"Only two human-made structures on Earth are large enough to be seen from outer space: the Great Wall of China and the Fresh Kills landfill, located on the western shore of Staten Island," according to justlivegreener.com. We are slowly destroying our planet. If we keep throwing stuff into landfills, we will eventually run out of space. The answer to this problem is simple. Reduce, reuse, and recycle.

Lesson 5

Conclusions: Finishing Strong

The **concluding paragraph** (the **conclusion**) is the last chance to have any effect at all on the reader. Devise a paragraph for the highest impact your topic requires. You can use the same tools that you used in the introduction: question, statement, fact, story, or quotation. Be creative; you can mix and match tools. Use one for the introduction and another for the conclusion, if you wish. Or begin a story in the introduction and finish it in the conclusion.

In addition, your conclusion will be stronger if you are mindful of the items in this list (elaborations follow the list):

1. Avoid recounting each point your essay just made.
2. Avoid introducing a new thought or point here.
3. Include a rewritten version of your main idea (in this case, your opinion).
4. If you can tie your conclusion to your introduction, do so.
5. Leave your reader with some food for thought and/or draw some insightful conclusions.

1) Avoid recounting each point your essay just made. Sermons and speeches use the conclusion to review, but this is tedious for readers of short reports or articles. If readers want to review written information, they can simply reread a section. Recapping or summing up is insulting to the reader and can leave the reading experience as flat as warm, day-old soda.

If your report or term paper is very long (a few thousand words or longer), you may consider recounting your points. But state them in a different manner than you stated them earlier. Nonfiction books use this reviewing technique effectively. But they are books, not short essays.

2) Avoid introducing a new thought or point here. Introducing a new point in the conclusion is a common mistake. Beginning writers think they are leaving the reader with something interesting to think about by inserting a new point in the conclusion. However, this only confuses the reader and leaves him wondering why, if it were so important, the writer hid it in the conclusion with little chance of supporting it. Instead, try using a strong story or fact to illustrate your main point. Or leave the reader with a cud-chewing question or statement.

3) Include a rewritten version of your main idea. Stating your opinion in a new way can solidify it in your reader's mind. Avoid copying it from the first paragraph; find an engaging way to restate it.

4) If you can tie your conclusion to your introduction, do so. Tying the conclusion to the introduction can give the reader a satisfying experience. It is called the **full-circle technique**, and it has the feeling of neatly putting a bow around the subject. Here are some handy ways to tie your conclusion to your introduction:

- Answer the question you began with. Example: "Who hath believed our report, and to whom is the arm of the Lord revealed?" (Isaiah 53:1 KJV). The answer? The last two words in the chapter: "the transgressors."
- Create a contrast. Example: Psalm 23 ("The Lord is my shepherd…") begins with the sheep following the shepherd and living a homeless life in fields. It ends with mercy and goodness following that one sheep that's now in a permanent residence—"the house of the Lord, forever."
- Use synonyms or repetition. Examples: If you use *toxic* in your introduction to describe the effect of divorce on children, try using the word *poison* in the conclusion. When referring to drug usage and its dangers, mention a dangerous boa constrictor and its deadly coils in the introduction and repeat the word *coils* in the conclusion.
- Finish a story or refer to it. Example: The story of a car accident that begins in the introduction can be finished in the conclusion to show the negative effects of texting while driving.

5) Leave your reader with some food for thought. Your conclusion is your last chance to sway your reader or make an impact. Leave your reader with something intriguing to think about. Draw stellar conclusions. Make brilliant observations.

Practice 2.7   For review, fill in the tools next to each letter. Write as many as you can remember before you turn back to get the rest:

Q:

S:

F:

S:

Q:

Here's the conclusion of a student's paper on recycling. Read it and write a grade in the margin based on how effective you think her conclusion is.

> We all need to step up and take responsibility for the world we live in. It does not take much to make a change. Throw that soda can into the recycling bin instead of the trashcan, bless someone else with that toy you have outgrown, or buy a reusable water bottle instead of disposable one. Will you seize the opportunity to make a difference? St. Clement of Alexandria once wrote, "We are not to throw away those things which can benefit our neighbor. Goods are called good because they can be used for good; they are instruments for good, in the hands of those who use them properly."

Keep going! There's more! Good introductions and conclusions don't just lie there like a headboard and footboard. They *do* something. They have a purpose. Use them to your advantage.

Below are three sets of introductions and conclusions. They are all written by students and are on the topic of heroes. Read each set and then answer the questions that follow.

*Set 1
Intro and
conclusion*

> When I was a little kid, I loved Superman. He was my favorite super hero. I had Superman pajamas and red cowboy boots that I wore around the house. Saving the world was easy with my super powers. The only thing that stood in my way was bedtime. But when I got older, I had to accept the fact that there is no such thing as a person with super powers. Heroes, though, still exist, and they have many qualities in common that make them heroes.

> Even though I can't be Superman like I wanted to be when I was little, I can still be a hero. All it takes is a little courage.

Set 2
Intro and
conclusion

What makes a hero? Is it the clothes? Is it the adoring fans? Actually, it is none of the above. Heroes come in all shapes and sizes. It does not matter how old they are. It is the character qualities that they possess that make them heroes.

None of these people became heroes because of lucky circumstances. Their heroism came straight from the character qualities within themselves. That is what makes a true hero. If you do not think you have the makings of a hero, think again. There are qualities within you that are exactly what makes a hero. All you have to do is let them shine.

....

Set 3
Intro and
conclusion

He's the lonely kid in school: too short to play on the basketball team, too freckled to attract the girls, and too shy to make friends. He rarely raises his hand in class, and when he does, the teacher doesn't seem to care. Though his eyes never leave the floor, this kid longs more than anything to have others raise their eyes to him in respect. What this student and many others may fail to recognize is that the qualities of a hero are never based fully on circumstances. Rather, heroism is achieved through strength, courage, and selflessness many ordinary people are willing to develop.

He may not have the good looks or high grades to make him popular, but that lonely kid in school does possess the ability to become a hero. Whether he goes out of his way to encourage a struggling classmate, supports a fundraiser at school for the local rescue mission, or merely exhibits a selfless attitude, that kid can, in his own way, become a hero.

Answer the questions:

1. Which introduction do you like the best? Explain.
2. Which one seems to introduce the topic of heroes best? Explain.
3. Which conclusion do you like the best? Explain.
4. Which conclusion seems to wrap up the topic best? Explain.
5. Give each set a grade. Yes, explain.

On a separate piece of paper, write a concluding paragraph for your opinion on teens owning credit cards. Make it sparkle. Include at least one of the QSFSQ tools and leave your reader with some perceptive food for thought.

Practice 2.8

A few more pages, and you're through with this lesson . . .

First Sentence Anxiety Disorder

Notice what you did *not* do in this chapter. You did not begin by wrestling with the introduction, pounding your way through paragraphs of points, and sweating out a conclusion.

You began writing in the middle—in the body of your paper. That's a helpful technique to use, especially when it's difficult to find a way to start writing. Beginning in the middle avoids **First Sentence Anxiety Disorder** (a completely fictitious and made-up name—but the anxiety is real). FSAD can strike beginning and professional writers alike. Concentrating first on the body of your paper will save you from staring at a blank piece of paper or an empty computer screen for hours, trying to come up with a witty first sentence. *After* you write the body, you can backtrack and write the clever beginning and the powerful ending.

Some professional writers know what they want in their conclusion before they write the rest of the article, so they write their conclusion first and fill in everything else later. Some writers have a great hook or thesis statement in mind as soon as they sit down to write; they, like Julie Andrews in *The Sound of Music*, begin at the very beginning.

"What about the thesis statement?" you ask. "Shouldn't I develop that first?" The truth is that writers often mentally flow back and forth between determining their thesis statement (main idea) and their points or reasons. Frequently what they learn about their topic helps inform or determine their thesis statement. So don't sweat it. Start writing wherever you can and adjust everything later. (More on the thesis statement in chapter 3.)

No doubt, when you examine your topic and work habits, you will figure out where you want to begin writing, especially if you have an informal list or bunch of sticky notes you've arranged into a formidable order.

First Drafts

A word about first drafts: **Never.** Here are the rest of the words about first drafts: **Never** submit a first draft to your teacher. An orchestra tunes up before playing, but its members would never consider this the real concert. Neither would a carpenter consider a framed-in house complete. In the same way, you never should consider your first draft as the completed work. Print off your draft and read it aloud—slowly—to catch as many mistakes as possible.

Professional Tip
Editors expect writers to submit their work double-spaced. This way, the editor can read it more easily and can make comments or corrections on the paper.

You will learn specifics about proofreading in later chapters, but for now, catch all the mistakes you know about. The draft you hand in should be your third or fourth. Really. I am not kidding.

How Much Time Is This Going to Take?

Writing takes time. For every 100 words you are assigned, set aside **at least** one hour. If any researching is needed, add more time. Rule of thumb, no joke:

100 words = 1 hour

Because your first assignment is at least 300 words, you'll need at least three hours to complete it.

Write an Essay

Write your opinion paper on teens owning credit cards. You may use the parts you have already written in this lesson for your essay. Use your skeleton and fill it out, putting the introduction, the three (or more) reasons, and your conclusion into their separate paragraphs.

If that topic leaves you cold, discuss one with your teacher and write your opinion of the new topic.

Discuss your points or reasons with your teacher before writing your opinion essay.

Look for interesting facts, examples, or anecdotal information (true stories) to support your points.

Don't worry about citing your sources for facts or quotations for now. Use them if you know how to; if you don't know how, leave them off. You'll be learning about them soon.

Ditto with a thesis statement. Use one if you know how to, but don't fret about it if you do not. We'll get to it soon enough.

Word count for **beginning** writers: at least 300 words.

Word count for **intermediate** and **accomplished** writers: at least 350 words. Check with your teacher for the date this is due.

This chart will help you organize your tasks. **Read the next two pages.** Unless your teacher gives you a different format, use the one on the next page for **all** of your homework.

Day 1	Day 2	Day 3	Day 4	Day 5	Day 6
Brainstorm reasons or points. Arrange them into an effective order.	Research, if needed. Write the body (the point or reason paragraphs).	Write introduction and conclusion.	Proofread. Does each point flow from one to the next? Is each point strong?	Proofread again; read once out loud. Print out essay and adjust as needed. Print final draft.	Submit essay to teacher.

1. Type or computer print in plain, size-12 font, something like Times New Roman or Calibri, which this is.

2. Double-space every assignment.

3. The heading of the first page belongs on the **top left** and should look like this:

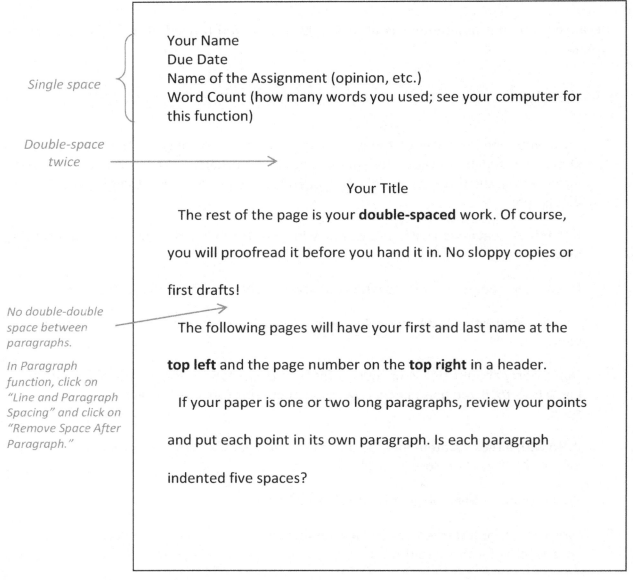

Single space

Your Name
Due Date
Name of the Assignment (opinion, etc.)
Word Count (how many words you used; see your computer for this function)

Double-space twice ⟶

Your Title

The rest of the page is your **double-spaced** work. Of course,

you will proofread it before you hand it in. No sloppy copies or

first drafts!

No double-double space between paragraphs.

In Paragraph function, click on "Line and Paragraph Spacing" and click on "Remove Space After Paragraph."

The following pages will have your first and last name at the

top left and the page number on the **top right** in a header.

If your paper is one or two long paragraphs, review your points

and put each point in its own paragraph. Is each paragraph

indented five spaces?

4. Leave a 1" margin all around.

5. From page 2 on, number each page on the **top right**. Learn to do this on your computer (find Header and Footer or double-click at the top of your page). Put your first and last name on the **top left** of each page after page one. Click "Different First Page." This head**er** is different from the first-page head**ing**.

6. Paper clip the pages together. Do not staple them.

ALL of your rough drafts and final drafts should be double-spaced, even the final one you hand in to your teacher. This helps you make corrections. Also, professors and editors expect double-spaces in any submissions.

No more single-spaced papers.

This is how to make your paper double-spaced in Microsoft Word. On the Home tab, find the box marked Paragraph:

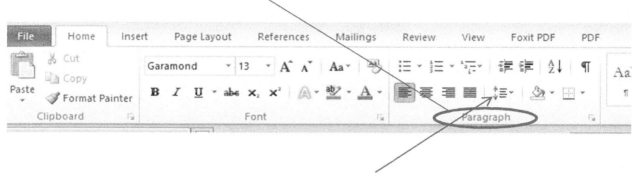

Next, click on the lines with the up and down arrows to get a pull-down menu. The menu will give you choices: 1.0, 1.15, 1.5, 2.0, 3.0, and so on. Choose 2.0 and begin typing.

If your paper is already single-spaced, highlight the paragraphs, click on the up and down arrows, and select 2.0 from the menu. Your paragraphs should automatically change to double-space.

If you are beginning a new file, type your heading on the left, single-spaced, and then type your title (centered). Next, hit Enter and go to Align Left (the gray box in the Paragraph box above). Then click on the up and down arrows. Last, select 2.0 from the menu. The rest of your paper will be double-spaced.

For this first essay, here's what you'll be graded on:
- ❑ Did you communicate your ideas clearly and express them well? 1-10 point
- ❑ Is there something noteworthy about the ideas or writing such as humor, insightfulness, obvious delight for the topic, and so on? 1-10 points
- ❑ Is the QSFSQ intriguing? 1-10 points
- ❑ Does the introduction clearly introduce the topic and opinion? 1-10 pts
- ❑ Do the points support the opinion? 1-10 points
- ❑ Are they arranged in an effective order? 1-10 points
- ❑ Does the conclusion adequately sum up topic and opinion? 1-10 points
- ❑ Are there separate paragraphs for the intro, each point, and the conclusion? 1-10 points
- ❑ Was the paper handed in on time? 1-10 points
- ❑ Did the student follow written instructions? 1-10 points

Part 2: Persuasion

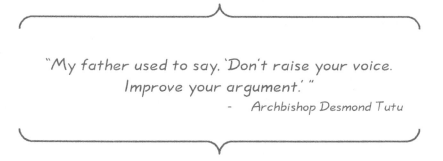

"My father used to say, 'Don't raise your voice. Improve your argument.' "

- Archbishop Desmond Tutu

Chapter 3: Persuasion Essentials

Lesson 1

Persuading—you do it all the time.

You and your friends want to get something to eat. You're salivating for pizza, but they yearn for burgers. What happens? You try to convince them to order a pizza; they try to talk you into going for a burger. The reasons you give are aimed at convincing each other and eating the food of choice.

But what if you have to write it down instead of speak it?

What Is Persuasion?

Writing a persuasive paper is a step beyond writing an opinion paper. In your opinion paper from chapter 2, you simply stated your opinion and backed it up with solid reasons. But in a persuasive paper, your aim is different. Writing persuasively is writing to convince readers to **believe** something and **behave** a certain way. In other words, you want readers to agree with your viewpoint on a certain topic and take specific actions.

Think about your **readers**. What do they need to know in order to think as you do or take action as you want them to?

Your opinion paper from chapter 2 was centered on you and your opinion. It answered the question "Why do I like this?"

But a persuasive paper focuses on the reader and what it will take to bring him or her to your point of view. It focuses on the question "What can I write to change the reader's mind?"

Do not be fooled. Many students believe that simply writing their opinion should be enough to persuade readers to change their minds. It is not.

Here's an example of how an opinion paper and a persuasive paper might differ, using a list of reasons about a car:

Opinion: I like my Honda CR-V.	**Persuasion:** You should buy a Honda CR-V.
Reasons why I like my Honda CR-V:	Reasons why you should buy a Honda CR-V:
1. It's my favorite color.	1. It gets good gas mileage.
2. It's just the right size for me.	2. *Consumer Reports* gives it high ratings for reliability.
3. I like the height of the driver's seat.	3. It's a mid-range size that suits many people's needs.
4. The radio, tape player, and CD player work.	4. It's less expensive than large SUVs.
5. I like to drive it.	5. Its four-wheel drive feature will come in handy.

This Venn diagram shows that the two lists overlap in one place only. Some subjects or reasons will overlap more than others:

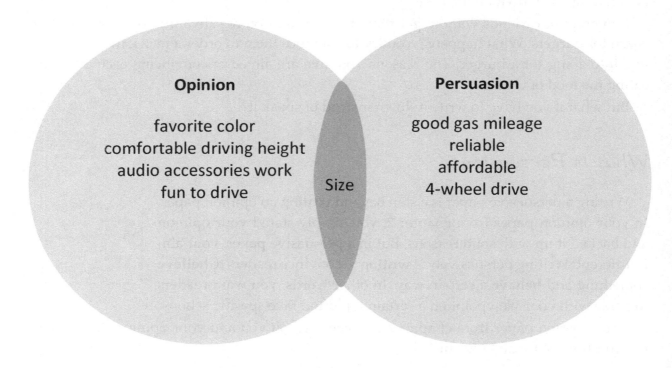

In persuasion, be focused on giving reasons why your readers should think as you do about your subject. If you want to convince your readers that gun control is detrimental, use facts and true stories to show how gun control has hurt people. If you believe in tighter gun control laws, use facts and true stories to show how gun control will help citizens. Just stating your opinion on gun control will convince no one.

How will you sway your audience? Develop a rock-solid argument.

Argument does not mean *fight*. It is simply an official term for writing persuasively. You won't need your boxing gloves.

Choose something you feel strongly about and write it in the margin. If you cannot think of something, brainstorm ideas and choose a topic from your resulting list.

Practice 3.1

Next, choose a specific audience: children, peers, parents, the girl next door, the principal, the Martians listening to all of our radio and TV shows—anyone.

Then, in the space below or on a separate piece of paper, brainstorm a list of reasons or points that you could use to convince your reader to believe as you do. Be imaginative. Some reasons can be silly and others serious. Brainstorm with another student, if possible.

When you have finished brainstorming points/reasons, choose the three that will best convince your target audience. Then go to Practice 3.2.

Review the methods of putting your ideas into a logical order (chapter 2) or devise one that logically fits your ideas. Then put the three reasons you chose in Practice 3.1 into one of those orders. Move them around until you get just the right combination of reasons and order. Aim for the reasons and the order that will build the most convincing case for your specific audience.

Practice 3.2

ORDER: _____

1.

2.

3.

Lesson 2

Purpose Statement

In every persuasive paper you write, you will develop a statement that will help you stay on target. It is called the **purpose statement**, and it reflects that you are trying to change your reader's mind. When you concentrate on writing your paper for a reading audience—and not a particular teacher—you will develop a purpose statement easily. Your purpose statement for persuasion begins with this formula:

I am going to convince the reader . . .

For instance, if your paper is on why teachers should not give homework, your purpose statement might be this: "I am going to convince the reader that teachers should not give homework," or, "I am going to convince teachers that they should not give homework." And good luck with that, by the way.

Perhaps you'd like to encourage readers to donate to the local food bank (changing their *behavior*). In that case, this might be your purpose statement: "I am going to convince the reader to donate money and food items to our local food bank."

If your paper is about cities using cameras at intersections, your purpose statement might be two-part: "I am going to convince the reader that when cities use cameras to identify and ticket stoplight violators, they are infringing on our privacy. In addition, I want to convince the reader to write a letter of protest to the mayor."

<u>Your purpose statement will never appear in your paper.</u> It is for your eyes only, and it exists to guide everything you write about your topic.

Practice 3.3   In the space below, write a purpose statement for the topic you chose in Practice 3.1. Use the formula.

PURPOSE STATEMENT:

The Main Idea

Another difference between opinion and persuasive papers is that writing persuasively incorporates a main idea called the **thesis statement**.

Your purpose statement helps *you*; the thesis statement guides *your reader* and tells her what to expect in the next paragraphs. It focuses her attention and shows her the topic's direction. The thesis statement is also called the controlling idea—it controls the direction of your paper like a steering wheel controls the direction of a car.

If your purpose statement for the humorous paper on homework is "I am going to convince the reader that teachers should not give homework," then your thesis statement might be this: "The toll on students, families, and teachers for this nightly battle is not worth the trauma it causes." The rest of the paper, according to the thesis statement, will first address the toll on students, then on their families, and last, the horrendously painful toll it demands of those poor, suffering teachers.

Here is the food bank topic again:

> **Purpose statement:** I am going to convince the reader to donate money and food items to our local food bank.

> **Thesis statement:** Our city's efficient food bank needs your help right now.

Thesis statements come in different forms. The above thesis statement is a **declarative sentence** that summarizes your controlling idea.

You may want to write your thesis as a **question**:

> Do we need to be concerned about global climate change?

The rest of your paper will answer that question by showing readers proofs (facts) about global climate change and why they should or should not be concerned.

Below is an introductory paragraph written by a student. Her thesis statement appears at the end of the paragraph and is a question:

> Should we require students to learn cursive? Forty-one out of fifty states no longer require students to learn it. *Detroit News* columnist Marney Rich Keenan laments the loss of handwriting: "Apparently, with the ubiquitous keyboard at our very fingertips, handwriting skills are now deemed irrelevant to the real world. Never mind that in the

1700s and 1800s, before the advent of the typewriter, professional penmanship was actually a noble career. Cursive writing is now becoming a dinosaur; hieroglyphics to the coming generations." So one would think cursive is no longer relevant or necessary, right?

If you guessed that this student goes on to defend learning cursive in school, you would be right.

In a **compare-and-contrast** paper (see chapters 6 and 17), your thesis statement will reflect the two things being compared and contrasted. Here are two examples, one from science and the other from history:

The current global-warming scare has many similarities to the global-cooling scare of the 1970s.

Although France aided America with its revolution, the French Revolution that soon followed had few of the qualities or features of the American Revolution.

Where does your thesis statement go? It's typically the last sentence in the introduction. If your introduction is two or more paragraphs long (as in some longer reports or term papers), insert your thesis statement at the end of your introductory paragraphs.

Consider your thesis statement to be in flux until you finish your research and put your paper or report together.

As you research and plan your paper, you will learn more about your topic and, perhaps, change your paper's direction. You may want to revise your thesis statement to reflect the new information you have learned.

Practice 3.4   Read the two separate introductory paragraphs below from different students. Underline the thesis statement in the first introductory paragraph. Then answer the questions that follow the paragraph.

A man with a foreign accent rattles off something to a tall, blonde, American woman. The lady answers with a blank stare and asks him to repeat himself again, and again, and again. This scene is not uncommon in America, the universal destination of immigrants, nor has it ever been. While some concerns—and frustrations—have always existed, immigrants undergird America's economy with human labor. Without them, America could not exist.

Answer these questions:

1. What is the topic of this student's paper?

2. Is she for it or against it?

3. What does she promise to show the reader?

This paragraph introduces the topic of the TV remote:

> The TV remote control seems to be an innocent device. We have grown very dependent on it and might not even want to watch TV without the ease of this automatic control box. The inventor of this infrared communications device is Robert Adler. He worked at Zenith for sixty years and invented the Zenith Space Command remote control in 1956. Many people have asked him if he feels guilty for inventing such a laziness-inducing product. His response is, "That is ridiculous. Every person should be able to change the channel from where he or she is sitting." One wonders, however, how the remote control has affected our culture.

Answer these questions:

1. Is he for the TV remote or against it?

2. What would you expect to learn in the rest of the paper?

3. Underline the thesis statement.

Please continue with today's lesson.

Your introduction—in any persuasive paper you write—should include these four things:

- ✓ A QSFSQ tool
- ✓ The topic
- ✓ Your view (for it or against it)
- ✓ Your thesis statement

Reread the introductory paragraph on immigration in Practice 3.4. The student doesn't have to write, "This paper is about immigration," and she doesn't state, "I'm for it." How does she announce her topic and her view without being so elementary and obvious? Write your answer here:

If you write a persuasive paper on the dangers of using a remote control, you might organize it like the illustration below. The introduction ends with the thesis statement.

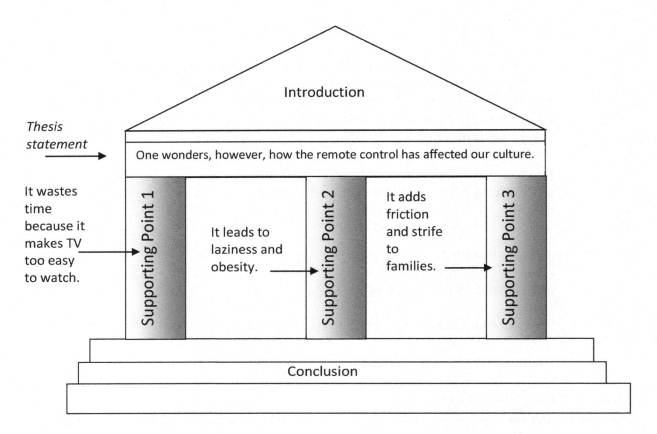

The **Greek temple** is one way to organize a paper. When you put the thesis statement where the temple's decorative frieze or pediment used to appear, and when you use your points to support your thesis statement, you have a handy visual aid.

Practice 3.5   Earlier in this chapter, you brainstormed a list of reasons to support a topic you feel strongly about, and you put them into an order. Review your list now. Here's what you have so far:

1. The topic
2. Your view
3. Three reasons
4. A purpose statement (Review it now.)

Your next step is a thesis statement. Brainstorm a few thesis statements on a separate piece of paper, keeping your audience and three reasons in mind. The thesis statement will be a complete sentence. Choose one that fits your reasons and what you want to say in your effort to convince someone to think and act a certain way.

If you are a **beginning** writer, skip the Digging Deeper section below in lesson 3 and join the text again at lesson 4. If you are an **intermediate** or **accomplished** writer, read the Digging Deeper section for your next lesson.

Lesson 3

Digging Deeper: Introductions

Longer persuasive appeals need not limit themselves to one paragraph of introduction. Cramming everything into one paragraph is pointless when you have much to say. For instance, if you are writing to persuade your audience not to succumb to triskaidekaphobia (an abnormal fear of the number 13), you may define the phobia, perhaps tell a true story or two, or give examples in the introduction. You may need to give a historical context by showing how this fear developed in cultures throughout history. Then you would insert your thesis statement at the end of your introductory paragraphs.

To learn how this works, read the following introduction completely rewritten and transmogrified from Henry David Thoreau's long essay "Walking," written in 1862. If Thoreau were a high school student being forced to write essays for school today, he might call his essay "The Benefits of Taking Walks," and it might look something like this:

> Very few people today understand the art of walking, that is, the art of taking walks, which is best done at a pace called *sauntering*. The etymology of *sauntering* is fascinating. It comes from the idea of roving people in the Middle Ages who asked for charity on the pretense of needing money to go to the *Sainte Terre*, or the Holy Land. They would never actually get there, of course, but it made a good story.
>
> In one way, though, sauntering on long walks really is attempting to reach a kind of holy land; every walk of this sort is a mission to reclaim something sacred that we modern, technology-loving people have lost. Our walks today are not adventures but only tours: We go somewhere and we come back. We walk through the mall. We walk up and down the aisles in the grocery store. We take a short walk around a park's paved path and call it exercise. This is not the noble art of which I write. Not at all. We must be like the camel that is said to be the only animal that can ruminate while it walks. Long, rambling walks offer enormous physical, emotional, and spiritual benefits.
>
> Strolls through nature provide more air and sunshine in our thoughts. How many students would be stronger and smarter if, instead of sitting up so late, they would take a walk through the fields and woods? When we submit to that subtle magnetism in

nature, we can think more clearly, like a lightning's sudden flash that rids the night of darkness or like the sun burning off a mist. Submitting to the desire to wander through nature can give us a deep sympathy with intelligence and inspiration. As the farmer needs fertilizer for his crops, our very health may require many acres of meadow, wilderness, swamps, and forest.

Does this inspire you to take a walk? Underline the thesis statement.

This young naturalist states his topic in sentence one. He gets to the point quickly. By sentence two, it is clear that he supports the art of taking walks.

Thoreau's original essay is at least 84 paragraphs long; it has plenty of room at the top for a short lesson in word derivations and a paragraph or two to show the problem in a suitable context.

The student's thesis statement is this: "Long, rambling walks offer enormous physical, emotional, and spiritual benefits" at the end of the second introductory paragraph. In the very next paragraph, he begins writing about the physical benefits ("Strolls through nature").

Lesson 4

Call to Action

Conclude your persuasive paper with a **call to action,** which encourages readers to *do something*.

The advertising and marketing worlds use a call to action (CTA) everywhere they can. On Internet sites, you'll see eye-catching rectangular boxes with words like Download Here or Buy Now or Add to Cart beckoning to you to click the box. Those are CTAs. Facebook uses Like, Comment, and Share as their CTAs; Instagram uses Follow. Each action is specific and measurable.

You, too, will suggest a positive action in your conclusion. It might be to call a senator or mayor (you will provide the telephone number), write a letter to an official (you will provide the address), or take some other action (such as having your pet neutered or buying something at the next Boy Scout fundraiser). A "we can fix this" attitude goes a long way in trying to convince someone to change.

Give your reader something constructive to do.

Devise a call to action that is specific, measurable, and achievable. "Let's all work to eradicate hunger" is NOT specific, measurable, or achievable. It gives the reader nothing to do but think that eradicating hunger is a good idea. He may agree with you, but he may not do anything about it. Encourage the reader to take a positive step. Give him something to do.

The following example is neither specific nor measurable:

This is a growing problem. We need to do something about it. Don't let it get any worse.

That call to action may leave the reader in a sweaty lather, but it won't encourage him to act.

There are many ways to be specific. Any of the following conclusions are appropriate as a call to action about teenage drinking [The targeted audience is in each bracket]:

1. Log onto www.madd.org to learn the warning signs of teenage drinking. Then talk to your teens about ways to avoid alcohol consumption at parties and in other social situations. The life you save might be your daughter's. [This is directed toward a parent or guardian. The first part mentions a specific action; the last sentence gives readers something to think about.]

2. You know what it is like at the prom. Even the good kids can go overboard and do things they normally would not do. If you see a friend drinking alcohol, remind him or her of the pact you made earlier and try to get your friend away from the temptation. And if you are tempted, grab your friend and recite your pact together. Only good can come from it. [This conclusion is directed toward the teen. The first part gives specific ideas; the last sentence gives food for thought.]

3. Now is the time for all good folks to come to the aid of their teens. We have this chance to make a life-saving law now. Once a drinking age goes down, it rarely goes back up again. Help protect our teens by calling your U. S. senators at 1-800-555-5555. Ask them to vote yes on SB5. [This is aimed at voters and gives a specific action, including the phone and bill numbers to make the action easier.]

Notice how specific and measurable those calls to action are. Readers make a pact ahead of time, or they don't. They talk their prom friend out of drinking, or they don't. They make the call, or, well, you get the point.

Read the conclusion for the paper on immigration. Is the call to action specific? Write your answer in the margin.   *Practice 3.6*

America as we know it would not exist without the aid of immigrants. Immigrants made her strong. Face it; except for the small population of Native American Indians, everyone who calls himself an American has ancestors who were immigrants. Don't stop our nation's lifeline.

Here is another example of a call to action. Is it specific? Read this student's conclusion and give her a grade:

Don't let casinos take over our state and steal our hard-earned money. Make a difference by calling your state senator or representative now. (Visit congress.org.) Tell them not to let money get in the way of morals.

You may recognize some of this list from chapter 2. It includes pointers for your **conclusion**:

1) Avoid recounting the points your paper just made. If your paper is long, however, you may sum up your points in a new way.
2) Avoid introducing a new thought or point here.
3) Include a rewritten version of your thesis statement.
4) If you can tie your conclusion to your introduction, do so.
5) Leave your reader with some food for thought. Issue a specific call to action in a persuasive paper.

Practice 3.7 Revisit your list of three reasons and your thesis statement on the topic you chose earlier. Based on the list and thesis statement, create a conclusion that includes a call to action. Remember to be as specific as possible; give your reader a measurable goal, something positive to do. Use a separate piece of paper.

Lesson 5

Paragraph Types

This lesson discusses four types of paragraphs.

The paragraphs in the body of your paper are the building blocks, no matter what type of writing you are doing. When writing a short essay, each reason typically gets its own paragraph. Longer reports or term papers may need more than one paragraph per point to adequately cover the topic.

Writing in paragraphs helps you organize your material. It also helps the reader by giving a visual break that signals a new idea.

Keep this in mind when writing for a newspaper, newsletter, magazine, or for an online source: Readers are more likely to read shorter paragraphs than long ones. Pick up any newspaper or read any article online and notice the short paragraphs that keep people reading. You know from your own experience that you would rather read a short paragraph than a long one. In fact, older fiction books can be frustrating to some readers simply because of the long paragraphs.

Paragraphs in school essays typically are longer than paragraphs written for periodicals or online sources. Even though the luckless teacher may grow bored reading countless long paragraphs, at least he or she knows that the student has covered the material completely and has a good grasp of the information and concepts. Vary your paragraph length according to the essay's purpose and readership.

Most paragraphs contain a **topic sentence**. If the thesis statement is the controlling idea for your whole paper, then the topic sentence is the controlling idea for your paragraph. It controls everything you put in the paragraph, and each paragraph develops only one point, as stated in the topic sentence.

Underline the topic sentence in the above paragraph. Which one did you underline? What is that paragraph about?

If you underlined "Most paragraphs contain a topic sentence," you hit the right one. That paragraph explains the topic sentence's task.

Some topic sentences are implied. Read the paragraph above that begins "Writing in paragraphs" and write in the margin a topic sentence that fits it best. (An answer is on the next page.)

In most of your writing for school, you will use topic sentences, not implied ones.

Paragraphs come in different types based on where the topic sentence is located in the paragraph or how the material is organized. We'll look at four types today. You are familiar with the most common type of paragraph, the **direct paragraph,** which organizes your material from *general to specific*. It begins with the topic sentence (*general*) and then proves, supports, explains, or illustrates it (*specific*). A great example of this is found in Ecclesiastes 4:9-12, paraphrased and arranged here in paragraph form. The topic sentence is in bold:

> **Friends are essential to a fuller life.** When friends work together, they accomplish more. If one becomes depressed, a caring friend can always pick him up. People who have no one to help them recover may be at risk for certain health and emotional issues. Friends look out for each other, sharing clothes and necessities; how can anyone do that alone? Whereas one person runs the risk of being attacked, two people have a better chance of defending themselves. Friends working together are like a chord made of three strands—it is not easily broken.

This direct paragraph begins with a general statement that is the topic sentence. It uses many specific examples to support it and then ends with an analogy that illustrates the point by giving the reader a word picture.

The **climactic paragraph** (using a *specific-to-general* order) begins with all the illustrations or proofs (*specific*) and then ends with the topic sentence (*general*). It builds its case first and ends with the clincher. Every statement in the paragraph builds to the last sentence, which is the topic sentence. Below is an example of a climactic paragraph, using the same passage from Ecclesiastes. Again, the topic sentence is in bold print:

Two people working together will accomplish more than if they had worked separately. If one of them gets into trouble, the other one is there to pick him up and get him back on his feet. Keeping warm and healthy is much easier for two than for one, and if attacked, two can fend off the bullies. Having someone by one's side is like being in a three-strand chord; it is hard to break. **Do not go through life alone.**

Answer from previous page: A possible topic sentence for the "Writing in paragraphs" paragraph is "Using paragraphs has its benefits."

You can build a case using the climactic paragraph, especially in persuasive writing. The many proofs or examples build upon each other until, finally, having guided your reader through the paragraph, you make your point.

Using a question as a topic sentence creates an **interrogative paragraph,** which uses the *question-to-answer* order to organize your material. The interrogative paragraph begins with a question and then answers it. Let's see how this works in the Ecclesiastes paraphrase:

In a world increasingly isolated by technology, what are the advantages to staying connected with others? When people work together in a joint effort, they will have better results than if they had worked alone. An attack on one's reputation can be devastating, but with friends who really know the truth, one's defense is built in. Not only will they continue to be friends but they will also squash rumors when they hear them. Friends can help with day-to-day realities like fixing a meal together or helping with homework. One piece of thread is easy to snap, but a whole rope twisted together is harder to break.

Every sentence in this interrogative paragraph answers its topic question. The advantage to this type of paragraph is that your reader begins to think about an answer and becomes engaged in the topic even as you present your material. It can build curiosity or help your reader care about the answer.

The **transitional paragraph** moves your reader from one phase of your essay to another. This example moves the reader from the importance of friends to the dangers of leaning too heavily on peers:

While it is healthy and advisable to maintain strong connections with a varied network of people, it is possible to become so dependent on others that one does not develop one's inner strengths.

Another type of paragraph is called the **turnabout paragraph**, but we'll get to that in chapter 5 (logical persuasion).

Develop a strategy for organizing your points, paragraphs, and paper based on these and other patterns you learn. Have you noticed that what can be done for the lowly paragraph can also be done for the whole essay? You've already learned about the general-to-specific order for the paragraph *and* the whole essay, for example. Keep your work from being a grab bag of random sentences. Plan!

Lesson 6

Unity and Completeness

Absolutely everything you write in a paragraph—explanations, illustrations, examples, quotes, and so forth—should be about that topic sentence. No sentence should go off the trail and introduce a new topic. When each sentence in a paragraph points to the topic sentence, you have achieved what is called **unity**.

The following paragraph does <u>not</u> exhibit unity. Figure out when the paragraph begins to veer off its true topic and write the sentence number in the margin:

> (1) Babysitters should have first-aid training. (2) This training can be anything from how to choose age-appropriate toys to performing CPR. (3) CPR stands for cardiopulmonary resuscitation and can be performed by one person or by a team in which one person works for a while on the victim and then a second person takes over. (4) CPR used to be performed by alternating phases of pushing on the chest and breathing in the victim's mouth, but the American Heart Association has developed a method that includes calling 9-1-1 first and then pushing on the center of the victim's chest.

In addition to unity, you will strive for **completeness**. Is the topic adequately covered, or did you stop far short of fully examining the assigned concept? Note how the following paragraph gives a shallow, incomplete treatment of the topic:

> Kudzu is another botanical pest. Originally from China and Japan, the vine flourishes here despite temperature or precipitation variations, growing almost as well in drought as in rain-forest conditions. It envelops anything it grows on and can cover whole houses if left unchecked.

This treatment of the kudzu topic is more complete:

Kudzu is another botanical pest. Originally from China and Japan, the vine flourishes here despite temperature or precipitation variations, growing almost as well in drought as in rain-forest conditions. Because it is so vigorous, it envelops anything it grows on and can cover whole houses if left unchecked. While the luxurious growth might create fantastical shapes and seem like a lovely green blanket on the landscape, this softening effect that hides rusting tractors and slows erosion has a dark side—literally. The climbing vines cover nearby foliage and block the sunshine. Healthy, useful plants then fall prey to kudzu's invasiveness. Given a few years, kudzu can even kill bushes and whole trees. Because the vines are not native to our area, they have no natural predators in place. Therefore, they continue to advance uncontrolled over the countryside.

That paragraph covers the topic more fully than the first paragraph about kudzu because it gives additional details of how troublesome the plant can be.

Just as you work to achieve unity and completeness in each paragraph, you will create unity and completeness in your whole essay. Every word, sentence, image, and example will point toward the thesis statement and enlarge upon it. Your thesis statement is the star of the essay; everything else is the supporting cast.

Answer from the previous page: The paragraph about babysitters and CPR veers from the topic sentence in sentence three.

Beginning writers may skip the Digging Deeper section and go directly to Practice 3.8 on page 52.

Intermediate and **accomplished** writers, please complete lesson 7 and then go to Practice 3.8 on page 52.

Lesson 7

Digging Deeper: More on Paragraphs

You have learned about the direct, climactic, interrogative, and transitional paragraphs. This section highlights four more types of paragraphs: *effect to cause, enumerative, comparison and contrast,* and *problem to solution.* These are simply four more strategies for arranging your material and can give you a greater freedom of choice when pondering the best way to present your information and ideas.

Also, in addition to unity and completeness, this lesson adds a third requirement for paragraphs. You want all the information in a paragraph to hang together, to stick together, to be connected, to be **cohesive**, like a drop of water on the hood of a well-waxed car. You can achieve this by salting your paragraph with synonyms, contrasts, repeated key words or phrases, or similar sentence structures in appropriate places. Stay tuned. The following pages will show you how to perform this truly amazing feat.

The four paragraph examples on the next pages use the topic of clowns to show the additional paragraph types <u>and</u> cohesion. (Cohesion is shown by the lines and arrows.)

Random point: I wrote these paragraphs on clowns because clowns give me the creeps. Yes, they do. In other words, I chose a topic I had a lot of feeling for, and that made it easier for me to write the paragraphs.

If you choose a topic you love or despise, writing will be easier for you as well.

Effect to cause

In this paragraph type, begin with the result and then show what caused it. The flow of this is similar to the question-to-answer order found in an interrogative paragraph.

Please read the following paragraph through a first time and ignore all the lines and arrows. Just get the idea of the paragraph and its effect-to-cause structure. Then read it through again, this time paying attention to the cohesion shown by the underlines and arrows.

Result: Children are afraid of clowns.

Cause: (1) Make-up that hides faces, (2) garish facial expressions, (3) no internal mechanisms to interpret make-up, (4) intuitive fear factor.

Children are often afraid of clowns, and it is no wonder. Infants primarily focus on faces and will look at a picture or image longer if it has a face on it. As children grow, they begin to size up social situations based, in part, by reading the facial expressions of those around them. Clowns and their make-up, on the other hand, are engineered to hide their faces under a mask of unnatural colors and shapes, often freezing a garish facial expression. The colors and abnormal shapes on the clown's face leave small children adrift in an emotional sea; they have no inner mechanisms which allow them to deal with the palette and illegibility of the greasepaint. In addition, children often have an intuitive sense that someone hiding behind a mask is not to be trusted. The fun factor is far outweighed by the fear factor.

Cohesion is achieved by . . .

- Synonyms (underlined words *make-up/greasepaint*)
- Repetition of key words (underlined words *faces* and *facial expression*)
- Contrasts or antonyms (gray arrows for *face/mask*, *reading/illegibility*)

The **effect** or result: Children are afraid of clowns. But why? The rest of the paragraph answers "why" or explains the **cause** of the fear by giving four solid reasons why children are afraid of clowns. Of course, it doesn't answer the question of why *I* am afraid of clowns, but that's another topic.

Enumerative

In the enumerative paragraph, begin with the number of parts (in this case, "three categories") and then write about each part. This order is sometimes referred to as the *partitive* or *whole-to-parts* order. Read the paragraph first for its content and enumerative qualities. Then read it again for its cohesive properties.

Modern clowns come in all shapes and sizes, but they can be divided into three categories. The first category is the happy clown, typified by the circus clown. His shoes are oversized; his clothing is colorful, mismatched, and usually baggy; his whitened face sports huge red lips, personalized markings, tousled hair, and, often, a large red nose. All this frivolity is designed to make onlookers grin. In fact, this clown is grinning. He is happy. He has tricks and gimmicks hidden everywhere and is often the butt of his own jokes. The famous Bozo and Ronald MacDonald are examples of this happy jester. The second category is the sad clown, often personified as a hobo. His clothing may be outsized and garish, but it is toned down by dark colors. The hobo's face is often painted with a frown and shapes under the eyes to symbolize tears. His goal is to remind viewers of the pathos and irony of life by making them feel sorry for him. The tragic Weary Willie, as portrayed by Emmett Kelly, is perhaps the most famous of this type. And the last category is the downright scary clown often found in horror movies or books. One peek at him, and no doubt remains that this clown is deranged. His clothing is askew. His greasepaint is ill applied and disordered. His grin is a leer. He is wicked to the core. The Joker, Batman's enemy, is a frightening example of this clown.

Cohesiveness achieved by . . .

1. *Repetitive sentence structure (shown by the underlining and black arrows)*
2. *Synonyms (underlining and gray arrows)*
3. *Contrasts (gray words)*

Comparison and contrast

The comparison-and-contrast paragraph, like the one below, begins with one feature or topic and moves to the next, using a transition. Or you may choose to begin with a topic sentence that forecasts your comparison or your contrast: "Although clowns and mimes, at first glance, seem to have much in common, their arts are quite different from one other," for example. Your strategy depends on your feature or topic.

Notice how the following paragraph begins with the "daytime" Harry Shankton and transitions to the "nighttime" Harry.

By day, quiet Harry Shankton is a self-proclaimed dullard working as a chemical engineer at the local automotive plant. Here he towers over others in intellect but not in social skills. He dresses plainly in soft-soled shoes, khakis, and

Transition from day to night

a short-sleeve, button-down shirt complete with pocket protector. Shankton does his job well and is as unobtrusive as a wavelet on the sand. But by night, he is a different creature, donning the bright clothing and

Note the contrasting words and how they add interest to the topic, emphasizing Harry's day-to-night contrast.

witty persona of Short Shanks, the children's birthday party clown. With typical size-46 clown shoes, red-and-white striped baggy pants, and a clashing orange shirt that sports a squirting flower, Short Shanks wows the kids with his games, antics, and tricks. He enjoys the thrill of making children laugh and loves to see the delight in their eyes when he performs his magic tricks. Height challenged, he finds that his short stature helps children feel comfortable around him, and he is often inundated by their happy shouts of "More! More!"

There are at least four sets of contrasting words in this paragraph. Find them, circle each word or phrase, and draw lines to connect each set.

Problem to solution

Begin with—yes—the problem. In this case, it is a fear of clowns. The rest of the paragraph is all about the solution or solutions. First read this paragraph for content and then read it for its cohesive devices that are shown by underlines, arrows, and a line.

Children are often afraid of clowns. What can you do about it? First, warn your child ahead of time if there is to be a clown at a party or restaurant. Many times, the child may not be afraid of the clown, per se, but is frightened by the suddenness of its appearance or of the unusual clothing or make-up. Second, show your child pictures of clowns before attending the event. Magazines and library books are innocuous sources of these images and can be used to talk to your child about why people dress up in this seemingly strange way. Third, when in the presence of a clown, pick up your small child or hold your older child's hand. Your physical presence can calm and reassure your anxious child. And last, choose events and venues that do not feature clowns. If your child continues to exhibit anxiety after desensitization efforts and reassurance, it is needless to continue exposing your child to this very normal fear. Childhood should be a happy, expansive time, with lots of "clowning" around. Be your son's or daughter's advocate in stressful times.

Cohesion is achieved by . . .

- Synonyms (underlined words connected with black arrows: *afraid, frightened, anxious, anxiety,* and *stressful*)
- Contrasts or antonyms (*afraid/happy*)
- Repetitive sentence structure (*first, second, third,* and *last*)

Practice 3.8 **All writers:** It is time to practice writing a paragraph. Turn to Proverbs 23:29-35 and read those verses. Write in the margin which type of paragraph that is (if it were all written in one paragraph).

Devise your own topic sentence. Paraphrase the Proverbs verses freely and add information as needed.

If you are a **beginning** writer, choose one paragraph type from the following list: direct, climactic, and interrogative. Then write that paragraph using the Proverbs material. Write with unity and completeness.

If you are an **intermediate** or **accomplished** writer, write one paragraph using any of the following paragraph types: direct, climactic, interrogative, effect to cause, enumerative, comparison and contrast, and problem to solution. Use the Proverbs material as the basis for your new paragraph. In addition to unity and completeness, make your paragraph hang together by using devices that create cohesion.

Write an Essay

Write a persuasive paper on the topic you chose in Practice 3.1. Take all the pieces that you have done so far—the thesis statement, the reasons in a logical order, and the call to action—and put them together in a fully completed essay.

If you are absolutely sick of that topic, choose another you have strong feelings about.

Save yourself some agony and many rewrites: Check your topic and points with your teacher before you begin your first draft.

Skillfully devise the types of paragraphs you use and, in the margins of the final paper you submit to your teacher, write the type of paragraph you employed for each paragraph in the body.

Beginning writers: Exhibit unity and completeness in your paragraphs. **Intermediate** and **accomplished writers:** Exhibit unity, completeness, and cohesion in your paragraphs.

All writers: Write your "secret" purpose statement on the back of your essay.

Word count for **beginning writers**: at least 300 words.

Word count for **intermediate** and **accomplished writers**: at least 400. If your topic needs some background information (as in "The Benefits of Taking Walks ") or if you need to define the issue for your audience so they understand its importance, you may choose to insert it before your thesis statement. You are not limited to three points and five paragraphs. Expand! Expound! Explore!

Check with your teacher for the date this is due.

Here's a suggested writing schedule to help you organize your tasks:

Day 1	Day 2	Day 3	Day 4	Day 5	Day 6
Brainstorm topics and points. Arrange points. Create a flexible thesis statement.	Research, if needed. Write the body (the point or reason paragraphs).	Adjust thesis statement and points as needed. Write introduction and conclusion.	Check for unity and completeness of paragraphs and essay. Proofread.	Proofread again; read once out loud. Print out essay and adjust as needed. Print final draft.	Submit essay to teacher.

Use this checklist for your persuasion paper:

- ❏ Are you trying to convince your audience of something (to change their minds and/or behavior)?
- ❏ Do you have a reader-grabbing QSFSQ?
- ❏ Is your thesis statement clear, and is it at the end of your introduction?
- ❏ Do all your succeeding paragraphs stick to and support your thesis statement?
- ❏ Are your points arranged in the order that will best highlight the topic or affect your audience?
- ❏ Do the topic sentences clearly state your points or reasons?
- ❏ Does each paragraph support its topic sentence with details, quotes, facts, and so forth?
- ❏ Does each paragraph in the body exhibit a logical internal order?
- ❏ Does your bedroom exhibit a logical internal order?
- ❏ Does each paragraph exhibit unity and completeness?
- ❏ Does your conclusion avoid conclusion pitfalls?
- ❏ Is your call to action specific and measurable?
- ❏ Did you write the type of paragraph next to each paragraph in your essay's body?
- ❏ Did you write your "secret" purpose statement on the back of your essay?
- ❏ **Intermediate** and **accomplished** writers: Are your paragraphs cohesive by use of selected repetition, sentence structure, contrasts, synonyms, antonyms, and so forth?

> "My most brilliant achievement was my ability
> to be able to persuade my wife
> to marry me."
>
> - Winston Churchill

Chapter 4: Persuasion—Next Level

Lesson 1

Not everything you write will persuade someone. Why is that?

People need to hear a new idea anywhere from three to one hundred fifty-one times before they believe it. Your essay may be planting an idea, not harvesting a direct result.

Some people have high sales resistance and are not easily persuaded. Others will not think your reasons are legitimate or important enough to make them change their minds. After all, most people have held their beliefs for a long time or have developed them with some sense of ownership. Their beliefs become their identity.

Or perhaps you simply used weak strategies.

This chapter shows you how to strengthen your persuasive-writing skills. The first two lessons explore how NOT to write. The last ones investigate strong persuasive techniques.

Don't Make These Mistakes

Under each mistake below, you will find a real or made-up letter to the editor and then a discussion of the letter with its shortcomings.

Note: You may find you agree with some of the writers. However, you are not reading to see if you agree with the views; you are reading to find poor persuasion strategies. Let's get started.

1. **Don't insult a person or an entire group of people.**

> Why are kids so stupid? Today's teens have turned themselves into human pincushions with all those tattoos and body piercings. Yesterday I ordered soup at a local restaurant, and when the waitress smiled at me, I could see her tongue was pierced. HOW GROSS! I almost lost my appetite.
>
> And what's with all the baggy pants? I'm tired of walking behind some kid who can't keep his pants up. PULL UP YOUR BRITCHES!

This writer is insulting the very people he hopes to persuade. Not a good tactic. Being derisive, angry, or insulting will only encourage readers to ignore you. Yelling puts the focus on the writer, not the issue; it will not engender respect or a positive change.

2. **Don't wander off your subject.**

What is this writer's real topic?

> I have been reading a lot about the old Crane factory and what people want to do with it. Why tear it down? If it is still in good shape, why not make it into an apartment building?
>
> If people want to tear something apart, why don't they tear out the old railroad tracks? No one uses those any more. They make street repairs cost more, and they are an eyesore.
>
> Speaking of eyesore, I would like the city to make my neighbor clean up his house and yard. His house is so full of junk that he is sleeping in a car up on blocks in his yard. And there are rats! I don't want rats in my yard or house. This is a public health nuisance.

This letter moves around. It begins with a factory, shifts to railroad tracks, and then tackles a neighborhood health issue. This weakens the effect.

Focus on one issue.

3. **Don't go on and on.**
4. **Don't contradict yourself.**

Kids today need to know their history. How can they appreciate their heritage and what they have today if they don't know where it all came from?

Without going into a history lesson about Westward expansion, which at one time was considered to be just west of the Appalachian Mountains and was encouraged by the government and helped by the Louisiana Purchase, land we bought from France, and by the War of 1812, fought with the British over land we thought we already had a right to, and even by our losses in the Texas Revolution that included the historic fight at the Alamo in 1836, which spurred us on, we have a great multi-cultural heritage.

How many words are in this looong sentence?

You've also got the Cumberland or National Road, which opened in 1818 and traversed the existing nation. Then came the Pony Express and the railroad system, which further connected the nation and made travel and commerce possible. Products like lumber, silver, and produce were now widely available. This benefited both the businessman and the consumer. The telegraph was developed in tandem with the railroad, and soon after followed the telephone, to say nothing of the vast system of interstates created in the wake of—and because of—the Cold War.

Do kids today appreciate their country's infrastructure or the technology that went into connecting us as a nation? Do they know anything about their history and how to preserve its importance? There is a lack of respect and feeling for our heritage and history.

Don't write incessantly and ramble. Few people will read a long letter from beginning to end. Did *you* read the whole thing? The longer the letter, the fewer people who read it. If you have something to say to the general reading public or to a legislator, you can do it in 200 to 300 words. Opinion articles or essays in some magazines can go on for pages. But you aren't writing for a magazine yet, so keep it short and succinct.

School assignments may have longer page/word requirements. Sorry.

Incidentally, that long sentence that is a whole paragraph is 89 words long. The general reading public is not ready for a sentence of that length!

As for contradicting yourself, if you say you are not going to give a history lesson but then you do, your readers will not trust anything else you write.

5. Don't rant and rave.

How dare you spell Christmas with an X! This is Christ's birthday, not X's! You may not wish to recognize Jesus or his birth or that Christmas really is the celebration of his birth, but that's what it is. Look at the word. It's got "Christ" in it! Don't insult Jesus and Christians just because we know the reason for the season!

Can you hear this writer yelling at you? It is perfectly all right to be angry about something. However, a writer needs to concentrate on using words and tools that will make the *reader* feel perturbed or concerned enough to do something constructive. Yelling, ranting, and insulting—all weak strategies.

6. Don't write without evidence; don't exclude facts.
7. Don't threaten your audience.

> I'm writing about genetically engineered crops. Have you people lost your minds? You don't know what you're messing with. Messing with crops before they've been tested long-term is insane. I won't eat the stuff and I know a lot of people who won't. You better stop messing with Mother Nature or you're going to get in trouble.

I get a kick out of reading this question: "Have you people lost your minds?" Which above guideline (#s 1-5) is this breaking? Write your answer here:

A case may be made for genetically engineered crops being harmful; however, this writer fails to use any facts. Telling readers that you are not alone in your belief is not a fact. It isn't even a random poll. And threatening readers, even with Mother Nature, won't win you any votes.

Other than answering the questions in the sidebars in #s 2 and 4 and the question in #7, you have no writing or practice assignment for this lesson.

Lesson 2

Avoid These, Too

Practice 4.1   Fill in the blanks to review the first part of the Don't List:

1. Don't _____ a person or an entire group of people.

2. Don't _____ off your subject.

3. Don't go _____ and _____.

4. Don't _____ yourself.

5. Don't _____ and _____.

6. Don't write without _____; don't exclude

   _____.

7. Don't _____ your audience.

More goofy mistakes are on the way. Read for weak strategies, not to see if you agree or disagree. Here's the rest of the Don't List:

8. Don't be vague.

> There's been a lot of talk about embryonic stem-cell research lately. The late Christopher Reeve (the Superman actor) was all for it, and so are other famous people. They want to have this research available so that people with diseases can benefit from it. In some countries, it is legal to do this kind of research.
>
> Other people think those embryos are human and shouldn't be messed with. After all, adult stem-cell research has had good results and is used in cancer patients today.

On which side of the issue is this writer?

Does this writer applaud embryonic stem-cell research or abhor it? It's hard to tell. Beginning writers often make this mistake when writing persuasive essays: They write the pros and cons of the issue, explaining both sides.

Although you may mention and refute an argument from the opposing view, you will not explain the ins and outs of both views. That is an expository essay—writing to explain something.

When writing persuasively, stick to one clear view and then support it. Choose a side. And I don't mean onion rings or applesauce.

9. Don't forget your audience.
10. Don't use jargon, lingo, slang, or technical words unless you define them right away.

> Automating the manufacturing process helps companies to improve productivity efficiencies while reducing labor costs. In many instances, the ROI for installing PLC-driven automation systems is less than one year.
>
> Management benefits from increased quality, reduced scrap of work in progress, less downtime, and increased throughput.
>
> Operator environment has increased safety with reduced ergonomic challenges and risks. Today, human/machine interfaces make troubleshooting to base causes simpler and faster. When machine vision is applied, the quality control gains are often exponential.

I am sure there is someone in this world who understands what this letter is saying, but there is too much technical jargon in it for the average reader. Jargon or slang tends to feel like a foreign language to most readers. It creates an "in" group and an "outsider" group, something you do not want to do when trying to sway readers. Bring them along; let them feel they are with the "in" group, the group that knows what is going on.

While you are avoiding jargon, avoid ambiguous terms, too. If you see "I'm pro-salmon and I vote" on a bumper sticker, would you know if the driver wants to protect salmon—or fish them? Until you read the rest of the stickers that show a love for fishing, you won't know what "pro-salmon" means. That term is ambiguous.

11. Don't be illogical; that is, don't draw wrong conclusions, make sweeping generalizations, present false dilemmas, and so forth.

> Our school board is thinking about requiring us to wear uniforms to school next year.
> That is ridiculous. Would *they* wear uniforms, too? They just want to take away our personalities and our right to express ourselves. They want to make us all look the same so we'll fit into their idea of perfection when we graduate and work in the "real world."
> Anyone who is for school uniforms is a traitor. Anyone who is against uniforms cares about us and our freedom of expression.

Discussions about school uniforms can be heated, and this letter is an example of how much is at stake for students. However, this writer has drawn some illogical conclusions about the school board's reasons and motives and has written a false dilemma in the last paragraph ("Either you are for us or against us"). You will learn more about fallacies (illogical thinking) in the next chapter.

There are two other "Don't" guidelines that belong on this list but have no accompanying letters. Read on.

12. Don't use "I believe…," "I think…," "It is my opinion that…," "I choose to believe…," or "I feel that…."

Keep "I" out of your opinion statement. Instead of conveying humility, it draws attention to yourself and weakens your argument. Instead of writing, "It is my opinion that breeding hairless dogs for allergy sufferers is cruel to the dogs," write, "It is cruel to intentionally breed a dog that will be miserable all its life," and then prove it. Instead of "I feel that abortion is wrong," write something like this: "Abortion harms children." Maintain an objective tone. That is, keep "I" out of it.

13. Don't announce what you are going to write. Just write it.

Avoid the "I am going to write about" trap. Some students believe that this is a chummy way to begin or that it warms up the audience. In reality, it only bores. Use your QSFSQ tools to create an interest and curiosity in the reader.

Here's the whole Don't List assembled for your viewing pleasure:

1. Don't insult a person or an entire group of people.
2. Don't wander off your subject.
3. Don't go on and on.
4. Don't contradict yourself.
5. Don't rant and rave.
6. Don't write without evidence; don't exclude facts.
7. Don't threaten your audience.
8. Don't be vague.
9. Don't forget your audience.
10. Don't use jargon, lingo, slang, or technical words unless you define them right away.
11. Don't be illogical; that is, don't draw wrong conclusions, make sweeping generalizations, present false dilemmas, and so forth.
12. Don't use "I believe...," "I think...," "It is my opinion that...," "I choose to believe...," or "I feel that...."
13. Don't announce what you are going to write. Just write it.

Practice 4.2

Brainstorm a list of your pet peeves on a separate piece of paper. Then choose one to write about. In this short paper, you are going to **break** as many persuasive Don't guidelines as possible. In other words, use as many of the items on the Don't List as you can. (*Do* rant and rave, *do* use jargon, and so on.) Yes, you heard me—**break these guidelines**.

Pretend you are going to send your paper to your local or school newspaper or post it on your favorite social media site. For fun, read your result aloud to other students.

This is the last time you will be allowed to write this badly!

Word count: at least 150.

Lesson 3

Powerful Persuasion Tools, part 1

Many of the following powerful tools correspond with the warnings on the Don't List. For instance, it makes sense that if you are not supposed to forget your audience, you would be miles ahead to understand for whom you are writing; in other words, "know your audience." Other tools, however, do not have a corresponding opposite on the Don't List. Still, they are solid strategies that will sharpen your persuasive skills. Which ones will you use?

Note: You are not reading the following letters to determine whether you agree or disagree with the writer; you are reading to discover effective persuasive techniques.

1. Know your audience.

The example letter for this tool is coming up soon.

In the past, you have written for your teacher, but now you will have chances to mentally choose a particular audience and write to them. Will your readers understand the religious or technical words you are using? Are they your peers? Teachers? Parents? Male? Female? Interior decorators? Auto mechanics? These factors will make a difference in how you write.

Professional Tip

Don't know who your audience is? Grab a copy of the current *Writer's Market* or *The Christian Writers' Market Guide*. Look up the magazine's title in the index and turn to a page loaded with readership information: age, gender, religious and political leanings, and so forth.

Each audience deserves specific vocabulary, sentence lengths and structures, and arguments. Your tone will vary. If you are writing for your own age group or a letter to the editor, using personal pronouns is acceptable: "If you are concerned about this non-use of the word *Christmas,* you can do something about it." More formal audiences may require an objective tone: "People concerned about this non-use of the word *Christmas* can do something about it."

Does your audience agree with what you are writing, do they disagree, or are they neutral on the topic? Knowing this is important. If they agree with you already, you are not convincing them but bolstering their beliefs, which is an important job. If they disagree, you most likely will not convince them right away. Instead, concentrate on stating facts and building bridges. What value do people of an opposing view share with you? Couch your argument in terms of this value (like "protecting our children," for example). Use neutral language. Show that you are civilized, not a slobbering troglodyte. Neutral readers are more likely to be swayed; be prepared to sway them.

Is the following writer trying to convince a neutral or opposing group, or is she validating her group's beliefs?

God Squad America launched yet another offensive in its secular jihad against the formerly free US-of-A this week. The target this time: preteen girls to whom the religiously consumed would deny a vaccine that promises 100 percent protection against cervical cancer.

That paragraph, written by syndicated columnist Bonnie Erbe, is directed toward an audience that already believes as she does. Aside from being medically incorrect (the vaccine protects against only some types of cervical cancer, according to the National Cancer Institute at www.cancer.gov), Erbe uses a tone and loaded words that are not calculated to win over the opposition but, instead, bolster the beliefs of those who agree with her view. You will learn more about neutral and loaded words in chapter 8.

2. Define your terms.

The code of chivalry, which is showing respect and honor to women, is being forgotten in today's society. Many young men don't even know what it is. And to make things worse, not very many efforts are being made to show the young men of today what to do.

It is a good thing that this writer defined *chivalry* for me because I was already on my way to the jousting match. Unknown terms and jargon are not the only words you need to define for your readers. What about *good gas mileage* or *wealthy* or *tolerance*? These abstract terms mean different things to different people. You even have to define the word *God* before you can go very far with a diverse audience.

3. Indicate your topic early.

Some people say there's nothing for teens to do in our little community. However, there are plenty of things to do.

There is no question about this writer's topic. You would expect him to list some interesting and safe things for teens in the area to do, and he does.

While some people like to keep readers guessing about their topic, there is no reason to do that. It does not raise suspense or create curiosity. It only confuses and frustrates.

4. Treat your reader intelligently.

> Kids are like little sponges: They absorb everything around them, including some things we'd probably rather they didn't. So shouldn't parents be careful about the messages inherent in their kids' toys?
>
> Not many parents want their daughters to value good looks and material possessions more than anything else. But the imaginary lives that toy companies assign Barbie dolls and others like them are completely centered on how they look and how much stuff they have.
>
> Advertisements scream at girls to buy countless dolls and numerous accessories for them. Without a doubt, these dolls contribute to selfish, shallow materialism in children.
>
> Many things influence how girls—tomorrow's women—view the world. While their dolls may not be the largest influence, they are an area parents can control to a great degree. Carefully consider the lifestyles and choices your children's toys promote; they have a bigger impact than you may realize.

Assume that your reader is not a dolt. This writer is not ranting about rampant consumerism, nor is she overreacting to girls playing with certain dolls. Her tone is polite and even. She makes a reasoned appeal.

5. Write about the opposing view fairly. Know the argument.

> People who are worried about global climate change say that too much carbon dioxide (CO_2) is escaping into the atmosphere and trapping heat there. To them, CO_2 is one of the bad guys. There are two facts, though, that they may not know. First, while CO_2 is a waste product of humans, it is necessary to plant life and photosynthesis. Plants need CO_2 so they can make food for themselves and oxygen for us. Second, NASA satellites have discovered that our planet sheds much more heat than we thought it did. In other words, "extra" heat is escaping out of our atmosphere and into space. According to Dr. Roy Spencer, U.S. Science Team Leader for the Advanced Microwave Scanning Radiometer on NASA's Aqua satellite, "The satellite observations suggest there is much more energy lost to space during and after warming than the climate models show." He adds that "there is a huge discrepancy between the data and the forecasts," especially when it comes to the dire warnings of CO_2 emissions that occur naturally over the oceans. James Taylor, a journalist for *Forbes*, asserts that "carbon dioxide emissions have directly and indirectly trapped far less heat than alarmist computer models have predicted." Perhaps our anxiety is unnecessary.

The writer of this paragraph is not freaking out; she states the opposing view fairly and gathers facts to refute it.

Controversial topics can best be discussed by stating an opposing view. Begin with the view you don't hold and then support your own view. This answers the unspoken "But what about...?" in the reader's mind, and it shows that you have chosen your view after careful thinking. In chapter 5, you will learn more about refuting an opposing argument.

6. Be concise. Stay focused on your objective.
7. Be logical and orderly.

> There needs to be a law against collecting money at intersections, even if it is for a good cause. It is a dangerous, potentially accident-causing distraction for drivers. It puts the firefighter at risk. It also gives impressionable youngsters who look up to firefighters the wrong idea that it's OK to play in the road. There have to be other ways to raise money that aren't an accident waiting to happen.

This letter to the editor is short and sweet; it is the opposite of the letter that gave the history lesson (see the Don't List). It states the topic early (#3 on the list of powerful tools), and then it follows with three sentences that succinctly delineate the three problems. And though it does not give a specific call to action, it ends on a positive note.

And so does this because it's the end of today's lesson.

Lesson 4

Powerful Persuasion Tools, part 2

Review tools 1-7 by filling in the blanks below: *Practice 4.3*

1. Know your _____.

2. Define your_____.

3. Indicate your topic _____.

4. Treat your reader _____.

5. Write about an _____ _____ fairly. Know the

   _____.

6. Be _____. Stay focused on your _____.

7. Be _____ and orderly.

The rest of the strategic tools await you. Dig in.

8. Identify yourself with regard to your topic (only if it adds weight to what you write).

> I've been incarcerated at the jail for the past 18 months. During my stay, I've heard numerous complaints by my fellow inmates as to the condition and treatment received by jail staff. For the most part the guards do their job. There are a few who abuse their authority but you have that in any job with authority status. Those certain few cause unnecessary anger and resentment in inmates and they shouldn't be hired for such a job.

This fellow is writing from jail. In a letter about needed changes in a jail, it makes good sense either to be an inmate or someone who works there. Insiders tend to have more credibility than those writing from outside a situation. Because the writer identified himself with respect to his topic, he seems more knowledgeable.

9. Quote people, experts, or the Bible.

Below are the first and last paragraphs from a letter to the editor about gun control.

> Close your eyes for a moment and imagine a world without guns. Although many people think of this as peace, gun control and peace can never coincide.

***

> Alexander Hamilton, the first United States Secretary of the Treasury, said, "The best we can hope for concerning the people at large is that they be properly armed." The right to own and use a firearm is a right that should not be taken away by any man, government, or army.

Quotations are important when supporting your views. This writer chooses someone close to the time when the American Constitution was being written. In addition, the expert's credentials give the quote more weight.

Another helpful practice is to gather quotations from friends, family, and acquaintances. Although these may not be experts, you can use their quotations to neatly sum up the beliefs on one side or the other. Other quotations may come from books, magazines, newspapers, sermons, the Bible, research doctors, family physicians, government offices, scientists, teachers, or reputable sources on the Internet. Be aware that doubters may ignore the "man on the street" quotations but value quotes from scientists and other experts in their fields.

10. Tell a relevant story.

Here are the first and last paragraphs from a letter about the harmful effects of smoking:

My dad struggled with tobacco addiction for almost 25 years. Sometimes I wonder if he would have ever started if he had been better educated on the harmful effects of cigarette smoking. If he had known about the addictive quality of smoking, would he have started? I wish he had known then what I know today.

**

The facts are unavoidable. Smoking is harmful. It is addictive. But there is hope. My dad has been smoke free for years. If you are addicted, there is help. Log onto whitelies.tv for excellent tips to help you quit smoking. Good luck! My dad did it, and so can you!

This writer begins with a story and ends by referring to it in her conclusion, neatly tying her conclusion to her introduction. Her story is an effective jumping-off point for the facts in the body of her article.

If you have a personal story that adds to your persuasive article, use it. Personal stories pack a tremendous punch. Write it concisely and plainly, but use it. Or find someone else who has a story, as the above writer did, check its authenticity, ask for permission to use it, and then include it in your writing.

11. Use humor if the situation calls for it, but use it sparingly.

The following example of humor is an excerpt from a weekly newspaper column by Edward Vasicek. These are two of ten ways the author suggests to create a bratty child. The writer is being ironic and is focusing not on the child's behavior but on the parents' actions.

If you want to raise a brat, start by letting her watch loads of TV (get one for the minivan too) and do not supervise or limit her viewing; give her the choice. Buy her clothes and toys she sees during the commercials, and be sure she watches all the "hot" shows. Program her mind to become dependent upon the media; otherwise she might become creative and engage in destructive practices like artwork, making friends, tea parties or playing board games.

Second, never spank the child. Let him throw tantrums and get away with being a brat. This will help him feel insecure and let him know that there are no real boundaries. He will learn to make a game out of seeing how he can outfox his parents. Out-maneuvering his parents will help develop ego. If the teacher sends home a note, remember: She is just picking on your little darling.

Humor is a powerful tool. By saying the opposite of what he really means (irony), Vasicek makes his point in a clever way. Readers see themselves in the backwards advice and may try to change. Humor is also useful to diffuse sticky situations or help make a point easier to swallow.

A word of caution is needed here, though. Written humor can be misread. In fact, if it *can* be misread, it *will* be. People sometimes misinterpret humor as anger or flippancy, or they take the written word literally. Without being able to look at the writer to check his mannerisms, watch the body language, and hear the tone of voice, it is easy to make a mistake about what the words mean. Have you ever experienced that problem in e-mails or on social media sites?

12. Be positive. Have a "we can fix this" attitude.
13. Issue a specific call to action.

> "It's beginning to look a lot like Christmas." Well, maybe not Christmas because the word *Christmas* was not to be seen in any of Target's promotions earlier this season. Some people were boycotting Target stores because of this. However, if you look at other retail store advertisements, they were not using the word *Christmas*, either.
>
> A boycott of Target was put in place to send a message to retailers. If you were going to boycott Target, though, you needed to do some research and also boycott other stores that were not using the word Christmas. Here is a list of stores to help you see who was included: Kmart, Sears, Kohl's, J. C. Penney, Best Buy, Wal-Mart, Kroger, Lowe's, CVS, Walgreens, and Staples, along with Target.
>
> But some of these stores have changed their mind. Lowe's changed their "holiday tree" signs to "Christmas tree" signs. Walgreens has said that while all of their advertisements are printed for this year, next year the ads will be different and use the word *Christmas*. And Target has added *Merry Christmas* to their advertisements.
>
> If you are concerned about this non-use and last-minute inclusion of Christmas, you can do something about it. Instead of saying, "Happy Holidays," say, "Merry Christmas." When you buy your cards for next year, buy some with the word *Christmas* on them so everyone knows what you're celebrating.

The tone of this Christmas letter to the editor is so different from the "How dare you spell Christmas with an X!" letter. Though the writer is concerned in the above letter, there is no yelling or threatening. The letter maintains a positive, calm tone throughout.

The writer gives a specific call to action at the end. Underline her suggestions.

14. Maintain an objective tone, if appropriate.

Maintaining an objective tone means using third person. Instead of writing "You should eat jicama; it's good for you," write "Try some jicama today; it is a healthful addition to one's diet." Take out personal pronouns (*I, me, you, yours*, and so forth). Only in casual settings are personal pronouns acceptable—as in this textbook. *I* have been writing to *you*.

An objective tone also means **avoiding** such phrases as "I believe…," "I think…," "It is my opinion that…," or "I choose to believe…." These make your argument weak. Use them in casual conversations, if you wish, but avoid them in school and formal writing.

Obviously, you will use *I* when telling a personal story or identifying yourself with respect to the topic, like this: "I've just turned 18, and I'm going to vote this year. I hope you do, too." But inserting yourself in the writing elsewhere moves attention from the original topic and puts the spotlight on you. Let the argument be about the topic, not about you.

Below is the complete Do List (your powerful persuasion tools):

1. Know your audience.
2. Define your terms.
3. Indicate your topic early.
4. Treat your reader intelligently.
5. Write about an opposing view fairly. Know the argument.
6. Be concise. Stay focused on your objective.
7. Be logical and orderly.
8. Identify yourself with regard to your topic (only if it adds weight to what you write).
9. Quote people, experts, or the Bible.*
10. Tell a relevant story.*
11. Use humor if the situation calls for it, but use it sparingly.*
12. Be positive. Have a "we can fix this" attitude.
13. Issue a specific call to action.
14. Maintain an objective tone, if appropriate.

 * optional tools

A few words about the Don't and Do Lists: Avoid everything on the Don't List. There is nothing good in it for you. On the Do List, however, some tools are optional, like the story, humor, and sometimes quotations. You will note that you cannot cram all the tools into one persuasive paper. If you did, your reader would overload. What a crazy, restless paper that would be. Be selective about your optional tools and use the other ones to your advantage.

Practice 4.4

Read the following letter penned after a mother was caught on a store surveillance camera beating her little daughter. The letter exhibits items from the Don't List and from the Do List. Next to each paragraph, write the guidelines broken or followed (example: "Don't List # 3").

Also, underline the sentence that states the letter's true topic.

Thank you for your editorial of September 25th titled "An Unfit Mother." As you stated, Madelyne Gorman Toogood's beating of her four-year-old daughter was appalling. Her attempts to defend herself after she was apprehended, in light of the video evidence, were frustrating to watch. Any mother who would lift her hand in this way against her own child deserves punishment. Again as you pointed out, having her child taken away from her for a time and having to sit in a prison cell will hopefully do her good as she contemplates the evil of her actions.

This tragic event made me think, though, that a far worse atrocity is occurring against children every day in our nation. It also has been videotaped, though most choose to remain ignorant and unconcerned about this form of child abuse. It is the practice of abortion, where men and women take their unborn children purposefully into a clinic to have their life taken. I would describe what happens to the child, but it is probably more than your readers could stomach. Indeed, is it because we have become a nation of "Toogoods" that we cannot see how even more appalling this practice is?

If any of your readers would like to help inform the conscience of our community about what is happening, please join the Right to Life's Life Chain being held Sunday, October 6, from 2 to 3 p.m. This is a peaceful, prayerful protest where we hold signs up along Washington and Markland Streets that tell the truth about abortion. If you would like further information, please call Right to Life at 452-9300 or feel free to reach me at 555-3344.

Man's name
Church where he is the minister
City

Lesson 5

The Persuasive Attitude

In a letter to Dear Abby, someone running for office writes that "we all have to work hard, do our best, and fight those who do not always believe in us." His view—that of fighting *people*—is not unusual.

It is a common belief that we should be in a battle against people who don't agree with us. On the other hand, Leonard Pitts Jr., a syndicated columnist, uses his column "not to hammer the other side down, but to persuade persuadable minds." Who's right?

Look up these verses in the Bible and answer the questions concerning   *Practice 4.5*
person-to-person persuasion in spiritual, moral, or ethical issues:

❑ **Acts 17:16-17.** How did Paul interact with people who were breaking God's laws?

❑ **2 Corinthians 10:3-5.** How do a Christian's tactics differ from those who do not believe in Christ? What can these tactics do?

❑ **Ephesians 6:12.** Who is your enemy?

❑ **Philippians 4:5.** What should be evident and why?

❑ **2 Timothy 2:24-26.** How should you treat those who oppose you? Why?

❑ **1 Peter 3:15-16.** When telling people how you believe, what should be your approach? Why?

❑ **Jude 22-23.** How should you treat doubters?

Should you worry about offending your readers? There will be times when, even at your most gentle, your opinion will be offensive. Some opinions offend some readers. This is totally and completely unavoidable.

Some views are offense-laden. To a feminist, the pro-life view is an insult. To members of the NRA (National Rifle Association), gun-control issues are offensive. But if you have presented your view in a kind, thoughtful manner, you will have done your job well.

Even Jesus offended listeners, and the disciples tried to set him straight: "Do you know that the Pharisees were offended when they heard this?" (Matthew 15:12 NIV). How does Jesus react to this news? Does he give himself a dope slap and say, "What was I thinking?" Please look up the next verses (13-14) to see what he says.

Write an Essay

Write a persuasive essay on why children shouldn't watch horror movies.

✓ Identify your target audience. The reasons you write for babysitters are going to be different from the reasons you give for parents.
✓ Brainstorm possible reasons. Be creative.
✓ Arrange your points for the greatest impact, using one of the orders you learned in chapter 2.

✓ Use a QSFSQ tool to begin your introduction. Issue a specific, measurable call to action in your conclusion.

✓ Incorporate strategies from the Do List (your powerful tools) and avoid the mistakes from the Don't List.

If this topic falls flat for you, devise another one and check with your teacher about it.

Word count for **beginning** writers: at least 300 words.

Word count for **intermediate** and **accomplished** writers: at least 400.

Here's a suggested writing schedule:

Day 1	Day 2	Day 3	Day 4	Day 5	Day 6
Brainstorm topics and points. Arrange points. Create a flexible thesis statement.	Research, if needed. Write the body (the point or reason paragraphs).	Adjust thesis statement and points as needed. Write introduction and conclusion.	Check for unity and completeness of paragraphs and essay. Proofread.	Proofread again; read once out loud. Print out essay and adjust as needed. Print final draft.	Submit essay to teacher.

Use this checklist for your persuasion paper:

❑ Did you select a specific audience?

❑ Do you have a reader-grabbing QSFSQ?

❑ Is your thesis statement clear, and is it at the end of your introduction?

❑ Do all your succeeding paragraphs stick to and support your thesis statement?

❑ Are your points arranged in the order that will best affect your audience?

❑ Do the topic sentences clearly state your points or reasons?

❑ Does each paragraph support its topic sentence with details, quotes, facts, and so forth?

❑ Does each paragraph in the body exhibit a logical internal order?

❑ Did you know that the largest living organism on earth is not a whale but a fungus the size of 1,665 football fields spreading under the forest in the Malheur National Forest in eastern Oregon, according to scientificamerican.com? Camping, anyone?

❑ Does each paragraph exhibit unity and completeness?

❑ Is your call to action specific and measurable?

❑ Did you avoid the mistakes on the Don't List?

❑ Did you employ the strategies on the Do List (your powerful tools)?

"Two sorts of writers possess genius:
those who think,
and those who cause others to think."
- Joseph Roux

Chapter 5: Persuasion—Logical

Lesson 1

I'm sorry to have to tell you this, but there are many, many methods for writing persuasively. Each method uses powerful tools (the Do List) and avoids the Don't List, but each method is different from the others. When you wrote your papers in chapters 3 and 4, you were writing a generic persuasive paper. It was like a basic plan for a cell phone—a good place to start, but it doesn't fit every need.

In this course, you will learn four methods of writing persuasively: (1) logical, (2) compare and contrast, (3) moral/ethical, and (4) emotional appeal. Each is like a different plan for a mobile device because each has basic components (the Do List) but includes different features.

Why are there so many ways to persuade readers? First, there are many issues. Some issues are best treated with certain methods. Second, there are many kinds of readers. What convinces one person might not convince another, so you need an assortment of appeals that will reach a variety of readers. And last, we just like to keep you busy.

It is acceptable—and even advisable—to mix and match the methods of persuasive appeals you will learn here, using components of each, after you have learned them. However, for this course, you are going to learn and practice each one separately.

This chapter's method is the **logical appeal**. Each method of persuasion has a key sentence in this course to help you remember its essence. The logical appeal's key sentence is this:

"I'll prove it!"

This sentence, even though it sums up the logical appeal, will not appear in your paper. It embodies the focus of your work as you write to convince your reader to think in a new way and take action. (*Method*, *appeal*, and *approach* are all used interchangeably.)

Porcupine Park Goes Belly Up?

The following essay (577 words) is written in the logical method. Read it and answer the questions that follow in Practice 5.1. You will be referring to this essay in the next three lessons as you learn about the logical appeal guidelines.

Introduction

Tyrone Bishop can often be found walking the beautiful trails in Porcupine Park. A junior at Shipley High School, Tyrone goes to the park to think. "I've got so many decisions ahead of me and so much homework every day. Pounding these trails, enjoying these trees, it gives me a chance to think," Tyrone admits.

Natalie Levine agrees. She and her two young daughters visit Porcupine Park often. "We live on a major highway," Natalie says. "That's no place for little kids to play. We like it here. It's quiet. The girls can run and play and just enjoy the wide-open spaces."

The issue and the writer's opinion of it

But not for long, it seems. Mayor Tewkesbury wants to build a city street through the middle of the park.

Reason 1 against the street

Porcupine Park, consisting of 47.2 acres on the south side of Shipley, was established by the city in 1974 to provide its citizens a haven of nature and safety. Hector Ramirez, the mayor at the time, heartily supported the park and its reason for existing. In the speech he gave on June 22, 1974, at the ceremony that officially opened the park, he said that the city "has a responsibility to ensure that our good townsfolk do not lose these beautiful trees, vistas, and spaces. Our people and our environment deserve this restful, safe oasis."

Reason 2 against the street (continued on the next page)

Constructing a city street through Porcupine Park will cripple citizens' enjoyment of nature and endanger their safety. The proposed street will connect San Pedro Street at the north end with Morris Street on the south, using 6.8 acres of park land and cutting the park into two sections. The addition of traffic noises, the smell of exhaust, and the inevitable litter will pollute the once-peaceful park. According to the city's Web site, shipleyatyourservice.org, the two-mile hiking trail will be downsized to 1.2 miles and will lose the stand of old-growth oaks. This proposed street is not on the edge of the park. It is almost straight up the middle. The young children who currently play safely on the play equipment and in the open fields will become vulnerable to car accidents. City streets (as opposed to necessary park roads) through parks increase the chances of a vehicle hitting a child, a walker, or a bicyclist by 33 percent, as found in this month's issue of *Your Park*, our state's magazine for city park coordinators.

Many motorists would like this street to be constructed because it would connect the Ellison housing development with the city's major employer, Shipley Packaging. In a poll conducted by *Shipley Chronicle*, 90 percent of the workers who live in Ellison and work at Shipley Packaging support the street through the park as a shortcut to work. And, after all, isn't saving on gasoline important these days? In spite of the savings on time and fuel, however, constructing the street would be a mistake. What price can be put on the blessings we would lose: an old-growth forest, the quiet and enjoyment of an ecologically balanced space, and the safety of our children? Even city Councilwoman Miranda Anthony, who supports the street, admits on her Web site, "I regret the loss of those fabulous oaks." *Treatment of the opposing view*

Constructing a city street through Porcupine Park breaks the original intent of the park, as set up by then-Mayor Ramirez, and endangers the peace and safety of the citizens who enjoy the park. It should not be built. Please contact Mayor Tewkesbury at mayortewkesbury@shipleyatyourservice.org to voice your opinion of this street. *Conclusion with thesis statement*

Answer these in-depth, thought-provoking, time-consuming questions. *Practice 5.1*
Use a separate piece of paper or the space below.

1. Do you agree with this writer? Explain.
2. What is the tone of this essay?
3. What two reasons does this writer give for not building the street?
4. Stand on the other side of the issue for a moment. List two reasons why someone might believe that the city street *should* be built up the middle of Porcupine Park.
5. Do you wish this lesson were over? Don't explain.

Lesson 2

The Logistics of the Logical Appeal, part 1

In addition to the basic components on the Do List (the powerful tools from chapter 4), you will add the following when writing a logical appeal:

Logical Appeal Guidelines

1. Use reliable evidence.
2. Use logical thinking to build your case.
3. Avoid logical fallacies.
4. Know the argument. State an opposing view fairly and then refute it.
5. Use quotations from knowledgeable people in the field about which you are writing, especially when disproving an opposing view.
6. Cite your sources correctly.

The rest of this lesson and the next ones explain each guideline.

1. Use reliable evidence.

Many facts are mentioned in the Porcupine Park essay: the size of the park, how many acres will be lost due to the construction, the increased chances of a patron being harmed by a vehicle, and so forth. Where do these facts come from? For the most part, the writer relied on the city's Web site, a reputable magazine, and the city's own newspaper. These are generally trustworthy sources of information, as opposed to someone's blog, which should be considered unreliable.

Ask yourself if your facts are current and reliable. Is your source trustworthy? Can you find the same evidence in other resources? Make sure your evidence is valid.

Is the following information reliable? According to the real Web site www.dhmo.org, dihydrogen monoxide (DHMO) "is a constituent of many known toxic substances, diseases and disease-causing agents, environmental hazards and can even be lethal to humans in quantities as small as a thimbleful." The site goes on to say that this toxic substance has been present at the site of any school violence and that it is disreputable because it "improves athletic performance." The information seems reliable. The site looks official. But what, exactly, is DHMO? Take another look at the chemical name at the top of this paragraph and all will be made clear. DHMO is water (H_2O). The site is a humorous hoax. While each "fact" is true, it is slanted to show only water's negative aspects.

Have you ignored or manipulated any facts? This makes your argument weak and full of holes, and then you appear untrustworthy.

Be careful when using numbers and statistics. They can be misleading, even if often repeated. Take, for example, the statement that humans use only 10 percent of their brain. This popular "fact" is a myth that is widely believed. According to Snopes.com, "Brain imaging research techniques such as PET scans (positron emission tomography) and fMRI (functional magnetic resonance imaging) clearly show that the vast majority of the brain does not lie fallow." Additionally, the site asks this question, "Have you ever heard a doctor say, '...But luckily when that bullet entered his skull, it only damaged the 90 percent of his brain he didn't use'?" Posit Science maintains that "functional brain imaging studies show that all parts of the brain function. Even during sleep, the brain is active," and "if 90% of the brain was not used, then many neural pathways would likely degenerate" and those functions (such as vision) would shut down.

As Rex Stout, creator of the Nero Wolfe detective series, writes, "There are two kinds of statistics: the kind you look up and the kind you make up." Make sure your "facts" really are facts.

Numbers and statistics can be manipulated in a variety of ways. Be aware of this when you find them. Say a gal in high school weighs 120 pounds and she wants to lose five pounds in one month. At the end of that month, she weighs in and finds she lost only 2.5 pounds. Aside from fiddling with the scales to adjust the display, here's how the numbers can be reported and still be true:

Mother: "Wow, honey. You attained 50 percent of your goal. You're halfway there!"

Little brother: "All you have to do is lose 100 percent more."

*Each number changes the **perception** of how much weight was actually lost.*

Best friend: "What are you so thrilled about? You lost barely two percent of your body weight."

New best friend: "Looking good, girl!"

2. Use logical reasoning to build your case.

The structure of a logical appeal may feel upside-down to you, like a climactic paragraph. Instead of beginning with your thesis statement and supporting it, as you have been doing for your essays, the logical appeal uses solid statements called premises to build up to your thesis statement sitting in your concluding paragraph. Your thesis statement/conclusion will be drawn from your **premises**, certain propositions you assume to be true and that, when combined, lead to a logical conclusion. Choose premises that are strong, ones that most readers can agree upon.

Typically, your premises, in one form or another, become your topic sentences, and your conclusion becomes your thesis statement.

Practice 5.2   The following is an example of a syllogism (premises and a conclusion) that is weak. Identify the problems a parent might have with this syllogism:

Premise 1: Safe drivers should be allowed to drive the family car to the weekend campout.

Premise 2: I am a safe driver because I have been driving for one month and haven't had an accident.

Conclusion: I should be allowed to drive the family car to the weekend campout.

Why are those premises weak? Identify two reasons in the space below and then continue to the next syllogism.

Here's an example of a syllogism that is more trustworthy. You'll recognize it as the skeleton from which the Porcupine Park essay was written. After you've read the following syllogism, turn back to the essay; underline and label the premises and conclusion.

Premise 1: Porcupine Park was established to provide our townsfolk with a peaceful and safe environment.

Premise 2: Constructing a city street through the middle of the park will damage the peace of the park and endanger citizens' safety.

Premise 3: Although many support the street, the benefits of not building it far outweigh the benefits of building it.

Conclusion: A city street should not be constructed through Porcupine Park.

Lesson 3

The Logistics of the Logical Appeal, part 2

3. Avoid logical fallacies.

If you use sound evidence but faulty reasoning, you will undermine your opinion. Strong reasoning follows the rules of logic. Your appeal will be logical if you build a well-reasoned, solid case while avoiding faulty reasoning.

The field of logical reasoning is a course in and of itself, and books on the topics of logic, critical thinking, and debate abound at your local library. But let's pause anyway for a short, brief, compressed, and maybe even small lesson in logical fallacies and other pitfalls.

Fallacies are weaknesses or shortcomings in reasoning. A few are mentioned below so you can recognize them in others' arguments and eliminate them from your own.

Genetic fallacy: Accepting or rejecting an argument not on its own merit but because of its source. Try these examples on for size:

> Of course it's true. I got it off the Internet.

> You can't believe anything she says. She raises fruit flies for a living.

Ad hominem fallacy: Focusing on and/or attacking the person who holds the view. Related to the genetic fallacy, an ad hominem argument bypasses the view itself and does not address the real issues. Here's an example of the ad hominem fallacy from noted evolutionist Richard Dawkins:

> It is absolutely safe to say that if you meet somebody who claims not to believe in evolution, that person is ignorant, stupid or insane (or wicked, but I'd rather not consider that).

Circular reasoning: Using one of the premises as a conclusion. For example:

> Gun owners are violent because they own guns.

False dilemma ("either/or" fallacy): Being presented with only two choices when others may be available and viable. You may have seen this example on billboards sponsored by the Robertson Foundation and the Ad Council:

☐ Do nothing

☐ Fight global warming

Are there more than two choices in this debate?

Straw man argument: Misrepresenting an argument from the opposing view in order to prove it wrong. Sometimes the misrepresentation comes from choosing a belief held by only a small number of opponents on the extreme end of the issue. Refuting the extreme belief has the appearance of making a strong case when, in reality, no *legitimate* beliefs from the opposition are refuted. The smoking-ban topic gives us straw man arguments from both sides:

> Lawmakers who want to ban people from smoking in their own cars want to control everything about our lives.

> The people who smoke in their cars when a child is present don't care about their children.

Weak analogy: Assuming that because two things can be compared on some level, all things about them can also be compared and proven true. Run your peepers across this weak analogy:

> God is like Santa Claus because God sees you all the time and he knows what you've been doing.

Although there may be aspects of God and Santa Claus that are similar, the differences far outweigh the similarities, thus canceling the use of this as a good analogy.

Broad (sweeping) generalization: Applying a general statement too broadly. This often means using words like *all, none, no, always,* or *never* in a statement or implying the use of them:

> No computer geek has adequate social skills.

> [All] Cheerleaders are ditzy.

Hasty generalization: Making a general principle from one case. In other words, it is built upon insufficient or biased evidence:

> My sister is a vegan, but I've seen her eat meat before. What a hypocrite! From this I know that all vegans are hypocritical.

Reductionism: Saying there's only one reason for a result. Many issues are complicated and cannot be reduced simplistically to one cause, as this example would like us to believe:

> The Roman Empire fell because it was attacked by warlike tribes like the Goths, Vandals, and Franks.

Is it possible that the fall of the Roman Empire is attributable to many factors?

Find the fallacies in this excerpt from a letter to the editor. There are at least *Practice 5.3* three (fallacies, not editors).

> Why do [people] think it is more moral to wash [embryonic] stem cells down a drain than to use them to help save and improve millions of American lives? If opponents want to think of embryonic stem cells as "lives," why not think of them as soldiers who are sacrificed to protect us from the war we all are fighting: to keep our country healthy. By refusing to build an army to protect our nation, [politicians] are failing to help keep people healthy.

Lesson 4

The Logistics of the Logical Appeal, part 3

4. Know the argument. State an opposing view fairly and then refute it.

The writer of the Porcupine Park essay knew the argument. Revisit the *Practice 5.4* essay. Who are the people who disagree with her? What is their argument? Write your answers below:

If you want to win over someone who holds an opposing view, consider beginning with a story, fact, or other specific detail that both sides can agree upon. Why make an enemy in your first sentence? Another tactic is to agree with something from the opposing view. For instance, though the writer of the park essay is against constructing the city street, she agrees with the opposing view that saving gas and time are important. Work hard to find something with which you can agree. This shows that you are not an enemy but a concerned thinker.

Know the argument. If you demonstrate to your readers that you know both sides of the issue, you stand a better chance of gaining their respect. And if you treat the opposing view fairly, you will have earned the right to refute it (prove it wrong).

Obviously, you can't anticipate all the arguments or spend your whole paper refuting them all. Select one or two popular or well-known arguments from the opposing view and refute those. How do you find opposing arguments? How do you know which ones are legitimate and important? Consider these options:

- ✓ Ask a trusted expert for arguments on both sides of the issue.
- ✓ Research the topic to learn what each side considers its strongest arguments.
- ✓ Speak with people who hold an opposing view; pick their brains.
- ✓ Imagine yourself on the other side of the issue and ask yourself, "Yes, but what about…?"

Refuting an opposing view deserves a new paragraph type. You will remember from an earlier chapter some types of paragraphs: direct (topic sentence first), climactic (topic sentence last), and interrogative (topic sentence as a question). The logical appeal will benefit from another type—the **turnabout paragraph.** In the turnabout paragraph, begin with the opposing view and then refute it with facts or logic. The topic sentence goes in between the opposing view and the refutation, something like this:

- Opposing view
- Topic sentence
- Refutation

When you eventually present your view (after the opposing view), use words like *but, however, nevertheless, despite, contrary to, although,* or *in contrast to.* These types of words neatly move your paragraph from the opposing view to yours. The sentence upon which the whole paragraph pivots (the one that begins *your* argument) is the topic sentence.

Steven Ertelt, writing as the Public Affairs Director for the Indiana Citizens for Life, shows us how it's done in a paragraph:

Much misinformation has been presented concerning partial birth abortion. Some say that it is medically necessary to protect the health of the mother. But that's not true. Dr. Martin Haskell, who has performed more partial birth abortions than any other person, admits that "80% are for purely elective reasons."

His topic sentence? "But that's not true."

In this turnabout paragraph, the writer uses the words "Some say... but...." Other formats might include "Many believe that... but...," "According to some scientists...," or "It is commonly assumed that...." Words like *seem, appear,* and *evidently* tip off the reader that you are setting up an opposing argument.

That is an effective pattern to introduce both the opposing argument and the facts against it, like this:

Some say that running with scissors is fun, but Julie Nyquist, a nurse at Slash and Patch in Fiskars, California, reveals that soft and squishy torsos do not blend well with sharp, metal scissors.

When writing about your own argument, remember item 2 from persuasion's Do List: "Define your terms." If a mother says of a toddler, "He's a good eater," does she mean that he eats only healthful food, that he eats a lot of food, or that he doesn't complain when given new food items? A definition of "good" would be helpful here. In the same way, you will need to define terms that can take on different meanings to different people, words like *patriotic, good citizenship, family values, hate speech, middle class, family, education, death,* and *censorship.*

As you research and explore your chosen topic, you may want to change your thesis statement, your argument, or your whole opinion. This is natural and is part of the learning/writing process.

Cruising back and forth among the phases of writing (brainstorming, planning, researching, organizing, and writing) is also natural as you adjust your writing to accommodate new material.

Let a classmate read your paper while it is in the first-draft form. He or she can look for weak facts or reasons, faulty logic, or other places to improve. The give-and-take between the two of you will aid you in writing a stronger paper.

Practice 5.5

Here and on the next page are examples of turnabout paragraphs written by students using facts, quotations, paraphrases, and logical statements. As you read each one, underline the sentence that transitions the paragraph from one view to the other. (In these examples, the topic sentence may appear near the beginning, middle, or end of the paragraph.) Then give each a grade in the margin based on what you now know about refuting an argument.

1

Many people say that hybrid cars are too uncomfortable and expensive, and not without reason; the cars are much smaller and lighter, making it easier for the hybrid engine to run. Yet comfort won't really seem to matter so much when gas prices soar as wells dry up one by one. Our wallets will benefit tomorrow from a little inconvenience today.

2

One of the other problems people have with hybrids is that they think, with such high mileage, the cars must not be very powerful. It would seem that way; however, according to Wikipedia.org, the cars "can provide a normal driving experience when used in combination during acceleration and other maneuvers that require greater power." Hybrids are the best of both worlds and can deliver when called upon.

3

A few of the best-known proofs for evolution today are these: the finches that Darwin studied on his voyage and the peppered moths that changed colors in succeeding generations. For decades these have been some of the most feverishly argued evidences for evolution. These creatures indeed have evolved, but this is actually microevolution. Evolutionist Collin Patterson says, "No one has ever produced a species by mechanisms of natural selection. No one has gotten near it." Animals may change within their species, but they won't change from species to species.

4

Roundabouts are becoming more popular in small towns. While some say they're confusing and dangerous, roundabouts are much simpler and safer than other intersections. At a four-way intersection, there are sixteen points where a vehicle could hit another vehicle and sixteen where one could hit a pedestrian. But roundabouts have only four car-to-car points and eight car-to-pedestrian points. Clearly, this lessens the danger for accidents with either cars or pedestrians.

Lesson 5

The Logistics of the Logical Appeal, part 4

Practice 5.6   To review the first four guidelines of the logical method, fill in the blanks:

1. Use reliable _____.
2. Use _____ thinking to build your case.
3. Avoid logical _____.
4. Know the argument. State an _____ view fairly and then _____ it.

Now on to the last two items in a logical appeal:

5. Use quotations from knowledgeable people in the field about which you are writing, especially when disproving an opposing view.

Facts are more believable if they come from an expert in the field. You may quote famous people, historians, scientists, philosophers, reliable Internet sources, encyclopedias, the Bible, doctors, police officers, ministers, elected officials, teachers, soldiers, and so forth. Find a source or someone who is related to your topic and get a quote to support your point.

You may have noticed that Mr. Ertelt, in the turnabout paragraph example in the previous lesson, does not quote someone who is against abortion; he quotes a famous abortionist to prove the point against a certain type of abortion procedure. This is very powerful and can serve to validate your viewpoint in the eyes of your readers.

The logical appeal relies heavily on facts and quotes. Load your essay with them.

6. Cite your sources correctly.

Avoid plagiarizing. When you use a fact, idea, or example from someone else, let readers know that it comes from someone other than you. This way, you are not stealing or plagiarizing someone else's information. Citing your original source will help you avoid the deep pit of plagiarizing. Only facts of common knowledge need not be cited (the location of the North Pole, an author's birth date, the temperature of water when it freezes, and so forth).

From now on, you will be citing your sources to avoid plagiarizing.

The following sentences are examples of how to cite your sources:

> Dr. Acumen, the self-proclaimed human encyclopedia, reveals in his new book *I Know it All*, "When it comes to facts, I can never know too many. I'm great at trivia parties. Everyone wants me on their team."

> According to www.idontcare.edu, 79 percent of high school students are apathetic about persuasive appeals.

These are called **in-text citations**. Instead of using a footnote or endnote, the information about the source appears in the sentence. Newspaper and magazine writers call this an attribution; research writers call it an in-text citation. You will learn in a later chapter how to use parenthetical citations and works cited pages. But for now, use an in-text citation, which can be summed up as a mathematical equation here:

In-text citation = signal phrase + person or source + credentials

Signal phrases? Just as blinking lights at a railroad crossing signal a train's approach, a signal phrase alerts readers that a quote or borrowed fact is coming. Here is a quotation without a signal phrase:

> Despite the new health guidelines stating that pickles should not be eaten with applesauce, students continue to practice this dangerous habit. "I'm not going to give up eating pickles with applesauce just because someone says it's going to give me heartburn."

Who cares? The quote is just hanging out there and has no credibility. No one knows who said the quote or why we should pay attention to it. Here's the same quotation with a signal phrase. Notice how much more believable it is now:

> Despite the new health guidelines stating that pickles should not be eaten with applesauce, students continue to practice this dangerous habit. Jesse Dillman, president of Students for Lunchtime Liberation, admits, "I'm not going to give up eating pickles with applesauce just because someone says it's going to give me heartburn."

These and others phrases can be used as signal phrases: *according to...*, *states...*, *shows that...*, and *claims that....* These signal phrases are most often written in the present tense ("says") or present perfect tense ("has said"), even if the person is long dead.

Signal phrases, combined with the person or source of the information ("Jesse Dillman"), along with the person's credentials ("president of Students for Lunchtime Liberation"), make up an in-text citation.

Here are more examples of how to use signal phrases in your in-text citations, which can appear at the beginning, middle, or end of your sentence:

- The actress and screenwriter Emma Thompson reveals . . .
- . . . writes Ravi Zacharias, a well-known Christian apologist.
- ConAgra Foods, a multi-billion dollar parent company for many food products, insists . . .
- . . . contends Cara Greenberg, who witnessed the accident.
- . . . , notes scientist Carl Sagan, . . .
- According to answersingenesis.org, . . .
- Historian David G. McCullough notes in his book *1776* that . . .
- C. S. Lewis, after losing his wife to cancer just a few years into their marriage, writes . . .
- As Itzhak Perlman, the famous violinist who lost the use of his legs to polio at the age of four, advises young musicians . . .

The name of the person or source establishes where the fact comes from. The credentials or person's title shows that he or she is an expert or knows something about the topic. A Web site, an organization, or a real person can be referenced. If a person is cited, you will include his or her position or credentials ("Edwin Losage, a reformed gambler, states in his memoir *Just One More, . . .*").

Below are three sentences with facts and in-text citations written by students. Underlining is added to emphasize the citation. You won't underline yours.

1. As a result, there are 40 percent fewer collisions, 80 percent fewer injuries, and 90 percent fewer fatal injuries and deaths when using a roundabout, <u>according to the United States Department of Transportation.</u>

2. If you live with a pack-a-day smoker who smokes inside the house, you inhale about three cigarettes' worth of smoke a day, 21 a week, and 1092 a year, <u>states www.whitelies.tv.</u>

3. <u>A 1998 University of California, San Francisco, study done of bar workers in California shows </u>that after two smoke-free months, 59 percent of workers who had complained of respiratory problems no longer had any symptoms.

Now it's time to review the mechanics of using quotations. If you are punctuation challenged or about to fall asleep, now would be a good time to stretch, get a snack, or hope for an interruption.

Sometimes you will want to use a whole sentence or two as a quotation. Other times you'll join the quotation midstream or paraphrase your quotation to succinctly state the fact. Below are examples of each.

While an ellipsis (three periods in a row, like this: . . .) will show that you have taken words out of the middle, you do not need to use them at the beginning or end of a quote to show you have taken words off the beginning or end of the quote. Please note the punctuation in each example:

In *Experiment in Autobiography*, science-fiction writer H. G. Wells recounts the time he contracted tuberculosis and thought he was going to die. He states, "I was exasperated not to have become famous; not to have seen the world."

Direct quotation using a whole sentence

In *Experiment in Autobiography*, science-fiction writer H. G. Wells writes that when he contracted tuberculosis and thought he was going to die, he "was exasperated not to have become famous; not to have seen the world."

Partial quotation

Partial quotation with an ellipsis to show a few words left out in the middle

In *Experiment in Autobiography*, science-fiction writer H. G. Wells writes that when he contracted tuberculosis and thought he was going to die, he "was exasperated not to have . . . seen the world."

Paraphrase

In *Experiment in Autobiography*, science-fiction writer H. G. Wells remembers contracting tuberculosis and facing the possibility of death. He writes that he was disappointed to think about dying so young because he had not yet traveled or achieved fame.

Practice 5.7   Here are sentences containing quotations. The first sentence contains the complete quotation; the second contains a partial one. In the second one, determine where the partial quotation begins. Consult your grammar book or check the examples above to know how to correctly punctuate both sentences. Then insert the commas and quotation marks as needed.

The pepper shaker will not help.

1. Even though Mark Twain could poke fun at any form of government, he particularly hated one form above all others. In a letter to Sylvester Baxter in 1889, he writes I believe I should really see the end of what is surely the grotesquest of all the swindles ever invented by man—monarchy.

2. Even though Mark Twain could poke fun at any form of government, he particularly hated one form above all others. In a letter to Sylvester Baxter in 1889, he writes that he would like to see the end of what is surely the grotesquest of all the swindles ever invented by man—monarchy.

Write an Essay

Choose a current event (local, national, or worldwide) that interests you. Or choose an issue that is a hot topic today (abortion, immigration, book banning, the death penalty, a war, renewable energy sources, and so on). You have a wide range of possibilities.

Write a logical appeal based on your opinion of what people should believe and do about this issue.

Plan before writing. Brainstorm, list tentative premises and a conclusion, and arrange your supporting facts and points in a logical order.

Check your topic and your points with your teacher before you research. Adjust your thesis statement (conclusion) and points as you gather information.

Here's a preliminary checklist to keep you on track:

✓ Before you write your first draft, write your purpose statement to keep your writing on track ("I am going to convince the reader…").
✓ Refer to the logical appeal list.
✓ Include facts, short quotations, and logical thinking.
✓ Avoid logical fallacies.
✓ Mention and refute an opposing view in a turnabout paragraph.
✓ Cite your sources by using in-text citations.
✓ Issue a specific call to action.

You will be writing as a magazine columnist. That way you will have a specific reading public in mind when you write. Choose the magazine and write the name of it on the back of your essay.

Your magazine column will most likely use the structure below. The turnabout paragraph may be Section 2, 3, or 4 or an added paragraph in the body. A section may be one paragraph or longer:

- **Section 1**: Introduction including your topic and your view of the topic
- **Section 2:** Premise one
- **Section 3:** Premise two
- **Section 4:** Premise three, if necessary
- **Section 5:** Concluding paragraph with syllogism's conclusion (thesis statement) and a call to action

Word count for **beginning writers**: at least 350 words.

Word count for **intermediate** and **accomplished writers**: at least 500 words.

Prepare a personal schedule to help you complete the tasks for this assignment (see the suggested schedule at the end of chapter 4 for ideas about your own schedule):

Day 1	Day 2	Day 3	Day 4	Day 5	Day 6

Use this checklist for your logical appeal:

- ❑ Does your paper have an interesting title?
- ❑ Is it double-spaced?
- ❑ Is your reader's attention hooked by your riveting question, statement, fact, story, or quotation?
- ❑ Do you get to the point quickly? Do you stick to the point?
- ❑ Do you use a variety of topic sentences?
- ❑ Do you use the turnabout paragraph to refute an opposing view at least once?
- ❑ Do you show a reliable knowledge of the opposing argument?
- ❑ Does your paper logically progress from one point to the next?
- ❑ Is it easy to read and easy to understand?
- ❑ Are there many reputable facts from reliable sources?
- ❑ Are your premises sound?
- ❑ Did you write the premises and conclusion on the back of your paper, along with the magazine you are writing for?
- ❑ Do you avoid logical fallacies?
- ❑ Do you prefer Coke over Pepsi?
- ❑ Do you define any terms that are important to your argument?
- ❑ Are your in-text citations correct?
- ❑ Is your call to action specific and measurable?
- ❑ Is your thesis statement in your concluding paragraph and does it follow logically from your premises?

"*A man who has the knowledge but lacks the power clearly to express it is no better off than if he never had any ideas at all.*"

-Thucydides

Chapter 6: Persuasion—Compare and Contrast

Lesson 1

The Organization of the Picnic

What do a mailbox and a deadly car accident have in common? Or, for that matter, a dangerous box jellyfish and . . . well, keep reading to find out.

But first, a message from your Grammar Factoid.

Many writers of all ages make a common mistake. They mistreat their verbs. In fact, they treat them so badly they turn them into nouns. Here's an example:

The **organization** of the picnic is Rudy's job.

Who is organizing this picnic? Rudy. But it doesn't seem as if he's really organizing anything, and the sentence is a yawner. Here's another try:

Organizing the picnic is Rudy's job.

That's a little better. *Organizing*, in that sentence, is a gerund. A gerund is a word that uses an "--ing" ending but is no longer a verb; it is acting as a noun (in this case, the subject of the sentence). Grammar neophytes may mistake it for a verb, but it isn't one, and Rudy—who is supposed to be organizing the event—is still separated from *organizing*. Again:

It is Rudy's job to organize the picnic.

We're getting there. We've moved to an infinitive (to + a verb: *to organize*). But we can do better:

Rudy will organize the picnic.

Can you hear Rudy sighing with relief? We finally got it right. Rudy, the subject, is doing the verb (*will organize*).

You will notice two positive things when you change a noun into a verb: You generally use fewer words, and you change the sentence from passive to active. This makes your writing easier to understand.

Lawyers and businesses often utilize a kind of writing that disembowels excellent verbs, leaving them as panting, pathetic, powerless nouns, but you don't have to. Avoid this kind of unintelligible writing. Make yours come alive.

Practice 6.1   Below are some nouns. Write the verb form of the word next to each noun. Then fix the following sentences on a separate piece of paper; locate the subject and use an action verb. The first ones are done for you.

examination—examine	confinement—confine
prediction-	acknowledgment-
hibernation-	confirmation-
decision-	circulation-
appearance-	realization-
communication-	discernment-
confiscation-	acquisition-

1. It is the prediction of this committee that the float will be a failure. (Fixed: The committee predicts that the float will fail.)
2. The implementation of the fundraiser is still awaiting authorization from the principal.
3. The realization that I would finally own a parrot was exciting.
4. Defenestration is prohibited.
5. The establishment of the carnival committee will be enhanced by the creation of guidelines.

6. The success of the cross-country bicycle race depends entirely upon the utilization of a safety team.
7. In a healthy person, the circulation of the blood is uninhibited by clots, plaque, or bad cholesterol.
8. Our low price includes the replacing of the pads and the machining of the rotors.

Are those sentences hard to understand? That's what happens when writers change strong verbs into nouns. If you have to read a sentence four times before you understand it, someone wrote it incorrectly.

Keep using those great verbs. Make them strong. Make them move the sentence along. Your writing will be more concise and easier to understand.

Lesson 2

Similarities and Differences

Finally, the compare-and-contrast section of this chapter on persuasion. Just so you know, this type of essay can also be called *comparison* and contrast.

If you want to show your readers that attending a family reunion can be fraught with danger, you can attack the topic directly (Uncle Harry and his rock-polishing kit, and those creepy cousins who always beat you up). Or you can compare it with some other dangerous activity (say, sky-diving without a parachute), maintaining that your family reunion is much more dangerous than the sky-diving trick.

Compare-and-contrast may be just the tool you're looking for.

Here's the compare/contrast key sentence when writing persuasively:

"That is bad, but *this* is worse."

When you combine the key sentence with the persuasive purpose statement, it looks something like this:

"I am going to convince the reader that *that* is bad, but *this* is worse."

The key sentence sums up the type of persuasive paper you are writing. It does not appear in your paper. But you will follow its *order* by writing about, say, the dangers of sky-diving without a parachute and then transitioning to how attending family reunions is even more dangerous. You may also use a version of the key sentence later to develop your thesis statement.

The compare-and-contrast argument sometimes uses degrees—not the heat kind but the comparison kind. You may have learned in grammar class that adjectives and adverbs can have three degrees of comparison (positive, comparative, and superlative); for example, *good, better,* and *best* are all degrees of the same concept. *Bad, worse,* and *worst* show the degrees, too. Generally, if you use degrees in your compare-and-contrast appeal, you will begin with the positive degree (*dumb*) and move to the comparative (*dumber*).

When writing persuasively, you are not limited to writing about dangerous things. You may choose to write, "*That* is good, but *this* is better," in order to persuade your reader to do something more meaningful. For instance, Apostle Paul uses this argument in I Timothy 4:8 (NIV): "For physical training is of some value, but godliness has value for all things, holding promise for both the present life and the life to come." In other words, "Exercise is good, but godliness is better" or "Building your body is good, but building your spirit is even better."

Persuasive compare-and-contrast essays are often built upon similarities and differences.

To persuade readers that square dancing is dangerous, compare it to another dangerous activity—shopping in the mall on Christmas Eve—and highlight the **similarities** of the two activities, based upon their danger.

If you want to convince your readers that tent camping is far more enjoyable than vacationing in a hotel in the middle of a city, you will discuss the similarities and the differences, but your case will be built upon the **differences** between the two modes. The differences you mention will tip the scales and make tent camping appear the winner.

You already use this compare-and-contrast method when you shop—comparing the similarities of two or three items and contrasting the differences.

Practice 6.2   Call to mind the last time you made a purchasing decision. Write it in the margin. Chances are, you were interested in more than one item, and you had to choose between the two. For instance, were you torn between buying a pair of sandals or buying athletic shoes? Between two different athletic shoes? Was your ice cream choice between vanilla and Choca-Mocha-Berry-Coconut-Pistachio?

Write your two choices in the margin.

Then fill in the lists on the next page. What were the similarities in the two choices? What were the differences?

When you have finished making lists of similarities and differences, circle the feature that clinched the deal for you.

SIMILARITIES   DIFFERENCES

In terms of the compare/contrast key sentence, you could say that *that* is good, but *this* is better. Rewrite the key sentence, using the two items you chose between. (Examples: "*That* umbrella is pretty, but *this* umbrella is guaranteed for 10 years," "The *blue* tent is easy to assemble, but the *orange* one is lighter to carry in my backpack," or "This necklace is cheaper than that one.")

You may use the comparable features (ease of assembly versus ease of toting) or degrees (like "cheaper" or "more powerful").

Write your compare/contrast purchasing key sentence:

Lesson 3

Jellyfish—Not Just Another Pretty Face

The following is the script of an electric company's safety message. What two things are being compared and contrasted?

(MUSIC UNDER: OMINOUS)

Announcer:

One of the most dangerous creatures on the planet is the box jellyfish. Each year, these floating predators kill more people than sharks and crocodiles combined.

This sea wasp trails a bundle of 6-foot-long stinging tentacles. Their venom attacks the heart, the nervous system, and the skin of the unfortunate prey. The pain is excruciating, and victims can go into cardiac arrest.

And yet, touching a box jellyfish is nothing—compared to touching a power line.

Contact with a power line can be instantly fatal. Unlike any of nature's predators, there's no antidote for this kind of encounter. Power lines are so dangerous, even touching them with objects such as ladders, clippers or kite string can be deadly. Cinergy reminds you: always know where power lines are located and stay away. A message from Cinergy/PSI. For more safety information, visit Cinergy.com.

Other radio spots featured the dangers of the mamba snake and the funnel web spider, all dangerous but not as dangerous as touching a power line.

The first part of the script centers on the dangers of the box jellyfish, the second part around the dangers of power lines. What sentence is the transition or pivot on which the whole message turns? Underline it in the ad above.

The whole script can be summed up in one sentence: "The box jellyfish is dangerous, but contact with power lines is even more dangerous." It shows what is similar between the two things (both are dangerous), and it shows what is different (contact with power lines is much more deadly). In other words, "*That* is dangerous, but *this* is more dangerous."

Begin with the item that is least important and end with the one that is the most important.

In just a few sentences, the script compares similarities and contrasts differences, beginning with the less dangerous thing and ending with the most dangerous thing. The transition statement that you underlined in the Cinergy spot should be this: "And yet, touching a box jellyfish is nothing—compared to touching a power line."

Write your own warning script. Use the pivot or transition statement: *Practice 6.3*
"*That* is dangerous, but *this* is even more dangerous." Of course, you will fill in what "that" and "this" mean. Begin with the least dangerous and end with the most dangerous. Put your transition statement between the two things you are comparing and contrasting, just as the Cinergy script did.

If you prefer, you can write about something stupid and more stupid, important and more important, handy and handier, fun and more fun, and so forth. Use the space below or a separate piece of paper.

Lesson 4

A Mailbox and a Deadly Accident

I promised you a mailbox and a deadly accident. Here they are.

The compare-and-contrast method of writing a persuasive article is particularly effective because you are able to put your issue in a new light. Read the following letter to the editor (327 words). Notice that his real subject takes on a new meaning and pathos when he compares and contrasts it to his mailbox problem.

Comparing mailbox vandalism to a drunk-driving accident

Last Saturday my mailbox was hit with a baseball bat sometime after the mail was delivered. My mail was strewn across my lawn. Ten hours later, just two tenths of a mile down the road, a young man, driving drunk, ran through a stop sign. Three teens, who minutes before had been celebrating a birthday, now lay dead or dying on the road and in a bean field.

Contrasting how easy it is to replace a mailbox to how impossible it will be to replace the teens' lives

This morning I replaced my mailbox with a new one. For those living in the country this is an annual ritual that you either accept, buying the cheapest mailbox you can find, or fight, buying the super-deluxe hardened model mailbox.

Today I replaced my mailbox. Today two of the teens who were killed will be laid to rest. They will never be replaced. Their families and friends will mourn them and will miss them the rest of their lives. I know I will never forget them. And the young man who started an evening of celebration with his friends and ended the evening in a jail cell will live with the consequences of his actions the rest of his life.

How tragic and sad it is that our culture has such a tolerance for drinking and driving. We seem to accept the slaughter of our sons and daughters. We think it is a bad thing, but unlike some countries, we can't seem to get a handle on it.

So let's comfort and pray for family and friends who mourn. Pray also for the rescue workers who tried their hardest to save someone that evening. As we are reminded of the brevity of this life, those of us who trust in Christ for the next life should be ready to answer questions asked at this time. And if you are a parent, this would be a good time to talk to your child about celebrating events responsibly. And remember, more than he needs a critic, a child needs a model.

Practice 6.4　　Do you know someone who has been affected by this kind of accident? How does this letter affect *you*?

This writer gives a deeper meaning to his subject by comparing and contrasting the results of drunk driving with the results of his destroyed mailbox. Write his version of the key sentence in the blank below:

What are his calls to action in the last paragraph? There are five. Write three here:

How would *you* end this letter?

Despite the writer's strong beginning, his call to action is weak. His conclusion (paragraphs four and five) has too many directions and too much advice. Narrowing down his call to action will make more impact.

Also, his conclusion will be stronger if he ties it to the introduction, mentioning again some element he had included in his first paragraph. Something like this is appropriate: "I will never walk to my mailbox again without thinking of those precious lives."

You, too, will have a stronger conclusion if you adhere to the purpose of your writing. Remember your original goal for writing your essay or letter—and stick to it.

Maybe it's just too obvious to state, but when you compare and contrast something, you choose things that have related elements. The above writer chose something that is replaceable (his mailbox) and something that is irreplaceable (teens' lives). If he had compared the teen tragedy to, say, the exploration of Mars, he would have confused the issue and become ridiculous.

If you are a **beginning** writer, skim or skip lesson 5 and go to Write an Essay at the end of the chapter. If you are an **intermediate** or **accomplished** writer, complete lesson 5 and then go to Write an Essay.

Lesson 5

Digging Deeper: A New Structure

When first learning to write, high school students master the art of creating a fitting thesis statement and inserting it near the end of their introduction. This is good. But what if you are not a beginning writer anymore and you yearn for more adventure?

I have just the thing for you.

On the next page is an article that uses the compare-and-contrast tool, but its thesis statement is near the conclusion. Similar to the climactic paragraph, the proofs, facts, and anecdotes appear first—building a strong case for the argument—and then the thesis is stated.

Watch how this works in the following abridged compare-and-contrast article titled "The Evolution of Religious Bigotry" written by Jonah Goldberg, a syndicated columnist. Incidentally, the word *jihad* means a Muslim holy war against infidels (those who disagree with them).

First topic

I just watched "Fitna," a 17-minute film by Dutch parliamentarian Geert Wilders.

Released on the Internet last week, "Fitna" juxtaposes verses from the Quran with images from the world of jihad. Heads cut off, bodies blown apart, gays executed, toddlers taught to denounce Jews as "apes and pigs," protesters holding up signs reading "God Bless Hitler" and "Freedom go to Hell"—these are among the powerful images from "Fitna," Arabic for "strife" or "ordeal."

By here, we definitely know his opinion of worldwide reaction to "Fitna."

Predictably, various Muslim governments have condemned the film. Half the Jordanian parliament voted to sever ties with the Netherlands. Egypt's grand imam threatened "severe" consequences if the Dutch didn't ban the film.

This is his transition from one topic to the next.

Meanwhile, European and U.N. leaders are going through the usual theatrical hand-wringing, heaping anger on Wilders for sowing "hatred."

Me? I keep thinking about Jesus fish.

Second topic

Traditionally, the fish pictogram conjures the miracle of the loaves and fishes as well as the Greek word IXOYE, which means fish and also is an acronym for "Jesus Christ God's Son, Savior." Christians persecuted by the Romans used to draw the Jesus fish in the dirt as a way to tip off fellow Christians that they weren't alone.

In America, these fish appear mostly on cars. Recently, however, it seems Jesus fish have become outnumbered by Darwin fish. No doubt you've seen these too. The fish is "updated" with little feet on the bottom, and "IXOYE" or "Jesus" is replaced with either "Darwin" or "Evolve."

Opinion of the second topic

I find Darwin fish offensive. First, there's the smugness. The undeniable message: Those Jesus fish people are less evolved, less sophisticated than we Darwin fishers.

The hypocrisy is even more glaring. Darwin fish are often stuck next to bumper stickers promoting tolerance or admonishing that "hate is not a family value." But the whole point of the Darwin fish is intolerance; similar mockery of a cherished symbol would rightly be condemned as bigoted if aimed at blacks or women or, yes, Muslims.

Second topic's tie-in to the first topic

As Christopher Caldwell once observed in the *Weekly Standard*, Darwin fish flout the agreed-on etiquette of identity politics. "Namely: It's acceptable to assert identity and abhorrent to attack it. A plaque with 'Shalom' written inside a Star of David would hardly attract notice; a plaque with 'Usury' written inside the same symbol would be an outrage."

But it's the false bravado of the Darwin fish that grates the most. Like so much other Christian-baiting in American popular culture, sporting your Darwin fish is a way to speak truth to power on the cheap, to show courage without consequence.

Whatever the faults of "Fitna," it ain't no Darwin fish.

Wilders' film could easily get him killed. It picks up the work of Dutch filmmaker Theo van Gogh, who was murdered in 2004 by a jihadi for criticizing Islam.

"Fitna" is provocative, but is has good reason to provoke. A cancer of violence, bigotry and cruelty is metastasizing within the Islamic world.

It's fine for Muslim moderates to say they aren't part of the cancer; and that some have, in response to the film, is a positive sign. But more often, diagnosing or even observing this cancer—in film, book or cartoon—is dubbed "intolerant," while calls for violence, censorship and even murder are treated as understandable, if regrettable, expressions of anger.

It's not that secular progressives support Muslim religious fanatics, it's that they reserve their passion and scorn for religious Christians who are neither fanatical nor violent.

The Darwin fish ostensibly symbolizes the superiority of progressive-minded science over backward-looking faith. I think this is a false juxtaposition, but I would have a lot more respect for the folks who believe it if they aimed their brave contempt for religion at those who might behead them for it.

Thesis statement. In other words, "The reaction to 'Fitna' is intolerance, but the reaction to the Jesus fish is even more intolerant." Or perhaps "'Fitna' can be taken as an assault on a violent faction, but Darwin fish are an intolerant assault on a peaceful group." Both topics appear in his thesis statement, and both are clearly being compared and contrasted.

Insights and food for thought in his conclusion

Cohesion devices: "Juxtaposition" recalls its first use in paragraph two, along with the images in the film.

"Behead" reminds readers of the introduction.

Answer the questions on a separate piece of paper: *Practice 6.5*

1. Do you agree with this writer? Explain.
2. What is your reaction to the Jesus fish?
3. What is your reaction to the Darwin fish?
4. Have you seen any other religious or ethnic symbols misused?
5. In your opinion, does the shape of Goldberg's essay (where he puts his topics and thesis) contribute to or detract from his message? Explain.

Write an Article

Write a compare-and-contrast persuasive article. Write it with the intent that it will appear in a magazine of your choice, a school newspaper, or a particular Internet site. This will give you a specific audience.

Decide on your topic and write your version of the key sentence. Make a list of similarities and one of differences. This will give you material for your article.

Your treatment of the first topic, because it is not your true focus, will be brief. But interesting.

When moving from the first topic to the second, insert a sentence or two that will transition your paper from the first topic to the "real" topic. This most likely will be your thesis statement. It will include your two topics and the contrast.

Conclude with some thoughtful observations and a call to action.

Save yourself some heartache and check your topic and lists with your teacher before throwing yourself into your article.

On the back of your paper, write the name of the magazine or newspaper for which you are writing.

Word count for **beginning writers**: at least 350 words.

Word count for **intermediate** and **accomplished** writers: at least 500 words. If you have never written a compare-and-contrast persuasive paper before, consider using its traditional form (similar to the mailbox letter):

- ✓ Intro with brief but pithy treatment of topic one
- ✓ Transition statement that is the thesis
- ✓ Treatment of topic two
- ✓ Conclusions

If you have written a compare-and-contrast persuasive paper before, feel free to use the shape you find in the religious bigotry article:

- ➤ Topic one
- ➤ Transition to topic two
- ➤ Topic two
- ➤ Thesis clearly showing contrast
- ➤ Insights on topic one as it pertains to topic two
- ➤ Insights on topic two

Be clear about what your two topics are and include your opinions of those topics soon after you mention each topic in your article. And, of course, use the first topic to shed light on the second one.

Prepare a personal schedule to help you complete the tasks for this assignment (see the suggested schedule at the end of chapter 4):

Day 1	Day 2	Day 3	Day 4	Day 5	Day 6

Check your paper against this new-and-improved checklist:

- ❑ Are you comparing two things that make sense when they are compared?
- ❑ Does your article pack a punch because you used the first topic to shed light on the second, more important one?
- ❑ Does your article have an interesting title?
- ❑ Is your article double-spaced?
- ❑ Does the opening sentence or paragraph grab the reader's attention by using an interesting QSFSQ?
- ❑ Is your treatment of the first topic brief but interesting?
- ❑ Is your thesis statement between the two topics?
- ❑ Does it show that two topics are being compared and contrasted and that one is more important?
- ❑ **Intermediate** and **accomplished** writers: Are your topics and opinions on them so clear that when you finally present your thesis, it is no surprise?
- ❑ Does your article get to the point quickly? Does it stick to the point?
- ❑ Do you know an English word that rhymes with *purple*?
- ❑ Does your article adequately support the thesis statement?
- ❑ Are your topic sentences clear?
- ❑ Is there a logical progression from one point to the next?

❑ Is it easy to read and easy to understand?

❑ Do you use strong verbs instead of turning them into nouns?

❑ Do you tie your conclusion to your introduction?

❑ Do you leave your reader with stunningly awesome food for thought?

❑ Did you write the name of the periodical or Internet site for which you are writing on the back of your paper?

"It is curious—curious that physical courage should be so
common in the world and moral courage so rare."
-Mark Twain

Chapter 7: Persuasion—Moral/Ethical

Lesson 1

Prefer the Active Voice

What can you do when you view a commercial that crosses a line or when you learn that a company has been treating its employees unfairly? Use the moral/ethical persuasive appeal. Keep reading to find out.

But first, a brief message from the active voice.

When your teacher throws an eraser at you, you can record the event in one of two sentences:

"The eraser was thrown at me by my teacher."

or

"My teacher threw an eraser at me."

The first sentence is passive. The eraser, which looks like the subject, is not doing the throwing. In other words, the subject is not performing the verb. Many passive constructions use a form of the verb *to be* (*was* in that first example), they are too wordy, and they are hard to understand.

The second sentence is active. The teacher is doing the throwing. The subject is performing the verb. The meaning is much clearer, and the sentence is shorter. This can make your writing stronger.

Many writing texts will tell you to prefer the active voice, and this one is no different. **Prefer the active voice.**

There is one exception to this rule (you knew there would be): If the thing receiving the action is more important, then use the passive construction. For example, "Charles Darnay was accused of treason" is a passive construction but is acceptable here because Charles Darnay, who is being accused, is more important than the person accusing him.

Practice 7.1   Below are sentences that contain active and passive constructions. Put an "A" next to the active ones and a "P" next to the passive ones. Then, on a separate piece of paper, rewrite the passive ones and make them active. (Note: Put a star next to the sentence that is correct as passive.)

1. He was heard by someone from the RCA record label during the concert.

2. Sir James Barrie wrote *Peter Pan*, the story about a boy who never grows up.

3. The astronaut Vladimir Shostakovich was struck in the foot by a meteor while repairing the space station.

4. An escape was planned by the pandas in the zoo.

5. The crowbar was dropped by the intruder when he heard the police sirens.

6. Begin shoveling snow at the start of a snowstorm and you will regret it!

7. An injury was sustained in the head by the soccer goalie.

Lesson 2

Intro to the Moral/Ethical Appeal

Now, back to the moral/ethical appeal.

Laura Ingalls Wilder (of Little House series fame) wrote many articles for magazines and her local newspaper as an adult. One of those articles is titled "How About the Home Front?" It appeared in the *Missouri Ruralist* May 20, 1918. World War I was in full swing, and Mrs. Wilder was writing to warn her readers of a frightening tendency she had observed. Individuals and companies were hiking up their prices (today we call it price gouging) during the war in an effort to increase profits. Other people were doing things seemingly for the war effort but really for their own gain. She wrote that when citizens act out of kindness and altruism, they are gaining a victory. Conversely, when they act selfish and greedy, like the enemy, then the enemy will have won the war.

Her appeal was a **moral/ethical** one (*ethical* meaning the moral principles that dictate how people will treat each other and upon which they base their actions). She was stating, "Here's the line. Don't cross it." And that's one of the two key sentences for the moral/ethical appeal. Below are both possibilities:

"You've crossed the line."

"Here's the line. Don't cross it."

These key sentences typically will not appear in your paper. They exist to help you focus on what a moral/ethical appeal says.

The moral/ethical persuasive appeal can be used for the following moral, ethical, and social issues:

- A show that makes contestants do objectionable things for prize money
- A pharmaceutical company that allows unethical practices or develops a drug that has negative side effects
- A commercial, ad, or billboard that features objectionable pictures or material
- A celebrity's lifestyle
- A show that glorifies something that God speaks out against
- Anything such as embryonic stem-cell research, a religious person killing an abortionist, abusive treatment of war prisoners, violent or disrespectful song lyrics, an undesirable business in town, questionable biotechnology, and so forth

Practice 7.2   In the space below, write other situations or issues for which the moral/ethical appeal would be appropriate. Then proceed to the rest of today's lesson.

Structure for a Moral/Ethical-Appeal Essay

You'll study two formats for writing the moral/ethical appeal. The first is an essay, which is in today's lesson, and the second is a letter, which is in the next lesson.

When writing a moral/ethical persuasive **essay** about an issue, use the following format to have the most impact on your readers:

1. In the introduction, make sure your readers know the **topic** and your **view** of it. Then give your readers a little bit of **background** so they understand the importance of the issue and what has been done about it in the past. This gives a historical perspective and puts the issue in a "frame" for your audience. Although your introduction may be more than a paragraph in length, keep this section succinct and interesting; you don't want to lose your readers.

2. In the next paragraphs, write about the **moral or ethical line** that shouldn't be crossed. Include facts and quotations. State why crossing the line is wrong. Mention possible alternatives.

3. In the conclusion, **encourage** readers to seek positive moral solutions and to avoid crossing that line.

An example of this format comes from a *BreakPoint* radio script you'll find on the next pages. The topic is self-injury.

Writing Love on Their Arms

It is not unusual for people to lash out at others to release pent-up anger and hopelessness. At Prison Fellowship, we have seen this over and over again, with prisoners who resort to violence as a way of dealing with abuse, loneliness, and fear. But there is another way that people respond to these feelings—they take it out on themselves.

Today, between two and three million Americans resort to self-injury as an emotional and physical response to negative feelings. Self-injury includes everything from cutting oneself, burning oneself, to even pulling hair. It can be life-threatening, and it always points to a deeper issue.

The topic, the view, and some background

Recently on "BreakPoint," we talked about a movie called *Wristcutters* that attempted to normalize suicide—if not even glamorize it. While suicide is utter despair and self-injury is a coping mechanism, they are both external expressions of hopelessness. <u>To present either of these self-harming behaviors in a flippant manner is despicable, to say the least.</u>

The crossed line (underline added)

Obviously, Hollywood has plenty to say to those who take a razor to their wrist. But what are Christians saying? One group of young people from Orlando does not need to say much—their love speaks for them.

Several years ago, when 19-year-old Renee Yohe turned to cocaine and razor blades in an effort to deal with a lifetime of sexual abuse, depression, and suicide attempts, her friends stepped in. A rehab center had deemed Renee too great a risk to be admitted immediately, so her friends stuck by her side for five days straight. They bought her drinks from Starbucks, took her to concerts, reminded her that she was beautiful. On the last night before she was allowed to enter rehab, they gave her gifts, hugged her, prayed for her. In response to their love, she handed them her last razor blade. It was her symbol of pain.

Alternatives and quotes

The experience with Renee led one of the friends, Jamie Tworkowski, to start an organization called To Write Love on Her Arms to offer hope to people, like Renee, who are dealing with depression, self-injury, and suicide. The group has rallied the support of bands like Switchfoot with the simple message to love the brokenhearted.

Jamie writes on his website: "We are only asked to love, to offer hope to the many hopeless. We don't get to choose all the endings, but we are asked to play the rescuers. We won't solve all the mysteries and our hearts will certainly break in such a vulnerable life, but it is the best way."

Jamie and his friends have refused to buy into the culture's downplaying or even glamorizing of self-destructive behavior. Instead, they are shining examples of the love of Jesus—a countercultural love that refuses to stand on the sidelines. As for Renee, thanks to the loving intervention of her friends, she has been clean from drugs for two years!

Encouragement to do the right thing, specific call to action

With two to three million people in this country engaging in self-injury, there is a good chance you know of someone caught in a cycle of despair. Are you ready to step in? Maybe God is preparing to send you, in the words of Isaiah 61, to "bind up the brokenhearted."

Visit our website at BreakPoint.org to find out more, along with links to organizations that can offer guidance and help.

Practice 7.3   On a separate piece of paper, answer these questions:

1. Do you know anyone who is cutting him or herself?
2. Do you agree with the author's method of fixing the problem?
3. Write one other thing someone can do to keep a friend from hurting himself or herself.
4. This script mentions a film and how it glorifies suicide and destructive behavior. How can you respond to a movie that crosses that line?

Lesson 3

Structure for a Moral/Ethical-Appeal Letter

Letters in the moral/ethical persuasive method will be slightly different from the essay format. When writing a letter to a company, politician, or celebrity, you may not need to include historical or background information. Instead, you will begin by writing something positive. Use this format:

1. In the first paragraph, write something **positive** about the company, politician, or celebrity. Be genuine about it.

2. In the following paragraphs, write about the **moral or ethical line** they should not cross (or already have crossed). Explain why. You may also mention some natural consequences of crossing the line, but don't sound as though you are threatening them.

3. In the last paragraph, **encourage** them to do the right thing.

A word of warning: Something strange happens when people hear the words *nevertheless, however, but,* or *yet* in this context. When someone says something nice and then follows it up with "but…," listeners often wince, wondering what is coming next ("You did a very nice job cleaning your room, *but…*"). Something about our human psychology cancels out all the good we've just heard about ourselves when we hear the words *however* or *but*. Avoid those words after you state the positive message. You can still deftly deliver a strong one-two punch that will make an impact.

Below is the first paragraph of a real letter written to Anheuser-Busch. It uses *but* and cancels out its own good message. In the space below, fix it and then continue to Practice 7.5.

Practice 7.4

Dear Anheuser-Busch:

I often find your commercials humorous even though I do not drink Budweiser. They are light-hearted and clever. But one of your recent TV commercials crossed a line, and I'll bet you know which one I'm talking about.

Dear Anheuser-Busch:

There's more to this lesson on the next page.

Practice 7.5   Below is a letter written to a company by a student. She uses the moral/ethical method when writing to American Girl about an issue that she believes is morally inconsistent with their products. Please read her letter and answer the questions that follow it.

Dear Ms. Brothers:

American Girl has inspired girls of many ages to be better by offering role models who portray the characteristics that make societies great. American Girl dolls are modestly dressed, and your line of clothes is also appropriate and becoming. The girls in your books display good morals and use their intelligence and imagination to help those around them. Until recently, I wholeheartedly supported your company.

I was very surprised and disappointed when I heard of the support you are giving to a group that does not have values that parallel your own. Where your company encourages young girls to be wholesome, Girls Inc. endorses and glorifies lesbianism, the abortion of innocent babies, and an immoral lifestyle. You have crossed a line by supporting, thereby endorsing, their company.

By donating to Girls Inc., you have made a statement. You are providing financial support so that they can further their agenda. You are agreeing with their actions. Is this really the kind of statement you wanted to make? With this, all of the good morals and clean living you have set up for girls to emulate is trashed by Girls Inc.'s encouragement of immorality.

Your company has gained the trust of girls and their parents all over the country. Many are influenced by the decisions you make. Don't support a company that contradicts everything you have been trying so hard to teach girls. I strongly urge you to consider withdrawing your support for and affiliation with Girls Inc.

Sincerely,

[the student's name]

A Concerned American Girl

On a separate piece of paper, answer the following questions:

1. Sum up in one sentence her main point.
2. Do you agree with her?
3. What is the tone of her letter?
4. Why is her first paragraph an effective way to begin her letter?
5. What is her call to action for American Girl?
6. Based on what you now know about the moral/ethical method of persuasion, give this paper a grade. Explain.

Lesson 4

Culture Hits the Shift Key

It is often the case that readers today turn off their interest if they smell religion. If they suspect they are reading a "sermon" instead of an article or letter to the editor, they may quit reading. Jesus, the Bible, and the Christians who believe in them are sometimes marginalized, that is, pushed to the side as being unimportant. Some people are of the opinion that Christians who believe the Bible are simply a fringe group not worth listening to. Or worse, are dangerous.

If you are a Christian and have a moral or ethical warning, what do you do?

What is true in the Bible will be true in other places as well. For instance, scientific facts, medical facts, studies on society, and university studies will prove the rightness of God's way of living. Proof can be found in secular sources.

Rose Publishing prints an interesting poster titled "Why Wait?" On the left side, it lists 12 reasons from the Bible to support abstinence before marriage. The right side contains 12 reasons from studies in science, health, and psychology—24 good reasons culled from many sources, both religious and secular.

Laura Ingalls Wilder never mentions God in her article about greed during wartime. She never quotes Bible verses that easily would have supported her thesis. She simply speaks truths that moral people would agree with, things that make sense about living right and not being greedy.

You may feel uncomfortable about *not* using the Bible.

Some writers feel that getting the moral message out requires speaking in a language the readers understand. They reason that the truth is true whether you mention God or not. Others believe it is important to use reasons from the Bible or to mention God, even at the risk of alienating portions of their audience. After all, if it were not for the Bible, would there be a moral message to spread? In your personal writing, the choice is yours.

You may have noticed that arguments today are not waged on the basis of right and wrong but upon whether the issue is *compassionate, environmentally sound, expedient, merciful, fiscally responsible,* or *courageous.* Words like these tend to replace right and wrong in today's cultural arena. For instance, Kevin Clash, the voice of Elmo on *Sesame Street,* explains in *My Life as a Furry Red Monster* that it took "courage" for him to divorce his wife. Bernard Nathanson, a former abortion doctor who was instrumental in getting abortion legalized, reveals in "Confessions of an Ex-Abortionist" that he and others slanted the cause of abortion as "enlightened" and "sophisticated," while opponents were labeled as "socially backward."

When you find yourself floundering in the middle of a moral or ethical argument, look at the words upon which the argument is based. Be prepared to shift it to another set of criteria, if necessary.

I Am Sooo Offended

When you write about an issue, try NOT to sound as though you are freaking out, like you are *sooo offended* or enraged. Keep the emphasis off you and your feelings. Keep the focus on the moral or ethical line crossed. Simply write your view of the issue or circumstance and keep going. Facts will bolster your argument. Often, it is not one letter that changes a company's mind; it is the number of letters the company receives that creates change. So keep writing.

Keep in mind the word *appropriate*. Companies may ignore your letter if you write they have done something bad, wrong, sinful, or immoral. But most readers understand the word *appropriate* (or *inappropriate*) and do not cringe when they read it. Even the movie industry uses the word in their "do not pirate our movies" announcements: "Inappropriate for all ages." *Inappropriate* is an emotionally neutral word and will not shut down the reader.

Consider these other words and phrases for your moral/ethical appeal: in poor taste, not age appropriate, objectionable, unacceptable, goes too far, shows poor judgment, unsuitable for children, unpleasant, and harmful.

Be sure to include a positive message at the end of your letter or article. Encourage your readers to do the right thing. Point them in the right direction and write as though they are quite capable of responding in a positive manner.

Practice 7.6   Swearing in movies and song lyrics was once considered rude but now is seen as cutting-edge or reflective of real life. In the space below and on the next page, write two reasons why swearing in public is detrimental. (If you don't believe it is detrimental, pretend you do for this practice.) Do not use any religious reasons.

Write an Essay or Letter

Choose **one** of the following three assignments:

- o In a moral/ethical persuasive essay, write about a social ill in society at large or in your area.
- o Write a letter to a business about a problem you see with their advertisements or the way they do business.
- o Write a letter to a TV station or network about a particular show that crosses a moral line.

Write in the moral/ethical style of appeal. If writing an **essay**, use the essay format: background/why crossing the line is wrong/seek other solutions. If writing a **letter**, use the letter format: positive statement/why crossing the line is wrong/encouragement to do the right thing.

For this assignment, do not mention God or quote the Bible or religious people. Find facts elsewhere that support your view.

Try to sway people to your way of thinking and convince them to change their behavior (to do something about it).

Brainstorm, arrange your points in a logical order, and issue a call to action, just as you would for any persuasive appeal.

Discuss your topic with your teacher before writing your first draft.

Word count for the essay for **all writers**: 250-300 words. If you write an essay, consider sending it to your local newspaper as a letter to the editor. Follow the newspaper's requirements for word count and identification. After you have polished your work, and your teacher has okayed it, retype it and mail it.

Word count for the letter for **all writers**: 250-300 words. (If your letter is lengthy, you have a smaller chance that people will read the whole thing.) Find the correct name and street address or e-mail address to which your letter should go. Addresses do not count in the word count. After you have polished it, and your teacher has okayed it, retype your letter and mail it.

Intermediate and **accomplished** writers: You may have a topic that begs for a higher word count and a fuller treatment. In that case, scrap the word count and dig in. Write as though you are creating a newspaper column or a radio script such as "Writing Love on their Arms."

Use the format for a business letter, which you will find on the next page.

Business Letter Format

Your name
Your address
Your town, your state ZIP Code

The date

The senator, manager, or other person's name
Company
Address
Town, State ZIP Code [two spaces but no comma between state and ZIP]

Dear Ms. Important: ← | Colon, not a friendly comma |

Notice that in a business letter format, you begin your paragraphs on the left side of the margin. You do NOT indent each paragraph five spaces as you do for other writing. Also, you single-space the stuff in each paragraph.

Everything that is single-spaced in this letter should be single-spaced in yours. Everything that is double-spaced should be double-spaced in yours.

Double-space between each paragraph. This gives the reader a visual break, which you need because you don't indent. This way, your letter isn't one long clump.

In your closing, leave enough space between the "Sincerely" and your typed name to sign your name.

Sincerely,

{This space is for your signature.}

Your typed name

Prepare a personal schedule to help you complete the tasks for this assignment (or use the one at the end of chapter 4).

Day 1	Day 2	Day 3	Day 4	Day 5	Day 6

Use this dreaded checklist for a moral/ethical appeal:

- ❑ Does the opening sentence or paragraph grab the reader's attention by using an intriguing question, statement, fact, story, or quotation?
- ❑ Are your topic and view clear?
- ❑ Are they near the beginning of your essay or letter?
- ❑ Does your essay or letter get to the point quickly? Does it stick to the point?
- ❑ Is there a logical progression from one point to the next?
- ❑ Is it easy to read and easy to understand?
- ❑ Did you effectively use your toolbox of paragraph types?
- ❑ Did you avoid "yelling" at your reader or focusing on yourself and your feelings?
- ❑ Did you follow the essay or letter format for a moral/ethical appeal?
- ❑ Did you use the correct address?
- ❑ Did you follow the homework directions?
- ❑ Did you use strong verbs instead of turning them into nouns?
- ❑ Did you know that, according to cbc.ca, if it had been Alexander Graham Bell's choice, we would be saying "Hoy! Hoy!" into our telephones today instead of Thomas Edison's "Hello"?
- ❑ Did you use most often the active voice?
- ❑ Did you correctly use and punctuate your in-text citations?

And who can forget these last two?

- ❑ Check the spelling. Even a computer won't catch *there, their,* or *they're* mistakes.
- ❑ Check the punctuation. The most common punctuation mistakes are commas, but they

do not have the corner on the mistake market.

> "They may forget what you said, but they will never forget how you made them feel."
> -Carl W. Buechner

Chapter 8—Persuasion: Emotional Appeal

Lesson 1

If you think that an emotional appeal involves wringing your hands, begging on your knees, or crying copiously, you will be pleasantly surprised—because an emotional appeal is none of these. This type of appeal contains many planned-out elements, just as the logical or any other appeal does. You will learn the elements in this chapter and how to use them.

No Kleenexes®?

Put away your tissue box. You will not need it.

"Emotional appeal" would better be stated as "an appeal to the emotions." Instead of being strong on facts and logic, appeals to the emotions are designed to bypass the brain and incite a reaction. Most songs, works of art, and commercials belong in this category.

Here's a student listing reason and using **logic**:

> I want a car for my birthday. I'll drive myself to practice, and I'll be able to pay for the gas and insurance with my new job.

And here's a student using an **emotional appeal** (appealing to the parental sense of guilt or fair play):

> I want a car for my birthday. After all, your parents bought you a car when you turned 16. It's only fair that you should buy me one, too.

Stephen Leacock, a Canadian writer, explains that "Advertising may be described as the science of arresting the human intelligence long enough to get money from it." *Arresting the human intelligence.* That is exactly what an emotional appeal does—it bypasses the brain and goes for the gut.

Evoking fear, guilt, loyalty, jealousy, peace, patriotism, anger, superiority, a spirit of cooperation, a spirit of competition, hunger pangs, panic, frustration, regret, repentance, curiosity, or duty can be very effective. You will be astute enough to note that not all of those are feelings or emotions. An emotional appeal can appeal to our loyalties (our country or favorite ball team), our values (honesty, time with family, fair play), and our attitudes ("Anyone richer than me is greedy" or "All poor people are virtuous"). These are things that cause us to **react to instead of think through** an appeal.

Relax. You can write an emotional appeal without being moody. The employees that write those sentimental, tear-jerker commercials for Hallmark Cards are not sitting in their cubicles softly weeping.

Before diving into the emotional appeal, though, let's review the methods of persuasion you have already practiced. The topic is hamburgers. Each method will deal with hamburgers in its own way. Read the examples below and compare them with each other. Note how the emotional appeal treats the topic of hamburgers.

Persuasion and the Hamburger

Logical Two or three premises on the nutritional value—protein, dairy, vitamin content—of hamburgers will lead to the logical conclusion that your readers should eat more hamburgers. You can cite facts from experts on how many burgers people eat daily around the world, how nutritional they are, how the industry ensures the meat to be healthy, and so forth. You also can set up an opposing argument to be refuted by a quotation from a McDonald's executive or a government employee who works in the cattle industry stating how safe, healthful, and economically sound eating burgers is. Key sentence: "I'll prove it!"

Compare and Contrast   You can choose similar burgers from two fast-food restaurants and show the readers the similarities and differences of all the features, with an eye toward nudging the readers to choose one of the burgers over the other. Or you might select a burger and a chicken sandwich from the same restaurant and compare the features, taste, and nutritional values of both, guiding the reader to choose one. Key sentence: "*That* is bad, but *this* is worse" (or some variation: "*That* is tasty, but *this* is tastier").

Moral/Ethical   This method can be effective when writing about animal rights, humane treatment of the animals from which the burgers are made, or the ethics of a fast-food joint on every corner. Because this is a persuasive essay, you can convince readers to eat at burger joints more often, boycott them because of questionable practices, or join an animal rights' group that works for more humane treatment of animals tagged for slaughter. Key sentence: "You've crossed the line" or "Here is the line. Don't cross it."

Emotional Appeal   You might appeal to your readers' sense of hunger in this method. In other words, make them feel hungry! Write about the juicy, steamy, sizzling burger, the cheese that melts before your eyes, and the crisp lettuce wedged between the bun and the burger. Then you might describe taking large bites and tasting the soft coolness of the bun against the hot saltiness of the burger. Your readers will salivate. Their stomachs will growl. They'll buy the burger.

An appeal to the emotions isn't a *thinking* thing; it's a *reacting* thing. Often people will "react to instead of think through" an emotional appeal. Why do you think so many pizza commercials play near suppertime?

Here's the key sentence for the emotional appeal:

"Use an emotion to plant the notion."

Yes, that's corny, but work with me anyway.

When you combine the super-secret purpose statement with the key sentence, you may end up with this:

"I'm going to use an emotion to convince my readers . . ."

Appealing to your readers' emotions does not require you to shout, be rabid, or even be impassioned about your topic. *You* do not have to be emotional or in a sweaty lather, but you will use words that connect to your *readers'* emotions.

Is an emotional appeal underhanded? Some consider its tactics as coming in through the back door instead of knocking on the front door like a logical appeal. Is appealing to the emotions sneaky, unfair, and manipulative? Not necessarily. It depends entirely on the topic and to what emotion you are appealing. An appeal to the emotions is like using a car—you can get the family groceries in it, or you can steal one, strip it, and sell the parts. It's what you do with it that matters.

Appealing to emotions can be manipulative when employed to get one's own way or to lead readers to a wrong way of thinking (class envy, racial hatred, or fear, for instance). Because it makes you suspend your sense of order and logic, it can be misused in order to produce a desired reaction or behavior. That's the slippery thing when you read or listen to an emotional appeal: You have to re-engage your brain and determine what the issue and the means of obtaining the goal are.

Practice 8.1   You are a parent. Write a letter to your child, telling him or her to do a particular chore (choose the chore). What are you going to write to get your child to do the chore? Use approximately 100 words. And by all means, have fun!

Lesson 2

Can You Feel the Love?

Examine the letter you wrote as a parent. It probably is filled with appeals to your child's emotions. Below are some examples of emotions and what they might look like in a "clean your room" letter:

Guilt: You should have done it yesterday.

Embarrassment: What if _____ saw this room? (Fill in with the name of someone your child would like to impress.)

Spirit of competition or shame: Your *brother* keeps *his* room clean.

Spirit of cooperation: I'll help you. What can we do first?

Sense of fulfillment: Think how happy you'll be when you get it done.

Bribe or reward: You can ask a friend over when you get it finished.

How many of those did you use in your letter? Write in the margin any others you used.

Below are examples of people using an emotional appeal in order to plant a notion. Are you familiar with any of these strategies?

1. Apostle Paul "uses an emotion to plant a notion." He pulls out all the stops when he writes from prison to Philemon about Philemon's runaway slave Onesimus. Paul plants the notion that Philemon should either take the slave back on an equal footing as a brother in Christ or let Onesimus stay with Paul, where he has been so helpful to the prisoner. Look up the verses and fill in the blank in the text:

> Therefore, although in Christ I could be bold and order you to do what you ought to do, yet I appeal to you on the basis of _____. I, then, as Paul—an old man and now also a prisoner of Christ Jesus—I appeal to you for my son Onesimus, who became my son while I was in chains . . . . I am sending him—who is my very heart—back to you . . .. If he has done you any wrong or owes you anything, charge it to me. I, Paul, am writing this with my own hand. I will pay it back—not to mention that you owe me your very self. (Philemon 8-10, 12, 18-19 NIV)

Using words like "should" and "ought" appeal to a person's **sense of duty**. When Paul uses his age and station in life ("an old man and now also a prisoner of Christ Jesus"), it is not by accident. He is trying to gain some **sympathy** from his reader, Philemon. He is also appealing to Philemon's sense of **pity** and maybe even **guilt**. He also appeals to Philemon's sense of **fair play** when he writes that he will pay Philemon back for anything Onesimus stole. He ends with a direct hit to Philemon's sense of **moral obligation**: "You owe me your very self." As for the blank, Paul is appealing to Philemon's **sense of love:** "I appeal to you on the basis of love." Not all these things are emotions, but they are things that can cause us to react without thinking.

2. Cheerleaders and school slogans appeal to students' **pride, sense of competition**, and **school spirit**. Consider the following cheer:

> Yellow jackets, black and gold,
> We are fierce and we are bold.
> When we play the Bears tonight
> We will sting and we will bite.

When used at a pep rally or game, shouting a cheer back and forth to each other can increase **excitement** and **team loyalty**.

3. Listen to this rude employee yelling at another employee:

> "You idiot! Can't you do anything right? I told you to copy these on both sides, but you only copied one. Why do I even bother?"

Berating often evokes **shame, embarrassment**, or **humiliation**.

4. Listen to another employee speaking to the same worker who, again, forgot to copy both sides of the document:

> "Thanks for doing the copies, Chris. Would you go back and copy the backs, too? I would appreciate it, and so would the boss."

This calmer employee is appealing to a sense of **team spirit** or **cooperation** in the listener. Also, politeness usually elicits a calm reaction from others.

5. Here is an almost-graduated teen talking to his mom or dad:

> If you love me and want to prove how proud you are of me, you'd buy me that Mustang for graduation. Joe's mom and Erin's parents are buying them cars for graduation, and their grades aren't even as good as mine.

This teen is appealing to parental **guilt** ("If you loved me…") and to a **sense of competition** ("Other parents are doing it for their kids"). Will it work?

6. Have you ever heard the following from a counselor at a summer camp?

> All right, Mosquitoes, listen up. We're only five points away from the trophy, but the Panther cabin is closing in fast. If we want this trophy, we have to pass inspection two more times and win tonight's volleyball game. Let's all work together to be the best we can be. Now, I need two Mosquitoes to scrub the floor.

This camp counselor is appealing to the campers' **spirit of competition** (a desire to win or be the best) and a **sense of cooperation** (a desire to work together to accomplish that goal).

7. Have you ever heard anyone saying this next one?

> I thought long and hard about this decision. It's the most difficult one I've ever had to make.

Usually that comes just before a moral misstep, a bad decision, or an unpopular decision. Not surprisingly, it is a bid for **sympathy**.

8. Here's a frustrated teen:

> Mom, why does Sam get to go on a road trip? You wouldn't let me go until I was 17!

This student is using **guilt** and is appealing to his parent's **sense of fair play.**

9. One last example of someone who knew how to "use an emotion to plant a notion" is the prophet Nathan when dealing with a sinful king. After King David sinned with Bathsheba and had her husband killed, Nathan told the following story (2 Samuel 12:1-4 NIV):

> There were two men in a certain town, one rich and the other poor. The rich man had a very large number of sheep and cattle, but the poor man had nothing except one little ewe lamb he had bought. He raised it, and it grew up with him and his children. It shared his food, drank from his cup and even slept in his arms. It was like a daughter to him.
> Now a traveler came to the rich man, but the rich man refrained from taking one of his own sheep or cattle to prepare a meal for the traveler who had come to him. Instead, he took the ewe lamb that belonged to the poor man and prepared it for the one who had come to him.

That's the end of Nathan's story, but it is not the end of David's. To what was the prophet trying to appeal in David's heart? To the king's sense of **justice**, **fairness** or **fair play**, **pity** for the poor man, and, ultimately, his **guilty conscience** for David's double sin. Did it work? Did David have an emotional reaction that enabled him to do something constructive? Read II Samuel 12:5-7a and report his reaction here:

Stories have tremendous power to sway people. We'll study stories later in this chapter.

Practice 8.2   Below are some examples of emotional appeals. Read the examples and fill in the blanks with what the writer is appealing to. Most examples have more than one correct answer, so be creative. If you have trouble thinking of names of emotions, search the Internet for a list of emotions.

1. Here are two paragraphs from Jonathan Edwards' famous "Sinners in the Hands of an Angry God" sermon, which he read from his notes in a quiet, even voice:

> If you are not a child of God, that world of misery, that lake of burning brimstone, is extended abroad under you. Below you is the dreadful pit of the glowing flames of the wrath of God; hell's mouth is gaping wide open; and you have nothing to stand upon, nor anything to take hold of. There is nothing between you and hell except the air; it is only the power and mere pleasure of God that holds you up . . . .
> Your wickedness makes you as heavy as lead; it drives you down, with great weight and pressure, toward hell. And if God were to let you go, you would immediately sink and swiftly descend and plunge into the bottomless gulf. At that moment, you will see that your health, your own care and prudence, your best contrivance, and all your righteousness have no more influence to uphold you and keep you out of hell than a spider's web has to stop a falling rock.

Edwards is appealing to the listeners' sense of _____ .

2. "Good riddance. The guy's a jerk and shouldn't be allowed to tell us what to do. He has too much money and not enough brains. We need someone who thinks like us and knows what it's like in the real world."

This writer is using ridicule (*ad hominem* argument) and is appealing to the reader's

_____ .

3. "Hurry! Hurry! Hurry! Step right up! See the bearded lady swallow a goldfish while the two-headed parrot sings a duet with himself!"

This barker is appealing to _____ .

4. Satan tempts Eve in *Paradise Lost* by John Milton:

> His fraudulent temptation thus began:
> "Wonder not, sovereign Mistress . . .
> Fairest resemblance of thy Maker fair . . .
> Empress of this fair World, resplendent Eve . . .
> Queen of this Universe, do not believe
> Those rigid threats of Death; you shall not die."

Satan is using _____ to appeal to Eve's sense of
_____.

5. "Our troops need our support. Show your support! Fly the flag! If you don't, you are unpatriotic. You are telling our men and women you don't care about them! If I don't see a flag in your window or yard, I'll know that you're against what they're doing for us."

This writer is appealing to _____.

6. "If you let their kind move in here, the neighborhood will never be the same. We will all lose our property values, and our kids will start playing with their kids. And what happens if our daughters want to start marrying their sons? You know what their people are like!"

This writer is appealing to _____.

7. "We can fix this problem if we all work together. Nothing will be too hard for us when we join hands and help each other out."

This is appealing to a sense of _____.

8. "Everyone knows that the most important issue facing our country today is the economy."

This writer is appealing to the reader's sense of _____.

9. "In the past, you have responded quickly and generously. You sent enough money and supplies to keep us afloat. We were able to fix our buildings and give food and supplies to the children in our neighborhood who lost their homes after the earthquake. Now we need your help again."

This appeals to a sense of _____.

10. "The prisoner before you may not look like much now, but he was forced out of his home and onto the streets when his business failed. You know it could happen to you. When deciding upon his fate, I ask you to keep an open mind and imagine him before he was forced to take the label *homeless*."

This appeals to a sense of _____.

11. The following are some things that the creationists at the Answers in Genesis booth were told at the annual convention of the National Education Association in Los Angeles:

"Oh, *God*, I am so tired of you people."
"I don't believe in fairy tales."
"You idiots."
"A young earth? Are you crazy?"

These people were using _____ and were trying to make the listeners react by feeling _____.

12. This sentence is from an Andersen® window company advertisement. The ad features a picture of a smiling couple standing in front of their new windows, and one of an efficient-looking Andersen® installer:

"Your neighbors are getting their windows replaced."

This ad is appealing to the homeowner's sense of _____.

13. This appears in an ad by Duke Energy, a power company, accompanied by a picture of a house being struck by lightning in a storm. The capitals are original to the ad:

"Your Electronics and Appliances Could be Gone in a Flash. Protect Them Today."

This ad is appealing to _____.

Lesson 3

A Speech Loaded with Appeal

So, you're sitting in the locker room just before the big game. Your team is sitting there with you, but they're in sorry shape: one was in a car accident yesterday and has broken ribs. Another is having trouble concentrating because of trouble at home. And you're not feeling so hot. Add to that the fact that you're playing on the opposing team's turf. It's their gym, their officials, and their home-team crowd.

Your coach steps in front of the team, hitches up his pants, and begins a "rally the troops" speech. He encourages you. He appeals to your sense of team pride, your sense of value in your home community. He says you may be small and injured, but think of the glory to be had if you win today, of how special it will feel to hoist that banner back home declaring your team the champions. (I'm using *he*, but your coach could be a *she* without the hitching of pants.)

This is just the sort of speech Henry V (Henry the Fifth) gives his battle-weary troops in Shakespeare's play *Henry V*. Eyewitnesses report there really was a speech and that the king ended it with the warning that the French had promised to cut off two fingers from every

English archer, rendering the men useless. I'd call that an appeal to fear or an attempt to provoke his men to fury, wouldn't you?

The speech in real life and in the play occurs just before what is now known as the Battle of Agincourt (or Azincourt), in northern France, October 25, 1415, which is Saint Crispin's Day in the church calendar. In a strange twist, Saint Crispin's Day commemorates twin martyrs.

A short history lesson: The English and the French had been fighting for years, nay, centuries. You may remember the Norman conquest of England beginning in 1066 (the Battle of Hastings, for instance) in which the French defeated the English on English soil. Almost 400 years later, the countries were still fighting for land and supremacy.

At the time of this speech, the English King Henry V had invaded northern France to regain land that he believed should belong to England. This was not unusual, as there had been English kings from time to time over some of what is now called France.

You can watch a rousing rendition of this speech given by Kenneth Branagh, who plays Henry V in his movie of the same name, here: https://www.youtube.com/watch?v=A-yZNMWFqvM. It begins with the king's men talking about how the odds are five to one against them and how the enemy's men are fresh, not worn out like the English are. Or read the scene here: http://www.shakespeare-online.com/plays/henryv_4_3.html.

Below is a paraphrased and altered version of the Saint Crispin's Day speech from Shakespeare's *Henry V*, Act IV, Scene III.

Note: The names listed with "Harry the King" ("Harry" being a nickname for "Henry") are those of his right-hand men there on the battlefield that day. The king would have pointed or nodded to each as he spoke the names.

And now, the moment we've all been waiting for . . .

> We stand here together on the cusp of a momentous and noble battle, and I hear your complaints. You're hungry. You're ill. You're weary. And you're outnumbered.
>
> Yes, we're outnumbered, but I say the fewer the men, the greater will be our share of honor. In God's name, I bid you, do not wish for one man more.
>
> Do I stand here for the promise of wealth or even to gain more subjects to the throne? No! I'll tell you what I desire. I desire honor, and if it is a sin to covet honor, I am the most offending man alive.
>
> You may wish for a few thousand more men from England who have nothing to do today. I wish for greater honor, the honor that comes from the glory of a hard-fought battle against tremendous odds.
>
> I will be fighting alongside you, men. You will not see me cowering and simpering like that weak-kneed ox with pudding for a belly who calls himself the king of France. He is no shrewd David who playacts the fool. He truly sports a jester's cap and sends his paltry underlings to defend what they have stolen from us. What are those men to us?

Frogs squatting in the mud. Crooked beanpoles that are no match for our archers' arrows.

Some of you may have no stomach for this mismatched battle. You may leave. I give you permission to go and even will line your pockets with enough money to make your way back home. Understand this: If you do not want to die with us, we do not want to die in your company.

This day. This day is called Saint Crispin's Day, and he who outlives it and comes home safely will stand tall and proud when this day is pronounced. He will hear the name "Crispin" and will lengthen his stride.

He who outlives this day and sees old age will celebrate with his neighbors and say, "Tomorrow is Saint Crispin's Day," and will roll up his sleeves and show his scars and say, "These wounds I earned on Crispin's Day."

Old men may be forgetful, but not he. He'll remember what feats he did that day. Then, with our names on his lips, familiar as household words—Harry the King, Bedford and Exeter, Warwick and Talbot, Salisbury and Gloucester—he'll toast the day.

This good man will tell the tale to his son, and Crispin's Day will never go by, from now till the end of the world, but that we here will be remembered—we few, we happy few, we band of brothers.

For today, he who sheds his blood with mine shall be my brother. He'll be a true gentleman, and those gentlemen now in bed in England shall think themselves vilely accursed that they were not here and despise themselves while brave warriors who fought with us proclaim our exploits here on this Saint Crispin's Day.

Practice 8.3   Answer the following questions:

1. If you had been among those outnumbered men that day, would you have been moved by anything the king said? Explain.

2. What vision of the future is he giving those who will survive the battle?

3. At a time when people were locked into a certain socio-economic status at birth, what unusual thing is the king offering his men who stay and fight with him?

4. What sticks out to you about this speech?

5. What is King Henry asking his men to believe?

6. What is he asking his men to do?

7. To what is he appealing? (There is more than one right answer to this.)

Lesson 4

For the Children

You will remember the Do List for writing persuasively (chapter 4). Please take a few moments to review it. In addition to that helpful list, you have specialized tools at your disposal for creating an emotional appeal. Treat the list below as a smorgasbord; you need not use all the items, only the ones that will have the most impact on your topic and audience. Each item will be examined more closely in this lesson and in the next ones.

Emotional Appeal Strategies

1. Do it "for the children."
2. Know when to use loaded words and phrases and when to use neutral ones.
3. Include shared cultural experiences that create a response or remind readers of an emotion.
4. Allude, even obliquely, to other writings (hymns, historical or patriotic documents, Bible verses or characters, Shakespeare, Greek or Roman myths, and so forth).
5. Use repetition. Repeat a key word or phrase for emphasis.
6. Use figurative language.
7. Relate a specific and loaded story to illustrate your point.
8. Use religious or patriotic words in ways different from their original meaning.
9. Use flattery.
10. Use ridicule.

The last three tactics are considered questionable but are included here so you can know when they are being used on you. More on that later in this chapter. Don't worry if you don't understand some of the ideas. All will be made clear as you read.

1. Do it "for the children."

Who doesn't want to help children? They are almost as cute as puppies and kittens and can be used to promote anything from grape juice to a new law. If the cause, product, or law can benefit people of all ages, children can help raise awareness of the issue. Folks respond better to children than they do to, say, a low-down, dirty-rotten gunrunner who might also benefit from the campaign.

Many new issues are introduced as being helpful to children. In fact, if you don't like a new proposal, you can be labeled as greedy, mean-

Emotional Appeal Strategies
- **For the children**
- Loaded/neutral words
- Cultural experiences
- Allusions
- Repetition
- Figurative language
- Story
- Different definitions
- Flattery
- Ridicule

spirited, or uncompassionate. The truth might be that you love children but dislike the proposal on some other grounds. It doesn't follow that if you dislike the proposal, you dislike children. But it *feels* that way.

The Modesto (California) *Bee* once ran this for its main headline: "Valley air hits children hardest." While it is true that polluted air harms children, it is also not so great for asthma, allergy, or emphysema sufferers and is also harmful to derelicts, criminals, and drug dealers. But innocent children make better mascots.

Pictures of babies or children pull more heartstrings and open more purse strings than pictures of looters or old men.

Correctly using children in your appeal makes it stronger. Be aware of when it is used on you!

Refer to the Saint Crispin's Day speech and write the clause where Henry V   *Practice 8.4*
appeals to his men by referencing children:

Keep going! There's more!

Loaded Words

2. Know when to use loaded words and phrases and when to use neutral ones.

This strategy is a lot of fun. A loaded word or phrase is one that has a strong emotion tied to it. Read these words from a Natural Resources Defense Council envelope, which tries to create anger, frustration, or panic in the reader. You are reading to identify loaded words, not to see if you agree with the topic. The loaded words are underlined:

Emotional Appeal Strategies
- For the children
- **Loaded/neutral words**
- Cultural experiences
- Allusions
- Repetition
- Figurative language
- Story
- Different definitions
- Flattery
- Ridicule

> [They are] taking <u>deadly aim</u> at the <u>world-famous</u> wildlife of
> Yellowstone National Park. Two of the park's <u>greatest living symbols</u> will soon be
> <u>stripped</u> of <u>protection</u>. Another is already being sent off to <u>slaughter</u>!

You'll notice that, as with advertising, this type of writing uses many adjectives, and, whew, are those adjectives loaded! It's easy to see how loaded words can have the power to incite people to action—or simply make them angry. Here is the same paragraph written with neutral words:

> [They are] changing wildlife policies at Yellowstone National Park. Two of the park's
> species may now be hunted due to overcrowding. Another is currently being harvested.

Few readers will have a strong reaction after reading that neutrally worded paragraph.

 Loaded words have emotional charges. The **denotation** (the dictionary definition) of any word can be fairly neutral, but its **connotation** (an implied meaning or feeling associated with the word, an emotional undertone) can put an entirely different spin on the word. Take, for instance, the word *niggardly*. Although its denotation is *stingy* or *tight-fisted*, the feelings associated with the word because it is spelled similarly to the unrelated racial slur can send up red flags in the readers' minds and create feelings of anger or insult. The strength of the implication or emotional undertone can cause readers to react.

Just as atoms have a positive, negative, or neutral charge, so can words and their connotations. Examples of words that might hold a positive charge (a positive connotation) are *adventure, honest, wholesome, fair, mouth-watering, cooperation, sublime*, and *free*. Some have a higher positive charge than others in the minds of readers. For you, *adventure* might be a +3; for someone else, it may be a +5. Words that might hold a negative charge (a negative connotation) might be *judgmental, divorce, war, liar, cold-blooded, betrayal, scheme, extremist*, and *slither*.

Practice 8.5   Here and on the next page are 16 pairs of synonyms. Each word in the pairs will have negative and positive charges based on the emotions they provoke. (*Provoke* has a higher emotional value than *elicit* or *bring out*, so I used it.) The first set of phrases is taken from the *Numb3rs* TV episode "Undercurrents." The phrase "join the workforce" was used to mean "be forced into prostitution."

Put positive (+), negative (-), or neutral (0) charges next to each word or phrase in each pair. Your charges will most likely differ from other students' numbers. There are no "correct" answers; your answers are based upon how you FEEL about the words or phrases. Use this scale to label your words.

After you finish the chart, please continue with today's lesson.

Negative connotation   Neutral   Positive connotation

-5 -4 -3 -2 -1 0 +1 +2 +3 +4 +5

The first one is done as an example:

join the workforce (0)	be forced into prostitution (-5)
impending	upcoming
pontificate	talk about
woman	broad
developmentally handicapped	retarded

a divergent reality	a lie
flag-waving	patriotic
diet	eating plan
rude	barbarous
iniquity	mistake
spouse	partner
gambler	risk-taker
euthanasia	murder
terrorists	insurgents
pre-owned	used
problem	issue

People on opposite sides of a moral or political issue use different words; some of the words are loaded and others are neutral. Consider the words *illegal aliens*, *undocumented workers*, and *migrants*, all of which have been used interchangeably. Some evoke high emotions, and others don't.

Readers can get pretty worked up about certain words, sometimes without even knowing why. In the moral/ethical chapter, you learned to use the words *appropriate* and *inappropriate* instead of words like *wrong*, *sinful*, *evil*, or *wicked* when asking a company to change something. People reading *inappropriate* will not foam at the mouth while people reading *wicked* might. When you write an emotionally neutral word, you are using a **euphemism** (YOU fa mizm).

Neutralizing some words can be done by putting them together, much like positively and negatively charged atoms. For example, *mistake* can be neutralized by adding *honest*:

honest (+2) + mistake (-2) = an honest mistake (0)

Here are other examples of words made neutral by adding a word of the opposite emotional value:

momentary (+2) + lapse (-2) = a momentary lapse (0)

fallen (–4) + hero (+3) = a fallen hero (-1)

youthful (+3) + indiscretion (-2) = a youthful indiscretion (+1)

amicable (+4) + divorce (-4) = an amicable divorce (0)

How cool is that? And weird.

Your positive or negative values might differ from those above. In that case, you will end up with different emotional charges for the end-result words. And that's why connotations can cause trouble. People attach differing emotional values to the same word. Be aware of your readers and how they view certain words.

Here's another strange thing that contributes to how people *feel* about words:

- Soft consonant sounds from an *s*, *m*, or *w* have a positive connotation and tend to smooth away harshness.
- Hard consonant sounds from letters like *k*, *t*, or *q* can add a sharp, grating quality to what you are writing.

Mary may maul her mouser without anyone noticing, but if Karl kicks his kitten, there's going to be an investigation. Be aware of this in your word selection.

Warning: Words that inflame people will make readers focus on the negative feelings, not on the issue or your great solution for the problem.

What's the key to all this stuff about loaded and neutral words? **Know your audience**.

If you are writing for a friendly audience that agrees with your viewpoint, you may use loaded words more often.

If you are unsure of your audience or you know they will disagree with you (in other words, you are trying to convince them), use neutral, almost-neutral, or positively charged words. You will hold their attention longer and have a greater chance of convincing them if you choose words that will not offend or inflame them. Consider using a bridge—a common word, point, philosophy, or value—that both sides agree upon, and across that bridge your argument will walk. If readers are going to take offense, it might as well be with the meat of your issue—with the issue itself and your view of it—not the words you use.

Practice 8.6   Refer to the Saint Crispin's Day speech and write two places where the king uses loaded words or phrases:

Lesson 5

Cultural Experiences, Allusions, and Repetition

3. Include shared cultural experiences that create a response or remind readers of an emotion.

Shared cultural experiences can have a great effect on your emotional appeal and can be a powerful tactic. Near voting time each year, voters are treated to candidates' commercials loaded with these experiences. How? The next time you see a political ad, notice the pictures of firefighters and policemen, children in school, the most recent natural disaster and rescuers, active and retired soldiers, and famous landmarks or symbols from the voting area. These are all shared cultural experiences that politicians like to cash in on.

Emotional Appeal Strategies
- For the children
- Loaded/neutral words
- **Cultural experiences**
- Allusions
- Repetition
- Figurative language
- Story
- Different definitions
- Flattery
- Ridicule

What are some of your generation's shared cultural experiences? They are usually things that are super-good or super-bad: a popular television show, a serial killer finally rounded up and given justice, the Olympics being held nearby, an earthquake or other natural disaster, an assassination, a terrorist attack, the destruction of an important landmark, and so forth.

Referring to these things can have an impact on your reader. It calls to mind personal reactions and emotions. For example, if there was a time in your town's history when everyone pulled together for some effort, refer to it when trying to persuade people to rally around an important issue. If there was something physically destructive in your town or county (say, a flood), you can use it, for example, to say that allowing gambling in your area will be just as devastating as that flood—and just as hard to clean up after.

Write one shared experience that has meaning for your town, area, or school. Then write one shared experience that has meaning for the nation.

Practice 8.7

What are two of the cultural experiences shared by the king's listeners? Write them here:

Read on! This lesson continues on the next page.

4. Allude, even obliquely, to other writings (hymns, historical or patriotic documents, Bible verses or characters, Shakespeare, Greek or Roman myths, and so forth).

Emotional Appeal Strategies
- For the children
- Loaded/neutral words
- Cultural experiences
- **Allusions**
- Repetition
- Figurative language
- Story
- Different definitions
- Flattery
- Ridicule

An **allusion** refers to something without saying what it is or where it comes from. Examples abound: A sailor is called a Jonah if he brings bad luck. A greedy, grasping, argumentative woman is sometimes called a Harpy, referring to a Harpy of Greek myth, someone you wouldn't want to meet in the forest on a dark night because of her claws and her tendency to want to shred things to pieces. Someone may say he is under the sword of Damocles (another Greek myth) if he feels under great pressure that may give way at any minute. A political situation might be so complicated as to be called a Gordian knot, an impossibly difficult knot to untie (from another myth).

If you love your country from sea to shining sea, you are giving your readers a cue to think about the patriotic song "O Beautiful for Spacious Skies," written about the United States. It gives a positive spin to your words. When an intelligent audience reads that someone is going to get his "pound of flesh" (*The Merchant of Venice*, Shakespeare), it understands that someone is going to take what is owed to him, whether he should or not. It gives a negative connotation to the action.

Allusions are best sprinkled in lightly, not poured in. And, of course, consider whether your audience will understand your allusions. Martin Luther King Jr. knew that his audience was well aware of the many historical and biblical allusions he used. The second sentence in his powerful "I Have a Dream" speech contains one: "Five score years ago…," referring to the "Four score and seven years ago" of President Lincoln's Gettysburg Address. In referring in this way to Lincoln, he puts liberation and emancipation in the minds of his listeners, and he gives a positive connotation to the words that follow because of the reference to a loved president.

Practice 8.8   List one allusion the king uses. Then read on. There's one more section to today's lesson.

5. Use repetition. Repeat a key word or phrase for emphasis.

Repetition is tricky. If done poorly, it will be redundant—using the same word over and over. If done well, it will enhance your writing by emphasizing the meaningful word or phrase.

The trick is to choose an important word or phrase. In Martin Luther King Jr.'s "I have a dream" speech, he repeats the words "I have a dream" nine times. It is a signal to the listeners that what comes next is a positive image about the future, something obtainable through hard work and cooperation. It creates an image, an expectation, and a positive connotation.

Below is an example of repetition written by Winston Churchill. Read it aloud:

Emotional Appeal Strategies
- For the children
- Loaded/neutral words
- Cultural experiences
- Allusions
- **Repetition**
- Figurative language
- Story
- Different definitions
- Flattery
- Ridicule

> We shall go on to the end, we shall fight in France, we shall fight on the seas and oceans, we shall fight with growing confidence and growing strength in the air, we shall defend our Island whatever the cost may be, we shall fight on the landing grounds, we shall fight in the fields and in the streets, we shall fight in the hills; we shall never surrender . . . .

Notice how skillfully England's then-Prime Minister Churchill, in a June 4, 1940, speech, uses "we shall." Note, too, how all the "we shall" clauses accumulate and add a stunning contrast to the "we shall never" clause.

Write two examples of repetition in the king's speech: *Practice 8.9*

Lesson 7

Figurative Language & Stories

6. Use figurative language.

The term **figurative language** encompasses many writer's devices, but it always does one thing—it paints a word picture for your reader. Your emotional appeal will benefit from figurative language.

Emotional Appeal Strategies
- For the children
- Loaded/neutral words
- Cultural experiences
- Allusions
- Repetition
- **Figurative language**
- Story
- Different definitions
- Flattery
- Ridicule

Figurative is the opposite of *literal*. A literal statement is this: "The sun was bright and hot today." A figurative statement about the sun is found in Psalm 19:4b-5 (NIV): "In the heavens he has pitched a tent for the sun, which is like a bridegroom coming forth from his pavilion, like a champion rejoicing to run his course."

Not only has the psalmist anthropomorphized the sun (given it human characteristics) but he also has anchored the words "power" and "strength" in our minds by the word pictures he painted.

Literal or concrete language can talk about a ballgame, the ball, the rules, the uniforms, and the field. But abstract—or figurative—language can tackle such things as team spirit, momentum, sportsmanship, victory, success, enthusiasm, and anticipation—all hard to describe because they are not nouns you can touch.

Figurative language and other writer's devices such as simile, metaphor, analogy, personification, alliteration, and assonance can lend creativity and depth to your work.

Even in nonfiction writing, figurative language can help make your point stronger. It cannot make a point for you, but it can illuminate your point and give it interest.

Below are some examples of simile, metaphor, extended metaphor, and chiasmus. Which ones are you already familiar with?

Simile A comparison between two things, a simile (SIM ə lee) uses the words *like* or *as*.

> The florid countenance of Mr. Stryver might be daily seen bursting out of the bed of wigs <u>like</u> a great sunflower pushing its way at the sun from among a rank gardenful of flaring companions. (Charles Dickens, *A Tale of Two Cities*)

> Each day, tension met us as we walked into the theater and lay <u>like</u> low morning fog in the aisles. (Maya Angelou, *The Heart of a Woman*)

Metaphor Using a metaphor (MET ə fōr) is like sending in a sub at a ball game. You take out the literal word and substitute a word picture. Instead of writing "She stood still and didn't move," you could write "She stood rooted to the spot." The figurative takes the place of the literal; in this case, the unmoving girl leaves the game and a tree gets substituted in. But because you didn't use *like* or *as* when you describe her as *rooted*, your device is a metaphor. Some examples:

> A book must be an ice-axe to break the seas frozen inside our soul. (Franz Kafka)

> If you do what is right, will you not be accepted? But if you do not do what is right, sin is crouching at your door; it desires to have you, but you must master it. (Genesis 4:7 NIV)

Can you envision a wild, slathering animal crouching at Cain's door, waiting to pounce on him and eat him alive because he is contemplating killing his brother?

An **extended metaphor** (longer than a phrase or sentence) takes an image and runs with it:

> Remember your Creator in the days of your youth . . .
> before the sun and the light
>   and the moon and the stars grow dark,
>   and the clouds return after the rain;
> when the keepers of the house tremble,
>   and the strong men stoop,
> when the grinders cease because they are few,
>   and those looking through the windows grow dim;
> when the doors to the street are closed
>   and the sound of grinding fades;
> when men rise up at the sound of birds,
>   but all their songs grow faint . . . (Ecclesiastes 12:1a, 2-4 NIV)

If "grinders" is a substitute for "teeth," what is the rest of the extended metaphor about?

Anthropomorphism   Giving human attributes to an animal, object, or even a god, as in the Greek and Roman myths. If you want to save a landmark building in your area that is slated for demolition, try writing about it as though it were a person who has seen so many important events and who deserves to be taken care of and preserved.

Chiasmus   A fun figure of speech is the **chiasmus** (kī AZ mus) in which you write a sentence or phrase and then reverse the important words in the next sentence or phrase. It becomes a kind of reverse parallelism, like these sentences from President John F. Kennedy's inaugural address in 1961:

> And so, my fellow Americans, ask not what your country can do for you; ask what you can do for your country.

> Let us never negotiate out of fear, but let us never fear to negotiate.

A word of caution about figures of speech: Beware of the dreaded **cliché** (klee SHAY). Overused phrases create boredom in the reader. "She stood rooted to the spot" (yes, I used that before) is a cliché, a worn-out metaphor that could use a new coat of paint. This would work better and create a fresh word picture: "She stood immobile, as though her shoes were nailed to the floor."

In your first draft, don't pay attention to any clichés you write. Just keep the flow going and write as many as you like. But when you examine your work later to fix it, delete those common phrases. Throw out the first thing that comes to your mind; use the second or third. That way, your similes and metaphors will be fresh and interesting.

Practice 8.10   Find two examples of figurative language in the king's speech. Then continue today's lesson with strategy #7.

7. Relate a specific and loaded story to illustrate your point.

Emotional Appeal Strategies
- For the children
- Loaded/neutral words
- Cultural experiences
- Allusions
- Repetition
- Figurative language
- **Story**
- Different definitions
- Flattery
- Ridicule

Well-told stories have a lot of power and can heighten an emotional appeal tremendously. Consider the following story that introduces a persuasive article on learning disabilities:

> My two best friends and I had just won the regional chess tournament when one of the judges, a former teacher, came up to us. We still wore our gold medallions around our necks and were grinning like we'd just won a NASCAR race.
>
> The judge turned to my friends. "I expect great things from you two in the coming years." He shook their hands and smiled. Then he turned to me.
>
> "You'd better beat that dyslexia problem, Ian, or you'll never get anywhere," he said. I could feel my grin disintegrate as he walked away.

This short story appeals to the reader's sense of pity, sympathy, and fair play. You want to engage all those emotions and have them on your side when you write about learning disabilities and how the public can treat better those who have them.

If you have a personal story about an issue, use it to your benefit. It will powerfully introduce your topic or support your points. If a friend, neighbor, or family member has a story you could use to introduce or support your topic, ask for permission before you use it. Then use it!

Stories have power, and politicians of all varieties know it. When they push for a new law, they find a person who will be helped by this new law and they tell that person's story. This person will always seem deserving and worthy: a hard-working college student, a single mother, a virtuous retiree, or a child of any sort—basically, the underdog. Some of these laws might be helpful and some harmful. When reading a story, look at the issue and the proposed solution, not at the story.

> King Henry V does not use a real story but a scenario (in this case, a series of possible events) to illustrate points in his speech. What scenario does he describe?

Practice 8.11

Lesson 8

The Slimy Strategies

Strategies 8, 9, and 10 are considered questionable and manipulative in some circles. They are included here, though, so you will recognize them when they are being used on you because they are common in emotional appeals.

8. Use religious or patriotic words in ways different from their original meaning.

Examine the following humorous example of this tactic, taken from the back of a *TV Guide*. The "joyless 1.7%" refers to people in the United States who do not own a television.

Emotional Appeal Strategies
- For the children
- Loaded/neutral words
- Cultural experiences
- Allusions
- Repetition
- Figurative language
- Story
- **Different definitions**
- Flattery
- Ridicule

> We at ABC are determined to convert the unconverted. To bring those joyless 1.7% into the fold. So that no American will be left unfulfilled and un-entertained. And come this November, Hoover's promise shall become a shining reality when America has a chicken in every pot, a car in every garage, and a TV in every living room.

This example is a lighthearted recycling of religious words and patriotic references. Underline the religious words that are used in a different context from their original meaning. Put a check mark next to the patriotic reference used in a different context.

When you come across a familiar religious or patriotic phrase in an article, ask yourself what is meant by that phrase. Don't be snookered simply because you recognize and like the word. If someone says a familiar religious or patriotic word, ask him or her to define it for you. It might have quite a different meaning than you originally thought, and it could change the whole argument.

9. Use flattery.

Emotional Appeal Strategies
- For the children
- Loaded/neutral words
- Cultural experiences
- Allusions
- Repetition
- Figurative language
- Story
- Different definitions
- **Flattery**
- Ridicule

John Milton in *Paradise Lost*, as you've already discovered, gives an excellent example of flattery in the section where Satan tempts Eve (Book IX). The whole time he is tempting her, he is also buttering her up, moving her from a lowly earthly ruler to the queen over the whole universe. He exalts her status with each phrase.

"I'm sure well-educated, intelligent people like yourselves won't believe…" is a form of flattery. If you disagree with this person, the flattering setup implies you are not well educated or smart. Flattery puts you into the bind of illogical thinking.

As a writer, avoid using flattery.

Flattery is different from a genuine compliment because it implies that you are using the positive statement to get something. As a reader, you should be aware when flattery is being used on you, inviting you to believe or do something you normally would not.

10. Use ridicule.

Emotional Appeal Strategies
- For the children
- Loaded/neutral words
- Cultural experiences
- Allusions
- Repetition
- Figurative language
- Story
- Different definitions
- Flattery
- **Ridicule**

The *ad hominem* argument, as discussed in the chapter on the logical method, is Latin for "to the man"; in other words, this tactic focuses on the person, not the reasoning. "Don't listen to him. Look at the way he dresses" is an example of this argument. It ignores the issue and attacks the person with sarcasm, ridicule, and mockery.

People who believe that God created the earth in a literal six-day time period are sometimes viewed as being nonintellectual, illogical, or "flat-earthers," those mentally in the Middle Ages where scientific inquiries were, at times, squelched. Or they may be laughed at as still believing Sunday school stuff. Who wants to be seen as stupid or backward? Who wants to be accused of being "against science"?

Ridicule is glorified name-calling. People who use this tactic, whether they know it or not, are attacking the person who holds the belief, not the belief itself.

Ridicule or name-calling trivializes the opposing view, even if the ridicule is humorous or comedic. It also marginalizes the ones who hold that view, pushing them to the periphery of the argument as though they do not count. If you believe God and His word to be true, do not minimize your influence in the world simply because someone has artfully made fun of you.

The next time someone uses an *ad hominem* argument on you, even if there is a little bit of humor sprinkled in, turn the tables. Ask the person to talk about the issue and the opinion, not what he thinks about the people who hold this opinion.

Here are the strategies again, put together in one list for your viewing pleasure:

Emotional Appeal Strategies

1. Do it "for the children."
2. Know when to use loaded words and phrases and when to use neutral ones.
3. Include shared cultural experiences that create a response or remind readers of an emotion.
4. Allude, even obliquely, to other writings (hymns, historical or patriotic documents, Bible verses or characters, Shakespeare, Greek or Roman myths, and so forth).
5. Use repetition. Repeat a key word or phrase for emphasis.
6. Use figurative language.
7. Relate a specific and loaded story to illustrate your point.
8. Use religious or patriotic words in ways different from their original meaning. ⎫
9. Use flattery. ⎬ *The questionable tactics*
10. Use ridicule. ⎭

Write a Letter or Speech

You have been granted the opportunity to study overseas for three months. Write a persuasive letter to your parent(s) or guardian(s) convincing them to let you go. Use the emotional appeal. Below are the decisions you need to make:

- what country you will visit,
- what subject you will be studying,
- which **two** emotions you are going to appeal to (guilt, fear, pride, hope for the future, a spirit of cooperation, a sense of duty, and so forth),
- and which **three** emotional-appeal strategies you are going to use from the list.

You are choosing only three strategies from the list. Using more in a short letter would be confusing. On the back of your paper, write the two emotions you are appealing to and the three strategies you decide to use.

An emotional appeal still requires good points or reasons. Abandoning your brain at this point could be dangerous.

Beginning writers: Use at least 300 words.

Intermediate and **accomplished** writers: Use at least 400 words. If you have had practice in writing an emotional appeal, you may want to choose the following essay instead of the letter to a parent: You are in charge of a group of people who have become lazy or dispirited. Write a speech to motivate them to action. Decide what emotions you will appeal to and which emotional-appeal strategies will help you get there. Word count: at least 400.

When you finish writing your letter or speech, check the list below and make any changes needed. Note the new items on the checklist.

Use this checklist for your emotional appeal:

- ❑ Is your letter double-spaced?
- ❑ Did you concentrate on using points and strategies that will best convince your parent(s) or readers?
- ❑ Does the opening sentence or paragraph grab the reader's attention by using an intriguing QSFSQ?
- ❑ Is your thesis statement near the end of the introduction?
- ❑ Are there clear and focused topic sentences?
- ❑ Does your letter get to the point quickly? Does it stick to the point?
- ❑ Is there a logical progression from one point to the next?
- ❑ Is it easy to read and easy to understand?
- ❑ Did you appeal to two emotions?
- ❑ Did you write them on the back of your letter?
- ❑ Did you know that a footful used to mean "as much as can be grasped with the foot," according to Noah Webster's New International Dictionary (1952)? Makes you wonder what people used to grasp with their feet. And why.
- ❑ Did you use three emotional-appeal strategies from the list?
- ❑ Did you write them on the back of your letter?
- ❑ Did you use good, strong verbs instead of turning them into nouns?
- ❑ Did you use the active voice?
- ❑ Check the spelling.
- ❑ Check the punctuation.
- ❑ Check the grammar.

Day 1	Day 2	Day 3	Day 4	Day 5	Day 6

Fill in this chart with the tasks it will take to finish your letter on time. Use the chart at the end of chapter 4 for ideas, if you wish.

Your Turn to Write Again

What?! Another essay? You've got to be kidding!

This essay is completely optional, but it's a great (and quick) way to see your name and ideas in print.

Write a letter to the editor of your local paper or your school paper. Use the business letter format you find at the end of chapter 7. Find out what personal information the paper requires (phone number and so on); include it beneath your address. Also find out what the word restriction is and stay below it.

Your letter can be on any topic you choose and can use any method of persuasion you have learned in this course: logical, compare and contrast, moral/ethical, or emotional appeal.

Issue a specific call to action.

Check your topic and your points with your teacher before writing your letter.

When you have finished writing your letter and have thoroughly proofread it, ask your teacher to read it. When it is approved, retype it and mail it to the paper.

Incidentally, you will have a better chance of getting published if you key your letter to some current event, holiday, or event of local or national interest. For instance, Earth Day is a great time to talk about ecological issues; Mother's Day can be used to write about adopting instead of aborting.

Part 3: Proofreading

"I never made a mistake in grammar but one
in my life but as soon as I done it I seen it."
-Poet and author Carl Sandburg

Chapter 9: Proofreading

Lesson 1

Proofreading Marks

You may bemoan the writing process because you think you have to Get It Right as soon as your fingers touch the keyboard. Let me assure you: No one gets it right the first time, not even professional writers.

Writing, you will remember, is a three-step process:

- ✓ Plan (brainstorm and organize)
- ✓ Write
- ✓ Fix

Writing is only the second step, and, often, you will find yourself gliding back and forth between the steps many times as you write an essay or report. This is natural and even helpful as you develop your work.

Try ardently, however, NOT to plan, write, and fix at the same time. Fixing while writing is actually detrimental to the creative process needed for a well-written assignment. Write, *then* fix.

If you do not proofread, you are not really writing. Writing without fixing is like running the first laps of a race but conking out on the last lap and never crossing the finish line.

Double-space homework drafts and final drafts. There are two reasons for this: (1) It gives you space to correct your work, and (2) it gives your teacher room to make remarks and/or corrections. Any work you submit to a publisher will also be double-spaced.

Never rely solely on correcting your work from a computer screen. Print off your work and use a colorful pen to make corrections.

Instead of erasing or scratching out mistakes, use the official proofreading marks in the chart below. They are recognized universally and are efficient ways of making changes. Imagine the marks in red. They really are delightful in red:

Proofreading Marks

Mark	What it means	How to use it	The results
ℓ	Take it out	Give it it to me.	Give it to me.
ℓ	Take it out	Use a picture, or school ID.	Use a picture or school ID.
⌒	Close the gap	ab o ut	about
⌣	Close the gap	proof read	proofread
≡	Capitalize	Sydney Opera house	Sydney Opera House
/	Make lowercase	the President's job	the president's job
∧	Add	"No" she said.	"No," she said.
/	Add a letter	acknowledgment	acknowledgement
∧	Add word(s)	When I nod my head	When I nod my head
∽	Transpose	There is it again.	There it is again.
—	Italicize	The Scarlet Letter	The Scarlet Letter
¶	New paragraph	at night. The next day,	at night. The next day,
⌁	No new paragraph	sometimes. He threw	sometimes. He threw
⟲ sp	Check spelling	imput sp	input
◯	Spell out	Gen. Black	General Black

Copyright (c) 2012 by Sharon Watson
WritingWithSharonWatson.com

Below are the proofreading marks used in a few paragraphs of a student's report on the origin of communes. Her original work was correct, but I added plenty of mistakes so I could show how to use the proofreading marks. To download color copies of the proofreading marks and these paragraphs, go to http://writingwithsharonwatson.com/using-proofreading-marks. Study these paragraphs and then continue to the next page.

Practice 9.1

Communes first appeared in belgium, France and Italy at the end of the 11th century. They were actually a town where everyone agreed to take an oath of mutual aide. Communes were formed because Europe had just finally turned away the attacks form the Barbarians, and the people needed better protection and better legal and economic systems.

Communes then were sort of like districts or states that were usually respected by the King of that country. Sometimes king would honor it with a charter.

At different times, living in a commune could mean simply a local self-government and at other times, it could mean a complete independence from the reigning authorities. All of the communes were different but there were fundamental similarities between them. Similarities, like, loyalty to your fellow communers above all else, she sharing of common expenses, like the upkeep of fortifications, a group of elected officials who who were the political authority, an authoritative structure that was directed toward keeping the peace an protecting the community members, a communal court where disputes were judged, and all economic affairs, like taxes and trade, being regulated in the community's best interest.

Answer the following questions about the paragraphs on communes. Use a colorful pen to make your marks easier to locate.

1. Find one instance where something was deleted. Now make the proofreading mark to delete this: x

2. Find one place where something was converted to a capital letter by a proofreading mark. Now make the proofreading mark to make the name of this park capital:

banff national park

3. Find where the word form is changed to the word from. See how the up-and-down movement switches or transposes the two middle letters? Now use that same mark to transpose the end punctuation in the following sentence. The period should be inside the end quotation mark:

Gabriel said, "You really should wear pink to the game" .

4. Find one place where something is added with a V, which is called a caret. Now add the word "his" where needed to the following sentence:

Nothing in remarks convinced me to wear pink to the game.

Don't quit yet! On the next page is a section of a student's paper that needs your corrections. Use the proofreading marks and a colorful pen to fix it. You are editing for punctuation, capitalization, paragraphing, clarity, and conciseness.

"John Newton"

You may know John Newton as the man who wrote Amazing Grace, but do you know

how he came to wrote the famous Hymn?

Or do you know what kind of a man John Newton was? No he was not a highly religious

man. He was a sailor and he was an excellent sailor. Did you know that there was a time in

his his life when he would've been ashamed to be scene with a bible? We'll start our story,

when John was twenty three. It was around 1750 in england. It was at that time when John

was made captain of a slave ship. He make many voyages to africa and made a profitable

living. He did his job well. He stood with whip in hand, forcing Africans into submission.

Yes, this was the same man who wrote that he was amazed at how God could "save a

wretch like me".

ALERT: Your computer will not catch all of your mistakes. While there are at least a dozen mistakes in the John Newton paragraphs, the computer upon which this is written is only catching three. Plus, a computer will not tell you if your paragraphs are a mess or your ideas are expressed badly. **It is your job to be your own editor.**

Lesson 2

Be Your Own Editor, part 1

 Read your paper through **at least three times**. Read it out loud. Read it from printed copies of your paper, not just the screen. You will catch more mistakes this way.

Check your original assignment. Occasionally, a student will write a great paper that deserves a high mark, but the paper will not fulfill the requirements of the assignment. Therefore, the grade will be lower. Carefully read the assignment and all the information the teacher gives you; make sure to write what is assigned.

When you read your paper through the **first** time, answer the following questions (some of which will already look familiar):

Professional Tip
When you get your work back from an editor or teacher and it is all marked up, rejoice. That's a **good** thing. Read the corrections, additions, or changes. Learn from each remark, make the necessary changes, and resubmit the article if the editor asked you to. Or submit it elsewhere.

- ❑ Does your paper have an interesting title?
- ❑ Is your paper double-spaced?
- ❑ Does the opening sentence or paragraph grab the reader's attention by using an intriguing question, statement, fact, story, or quotation?
- ❑ Is your thesis statement near the end of your introduction?
- ❑ Does the paper support the thesis statement?
- ❑ Does your paper get to the point quickly? Does it stick to the point?
- ❑ Are the topic sentences clear and fitting for each paragraph?
- ❑ Do the paragraphs support the topic sentences?
- ❑ Is there a logical progression from one point to the next?
- ❑ Is it easy to read and easy to understand?
- ❑ Does it deliver what your title, introduction, and thesis statement promise?
- ❑ Did you follow the assignment directions?

In this way, you are checking the content of your article and the flow of what you wrote.

Practice 9.2   Choose any paper you wrote this year and print it off. Then proofread it using the above boxes. Do not skip any boxes.

Use the proofreading marks and a colorful pen to correct your paper. Then make the corresponding corrections on the computer.

Your teacher may ask you to hand in the old copy with your written revisions, along with the new, corrected copy.

Sometimes it is easier to proofread someone else's assignment. If this option is open to you, consider switching papers with another student and proofreading that paper instead of your own.

Hold on to your old assignment. You are going to need it again in Practices 9.3 and 9.4.

Lesson 3

Be Your Own Editor, part 2

In the **second** reading, check these:

- ❑ Read your paper aloud. Are words missing? Are you too wordy? Are you redundant? Are you really saying what you want to say? Are you using clichés?
- ❑ Streamline your writing for more impact. Do you use strong verbs instead of turning them into nouns? Do you most often use the active voice? Do you write with a specific audience in mind? Do you vary your sentence lengths and structures? Are you careful with your word order?

You'll want to be able to say "yes" to questions in the second box. You may be unfamiliar with some of the items or questions in the above list. Don't worry. You'll learn all of them by the end of this course. For now, double-check the things you know about.

Practice 9.3

Use the same printed-off assignment you used in Practice 10.2 and check it against the two boxes above. Check the things with which you are familiar. Use a colorful pencil or pen. Then make the corresponding changes on the computer's copy of your paper.

Your teacher may ask you to hand in the old copy and the new, corrected copy.

Lesson 4

Be Your Own Editor, part 3

In your **third** reading, check these mechanical items:

- ❑ Check the spelling. Even a computer won't catch *there*, *their*, or *they're* mistakes.
- ❑ Check the punctuation.
- ❑ Check the grammar. Don't rely entirely on your computer. Use your head and a good reference book.
- ❑ Use these tricks to catch more mistakes:
  - Proofread from a printed copy of your paper, not the screen.
  - Resize the font or choose another font to aid in your editing. This moves the words into new positions, making it easier to catch mistakes you normally would read over.
  - Read your paper aloud. Your ears will catch some mistakes for you.

If you let your paper lie dormant for a few days, you'll catch more mistakes. This will require you to write your paper not at the last minute but a few days before it is due.

Practice 9.4   Using the same printed-off assignment from Practices 10.2 and 10.3, check the items above—one box at a time. Do not skip any boxes. Use a colorful pen or pencil.

Make any corresponding changes on your computer's copy of your paper.

Submit your old assignment (with all the proofreading marks on it) and your corrected one (printed from the computer) to your teacher.

To have some fun proofreading someone else's written mistakes, go to http://WritingWithSharonWatson.com and search "cheerleaders."

On the next page, you'll find the complete list assembled with all its parts. Dog ear that page so you can use it every time you write anything.

If you are a **beginning** writer, your part of the chapter ends after you have perused Be Your Own Editor on the next page.

If you are an **intermediate** or **accomplished** writer, read Be Your Own Editor on the next page and then complete lesson 5.

BE YOUR OWN EDITOR

"Write down the revelation and make it plain . . . ." (Habakkuk 2:2)

1. **Reread** your paper:

   - Does it have an interesting title?
   - Is it double-spaced?
   - Does the opening sentence or paragraph grab the reader's attention by using an intriguing question, statement, fact, story, or quotation?
   - Is the thesis statement near the end of the introduction?
   - Does your paper support the thesis statement?
   - Does your paper get to the point quickly? Does it stick to the point?
   - Are the topic sentences clear and fitting for each paragraph?
   - Do the paragraphs support the topic sentences?
   - Is there a logical progression from one point to the next?
   - Is it easy to read and easy to understand?
   - Does it deliver what your title, introduction, and thesis statement promise?
   - Did you follow the assignment directions?

2. Read your paper **aloud**. Are words missing? Are you too wordy? Are you redundant? Are you really saying what you want to say? Are you using clichés?

3. **Streamline** your writing for more impact. Do you use strong verbs instead of turning them into nouns? Do you most often use the active voice? Do you write with a specific audience in mind? Do you vary your sentence lengths and structures? Are you careful with your word order?

4. Check the **spelling**. Even a computer won't catch *there*, *their*, or *they're* mistakes.

5. Check the **punctuation**.

6. Check the **grammar**. Don't rely entirely on your computer. Use your head and a good reference book.

7. Use these **tricks** to catch more mistakes:

   - Proofread from a printed copy of your paper, not the screen.
   - Resize the font or choose another font to aid in your editing. This moves the words into new positions, making it easier to catch mistakes you normally would read over.
   - Read your paper aloud. Your ears will catch some mistakes for you.

Lesson 5

Digging Deeper: Critiquing

 **Critiquing** does not mean being nasty and *criticizing*. It means you look for the commendable things the writer did and for some areas of improvement.

You have already critiqued a number of other high school writers in this course. As you read each example of a certain type of writing, you evaluated whether they were logical, orderly, clear, and interesting and whether they had completed their assignments correctly. You've even given grades to these students' papers and explained how you arrived at them.

Critiquing a classmate's assignment is a valuable skill to develop. It sharpens your ability to look for mistakes and trouble spots in your own papers. It shows you some favorable ways to write. And it makes you a better writer.

When you have the chance to critique or evaluate a classmate's assignment, keep this advice in mind:

- ✓ Be kind. While you are critiquing a classmate's work, a classmate is critiquing yours.
- ✓ Read the paper through carefully and thoughtfully before you make any remarks. This way, you understand where the paper is heading and what the writer is saying (or trying to say).
- ✓ Look for positive, specific things the writer achieved. Here are some evaluation examples:

  - "I like the way you support this point. It is interesting to me because I have never thought of that example before."
  - "Great story in your introduction. It sets the tone for the rest of your paper."
  - "Just when I was wondering what opponents might think of this issue, I came across this paragraph. Great statement of the opposing view and refutation!"
  - "Your humor made me smile. It is very fitting for this topic."
  - "Your use of synonyms for the word *wild* (plus your contrast in the third paragraph) really makes your paper feel cohesive."

- ✓ Look for specific ways the writer could improve. Here are some evaluation examples:

  - "I like the way you begin your paper. I thought it was going to be about the value of flossing; instead it turned out to be about how pets need dental care. Is there some way you could make your introduction match your true topic better?"

- "Consider using more points. It feels like your paper is too short to support your thesis well."

- "Your conclusion is not as hard hitting as the rest of your paper."

- "It seemed like you wrote too much about Greeks and not enough about the Romans."

- "In this paragraph, it feels like you are yelling at readers."

✓ Your teacher may quantify your remarks with an assignment like this: "Find two commendable things and two places for improvement."

✓ Your teacher may also want you to look at grammar, punctuation, and mechanics (paragraphing, citing sources, word usage, and so forth). If so, use a colorful pen (not red) and the proofreading marks to make any corrections.

Critiquing is sometimes called **peer review**. Whatever you call the task, it is well worth the effort.

Trade papers with a classmate or friend and put your name somewhere *Practice 9.5* near the top of the first page. Read his or her homework carefully and thoughtfully. Then begin critiquing. Remark on two things this student did well and on two things that you think can be improved. Write your remarks in the margins of the classmate's paper or at the end. Include two or three grammar, punctuation, or mechanical corrections.

> "A word to the wise is not sufficient
> if it doesn't make any sense."
> —James Thurber

Chapter 10: Common Grammar Mistakes

Lesson 1

The title of the chapter isn't the most exciting. In fact, you might find it downright boring—or even intimidating.

I've been known to zone out when people try to explain football rules and lingo to me. My eyes glaze over. My ears hear a voice but no real words. Everything grows dim. The same may be true for you and the subject of grammar.

I'd like to make some concepts as easy as possible to understand.

You've just learned quite a bit about proofreading skills, some of which you've already been applying to your essays. This chapter highlights some common mistakes in punctuation and homophones (words that sound the same but are spelled differently). Knowing how to avoid these mistakes will set you apart from the average writer.

Commas and Compound Sentences

Commas are beastly things. Let's tame them.

A compound sentence is made of two independent clauses. An *independent clause* has a subject and a verb (or subject and predicate) and can stand alone as a complete sentence. Comma mistakes in compound sentences are rampant.

The infographic on the next page is your tutorial and shows you what **compound sentences** are, what **coordinating conjunctions** are, and where the comma goes in a sentence of this sort. It also explains the exceptions. Imagine it in color. It's really lovely in color. Before we go any further, here are some important terms and examples.

An **independent clause**:

Jesse hates to do homework.

A **dependent clause**, one that cannot stand alone (This one is missing a subject):

Which is not good.

A **compound verb**, often confused with a compound sentence:

Olivia bakes cupcakes and takes them to youth group every week.

You cannot make a complete sentence out of the second half of the sentence: "takes them to youth group every week." Therefore, it is *not* two independent clauses joined together to make a compound sentence. It is a sentence with a coordinating conjunction (*and*) that joins two verbs (*bakes* and *takes*).

A **compound sentence** with a *coordinating* conjunction (*and*). Note the comma before the coordinating conjunction:

Olivia bakes cupcakes, and she takes them to youth group every week.

A sentence with a *subordinating* conjunction (in this case, *because*)—which does not get a comma:

Olivia bakes cupcakes because she takes them to youth group every week.

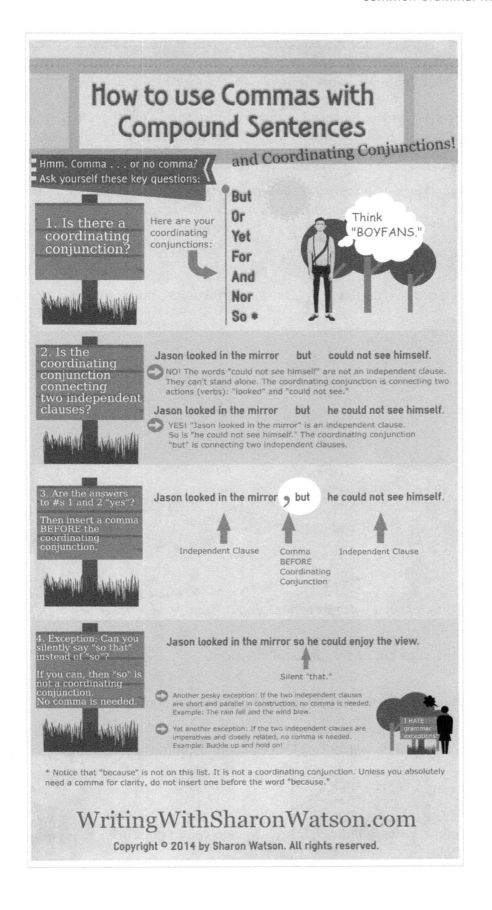

Practice 10.1   Feel free to download a colorful version of the infographic by going here: http://writingwithsharonwatson.com/commas-compound-sentences-coordinating-conjunctions/ .

In numbers 1-7, write the coordinating conjunctions. In numbers 8-20, read each sentence carefully. If it is a true compound sentence with a coordinating conjunction, place the comma correctly. If it is not a compound sentence, leave the comma out.

Just so you know, an imperative sentence (subject: *You*) with two verbs does not get a comma: "Spit your gum out and throw it away."

To delete a comma, do this:

To insert a comma, do this: ∧   Use a colorful pen so you can see your corrections clearly.

1.

2.

3.

4.

5.

6.

7.

8. I love to play the tuba and will enter the Oompah Contest next week.

9. Seymour fed the dogs but he forgot to tell his mom.

10. Doctors study ethics for they make many life-and-death decisions every day.

11. Jason doesn't know if he will write a letter of complaint to the NFL about the godaddy.com commercials or send a short e-mail.

12. He fixed a peanut butter sandwich for me so I wouldn't faint during my comma quiz.

13. The costume designer shopped all day yet did not find the right material for Anna's and Elsa's dresses.

14. Jeremy loves to read *The Three Musketeers* but he refuses to watch the movies.

15. Johnny Depp bought a private island for his family in 2004 because he wanted them to have a safe haven.

16. I quit gardening for I couldn't stand the worms and fat grubs.

17. I quit gardening because I couldn't stand the worms and fat grubs.

18. The soles on my new sneakers are flapping so I bought a new pair.

19. Write your essay this week and hand it in by Friday.

20. *Castaway* uses no music while the main character Chuck Noland is deserted on the island and I didn't even notice!

Lesson 2

"So That" + Correlative Conjunctions

So that

You'll notice in the infographic in lesson 1 that there is an exception to the coordinating conjunctions. It's the words *so that*:

> Jason looked in the mirror so he could enjoy the view.

Yes, it looks as though *so* is a coordinating conjunction joining two independent clauses. After all, these two are complete sentences:

> Jason looked in the mirror.   He could enjoy the view.

However, there is a silent *that* after the word *so*:

> Jason looked in the mirror so {that} he could enjoy the view.

Anytime you have a silent *that* following *so*, you do not have a true coordinating conjunction in the word *so*. It is actually a subordinate conjunction, and it does not get a comma before the *so*.

So, when two independent clauses seem to be linked with a *so*, try to wedge in a silent *that*. If you can, you do not need a comma.

Correlative Conjunctions

I have a pet peeve, grammatically speaking, and I'm sure you're dying to know what it is. Well, I have many, but let's stick with one today. So, without further ado . . .

If you use the words *not only . . . but also*, you do not need a comma before the word *but*. *Not only . . . but also* is called a **correlative** (co REL ative) **conjunction**. Examples abound:

> **Not only** do I despise Fluffy **but I also** cannot stand Fifi.

> **Not only** are there too many books in the world **but** there are **also** too many textbooks floating around.

> He **not only** gives me the creeps **but** he gives me the heebie-jeebies **as well**.

> The Great and Terrible Oz **not only** grilled Dorothy about the silver shoes **but** demanded that she do something for him.

In that last example, the *also* is silent. (And, yes, they are ruby slippers in the movie but silver shoes in the book.)

Correlative conjunctions come in pairs. They are related. They are relatives, like these:

- Not only . . . but also
- Either . . . or
- Neither . . . nor
- Both . . . and
- Whether . . . or

No comma is needed before the conjunction:

> **Either** you get a job **or** you go to school.

Practice 10.2   Now you try it. On the next page you'll find a few sentences on coordinating conjunctions, *so that* versus *so*, and correlative conjunctions. Correct them by placing a comma where needed or deleting an unnecessary comma. If the sentence is correct as it stands, mark it with a "C." (Hint: Seven are correct.)

To delete a comma, use the delete mark, like this:

To insert a comma, use the caret, like this: ∧ Use a colorful pen.

1. Not only did Landon send her flowers at work but he sent her candy, as well.

2. Either you drive this car across the bridge, or I'm going to slam my foot on the accelerator and force us across.

3. We value your opinion, and truly appreciate your business.

4. Neither the faucet worked, nor did the water fountain.

5. Alex wrote a note to himself, and put it on his dashboard; otherwise, he would forget to pick up his mother.

6. Not only did the hurricane displace thousands of people but it also shut down hundreds of businesses.

7. Roberto did the written assignment, and handed it in two days before it was due.

8. You may either call me Mrs. O'Leary, or you may call me Betsy.

9. Bianca's health has improved since she began doing daily exercises.

10. Bianca's health has improved because she began doing daily exercises.

11. Bianca's health has improved for she began doing daily exercises.

12. Not only did Liz sneak in late, but she also lied about it to her mother the next morning.

13. Bees have helped humans for years, and live everywhere on earth but the North and South Poles.

14. The picture clearly showed your feet but your head was cut off.

15. I can only hope that you will not only sneeze into a tissue, but you will throw it away, too.

16. My mother lost her favorite earrings so I will buy her another pair for her birthday.

17. My mother hid her favorite earrings so I would buy her a new pair.

18. Don't forget to rake the leaves, and clean the garage.

19. I did my homework on Thursday so I could proofread it today.

20. I'm going to wash my Colts hat so I can wear it for the big game Sunday.

Lesson 3

Comma Splices

You want to avoid comma splices.

A comma splice occurs when you mash up two sentences or independent clauses incorrectly, like leaving out a conjunction.

Here's an example of a comma splice:

There is a skunk in the aisles, I am sure that is against store policy.

You can fix it either of these ways:

Add a semicolon   There is a skunk in the aisles; I am sure that is against store policy.

Add a coordinating conjunction   There is a skunk in the aisles, **and** I am sure that is against store policy.

Or you can take the skunk out of the store.

Here's the skinny on comma splices:
- Do not put two complete sentences (independent clauses) together with only a comma.
- To link two complete sentences (independent clauses), use a coordinating conjunction like "and" or use another type of conjunction like "because."
- If the second sentence (independent clause) begins with any of the following words, use a semicolon instead of a comma to connect them: *nevertheless, furthermore, moreover, consequently, therefore, in fact, however,* and *then*. All of those words need a comma after them in the second independent clause. Exception: *then*.

Correct example   They told me not to go into the basement; **nevertheless,** I sneaked down the rickety steps into the tarry darkness below me.

Short sentences in parallel construction do not need conjunctions, like this:

"I came, I saw, I conquered." – Julius Caesar

"We have wronged no one, we have corrupted no one, we have exploited no one." –II Corinthians 7:2

The following sentences are all comma splices. Fix them by inserting a conjunction or a semicolon as needed. *Practice 10.3*

If you add nevertheless, furthermore, moreover, consequently, therefore, in fact, or however, add a comma after it.

Use a separate piece of paper.

1. First impressions can be misleading, hasty judgments are often wrong.
2. The Depression in the 1930s caused much unhappiness in some families, others it brought closer together.
3. Horror movies are not good for children to watch, in fact they have an adverse effect even on adults.
4. The painting was not valuable, the museum offered only five thousand dollars for it.
5. Many mystery writers have been helpful to the police in real crime cases, Sir Arthur Conan Doyle is one example.
6. I saw the cutest puppy at the animal shelter, I brought him home.
7. New York was our capital at one time, George Washington was sworn in as president there.
8. Dad refused to eat the mushrooms, he was afraid they were poisonous.

Lesson 4

Punctuation with End Quotation Marks

This lesson answers such thorny questions as this one: "Does the period go *before* or *after* the last quotation mark?" And if that doesn't create some excitement, I don't know what will.

The infographic to teach the facts is on the next page. There are only two rules (can you believe it?), and they are easy (again, is it to be believed?). Imagine it in shades of orange and aqua. Download it in all its glory here: http://writingwithsharonwatson.com/quotation-marks-and-punctuation/ .

Although the rules are similar, this lesson does not cover quotation marks in dialog. Tarzan will hit that in lesson 5.

As you'll notice by the infographic, these two rules are for American English conventions. The British English system handles punctuation with end quotation marks differently. Observant readers have noticed the difference between the American and the British ways of handling the punctuation and most likely have been confused about this huge and dire issue. But no more.

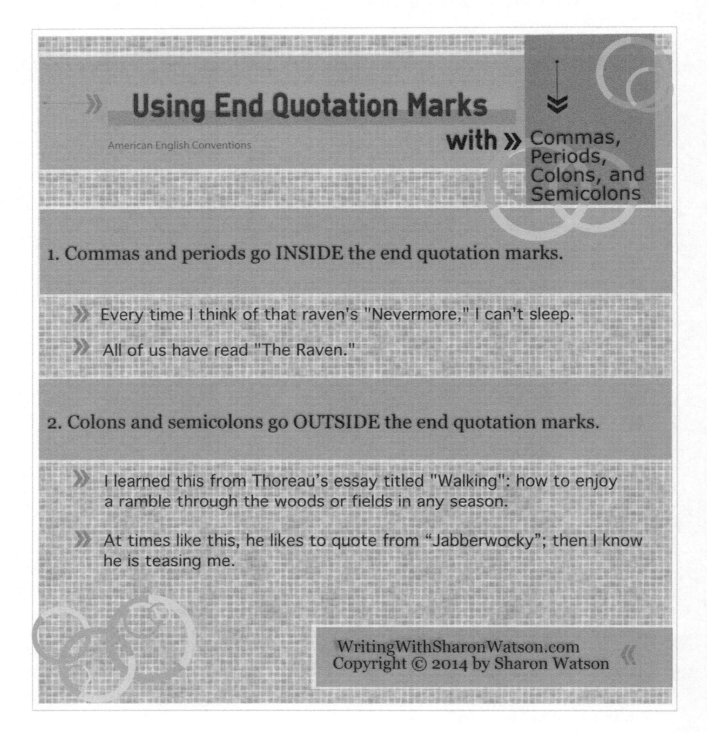

» Using End Quotation Marks

American English Conventions

with » Commas, Periods, Colons, and Semicolons

1. Commas and periods go INSIDE the end quotation marks.

» Every time I think of that raven's "Nevermore," I can't sleep.

» All of us have read "The Raven."

2. Colons and semicolons go OUTSIDE the end quotation marks.

» I learned this from Thoreau's essay titled "Walking": how to enjoy a ramble through the woods or fields in any season.

» At times like this, he likes to quote from "Jabberwocky"; then I know he is teasing me.

WritingWithSharonWatson.com
Copyright © 2014 by Sharon Watson

Practice 10.4   Use your new powers of punctuation to correct these sentences. You'll use the up-and-down motion to transpose punctuation, like this (except yours will be in red or another eye-catching color):

Only one sentence is correct as it stands. Mark it with a "C."

1. Roxanne promised, "I'll go to the party with you". However, she sent her sister instead.

2. You must admit one thing about deliveries marked "rush order;" they eventually arrive.

3. Someone stole her books, her magazines, and her file labeled "How to do a triple Lutz".

4. The first story Mark Twain ever wrote, "The Jumping Frog of Calaveras County", was an instant success.

5. I just read Carl Sandburg's poem "Fog;" I've never thought before of fog as a stealthy cat.

6. Uncle Art looked up and snapped, "It's time you learned to be accurate"; then he went back to checking the columns of figures.

7. I answered, "That's very good of you", but I didn't mean it.

8. I had to look up these words from the poem "The Bells:" *tintinnabulation*, *euphony*, and *expostulation*.

Lesson 5

Punctuation in Dialog or Quotations

A tiff between Tarzan and Jane in this fun tutorial will guide you through the punctuation-in-dialog jungle. The rules are the same whether you are using them in dialog or for quotations in essays and reports.

Yes, *dialogue* can also be spelled *dialog*.

Take special note of where the commas, periods, and quotation marks appear in the sentences on the next page.

To download a full-size, colorful version of the tutorial in PDF format, go here: http://writingwithsharonwatson.com/punctuation-in-dialog/ .

Punctuation in Dialog

American English Conventions

Here's your guide to life, love, and dialog punctuation!

Dialog, then attribution *	"Jane, I don't love you anymore," said Tarzan. **
Dialog broken by attribution	"Tarzan," said Jane, "you always were more interested in your elephants than you were in me."
Attribution, then dialog	Tarzan said, "I find their conversation more stimulating than yours."
Dialog, attribution, then new sentence of dialog	"I'm going back to my father in Baltimore," said Jane. "I'm taking my leopard-skin outfit with me."
Dialog broken by attribution	"And I," said Tarzan, "am keeping the tree house. There are plenty of baboons that will be glad to share it with me."
Dialog ending with an exclamation point	"And to think that I almost gave up civilization for you, Monkey Boy!" said Jane.
Dialog ending with a quotation mark	"Monkey Boy?" asked Tarzan, a tear forming in the corner of his eye.

* attribution = speaker tag = said Tarzan

** After each speaker is made obvious in real dialog, only a few attributions are needed for clarity.

{ Tarzan dialog taken from Writing Fiction [in High School]. Copyright © 2010 by Sharon Watson. All rights reserved. }

WritingWithSharonWatson.com

The following sentences are real dialog from the original *Tarzan of the Apes* by Edgar Rice Burroughs. However, they are missing some punctuation and quotation marks. Fill them in correctly according to what you just learned from the infographic.

Practice 10.5

To insert an exclamation point, question mark, or quotation mark, do this with a **colorful**

pen: \?/ or \"/

To insert a comma or period, do this: /\

The first one is done for you. Note the circle around the added period in sentence 7. This helps you spot your lonely addition at the end. To insert a period, you can use a circle instead of a caret, if you wish.

1. "Close and bolt the door, Alice," cried Clayton. "I can finish this fellow with my axe!"

2. "Back, Alice   shouted Clayton   "for God's sake, go back

3. "Come back to me   she whispered. "I shall wait for you—always

4. "Mercy, Mr. Philander   interrupted the girl.   I never can remember so many questions

5. Jane asked   Where is the forest man who went to rescue you? Why did he not return?

6. "What are you Tarzan?   he asked aloud   An ape or a man?

7. "Then you knew your mother, Tarzan   asked D'Arnot .

8. "Yes. She was a great, fine ape, larger than I   replied Tarzan   and weighing twice as much

9. "Oh, I beg your pardon!   she exclaimed, pausing on the threshold.   I thought you were alone, papa

10. "What shall I call you   she asked   What is your name

11. "I was Tarzan of the Apes when you first knew me   he said.

12. "Tarzan of the Apes!   she cried   And that was your note I answered when I left?

13. "This is not an African jungle   she said   You are no longer a savage beast. You are a gentleman, and gentlemen do not kill in cold blood

14. "I am still a wild beast at heart   he said, in a low voice, as though to himself.

15. "Jane Porter   said the man, at length   if you were free, would you marry me

Lesson 6

~~Its~~ It's Confusing

It's easy to mix up certain words that sound the same when you write the first draft of your assignment, especially when its due date is fast approaching!

So, let's talk about *it's* and *its*.

It's = it is. It's a contraction for *it is.*

Its—without the apostrophe—is a possessive pronoun.

But don't possessives get apostrophes? "The dog's bone" and "the parrot's scream" both show how nouns that possess something use apostrophes. The bone belongs to the dog; the scream belongs to the parrot.

Here's the crazy thing: **Pronouns do not use apostrophes when they are possessive.**

The only time *it's* is correct is when you can take it apart and say, "It is." If you can't take it apart in your sentence and say, "It is," (and have it make sense) then do not use an apostrophe.

Examine the infographic on the next page and then complete practice 10.6. Download a colorful version of it here: http://writingwithsharonwatson.com/confusing/ .

~~It's~~ ~~Its~~ Confusing!

You can say, "It is."

- **it's** = a contraction meaning "it is": Look at my guppy; it's sick.

You CANNOT say, "It is."

- **its** = a possessive pronoun: Its fins are not moving.

You can say, "You are."

- **you're** = a contraction meaning "you are": You're not supposed to pet my guppy.

You CANNOT say, "You are."

- **your** = a possessive pronoun: Get your hands off my guppy!

- **they're** = a contraction meaning "they are": Look at the eyes. They're glossing over.

You can say, "They are."

You CANNOT say, "They are."

- **their** = a possessive pronoun: When did their cat play with my guppy?

- **there** = an adverb: Put my guppy in there and then flush.

You can say, "Who is."

- **who's** = a contraction meaning "who is": Who's going to give the eulogy?

You CANNOT say, "Who is."

- **whose** = a possessive pronoun: Whose turn is it to buy a new guppy?

Strange Fact! When you make most NOUNS possessive, you add an apostrophe and an "s," like this: Luke's guppy.

However, when you make most PRONOUNS possessive, you do not use an apostrophe. You simply add an "s," like this: yours, his, hers, its, ours, theirs, whose.

Practice 10.6   The sets of words in the parentheses below are called **homophones**. That means they sound alike but are spelled differently, like *piece* and *peace*.

Circle the correct words in each set of parentheses.

1. (It's   Its) not a secret.

2. (It's   Its) easy to fall off this cliff because (it's   its) trail runs too close to the edge.

3. (You're   Your) not really going to eat that, are you?

4. (You're   Your) stomach will revolt if you ride the Tilt-O-Wheel after eating three chili dogs.

5. (You're   Your) experience at the theme park will be better if (you're   your) not sick on the rides.

6. They really want to eat (they're   their   there) chili dogs anyway.

7. The Lambert Stone Crushers' Chess Club has (they're   their   there) meet tomorrow; (they're   their   there) going to walk all over the Humbolt Honeybees.

8. (They're   Their   There) is every reason to believe (they're   their   there) going to win (they're   their   there) trophy back.

9. (Who's   Whose) dog has been chewing my shoes?

10. (Who's   Whose) the clown in the purple polka-dot suit?

Lesson 7

Commas with Dates and Addresses

On the off chance that you've been wondering where to put the commas in dates and addresses, I've included this lesson. So, where do they go?

In dates, you need a comma between . . .

Day and date   Friday, September 13
Date and year   September 13, 2016
Elements in a sentence   Friday, September 13, 2016, is an important date.

No comma is needed between . . .

Put a comma here if you've written the date and the year.

Month and date   September 13 is not really a Friday.
Month and year   September 2016 contains five Fridays.

In addresses, you need a comma between . . .

Street address and city   123 Klickitat Street, Portland
City and state or province   Portland, Oregon
                                    Toronto, Ontario
Elements in a sentence   The residence of the Prime Minister of the United Kingdom has been 10 Downing Street, London, England, since 1732.

Commas surround the state or country if you've also written the town.

I visited Hannibal, Missouri, and saw the famous island in the middle of the Mississippi River Mark Twain used in *Tom Sawyer* and *Adventures of Huckleberry Finn*.

The address of the Very Large Array is Old Highway 60, Magdalena, New Mexico 87825.

Practice 10.7   Insert commas as needed. Use your proofreading marks (You know, those carets) and a colorful pen. Three sentences are correct. Mark them with a "C."

1. James Marshall found gold in a river at Sutter's Mill on January 24 1848 in California.

2. Few caught the fever, however, until President James Polk stated in his inaugural address in December 1848 that there was an "abundance of gold."

3. Poe's short story "The Gold-Bug" takes place on Sullivan's Island South Carolina and is not about the Gold Rush. It's about a man being bitten by what he thinks is a gold-colored bug.

4. In fact, it was published in June 1843 and predates the Gold Rush.

5. Jack London was born January 12 1876 and wrote of the Klondike Gold Rush in his popular book *The Call of the Wild*.

6. On July 12 1897 Jack London sailed from San Francisco California to try to find gold in the Klondike.

7. He lived in Dawson City Yukon Canada for almost a year as he searched for gold. There he developed scurvy and lost some of his front teeth to the disease.

8. The *Call of the Wild* was first published in August 1903.

9. On another topic entirely because I ran out of the gold one, the *Titanic* departed

Southampton England Wednesday April 10 1912 on its unsuccessful voyage to New York City

New York.

10. On yet another topic, the Smiths moved into their new home at 24 Wistful Vista Hollywood

California on August 21 2010 and moved out in December of 2015.

Part 4: Exposition

"When your true love writes, *Dear Light of My Life, Joy of My Heart, O Lovely Pulsating Core of My Sensate Life,* some response is called for."
- *Garrison Keillor, humorist*

Chapter 11: Letters & E-mails

Lesson 1

In this chapter, we'll be studying how to write letters of condolence and thank-you notes. We'll also hit e-mail etiquette—not the most hard-hitting chapter in this course, I'll admit, but, hey, the homework will be light. Also, we'll go deeper into items 2 and 3 of Be Your Own Editor.

You can find the format for a business letter at the end of chapter 7.

Old letters are fascinating to read. Whole books have been published that contain only letters and journal entries of famous people, and they are a wealth of culture and history. Will future readers find letters from your generation as they seek to understand this era and peel back the layers of time?

Some say that, in the face of social networking habits of short bursts of communication, personal letter writing is a dying art. Others disagree and love the feel of the paper in their hands as they tear into the envelope and read a personal letter in a friend's handwriting. Did she use purple ink? Was he so angry that the words can be felt through the back of the paper? Perhaps some letter you receive will have so much meaning that you'll save it in a box under your bed to take out and read years from now.

Below is a humorous letter from Samuel Clemens, otherwise known as Mark Twain, to his acquaintance Rudyard Kipling (author of *Kim* and *The Jungle Book*). Check out how many words Twain misuses in order to amuse Kipling:

August, 1895

Dear Kipling,

It is reported that you are about to visit India. This has moved me to journey to that far country in order that I may unload from my conscience a debt long due to you. Years ago you came from India to Elmira to visit me, as you said at the time. It has always been my purpose to return that visit and that great compliment someday. I shall arrive next January and you must be ready. I shall come riding my ayah with his tusks adorned with silver bells and ribbons and escorted by a troop of native howdahs richly clad and mounted upon a herd of wild bungalows; and you must be on hand with a few bottles of ghee, for I shall be thirsty.

Affectionately,

S. L. Clemens

Thinking about drinking a bottle of ghee (clarified butter) may make you feel nauseated, but Twain's silliness probably made Kipling smile. (An *ayah* is a nanny; a *howdah* is the seat on an elephant's back; and *bungalows* are small, one-story homes.) What fun it must have been for Kipling to read that short letter. And he must have saved it, for it appears in a book of letters that Twain wrote.

Who knew personal letters could be so interesting?

Letters of Condolence

You will have friends who go through losses in their lives. Maybe they will experience an accident or will have to leave all their friends behind to move to another city. Perhaps someone close to them will die, and you will want to write something to them. How do you begin? How do you know what to say? Humorist and writer Garrison Keillor gives some advice:

Sit for a few minutes with the blank sheet in front of you, and meditate on the person you will write to, let your friend come to mind until you can almost see her or him in the room with you. Remember the last time you saw each other and how your friend looked and what you said and what perhaps was unsaid between you, and when your friend becomes real to you, start to write.

As Keillor advises, focus on your friend or acquaintance, not on your uneasiness about writing. Writing a letter of condolence is about your friend, not you. Because of this, you will **avoid recounting any stories about you** when you lost someone dear to you. People in pain do not have the brainpower or the emotional energy to take in such stories, and they usually do not care how you reacted or what you felt. They are doubled over on themselves and cannot focus on you.

Second—yes, this is a list—**keep it short** ("I am sorry for your loss, and I'm keeping you in my prayers") or write a longer letter that includes a memory you have of the person she just lost. These shared memories are healing, and they affirm the good qualities of the dearly departed.

Third, **avoid teaching life lessons** or writing something hurtful. This includes, but is not limited to, the following:

- **"At least you had him for _____ years."** The number of years will vary, but the callousness of this statement does not. It negates the grieving person's pain and implies he should be happy or thankful. Incidentally, anytime you hear yourself say, "At least…," clap your hand over your mouth because your next words will most likely do nothing but hurt.

- **"It's all for the best."** Even if the person was sick and in great pain, a death rarely feels like it is "for the best." Family and friends will miss the person or cherished pet who died. They will mourn him. Say something about the loss; do not write platitudes.

- **"I know what you're going through."** While each grief shares similar emotions, there is no way you can get inside your friend's head. "I had a similar experience" or "I lost my brother, too. Do you want to talk to me about it?" are two better ways of letting your friend know you are there for him. This tells the person that you understand the pain, but it doesn't burden him with your long, sad story.

And last, **be specific about what kind of help you can offer**. Instead of writing that you will call sometime soon, write that you will drop off a dessert on Thursday, feed and walk the dog on the day of the funeral, or call on Tuesday to ask what you can do. "Call me if you need anything" means little to the overwhelmed mourner and will not be taken seriously.

Practice 11.1   In the space below, write the items in the above lists that are new to you. If you have suffered a loss in your life, write things people told you that were helpful. Then proceed to Practice 11.2.

Practice 11.2:
Do they make
the grade?

Below are three sympathy letters written for assignments by students. Read the fake letters and answer the questions that follow them. Then proceed to Practices 11.3 and 11.4.

1. Dear Friend Katie,

I am so sorry for your loss. I can't imagine what it might feel like to lose my father at such a young age. Although my words may not be the most comforting, please know that you and the rest of your family are in my prayers.

I will call you after the funeral. I want to bring over a snack and look at your old photo albums with you.

With my deepest sympathy,

2. Dear Al,

Everyone's so sorry that you lost your father to cancer, but it's times like these when we need to remember the happy times.

I'll always remember the time when we were in the car with your dad, listening to Bill Cosby. Bill was working with Ray Charles, who is blind, and said, "Well, Ray, why are you shaving in the dark with the lights out?" That's when your dad's drink came out of his nose and went all over the CD player! The CD player broke, but it was worth the memory.

Just know you'll see him again, and you're in our prayers.

Your friend,

3. Dear Bob,

I give you my utmost condolences for the loss of your grandfather. I do not say this out of mere ritual but from true, heartfelt emotion. But do remember that if "home is where the heart is," then your grandfather is walking the golden streets right now. He led a productive life and has left a fine legacy and fond memories behind.

Remember that time when you invited me to your family picnic at the park? Your grandpa insisted that he could play football, but, attempting to catch the ball, he crashed into Aunt Bess. Bess was carrying a casserole dish, which went flying, almost as if it were in a cartoon. The dish hit Uncle Ben, and he tripped, crashed into the table, and upset the tower of health food muffins that your grandpa brought. The whole place was a mess, but your grandpa was ecstatic. His only remark was, "I caught it! I caught it!"

But if we walk backwards into the future, we are sure to bump into something. So let's leave the past behind us. After all, time heals all wounds. But then again, absence makes the heart grow fonder. On that note, don't mourn, for we do know where he has gone, and we will someday join him.

Signed,

Answer the following questions:

1. What did the writer do correctly in letter #1?
2. What did the writer do correctly in letter #2?
3. In letter #2, underline the part he should have left out. Explain why he should have left it out.
4. What did the writer do correctly in letter #3?
5. In letter #3, underline the parts he should have left out. Explain why he should have left them out.
6. In the margin next to each fake letter, grade each student based on what you now know about writing a letter of condolence.

Write a letter to a real friend as though your friend's mother, father, or close pet has just died. Go beyond pretending; immerse yourself in the idea and identify with your friend. Write a letter of sympathy to your friend, remembering what you've learned to say and not say. Put yourself into this situation as much as possible in order to stay focused and be compassionate.

Practice 11.3

Compile lists of hurtful things and healing things people can say to each other at a time of grief. In order to do this, talk to people and ask them what others said to them that hurt and helped. Add to these lists things people have said to you in times of grief.

Practice 11.4

Lesson 2

Thanks but No Thanks

You have probably written a few thank-you notes in your life. Do you find it as easy as gliding across a polished floor in your socks, or is it a heart-palpitating, sweaty-faced, teeth-grinding chore? Here are a few handy tips to make any thank-you note a breeze to write.

Buy a pack of small note cards and have them on hand for note-writing occasions. Writing a thank-you note is harder if you have to scramble to find a card and, when you find one, it's an old, flowery, goofy-looking card that would be too embarrassing to use. Choose some inexpensive ones that fit your style or make some by hand or on your computer. Small note cards, incidentally, are less intimidating to fill in than regular sheets of paper.

If you receive many presents at one time (a graduation or birthday), **make a list of each gift and giver**. That way, when you write the notes, you will have a clear record of who gave you what. Writing thank-you notes within one month of receiving the gift is considered polite. Strive to be timely. If one month has passed and you still haven't written, duct tape your hand to a pen and include in your note an apology for your tardiness.

The same good sense you used in a letter of condolence will be useful when you write a thank-you note. **Focus on the person** to whom you are writing.

Unless you are very close to the person who gave you the gift, you will only crash and burn if you mention that you already have that item, that you had tried one on last week and decided not to buy it, or that you look horrible in neon orange.

If your Aunt Ruby gives you a present that you think is strange, she's going to want to know if you like it. Say something as positive as possible about it and then move on. Mention her kindness or thoughtfulness. If this is a graduation present, mention a little about what you are planning to do in the near future. If this is a birthday present, tell her a little about your year or recall her recent visit. Keep the tone chatty.

Practice 11.5 Uncle Roger sent you a hand-knit sweater. He knit it himself while recuperating from a broken ankle. The sweater is hideous. It is lime green with black stripes through it. Occasionally, there are white dots with animal appliqués sewn on them. The sweater is too small for you.

Write a thank-you note to Uncle Roger.

Lesson 3

Be Your Own Editor: Item #2

Before moving to e-mail etiquette, let's pause here for a moment and schmooze with your proofreading guide.

You will remember that item #1 on Be Your Own Editor asks questions about your thesis statement, the logical flow of points, and so forth. (See page 158.)

Item #2 on Be Your Own Editor asks these questions:

> 2. Read your paper aloud. Are words missing? Are you too wordy? Are you redundant? Are you really saying what you want to say? Are you using clichés?

Here's what all that means:

Read it! Reading your paper out loud has almost magical qualities. You suddenly see—and hear—mistakes that weren't there before. They materialize as you hear yourself read your work, and you discover sentences that are awkward or unclear.

Missing words? Every now and then, you leave out a word. Sometimes you do it on purpose. It's smart to leave a blank when your writing is "hot" and you are writing down your ideas as quickly as you can but can't think of the perfect word. Just don't forget to go back and fill in that word or phrase later. Sometimes the omission is a total oversight. You will catch it when you try to speak a word that should be there but is not.

Too wordy? Being too wordy is a common mistake. In small ways, you can tighten up your work. For instance, use *every* instead of *each and every*. In larger ways, make sure you don't ramble. Being too wordy also includes the vice of using words that are complicated or that you found in the thesaurus but are unfamiliar with. Using words that sound sophisticated can lead to mistakes like the man who wanted to write that he was no good at making apologies but who wrote instead, "I'm no good at apologetics." This is a real example from a real book (*Murder in Mackinaw*). Nix the complicated; prefer the simple.

> "I find the practice of using long words where short ones will do utterly reprehensible."
> –Winston Churchill

Redundant? Have you ever heard of the Department of Redundancy Department? Being redundant simply means using the same word too many times or expressing the same idea more than is necessary. If you are writing about a dog, the word *dog* can appear too many times in your writing. Vary your words; use *pet*, *he* (or *she* or *it*), or *your canine* once in a while. Once in a while. If you overdo the clever use of other words, your writing can get tiresome.

Huh? Are you really saying what you want to say? "We had to fix the snacks and punch ourselves" will mean one thing to the writer and another thing to the reader! Check to see that you are clear and that your writing is not muddled.

Clichés? A cliché is simply an overused phrase or image. If you write that someone eats like

"Everything stinks until it's finished."
—Theodor Geisel (Dr. Seuss)

a horse or is as wise as an owl, you are weakening your writing by using these clichés. Sure, you can use them in your first draft, but when you revise, pull them out and create something new and interesting. In other words, avoid clichés like the plague.

Review Be Your Own Editor's item #2 each time you proofread your work. This will make you a smarter writer.

Practice 11.6   Grab an old assignment, print it off, and put it up against the expanded, explained version of Be Your Own Editor #2. Use a colorful pen and mark your changes using the proofreading marks you learned in chapter 9.

Your teacher may ask for the old and new versions of your assignment.

Lesson 4

Be Your Own Editor: Item #3

Item #3 in Be Your Own Editor reads as follows:

> 3. Streamline your writing for more impact. Do you use strong verbs instead of turning them into nouns? Do you most often use the active voice? Do you write with a specific audience in mind? <u>Do you vary your sentence lengths and structures?</u> Are you careful with your word order?

One hopes those questions can be answered with a resounding "Yes!"

You are already familiar with the first part of #3 (strong verbs, active voice, and specific audiences). Now you are going to explore the underlined portion: **Do you vary your sentence lengths and structures?**

Locate a recent assignment, print it off, and do this to a **long paragraph:**

Practice 11.7

1. Count the **number of words** in each sentence. In the left margin of your paper, next to each sentence, write the number of words in each sentence.
2. Label each sentence according to its **type**. In the right margin of your paper, next to each sentence, write these abbreviations for the sentence types:

D = declarative (simple sentence with a subject and a verb):

> *Your dog ate my cat.*

I = interrogative (a question):

> *Do you know that your dog just ate my cat?*

Imp = imperative (a command, with "you" as the understood subject):

> *Tell me the truth.*

E = exclamatory (something that deserves an exclamation point):

> *You've got some nerve!*

SS = compound subject:

> *<u>You</u> and <u>your dog</u> have been nothing but trouble for me.*

VV = compound verb:

> *Your dog <u>terrorized</u> my cat for weeks and <u>ate</u> her this morning.*

IP = introductory phrase or clause:

> *When I called my cat this morning, all I found was her tail.*

CS = compound sentence:

> *I began to cry, and then I saw you smile.*

F = fragment:

> *Which was not nice.*

RO = run-on sentence:

> *Your dog ate my cat so I called the pound but they can't come until tomorrow and I'm going to put the tail in my freezer for evidence so don't look so smug.*

Some sentences will have more than one label.

Finish Practice 11.7. On the next page, we'll examine what you found.

How many words were in each sentence in the paragraph you evaluated? Around 20 words per sentence is a good amount, but if you find that your sentence lengths don't vary much, your work could become tedious to your readers. Use a variety of sentence lengths.

Did you vary your sentence structures, or did you consistently use the same types of sentences? If you often use compound sentences, consider breaking them up into separate sentences or connecting them with a semicolon instead of a coordinating conjunction (*and, but, for, or, nor, so,* and *yet*). If declarative sentences are all you have written, play with them: Add introductory phrases, combine them into compound sentences, or find other ways to make them interesting.

A word about fragments: Avoid them in school writing. If you cannot identify fragments in your own writing, learn how to write complete sentences first. Also, read your work out loud to find the correct sentence breaks. Later you can branch out into using an occasional fragment—and by then it will mean something. It will be used intentionally in order to make a point, not simply because you don't know what you are doing.

Lesson 5

Be Your Own Editor: Word Order

The last sentence in #3 of Be Your Own Editor is this: **Are you careful with your word order?** It's time to find out what that means.

Place modifiers as close as possible to the words they are modifying. Modifiers are words or phrases that adjust the meanings of nouns and verbs. Adjectives and adverbial phrases, for example, should sit next to the words they are modifying. If not, you get a sentence like this:

Angie sewed the material her aunt gave her <u>with great pride</u>.

Is Angie proud of her job, or is her aunt proud of the gift she gave her niece? Probably the sentence was supposed to look like this:

<u>With great pride</u>, Angie sewed the material her aunt gave her.

Watch out for the word *only*. It can trip you up if you do not pay attention to where you put it in your sentence. Here's the sentence we're going to play with:

Tarzan said that he loved Jane.

That's pretty straightforward. But try adding an *only* to it in different places and watch what happens. Below is the same sentence with extra room added. Insert *only* before each word and after *Jane* and notice how it changes the meaning. The first two are done for you:

Tarzan   said   that   he   loved   Jane   .

<u>Only</u> Tarzan said that he loved Jane. (Poor, lonely Jane.)

Tarzan <u>only</u> said that he loved Jane. (He said it, but is he going to do anything about it?)

Just is another troublesome word to watch out for. So many ways to go wrong!

Being unaware of word order can lead to other problems, too. The following are examples of misplaced modifiers, that is, modifiers that should be closer to the actual words they are modifying:

I packed lunch for my friends in the picnic basket.

Rhea Sanderson, our soloist, warned her pianist with a raised eyebrow.

Were the friends in the picnic basket? Did the pianist own the raised eyebrow or did the soloist? And here's one I can't resist. It comes from a radio ad for a medical clinic:

Are you tired of waiting in the emergency room for an injury?

Think about it. It will come to you.
    These mistakes can be fixed easily with a little attention to detail.

Word order is also related to **where in the sentence you stash the important stuff**. Have you ever seen the following paragraph?

The Paomnnehal Pweor of the Hmuan Mnid

Aoccdrnig to rsceearch at Cmabrigde Uinervtisy, it deosn't mttaer in waht oredr the ltteers in a wrod are. The olny iprmoeatnt tihng is taht the frist and lsat ltteers be at the rghit pclae. The rset can be a ttoal mses and you can sitll raed it wouthit porbelm. Tihs is bcuseae the huamn mnid deos not raed ervey lteter by istlef, but the wrod as a wlohe.

Do you understand what that is saying? According to the research, you can.

In the same way that the human mind reads the beginnings and ends of each word, it also pays attention to the beginnings and ends of sentences. The middles get muddled. You know from your own experience that you don't pay as much attention to the middles of sentences; you skim those. So why would you put the really important information in the middle of a sentence? Consider the following misquotation:

> **It is time for all good men to now come to the aid of their country.**

It lacks punch because the important word—*now*—is buried in the middle of the sentence. Here it is as it should be:

> **Now is the time for all good men to come to the aid of their country.**

Ah, now we understand that the decision about aiding the country needs to be snappy. (*Snappy* is on the end of my sentence to emphasize the time factor.)

When talking about word order, well-written sentences come in two varieties: **loose** and **periodic**. A *loose* sentence structure means that the important stuff is at the beginning of the sentence: "Tuesday morning, your report is due." A *periodic* sentence structure means that the important stuff is at the end (near the period) of your sentence: "Your report is due on my desk Tuesday morning." Either way, you have emphasized Tuesday morning by placing it at the beginning or the end of your sentence.

What is the "important stuff"? Most likely, because you wrote the sentence, you will know what is important. You know what you want to say, and you know what you want to convey to your audience. So if the crux of the sentence is buried in the middle, move it.

Watch out for these kinds of sentence structures (bold added for emphasis):

> **There was** a dramatic change in the country after the earthquake.

> or

> **It was** only after he ate all the donuts that he showed any remorse.

Take a moment to underline the important information in those two sentences.

The first sentence begins with *There was*, and the second begins with *It was*. These structures almost always bury important information in the middle of a sentence. Avoid them.

If you underlined *dramatic change* and *only after he ate all the donuts*, you are correct. Below are the sentences again, with the emphasis in more effective places. There are many right ways to fix them. Or many are the right ways to fix them. Or you can fix them many ways that are right.

A <u>dramatic change</u> occurred in the country after the earthquake. (loose)

After the country endured the earthquake, it experienced a <u>dramatic change</u>. (periodic)

<u>Only after he ate all the donuts</u> did he show any remorse. (loose)

He showed no remorse until <u>after he ate all the donuts</u> (periodic)

When you are writing your first draft, forget about all this editing stuff. Really. Don't worry about sentence lengths and structures, modifiers close to the words they modify, and loose and periodic sentence structures. Simply let your writing flow as you create your work.

Later, in the revising process, you will catch and fix these things. Writing while paying attention to the checkpoints on Be Your Own Editor is **impossible!** To repeat: Writing while editing is impossible! Write. Then fix.

Below are sentences taken from real students' papers. On a separate piece of paper, move the important stuff to the beginning or end of each sentence, creating either a loose or a periodic sentence.

Practice 11.8

Be creative. These sentences can be finessed in a number of effective ways.

1. Nicole, at the age of seventeen, found herself unmarried and pregnant.
2. The tensions were considerable that led up to the Civil War.
3. Norma McCorvey (called Jane Roe to conceal her identity) was an unmarried carnival worker who was denied an abortion in Texas in 1969.
4. A nation lying deep in the Middle East called Iraq is the seat for many conflicts throughout recent history.
5. Hundreds of thousands of people lost their homes because of Hurricane Katrina alone, and it will happen again if they move back.

Lesson 6

E-mail Etiquette

> We now return you to your regularly scheduled lesson on writing e-mails.

In the Dark Ages, people had to mail a letter, place a phone call, get up from their desk and physically deliver information to a co-worker, or send information on the back of a paper airplane, which led to eye poking, which is why e-mail was invented.

Today, as you well know, communicating electronically is quicker and easier—and often sloppier when it comes to actual communication.

It's time to fix that.

Consider the following guidelines for e-mail etiquette. The one overlying principle is this: **Be focused on your audience.** It's all about them. Write so they will understand you clearly and will know what you expect them to do next.

> ➤ **Think about your e-mail's purpose before you write.** Why are you writing? What reaction or response do you want? Tell your readers what their next step is; ask what yours should be. Don't assume they know what you are expecting. Be specific.

> ➤ **Avoid combining messages.** One e-mail, one message. If you have more than one subject to tackle, put each in separate e-mails.

> ➤ **Double-space between paragraphs only.** Don't indent your paragraphs. Simply begin at the left margin and single-space your lines. Then hit Enter twice to begin a new paragraph. (Your e-mail may add this extra space automatically every time you hit Enter. Experiment to find out.) This gives your reader a visual break and makes the information easier to assimilate. This is the format for any business letter, whether electronic or paper.

> ➤ **Don't use ALL UPPERCASE or lowercase letters.** Writing in all uppercase looks as though YOU ARE SCREAMING; forgoing capitals where they belong makes you look grammar challenged.

> ➤ **Keep the message short and to the point.** A one-screen e-mail has a better chance of being read, and it is a matter of politeness not to ramble. Of course, being too short can seem rude: "Ship that hot-air balloon now!" isn't as polite as "Please ship the hot-air balloon by the end of this week."

➤ **Avoid using emoticons or smileys in business communications.** In business e-mails (say, to a legislator or in a moral/ethical letter to a company), smileys signal a level of informality you want to avoid. In personal communications, universal smileys are acceptable.

➤ **Avoid informal acronyms.** You know—IMHO, LOL, and so forth. These are too informal for business communications but are considered acceptable for personal use. Be aware that some acronyms are not universal; not everyone knows or understands specific ones.

➤ **Sarcasm and humor do not come across well in e-mails.** Because readers cannot see your facial expressions, hear your voice tone, or see your body language to help them evaluate what you are writing, it is best to avoid sarcasm and humor.

➤ **All e-mail is public.** You may think you are sending a private communication, but you are not. Do not assume that you and your correspondent are the only two people who will read your message. Your message could be read out loud, forwarded to other readers, or printed off and distributed. Letters that arrive through the postal service and are stamped are often considered private, but e-mail is viewed as fair game.

➤ **Don't flame.** Flaming is sending messages with offensive material: insults, racially oriented or intentionally provoking words, and so forth. It also means letting loose with any angry, bitter, or vengeful messages. Avoid statements like "Jim's a jerk. Have you seen those stupid hats he wears?" There's no good reason to purposely flame. Reread your message to make sure you are not starting a conflagration.

➤ **Be specific in the subject line.** Instead of "Student Meeting," write "Soccer Fundraising Meeting Thursday." Also, if one subject has sustained a few volleys, it's time to change the subject line. That way your correspondent will be able to access pertinent information—with the right subject line—when she looks in her inbox.

➤ **If you send an attachment, write what it is and why you have included it.** Because an attachment does not have a subject line, it is best to tell your correspondent what the attachment is. A simple "The attachment is the map to my house for the party Friday night" will save your correspondent a lot of trouble.

➤ **Hide the names and addresses of the list of people you are e-mailing.** It is rude and an invasion of your correspondents' privacy to include all the names and addresses in the "To" or "Cc" line. Use "Undisclosed Recipients" or "Bcc" ("blind carbon copy") to hide the information. The only exception is when it is absolutely necessary for all recipients to have each other's information so they can communicate with each other.

> **Proofread everything you write before you click Send.** Electronic communication is easy to send, so why make it hard to read? Proofread it as you would anything else—at least three times. Make sure you are saying what you want to say and asking for a specific response or action.

When deciding whether to use a **formal** or **informal tone**, take these three things into account:

✓ **Consider your audience.** A letter to a company or a company's representative will require a more formal tone than a post on a social media site. Try to match your correspondent's style. This assures that you will communicate in a language she will understand and appreciate.

✓ **Consider the subject matter.** Is your subject matter of great significance, or is it trivial? Match the tone to the subject matter's importance.

✓ **Consider what the reader will do with your message.** Will the message be printed off for public use or read for personal use?

Writing an informal email to a friend or co-worker? Then it's okay to skip the comma after the "hi" and put it after the person's name, like this:

Hi Amy,

But when writing a more formal email, use any of these:

Formal business letter (use a colon)   Dear Leo:

Personal (use a comma)   Dear Leo,

Informal business (set off the name with a comma)   Hello, Ian,

By the way, check with your teacher, professor, or editor about whether to use a hyphen in this word: *e-mail* or *email*. Either way is correct. It's just a matter of style and preference.

Below is an e-mail message. Answer the questions that follow it and then write your own message in reply.

Practice 11.9

From: Dorian Gray <agelessgray@coldmail.com>

To: Oscar Wilde <bunbury@algernon.com>

Subject: That portrait

Dear Mr. Wilde:

The portrait you painted of me is deeply dissatisfying and somewhat disturbing. At first, it seemed a good likeness, but lately, it has been changing—yes, changing—of its own accord.

I assure you, I have not touched it, but each day it changes. To be more specific, it ages as I age. The painting is not the issue; I expect it to get old and show hairline cracks. It is the face itself that ages, and to this, I most strenuously object. I hold you, the artist, responsible.

You must come and do something about this, or I shall ask for my money back.

Sincerely,

Dorian Gray

Answer the questions:

1. How formal is this e-mail? What is your clue?

2. What is Mr. Gray's problem?

3. What is he asking Mr. Wilde to do?

4. What could he say to be more specific about the response he wants?

Respond to Mr. Gray as though you were Mr. Wilde. Use the same tone of formality Mr. Gray uses and be specific in your response about what you will do for Mr. Gray. Use the box on the next page.

From:
To:
Subject:

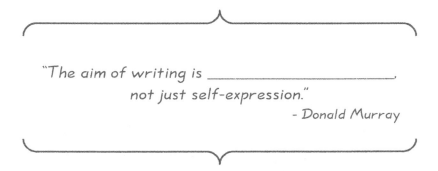

"The aim of writing is _____,
not just self-expression."
- Donald Murray

Chapter 12: Process Writing (How-to)

Lesson 1

You will notice that the quotation at the head of this chapter is not complete. Jot down some educated guesses as to what the aim of writing is:

Look for the correct word or words later in the text of this chapter.

Writers Have Audiences

Earlier in this course, you learned to have a specific audience in mind each time you write, choosing the age group, the educational level, the gender, and so forth. This advice is in #3 on your proofreading guide Be Your Own Editor on page 164 ("Do you write with a specific audience in mind?").

According to wordiq.org, comic books are written on a sixth-grade level, *Reader's Digest* on a ninth-grade level, and *TIME* on an eleventh-grade level. Most newspapers are written on an eighth-grade reading level. So how do you know the grade level of your own writing? How do you know if your writing fits your intended audience? Try the **Fog Index**.

The Fog Index has nothing to do with weather, ships, or lighthouses. Developed by Robert Gunning, it mathematically measures a writing sample to determine its grade level. In a simple formula, the Fog Index uses sentence length and difficult words as its criteria. A number of credible versions exist. The one included here varies slightly from Gunning's original formula.

Included in this lesson are a paragraph from *Benjamin Franklin's Autobiography*, the Fog Index material, and an example of how to use the equation. Let's see how the Fog Index reveals the age group for which Franklin is writing.

I began now gradually to pay off the debt I was under for the printing-house. In order to secure my credit and character as a tradesman, I took care not only to be in reality industrious and frugal, but to avoid all appearances to the contrary. I drest plainly; I was seen at no places of idle diversion. I never went out a fishing or shooting; a book, indeed, sometimes debauched me from my work, but that was seldom, snug, and gave no scandal; and, to show that I was not above my business, I sometimes brought home the paper I purchased at the stores thro' the streets on a wheelbarrow. Thus being esteemed as an industrious, thriving young man, and paying duly for what I bought, the merchants who imported stationery solicited my custom; others proposed supplying me with books, and I went on swimmingly.

The Fog Index

1. Select a medium-size passage (approx. 100 words) and count the words. Then count the sentences.

2. Figure the average sentence length: $\dfrac{\text{Number of words}}{\text{Number of sentences}}$

3. Count the number of hard words. (Hard words are three or more syllables, **not** counting proper nouns, hyphenated words, or words of three or less syllables that end in common suffixes such as *–ed, -es,* or *-ing*).

4. Figure the value of hard words: $\dfrac{\text{Hard words x 100}}{\text{Number of words}}$

5. Add #s 2 and 4 together.

6. Multiply the sum by 0.4 and round off the result to the nearest whole number. (This becomes the grade level for the writing.)

It's not fair that you have to do math in a writing course, but I'm going to try to make it as painless as possible. Here is the Fog Index in an equation:

$$\left[\frac{\text{Number of words}}{\text{Number of sentences}} + \frac{\text{Hard words x 100}}{\text{Number of words}} \right] \text{x } 0.4 = \text{Fog Index}$$

Follow along on the next page as we figure the Fog Index for this example from the Benjamin Franklin excerpt. (Note: *Printing-house* is considered one word. Because it is hyphenated, it is not considered difficult.)

$$\left[\frac{\text{Number of words}}{\text{Number of sentences}} + \frac{\text{Hard words x 100}}{\text{Number of words}} \right] \text{ x } 0.4 = \text{Fog Index}$$

$$\left(\frac{146}{5} + \frac{11 \text{ x } 100}{146} \right) \text{ x } 0.4 = \text{Fog Index}$$

$$\left(29.2 + 7.5 \right) \text{ x } 0.4 = \text{Fog Index}$$

$$36.7 \text{ x } 0.4 = \text{Fog Index}$$

$$14.68 = \text{Fog Index}$$

$$\text{Grade } 15 = \text{Fog Index}$$

Hard words

gradually
character
reality
industrious (2x)
appearances
contrary
diversion
wheelbarrow
stationery
solicited

The Fog Index is grade 15. Benjamin Franklin, it seems, is writing for people who can read and comprehend well.

Practice 12.1   Now try it on your own. Read the first few paragraphs from this *USA Today* article about the fear of flying:

> Businesswoman Marci Smith can pinpoint when things began to unravel at her last job. Two years ago, she boarded a flight in Atlanta en route to an important business meeting in Philadelphia.
> She panicked at the thought of the looming airplane trip and began to cry. She got off the plane and rented a car to drive to the meeting, which, to the deep disappointment of the import company that employed her, she missed.
> "Things went downhill from there, and I resigned" last May, Smith said.
> Fear of flying cripples—or at least burdens—the careers of millions of Americans. Also known as aviaphobia, it causes many employees to pass up promotions or miss out-of-town meetings, training sessions or sales calls.

Figure the grade level of this news article by using the Fog Index. (Note: The hyphenated *out-of-town* is one word and is not considered difficult.)

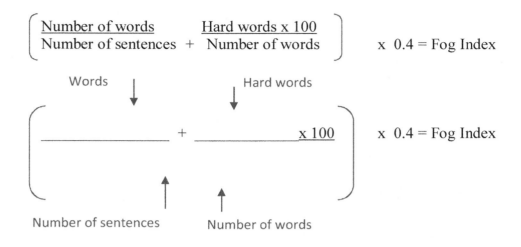

$$\left(\frac{\text{Number of words}}{\text{Number of sentences}} + \frac{\text{Hard words x 100}}{\text{Number of words}} \right) \quad \text{x } 0.4 = \text{Fog Index}$$

Words ↓   Hard words ↓

$$\left(\underline{\hspace{3cm}} + \underline{\hspace{3cm}} \text{ x 100} \right) \quad \text{x } 0.4 = \text{Fog Index}$$

Number of sentences ↑   Number of words ↑

$$\left(\underline{\hspace{3cm}} + \underline{\hspace{3cm}} \right) \quad \text{x } 0.4 = \text{Fog Index}$$

$$\underline{\hspace{4cm}} \quad \text{x } 0.4 = \text{Fog Index}$$

$$\underline{\hspace{4cm}} = \text{Fog Index}$$

Round off your answer. The grade level of this *USA Today* article is _____.

Print off one of your latest assignments. Then select a paragraph of approximately 100 words and determine its Fog Index with the help of the formula on the next page.

Practice 12.2

$$\frac{\text{Number of words}}{\text{Number of sentences}} + \frac{\text{Hard words x 100}}{\text{Number of words}} \qquad \text{x } 0.4 = \text{Fog Index}$$

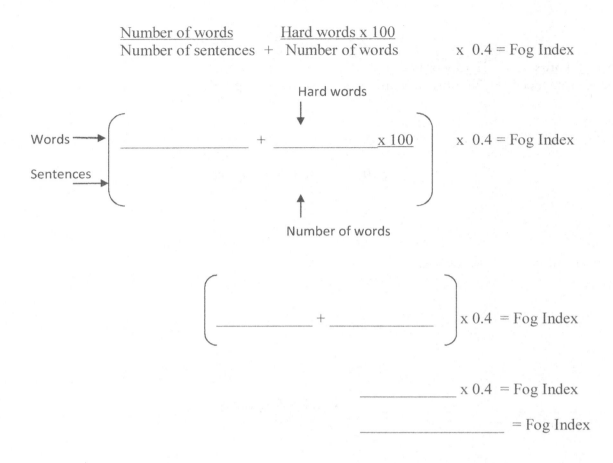

The Fog Index for your paragraph (rounded off) is grade _____.

Some more information on the Fog Index before you finish today's lesson: If you find that you have written for a grade level other than you intended, you can correct that easily. As a general rule of thumb, most sentences should have about 20 words or fewer.

If the Fog Index indicates a grade level lower than you intended, consider combining two shorter sentences or throwing in a few longer words. If the grade level is too high for your audience, there is hope. Cut some of your longer sentences down, throw in a short sentence occasionally, or use smaller, easier-to-understand words. These tips may not make your writing *good*, but they will make it more appropriate to your particular audience's grade level.

A word of caution: Don't write with the Fog Index in mind. Simply write now and fix later. Let your ideas flow in your first draft before you even think of changing words or sentence lengths. After you write and proofread, you can check your work against the Fog Index and make any necessary adjustments.

Incidentally, in the quotation at the beginning of this chapter, the aim of writing is *communication,* according to Donald Murray. Did you guess it? And do you agree?

Lesson 2

"Good" English

What is good English? Experts have been debating this for years. For the purposes of writing for your intended audience, however, good English is English that is appropriate for your audience. For instance, if you are writing for a journal for college professors, you are going to make sure your grammar is faultless and your tone is respectful and objective. If you are writing for your peers, your grammar occasionally can follow current trends and your tone can be more casual.

> *Professional Tip*
> Use strong verbs and specific nouns instead of cluttering your writing with many adjectives and adverbs. Instead of writing "He **forcefully hit** his brother on the head," write "He **struck** his brother on the head with a tomato."

Tone is how a writer sounds to a reader. Does the author sound friendly, authoritarian, enthusiastic, angry, or ironic? A folksy or casual tone might include a few contractions and a sprinkling of the pronouns *I*, *you*, and *we* ("So in the meantime, you'd better stay away from any downed power lines"). A more formal tone avoids contractions and prefers an objective style ("Residents are advised to stay away from downed power lines").

> **Casual:** You could feel the static electricity on your skin and hair when the storm moved in on Pikes Peak.

> **Formal, Objective, and Passive:** The static electricity could be felt on tourists' skin and hair as the storm engulfed Pikes Peak.

> **Formal, Objective, and Active:** As the storm engulfed Pikes Peak, tourists reported feeling static electricity on their skin and hair.

Avoid a casual tone in reports and term papers, which require an objective tone.

Learn to adapt your articles, essays, and term papers to your audience and your purpose for writing.

What Is Exposition?

News flash: You are no longer in the persuasive section of this course. In other words, you are no longer writing to sway readers to your point of view, nor are you required to give a call to action in your conclusion. This chapter and the next seven are exposition.

What is **exposition**? It is writing that explains or teaches. Newspaper articles are expository, as are textbooks, reference books, encyclopedias, instruction manuals, and cookbooks. Magazine articles that contain information on how to choose a motorcycle that is right for you or how to have healthy hair are expository. They are teaching readers something or explaining things to them.

This whole textbook is expository. It is teaching you how to write, explaining in detail the formats and nuances of language needed for the art of writing well and clearly.

When writing exposition, hook your readers by using your QSFSQ tools. Position your thesis statement near the end of the introduction. Arrange your points or reasons in a logical order and continue to use topic sentences and paragraph types. These things do not change.

But because expository conclusions don't issue a call to action, you end on a different note. Draw conclusions, recount a powerful illustration, give readers some food for thought, be insightful, or tie the conclusion to the introduction. You are not trying to convince readers; you are teaching, explaining, enlightening, or even entertaining. Your reason for writing has changed.

Below are the introduction and conclusion of an essay on gossiping. It begins with a story and ends by finishing up the story, neatly tying the beginning to the ending.

Introduction

One day I told a friend what I thought about another friend's haircut. I went on and on about how bad it looked and how I thought she should try another style. I even said, "Didn't she look in the mirror before she left the house?" To my horror, my other friend—the one with the bad haircut—was sitting at the next table. She had heard every word I said. From this humiliating incident I learned how horrible gossiping is.

Conclusion

Gossiping can cause a lot of pain. It is true what the Bible says: "Whoever repeats the matter separates close friends" (Proverbs 17:9). I lost not only the friend with the haircut but also the friend I had gossiped to. Who would want to be a friend to someone who disrespects her other friends? Tomorrow night I am going to meet them at the game and apologize to them both. That, too, will be humiliating, but at least this time it will be for a good cause.

The introduction is clear about the topic, and it includes a thesis statement at the end. The last paragraph draws some conclusions and wraps up the subject, but it does not tell readers what to do. Readers infer from this type of ending that gossiping is harmful and that they shouldn't do it; calls to action do not belong in expository writing.

Here's a student's set of introductory and concluding paragraphs for a how-to:

Introduction

"Aww, they're so cute!" Of course they are. They're three-year-olds in little pink tutus! But whoever thinks that they can easily teach three-year-olds to dance is slightly off their rocker. There are ways to survive the half-hour dance class, but only seasoned dance teachers know the secrets. If you ever find yourself in this predicament, there are some things you will need to know.

Congratulations! You have survived a class full of three-year-olds, and you can walk from the classroom with a sense of pride and accomplishment. *Conclusion* I have just one more suggestion. That hand sanitizer sitting on the counter— not such a bad idea.

Take a peek at this book's table of contents to see the types of expository writing you will be practicing this year. If you're prone to stomach cramps, you may not want to turn there at all.

Lesson 3

I Know How To . . .

You have learned how to do many things in your life, and you probably can tell someone else how to do some of them, too. Put a check next to the items on this page and the next that you already know how to do.

Avoid mowing the lawn

Train a horse

Make a friend

Drive a car

Play a sport

Prepare for and go hiking or camping

Survive a natural disaster

Shop

Change a tire

Ski

Get a job

Write a song

Sew an article of clothing

Tap dance

Know when someone is lying

Enjoy the woods

Play an instrument

Babysit

Ride a four-wheeler

Pluck a chicken

Build a Web site

Bake a dessert

Memorize Scripture

Stabilize a broken bone

Teach a Sunday school class

Throw on a potter's wheel

Procrastinate

Skateboard

Win a trophy

Build a dog kennel

Illustrate math notes with doodles

Read a map

Write other things you know how to do:

Before you write a how-to or process essay, make a list of steps. This is essential. Writing down the steps and then arranging them in the right order is a task that cannot be omitted.

Practice 12.3   For this exercise, you will need an unfrosted sheet cake or two unfrosted round cakes, along with some frosting (chocolate is messiest—I mean *best*). Number a piece of paper from 1 through 10 and then make a list of steps on how to ice a cake. You are not limited to 10 steps. Use more or less as needed.

Practice 12.4   Now give your list to a friend or classmate and ask him or her to do what is on the list. Then watch as your friend tries to follow your steps. How successful is the experiment? How complete and clear is your list?

Lesson 4

How to Write a How-to

A how-to paper is sometimes called a **process paper** because it shows the process by which something is done. In one sense, this whole course is one big how-to, showing you how to write all kinds of essays.

Here are the steps to writing a how-to or process essay:

1. **Write an introduction** to set the mood and tell readers what you are going to teach them.
2. **List items** or ingredients the readers will need.
3. Go **step by step** chronologically.
4. **Be clear** in your instructions.
5. **Use transition words** and phrases between the steps.
6. Include **charts or pictures**, if necessary.
7. **Define** any jargon.
8. **Write a conclusion** to tell readers what to do once they're finished.

Process writing can be used in both fiction and nonfiction work. Consider this humorous passage from Mark Twain's *A Connecticut Yankee in King Arthur's Court* in which he shows the process of putting on armor:

I had the demon's own time with my armor, and this delayed me a little. It is troublesome to get into, and there is so much detail. First you wrap a layer or two of blanket around your body, for a sort of cushion and to keep off the cold iron; then you put on your sleeves and shirt of chain mail—these are made of small steel links woven together, and they form a fabric so flexible that if you toss your shirt onto the floor, it slumps into a pile like a peck of wet fishnet; it is very heavy and is nearly the uncomfortablest material in the world for a nightshirt, yet plenty used it for that—tax collectors, and reformers, and one-horse kings with a defective title, and those sorts of people; then you put on your shoes—flatboats roofed over with interleaving bands of steel—and screw your clumsy spurs into the heels. Next you buckle your greaves on your legs, and your cuisses on your thighs; then come your backplate and your breastplate, and you begin to feel crowded; then you hitch on the breastplate and the half-petticoat of broad overlapping bands of steel which hangs down in front but is scalloped out behind so you can sit down, and isn't any real improvement on an inverted coal scuttle, either for looks or for wear, or to wipe your hands on; next you belt on your sword; then you put your stovepipe joints onto your arms, your iron gauntlets onto your hands, your iron rattrap onto your head, with a rag of steel web hitched onto it to hang over the back of your neck—and there you are, snug as a candle in a candle mold. This is no time to dance. Well, a man that is packed away like that, is a nut that isn't worth the cracking, there is so little of the meat, when you get down to it, by comparison with the shell.

Answer the questions: *Practice 12.5*

1. Underline any words that Twain uses to set the mood (for instance, *troublesome*).

2. Put a check next to the two similes and a metaphor he uses to enhance the mood.

3. Circle his transition words that move the reader from one step to the next.

4. Twain's passage is one long paragraph. Break it up for him into an introduction, one paragraph for the body, and a conclusion. Use your proofreading marks from chapter 9.

Lesson 5

Practice 12.6
Does he make
the grade?

Below is a process essay titled "The Art of Fishing," written by a student (695 words). Read it and answer the questions at the end of the essay:

A glorious sun rises over the pristine lake. You have a donut in one hand and a fishing pole in the other. Life awakens all around you as you sit waiting for your line to become taut. Then it happens. You feel a tug on your line, you set the hook, and the fight is on. After a thrilling battle, the fish is yours—a giant that has lived many years, a fish many have pursued. The smooth feel of its scales, the joy that shakes through your body: these are two of the incredible things that come with catching a gigantic fish. Many consider this exhilarating sport to be an old man's boring pastime. I disagree!

To begin fishing, gather these items: a fishing reel equipped with fishing line, a fishing pole with the fishing reel attached, #4 fishing hooks, clip bobbers, worms, lead split shot (little lead weights that can be found at Wal-Mart or any tackle shop), and, if you want, a bucket for water to keep your catch in.

Once you have reached your desired fishing spot, string your line from your reel through the metal rings on the rod and out the ring on the top. Then tie your hook to the end of your line and attach your split shot about 12 inches above the hook. After you have this completed, fasten your bobber above the split shot. The distance between the bobber and the split shot depends on how deep it is where you are fishing. In fairly shallow water, your hook should be one to two feet deep. This is usually good when you are fishing from the bank.

Now you are ready to add the worm. If this makes you squeamish, you can ask a parent or friend to help you. Or just thread the worm on the hook, leaving as little of the worm left hanging off the hook as possible.

Having finished with the worm, look around for a good direction in which to cast. The middle of a pond or lake is hardly ever the best place to catch fish. Fish like to live and hide near piles of branches, next to groups of weeds, or where shallow water gets deep quickly. Fish will not always be in these places, but those are your best chances for catching them.

After finding a good place to cast, face the area you are going to cast and raise your fishing rod until it is in the 10-o'clock position. If you have a spin-cast fishing reel, hold down the button on the back of the reel. Swiftly bring the rod tip down and forward until it reaches the two-o'clock position. At the same time, release the button on the reel. This should send the worm, hook, split shot, and bobber sailing, hopefully where you wanted to cast.

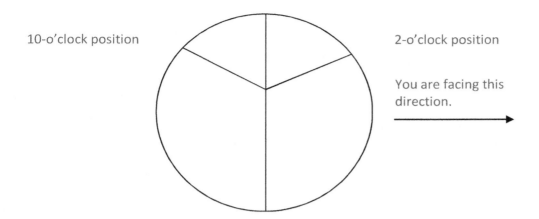

10-o'clock position

2-o'clock position

You are facing this direction.

Now that you have your worm in the water, all you have to do is wait. If you have the right amount of split shot on your line, the bobber should be halfway in and halfway out of the water. If it is under the water, there is too much weight, and you need to take a split shot off the line. If the bobber is just lying on top of the water, add more weight. Once your bobber is sitting in the water correctly, you will want to wait and watch your bobber. Once it goes down or starts to move around, jerk the tip of your rod up to the one-o'clock position. This should set the hook into the fish's mouth.

Now the fight is on. If the fish is really big, you don't want to just reel him in; you want to wear him out, or he might snap the line. After you have won the battle, the choice is yours. You can keep the fish as a meal or a trophy or just release him to fight another day.

This is not an old man's boring pastime. To some it is a passion. Don't miss out on the wonderful experiences that can be had in fishing. There's just nothing else like it. Grab your gear and meet me at the lake!

Answer the following questions:

1. Is there anything in this young man's how-to essay that makes you want to go fishing? Explain.
2. Is there anything in the essay that makes you want to avoid fishing? Explain.
3. Underline words and phrases in the introduction that set the mood for the essay.
4. In which paragraph does he include the items you need in order to fish?
5. Are his steps chronological?
6. Put an arrow next to any sentence or section you found unclear.
7. Underline words and phrases in the body of the essay that serve as transitions.
8. Is his chart helpful?
9. Does he use any jargon he doesn't define?
10. How does he tie his conclusion to his introduction?
11. Is his conclusion effective? Explain.
12. Give this paper a grade and explain how you arrived at it.

Lesson 6

Chronological, Schmonological

Some how-to writing does not require careful attention to the chronological flow. Will this result in anarchy? Pandemonium? A ghastly mess? Maybe not. In *Field and Stream*'s "50 Skills: Hunt Better, Fish Smarter, and Master the Outdoors," you will find tips on how to make waterproof matches, descend a cliff with a single rope, see in the dark, and kill fish humanely. Though each how-to is explained chronologically, the topics are in no chronological order but are grouped according to category (hunting, fishing, camping, hiking, and so on).

Shutterbug's *Digital Photography How-To Guide* includes an article on how to sharpen the images you get from your digital camera. The author gives four methods, each of which is separate from and does not rely on the others.

The how-to essay on the next page is written by a student. It contains 396 words and clever methods for eating a cupcake. Each method uses an internal chronological sequence, but the methods themselves are not chronological. Try not to drool on the page.

Professional Tip

Some technical jargon for writers:

SASE—self-addressed, stamped envelope

SAE—self-addressed envelope (send but don't affix stamps)

MS—manuscript

MSS—manuscripts

Query—letter you write to the publisher with your book or article idea

Proposal—information about your proposed book, including what need it will fill, targeted audience, chapter synopses, author bio, and so forth

Guidelines—special rules each publisher has for its writers, available online from publishers

---

Begins with a scenario (like a story, but hypothetical). Underlined sentence is her thesis statement.

You just finished your lunch and would like to have something sweet for dessert. You decide on Hostess Cupcakes. When you start to eat your cupcake, your brother comes in and says, "That's not the way to eat a cupcake." Well, that may not be the way *he* eats one. I asked everyone in my family how they eat a Hostess Cupcake and found that there are four ways to eat this snack.

The first way to eat a cupcake is the way my brother likes to eat them—I'll call it the Typewriter Method. He takes the cupcake and eats three bites across it; then he slides it back and takes three more bites out of the next row. He then repeats this process until he finishes the cupcake.

The internal structure of each paragraph uses transitional words to show a chronological order.

The second way to eat a Hostess Cupcake is the Squiggly Line Last Method. To eat a cupcake this way, you must eat to one side of the squiggly line in the middle of the cupcake. Then you turn the cupcake around and eat to the other side of the squiggly line. Last, as the name suggests, you eat the squiggly line. My dad eats the cupcake this way.

My youngest brother eats cupcakes a third way, and I have named the method after him: the Little Brother Method. He starts by eating all the cake around the filling and icing. Then he nibbles the icing to the squiggly line with his pinky finger out. Then he just pops the rest of it in his mouth and eats it (the cupcake, not the finger).

The last way to eat a Hostess Cupcake is the best way because it is the method my mom and I prefer. It is called the Inverted Method. First we turn the cupcake upside down and eat the cake and filling part of the cupcake. Then we use our teeth and scrape the rest of the cake off the icing, eating the icing around the squiggly line and, finally, the line. What could be better?

She saves "the best" for the last method.

You probably have your own well-developed procedure for eating these treats. Even though my family can't agree on a method, we agree on one thing—we like the desserts! The next time someone tells you that you are not eating the cupcake the right way, ask, "What's your method?" Then eat some together and call it research.

Brainstorm ideas for a magazine article that would not require a chronological list. Then mark one or two that interest you. Use a separate piece of paper.

Practice 12.7

Lesson 7

Parallelism

How-to and process essays often use a tool called **parallel writing** or **parallelism**. Parallel writing keeps sentences and phrases easy to understand because it repeats the same structures and word usage.

The Bible has many fine examples of parallelism. The following verses from Proverbs 6:27-28 (NIV) are in a parallel style:

Can a man scoop fire into his lap without his clothes being burned?

Can a man walk on hot coals without his feet being scorched?

The **sentence structure** for both verses is the same:

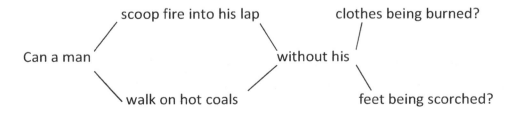

You most likely created parallel writing when you wrote your list for icing a cake (imperative sentences in the present tense), just as Chiquita® does for cutting a pineapple:

Verb	Preposition	Noun used as object of preposition
Cut	off	crown.
Cut pineapple	in	half lengthwise, then into quarters.
Cut	off	core.
Remove fruit	from	shell.
Cut	into	wedges or chunks.

Practice 12.8

Process writing benefits from parallel construction. It helps you stay organized, and its structure helps readers take in new information easily. If you were writing to tell your readers how to have a fun time at a local amusement park, you would not write this:

> Riding the Tilt-O-Stomach can be especially exciting if you remember to drink lots of milk shakes before you get on, you can down three chilidogs, and the eating of cotton candy.

Notice the shift from infinitive phrase to clause to gerund phrase. That mix of noxiously nonparallel writing is almost as bad as downing the milk shakes, chilidogs, and cotton candy before riding the Tilt-O-Stomach. Fix that nauseating sentence here:

Fix this next jumbled-up sentence in the space below, written by a student:

> MP3 players let you take lots of songs without a bulky CD wallet, some don't skip at all, and let you play any song you want, when you want it.

If you are a **beginning** writer, go directly to Write an Essay at the end of the chapter.

If you are an **intermediate** or **accomplished** writer and have written a how-to before, complete lessons 8-10.

Lesson 8

Digging Deeper: Four Types of Process Essays

You have just read about one sort of process paper, the how-to. But there are other kinds of process papers you can write for high school, college, or professional outlets such as magazines and Web sites. Below is a short list of possibilities, followed by examples.

This section is three lessons long.

1. The "I am going to tell you how I propose to fix this problem" paper.

This is called the **problem-solving process essay**. Although you could write an essay showing the process by which you are going to stop your sister from stealing clothes from your closet, this type of process essay usually is reserved for more earth-shattering problems. Consider these topics as fitting in this category: a) how you propose to stop bullying in school, b) the methods by which individuals can save energy and gasoline, or c) the process by which you would fix the problem of smart students being ostracized. You begin with a problem and then propose a solution, much like the problem-to-solution structure you learned on page 49.

2. The "I am going to tell you how this works or how it is done" paper.

Explaining how a GPS works, how birds migrate, or how the parasitic mistletoe can kill a tree are all topics that fit in this category of process writing.

3. The "I am going to tell you why (or how) it happened" paper.

This is called a **causal-process essay**; in other words, what caused the result? In this type of paper, you can explain why a character in a novel acted as he did (motivation, personality, circumstances, etc.), the process by which being overweight became the new cultural sin, or why a local bridge collapsed. The first paper will be for a literature class, the second for health, and the third for current events or physics. This structure is like the effect-to-cause paragraph you learned on page 46.

4. The "I am going to tell you how I did it" paper.

This paper is a personal narrative, not expository, but it fits nicely here because you explain how you accomplished (or did) something. Magazines often feature this type of article in which a celebrity explains how he or she achieved success.

Problem-solving process essay

In the **problem-solving process essay** ("I am going to tell you how I propose to fix this problem"), you will, yes, solve a problem. Overflowing landfills, toxic waste disposal, and the proliferation of the AIDS epidemic are real problems facing our world today. Students are often asked to present a solution to these and other problems and show that their solution is viable.

In the problem-solving essay, use your introduction—which you now know can be more than one paragraph long—to present the problem (the topic), a bit of its history (to show how it became so bad or why it needs to be fixed), and its ramifications (what it means to readers). Put your thesis statement at the end of your introductory paragraphs and then jump into the body of your essay, where you will show how you propose to solve the problem. If other methods of fixing the problem have been tried and have failed, they might be worth mentioning, but only briefly. A problem-solving process essay is all about how *you* would correct the situation, what process *you* would use to achieve a positive outcome.

Below is an example of this type of process paper. People today are concerned about using up the earth's resources and running out of energy sources. Would you be surprised to learn that people in 1919 were also concerned about where the next energy source was going to come from? "The Great Woods Have Been Destroyed," written by Laura Ingalls Wilder, shows the problem, some ways in which others thought they could solve it, and her idea of how to solve the energy problem. Here is an abridged version of her article:

What a frightful thing it would be if we were to wake up some morning and find that there was no fuel of any kind in the United States with which to cook our breakfast. Yet this astounding thing may happen to our grandchildren, our children or even in our own lifetime if our days should be "long in the land."

Her explanation of the problem

Too many of the forests of the United States have been made into lumber even though there never has seemed to be lumber enough, and the waste of timber has been great. The great woods of the East and the North of our country have been destroyed.

People then will not be able to use coal in place of wood, for the supply of coal is fast disappearing. The end of hard coal is in sight. Soft coal therefore must be the basis of the country's industrial life as well as its fuel. There is, to be sure, a great deal of soft coal left; but it is of poor quality and must be especially prepared for use to be satisfactory. The greater difficulties and more costly equipment in mining inferior coal and also the higher wages make prices higher.

What other people have proposed and why she thinks it won't work

But cost alone is not the greatest problem. There is danger of a power shortage which will stop all manufactories unless a way is found

Further explanation of the problem

to furnish a national power supply. Two-thirds of all our coal mined goes into the production of power. Eleven million persons are working in our manufacturing plants and more than double the power was used last year than was used in 1900.

Her proposal (thesis statement underlined)

Electricity is the only thing that can save the situation. One ton of coal used in generating electricity will furnish power equal to four tons.

Secretary [of the Interior, Franklin K.] Lane has a plan for furnishing electric power through a large central station. He urges a power survey of the whole United States, the locating of central stations and smaller supply stations.

It is known that in the territory between Boston and Richmond is situated one-fourth of the power-generating capacity of the country, and as an illustration of the plan, I quote Floyd W. Parsons in the *Saturday Evening Post*: "The logical development is a multiple-transmission line of high voltage extending all the way from Boston to Washington and on to Richmond. Energy could be delivered into this unified system by power stations located near the mine mouths and by hydro-electric plants located at the 20 or more water power sites tributary to this area."

An expert's opinion to support her solution

Thus might be created rivers of power flowing through the country and furnishing energy and power to our manufactories at much less than half of what it costs now.

They have one such great power line in California and another, 500 miles long, reaching from Tonopah, Nevada, to Yuma, Arizona.

Proof that her proposal has worked elsewhere

There is water power enough in the Ozark Hills to furnish power and light for that section of country and, if included in the national system with the coal of Kansas and Illinois, would do its part in caring for the whole. The railroads could be electrified also, and by the careful handling of our natural power and fuel, by a responsible head, that cold and dreary breakfastless morning might never arrive. It need never arrive if we see to it that our water power and what is left of our fuel supply is handled carefully and intelligently.

Ending on a positive, it-can-be-fixed note

A tie-in to her introduction

Her ideas of hydropower are not far from what we have today. What problem will you solve?

How it works/How it is done

Essays of science or technology can fascinate readers as they learn the complicated process by which the eye sees ("how it works") or how a cell phone signal can be used to triangulate a position ("how it is done"). How did Noah get all those animals to fit in the Ark? How does a team prepare for the big game? A skillfully written process essay can answer these and other questions of interest.

Here is an example of this kind of process paper (424 words), written by a student:

How a Mosquito Sucks Your Blood

You hear a high-pitched whining in your ear, and you swat in irritation at the small pest that is buzzing in circles around you. The creature is silent. Then you feel a slight itch on your neck and immediately slap the insect you know is resting there. But its reflexes are faster than yours, and you hear it whining once again. We all know that summer brings with it warm sun and vacations, but unfortunately it also brings pesky mosquitoes.

How do mosquitoes manage to be so annoying? The answer is quite simple. They suck your blood. Then they leave an itching, red lump as proof of their harassment.

Only the female mosquito is properly equipped to bite you and drink your blood. But she's not really biting; she's stabbing. When she has chosen you as her victim, she flies over and lands on an exposed portion of your skin. Then she extends her proboscis, the long, straw-like appendage she uses like a needle, and proceeds to stab you and drink your blood. How much blood? She only drains .002ml from your 4-5 liters and can become engorged on that amount. Contrary to popular belief, mosquitoes don't rely on human blood as a food source. They, particularly the males (who don't even have a proboscis), feed on nectar and other sugary substances. The females, however, do need a certain amount of human, mammalian or bird blood in order to obtain protein and other nutrients for their developing eggs.

Why is it that, even when you are watching her poke into your skin, you don't feel the stab? The female mosquito shoots an anesthetic through her proboscis so you don't feel the needle entering your skin. After the mosquito has "bitten" you and flown away, you are most likely left with an itchy, red welt. This is because when she stabs you with the anesthetic, she also injects you with anti-coagulant chemicals. This keeps your blood from clotting while she is busy stealing it. And it also keeps your body from quickly closing off or healing the small puncture. The chemicals in her saliva cause your body to react by enlarging the blood vessels, causing the red bump and releasing histamines, which causes the itchiness. Naturally, your next move is to scratch the mosquito bite; this only causes it to become irritated and inflamed, itching worse than before.

The next time you hear a mosquito whining in your ear, appreciate how far some mothers will go for their offspring. Then go get some bug spray.

Practice 12.9   Brainstorm some ideas for each type of process paper listed below.

Problem-solving essay:

How it works/How it is done:

Lesson 9

Causal-process essay

Effect: rising crime in your town. Why is it rising?

Effect: famine in the Sudan. What are the ecological, economic, and political factors that contributed to the famine?

Effect: a geological formation near you. What factors caused it?

Effect: a plane crash. What are the problems that caused it?

An effect—or a result—didn't just get there. Things had to happen that led up to the final result. In the **causal-process paper**, you explain the process by which something was achieved. You begin with the effect, say, the Dust Bowl in Oklahoma in the 1930s, and then show the possible causes or factors that made the Dust Bowl possible, such as over-farming, drought, and so on. The causal process seeks to isolate and discuss how these and other factors contribute to and create the particular result you are concerned with. You may also be asked to write what you think could have been done to alleviate the problem or avoid it altogether, along with recommendations for the future.

You can be sure that every plane crash will be investigated by teams of experts to find the reasons why that plane crashed—and to avoid other crashes in the future. The experts will examine the transponder, the black box, and the maintenance logs. What happened? Was it a mechanical failure? Operator error? Was a piece of the plane damaged or stressed? What part did nature or weather play in the accident? Had all the scheduled maintenance been performed at the right times by the right people? These and other factors are going to be examined in great detail.

In preparing to write your causal-process essay, you will research and isolate the various factors that led up to the effect you are writing about. Then you will discuss them in detail and explain how each factor aided in bringing about the result. In other words, you begin with the end result and figure out what made it happen.

Avoid **reductionism**. This is a fallacy in which writers maintain that the result had only one cause, much like saying, for instance, that a drop in graduation rates is due only to the need for older teens to find jobs. Most likely, many reasons or factors contribute to the end result, so include many possibilities.

Below is a causal-process essay written about an annual occurrence in a small town. As you read it, think of other factors that might have contributed to the problem:

> Yes, it has happened yet again. The Red Devil River has surged out of its banks and flooded our tiny town of Montgomery like a hungry mob of shoppers storming the doors of Wal-Mart at 4 a.m. on the Friday after Thanksgiving. It is annual. It is dangerous. And it is not a pretty sight. While folks say we need to do something about the flooding, it will behoove our community to examine the reasons Red Devil continues to flood. In addressing these issues, Montgomery has a better chance of fixing them.
>
> The first reason Red Devil River floods Montgomery every year is because we are downstream from other rivers and tributaries. Every major rainfall or snow-melting event swells its banks with the run-off of those waterways. This has been happening for hundreds of years and is so obvious that even our fourth-grade students know about it. We cannot change the course of nature nor the location of our town, so let's move on.
>
> Second, Montgomery, founded in 1812, was first settled in a troublesome location—on the banks of the Red Devil River at the end of the current Muskatoochee Street, near Red Devil Park. Casual observers will note that across Red Devil River from this site, the bank is high. In fact, three miles up or down the river will show high banks on both sides. The river does not flood there. It is only at the site of the original Montgomery that the land tips smoothly down to the river, a feature that must have made our founders' search for water much easier but has not been a blessing to us. Had Montgomery been founded up- or downriver, we would not have this problem today.
>
> A third factor in Montgomery's annual flooding is the Grable Bridge south of town. According to the date carved into the abutment, Grable Bridge was constructed in 1898. While it is still sturdy and usable today, it has a major flaw. It is too narrow. Its piers stand at the edge of the water, not farther back on land. This constricts the flow of the river and slows its progress when the river swells, forcing the muddy waters up the smooth bank and into town.
>
> Unfortunately, it is the fifty or so houses and businesses for two whole blocks to the west of the river at that point that suffer each year. Some say that those who live near the river should expect this yearly soaking and should not complain. After all, they know they are living in a flood plain; they should shut up or move. But this option is

impracticable. Those citizens have invested in their homes and businesses. They cannot move to higher ground *en masse.*

It is too late to move the town to higher ground, but it is not too late to solve this problem of yearly flooding. Building a new bridge just south of the current Grable Bridge will allow the flooded river to flow swiftly downstream without backing up into our little town. With foundations and piers in the correct places, the new bridge would be a boon to Montgomery and its inhabitants. Another solution is building a levee between the town and the river at the low spot. This will ensure safety for those houses and businesses most affected by the flooding. It will also have a positive effect on the land and housing values of that area. In addition, Red Devil Park will be available to our citizens year round and will cease being hazardous during flood season.

The annual flooding of Montgomery does not have to be as sure and destructive as Black Friday shopping. Instead of succumbing to the power of the river, we can take these safety precautions and fear its inevitable surges no more.

Practice 12.10   Answer these questions on a separate piece of paper:

1. To what does this writer compare the yearly flooding?
2. What is the thesis statement?
3. What are the three causes this writer attributes to the annual flooding?
4. What other factors might lead to annual flooding?
5. What is the one idea some folks have talked about but is not workable?
6. What are the two recommendations this writer proposes?
7. What other recommendation can you add?
8. How does this writer tie the conclusion to the introduction?

Lesson 10

The "How I did it" process essay

Have you seen a friend through a difficult situation? Have you survived a traumatic experience such as a disease or a car crash? Did you lead your team to victory? Did you overcome a bad habit? Did you survive a black night babysitting monster kids or win the local singing contest? Then you can write how you did it. In other words, you can explain the process.

Articles like "How I Overcame My Fear of Heights and Became a Parachuting Fool" abound in magazines because we like to read about how people Made It Big. Typically, we look for one of two criteria: 1) the person is famous, or 2) the person did something interesting (or made it *sound* interesting or humorous).

Most likely, you aren't famous yet, so opt for #2. Write about how you did something that might be of interest to others. Or write it in a way that will capture your reader, perhaps with humor.

Read this humorous how-I-did-it process narrative essay (697 words). It is written by a student.

How I Prepared for the Mini-Marathon

To do the Mini-Marathon (a 13.1-mile race), everyone says that you have to train for at least half an hour every day, eat healthful food, and make sure that you are mentally prepared. When I did the Mini-Marathon, I did all of the above. I trained twenty minutes on the treadmill on the days I felt like it. I ate an occasional salad when there was nothing else left in the fridge, and I even sang with my headphones from home to Indianapolis on the day of the race to get myself energized.

I start my day with training. First my alarm rings, and things just go downhill from there. I roll over and fumble around with the buttons until the alarm is quiet. Seven a.m. is definitely too early to go running. I groan and pull my blankets closer. Most days this is where my training session stops, but some days just before my eyes drift shut again, I force myself to roll out of bed. After finding a pair of shorts and a tank top, I sit on my bed, tying my shoes and resisting the urge to curl up on my bed and sleep for just a few more minutes; instead I head downstairs with as much enthusiasm as a three-year-old being sent to bed.

When I get to the kitchen, I drink a glass of orange juice before heading down to the basement, where I face the treadmill. I always start out walking. When I get bored of that, after two minutes, I start to run. The problem with treadmills is that you have to stare at the same wall while you're running, which can get monotonous. So, to solve this problem, I start watching the little screen that shows how many calories I am burning. This gets so boring that I calculate how many steps it takes on the different speeds to burn one calorie. On the fifth speed it takes twelve steps. And that isn't even the worst part.

What's worse is that—no matter how far the treadmill says I've run or even how far I feel like I've run—I never actually *go* anywhere. When I get off, I have this terrible feeling, partly because I just ran three and a half miles and partly because I did it without ever moving, even though my muscles tell me this is not true.

Once I successfully complete my training session, I hike up the stairs for a hearty breakfast of frosted-flakes cereal and an orange. This is my typical breakfast on the days I train. But to ensure that I perform well in the Mini-Marathon, I do what every great athlete does the night before the race. I carb load.

Carbohydrate loading is an athletic tradition. All you have to do is eat a ton of carbs. The night before the Mini-Marathon, my mom cooks a huge spaghetti dinner for our family and some friends who are also doing the race. We all load our plates and have dinner. After dinner we watch a movie and then go straight to bed. We have to get up at four a.m.

When my alarm goes off at four, I decide that running at seven wasn't so bad. But I drag myself out of bed and get dressed. My breakfast is extra healthful: a granola bar and gummy bears to snack on in the car. Mom read somewhere that they give you lots of energy and are recommended for runners.

When we get to Military Park, I know I am ready to do the Mini-Marathon. I don't know which part of my training helped the most. Was it the treadmill? The gummy bears? Maybe it's that I have a friend who drags me along the whole route. But I finish. I finish in two hours and fifty-four minutes, a full two seconds ahead of my older sister, which has been one of my goals from the very beginning. I finish after twenty thousand people and yet before ten thousand. For me, finishing the Mini-Marathon is a tremendous accomplishment because I worked toward that goal by training for weeks. What a fantastic feeling!

Practice 12.11   Brainstorm some ideas for each type of process paper listed below.

Causal-process essay:

Personal "how I did it" narrative:

Write an Essay

The following assignment is for a **beginning** writer:

Write a how-to essay. Teach your reader how to do something that you know how to do and have done before. Research to augment your instructions, if necessary. Follow the steps of how to write a process essay, as the student with the fishing essay did.

One topic you may not write about: how to write a how-to paper.

When you have finished writing your essay, proofread it with Be Your Own Editor on page 161.

Word count: at least 400 words.

Check out this assignment's checklist:

- ❑ Is the title interesting?
- ❑ Is there an introduction?
- ❑ Does it set the mood?
- ❑ Does it tell readers what is being taught?
- ❑ Is there a list of needed items/ingredients? *
- ❑ Are the steps chronological? *
- ❑ Are the instructions clear?
- ❑ Are there effective transitions?
- ❑ Is there something else you'd rather be doing right now?
- ❑ Is the chart or illustration helpful and clear? *
- ❑ Is the jargon well defined? *
- ❑ Is there a conclusion?
- ❑ Does it adequately sum up the subject?
- ❑ Is it clear that the paper is focused on a particular audience?
- ❑ Does the paper adequately describe the process?
- ❑ Are the instructions divided into paragraphs logically?
- ❑ Is parallel writing used where necessary?
- ❑ Is the paper double-spaced? * These items, depending on the topic, may be optional.

Fill in this chart to help you schedule your tasks or use the chart at the end of chapter 4.

Day 1	Day 2	Day 3	Day 4	Day 5	Day 6

If you are an **intermediate** or **accomplished** writer and have already successfully written a how-to sometime in your high school career, choose ONE of the following assignments:

○ Write a **problem-solving process** essay. This is the problem: In your town, some people do not have enough to eat. They go to bed hungry almost every night. Infants, children, fixed-income senior citizens, and anyone in between can fall prey to poverty and hunger due to job lay-offs, business failures, exorbitant health-care costs, natural disasters, or anything else that takes food from their mouths. This is a real problem in your town, and you have a chance to advance a solution.

Without proposing to use any government money, write a solution to the hunger problem in your town. You may need to research to see what has already been done or to find viable avenues for your plan.

If you have another problem you would rather solve, check the topic with your teacher to get approval first.

When you have finished writing your essay, proofread it using Be Your Own Editor on page 164..

Word count: at least 500 words.

○ Write a "**how it works**" or "**how it is done**" process essay, clearly showing the process by which something works or is done.

Check your topic with your teacher before writing.

Do the necessary research to better understand your topic.

Make sure your reader knows the tone of the essay and the topic in the first paragraph.

Use transition words and phrases as needed.

When you have finished writing your essay, proofread it using Be Your Own Editor on page 164.

Word count: at least 500 words.

○ Write a **causal-process essay** in which you begin with the problem or result and show what contributed to it or what caused it.

Check your topic with your teacher before writing.

Research your topic to give a full, in-depth look at it.

Suggest recommendations in your concluding paragraph, if this is appropriate to your topic.

When you have finished writing your essay, proofread it using Be Your Own Editor on page 164.

Word count: at least 500 words.

○ Write a **personal narrative** (your story) of how you did something. Describe the process. Choose an interesting topic or make it interesting by using humor or other devices.

Check your topic with your teacher before writing.

When you have finished writing your essay, proofread it using Be Your Own Editor on page 164.

Word count: at least 500 words.

"Opinions cannot survive if one has no chance
to fight for them."

- Thomas Mann

Chapter 13: The Position Paper and Documentation

EXISTENTIAL ALARM: In this chapter you will learn everything you need to know about the position paper—except why.

Lesson 1

A position paper is a glorified opinion paper. And it is an exposition paper; that is, you are not trying to persuade your readers. You are simply explaining your position.

When writing a position paper, you choose a debatable topic on which thinking, educated people may disagree: a current war, celebrating Halloween, a trend in the movie industry, embryonic stem-cell research, immigration, viable sources of energy, and so forth. Your topic should have political, social, cultural, economic, or religious relevance.

Writing your opinion of your new minister or priest has little meaning for any audience larger than your church, but writing your opinion of mega-churches is quite relevant for today's churchgoers. In the same way, an opinion of a new ice cream shop pales in comparison to an opinion on whether sexually oriented businesses should be allowed to set up shop in your city.

"The dangers of smoking" is not an appropriate topic for a position paper because few people deny that smoking is unhealthful. However, writing about whether smokers should be allowed to light up in their own cars when children are present is a debatable, controversial topic that has political, social, and health ramifications.

Below are some examples of topics important and deep enough to use for a position paper. You could write your view on . . .

- government and businesses using security cameras to tape employees, customers, and drivers
- corporate farming techniques
- gender-neutral Bibles
- women as priests or ministers
- gun control
- medical experimentation on humans or animals
- abortion
- the salaries of organized sports players
- buying products made in countries that violate human rights
- banning books
- Americans buying carbon offsets in other countries
- the death penalty

Take a moment to brainstorm three or four topics of importance that interest you. Use this space:

Although you may mention an opposing view, you need not spend much time refuting it. Concentrate on supporting your own view.

Writing a position paper (or any report or term paper) takes research. And that takes certain skills, some of which you already have learned in this course:

- ✓ brainstorm
- ✓ narrow down a topic
- ✓ develop a thesis statement
- ✓ arrange points in a logical order
- ✓ write topic sentences
- ✓ create paragraphs of differing formats
- ✓ use transition statements or sentences

✓ use the introduction to create interest or curiosity

✓ use the conclusion to sum up and give food for thought

✓ proofread your own work

In this and the next lessons, you'll learn about taking notes, plagiarism, and organizing your material. And if that doesn't keep you awake, I don't know what will.

Taking Notes

Taking notes means getting the essential facts. You'll take more notes than you will need in your paper, but until you write the paper, you won't know which facts to use.

Below is a format anyone can use to take notes. Reporters use a similar method when taking notes for their articles. Write your notes on the fronts of regular notebook paper. Do not write on the backs of the pages. This way you can find your information quickly. Head the tops of the pages according to subheadings within your topic (you may want to use two or three pages for the same heading). For instance, if your topic is the icons of evolution, your headings might look like this:

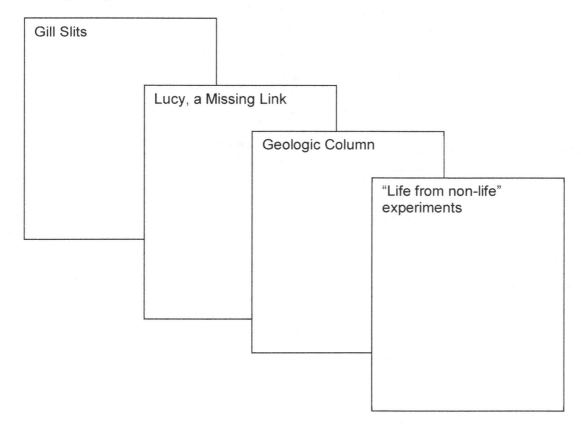

Don't worry if you don't know what to label your pages. You'll find out quickly enough when you begin to read your sources. In fact, if you are unsure of what possibilities are within your topic, skim chapter headings of books, magazines on the subject, and Internet sources.

Keep a separate notebook page for your source information. Sources can be books, magazines, Internet sites, interviews, newspapers, DVDs, and so forth. Write the information about the source (author, publisher, and so on) on your source page—see below—and label it with a letter. When you take notes from that source, put them under the appropriate page headings and put the source's matching letter and a page number next to it. That way you can keep your facts and sources straight and be able to refer to them correctly in your paper.

This is what it will look like in your <u>notebook</u> and the page for your <u>sources</u>:

Gill Slits

A Ernest Haeckel, Hitler's mentor, developed a theory in 1866 that human embryos go through all phases of human evolution. He even drew pictures of embryos from different animals and humans to compare them.

A As early as 1874, Wilhelm His proved Haeckel had doctored the drawings to make them look like he wanted them to. Haeckel was "barred from many scientific circles."

B Teachers and textbooks still teach this discredited theory today.

C "Gill slits" are really pharyngeal pouches. In humans, these become Eustachian tubes, the thymus, parathyroid glands, and other things.

B The thymus is part of the human immunity system, and the parathyroid glands are for calcium control.

D "In mammals, the jaws, inner ear, tongue, tonsils, and other organs are formed from these ridges." Page 73

D The pharyngeal pouches in mammal, bird, and reptile embryos "<u>never</u> [have] any openings in these structures like gills." Page 73

Source Page

A Morris, John. "Does the Human Embryo Go Through Animal Stages?" Institute for Creation Research, 1 Aug. 1989. Web. 29 Oct. 2012.

B Ham, Ken. "A Surgeon Looks at Creation." Answers In Genesis, June 1992. Web. 29 Oct. 2012.

C Lindsey, George. "Evolution – Useful or Useless?" Institute for Creation Research, 1 Oct. 1985. Web. 29 Oct. 2012.

D Moore, John N. *Questions and Answers on Creation/Evolution.* Grand Rapids: Baker Book House, 1985. Print.

The above source page uses the Modern Language Association (MLA) method of citing sources, which you will use for your position paper. Stay tuned for more on that in upcoming lessons.

The sources on the source page are in no particular order. They are not alphabetized but appear in the order the student used them. The capital letters on the Gill Slits page (A, B, C, and D) are all keyed to their corresponding sources on the source page. This enables your source documentation to run smoothly when writing your paper. In your notes, include page numbers from sources that have them because you will need them in your paper.

Always print any information you get from the Internet. This gives you a hard copy of the facts. Internet information is always in flux; what is on the site today may not be there tomorrow, and you need proof of your information.

Lesson 2

Plagiarism and Paraphrasing

Putting a fact into your paper without citing your source is considered plagiarism. Cite all facts except those of common knowledge, like the number of miles between the sun and Earth, for instance.

Plagiarism will earn you a lower grade on your report. It is also illegal. It represents someone else's work as your own.

To quote a source, carefully copy the quotation word for word into your notebook and put quotation marks around it or use a copier or scanner to get the quote right. This is perfectly legal if you are using the information for your own use (a school assignment, in this case).

In order to take notes without plagiarizing (using another writer's facts, words, ideas, illustrations, examples, or sentence structures), **paraphrase** the original text by putting it into your own words.

Consider this sentence and the following two paraphrases:

Original sentence: "The Eskimos used to kill their elderly by setting them adrift in ice floes floating out to sea!"

Incorrect paraphrase: Eskimos used to murder their old people by putting them on ice floes. [uses the same sentence structure as the original]

One correct paraphrase: Older people in the Eskimo culture were put to death by sending them out to sea on barren ice floes.

The reason the incorrect paraphrase is considered plagiarism is because it uses the same sentence structure as the original sentence.

To learn more about plagiarism and how to avoid it, go to plagiarism.org.

Practice 13.1 Go to plagiarism.org and write down two facts about plagiarizing that are new to you.

Practice 13.2 Look up Psalm 73 in your favorite version. Sum up what Asaph is pondering here but avoid plagiarism. Use the space below or a separate piece of paper. The ideas don't have to be complete sentences.

Lesson 3

Organize

Once you have taken your notes and recorded your source material, you'll organize your main points and supporting points. For this, try the cluster method, the Greek temple method, a list, or an outline. Examine the following methods on the next pages used for a position paper on the icons of evolution.

Cluster method

This cluster uses boring shades of black and gray. Yours can use colors of your choice to delineate the different levels of main points and supporting facts.

- Clever intro, thesis statement: "Many of evolution's icons are based on old or erroneous information and should be disregarded."
- Textbook example occurs nowhere on Earth
- Clams and other "simple" life forms are found in every layer.
- Conclusion
- Geologic column
- Created amino acids—building blocks but not life
- Worst of all--racism
- **Icons of Evolution**
- "Life from non-life" experiments
- Miller made left- *and* right-handed amino acids—the combo is detrimental to life
- Lucy: only ape qualities, no human ones
- Radioisotope dating
- Human embryonic "gill slits"
- Small cranial capacity, sloping face
- Pronounced curve of finger and toe bones
- Never develop into any breathing structures
- Recapitulation proved false over 100 years ago
- Really pharyngeal pouches, not slits
- Locking wrist bones—a knuckle walker

Greek temple method

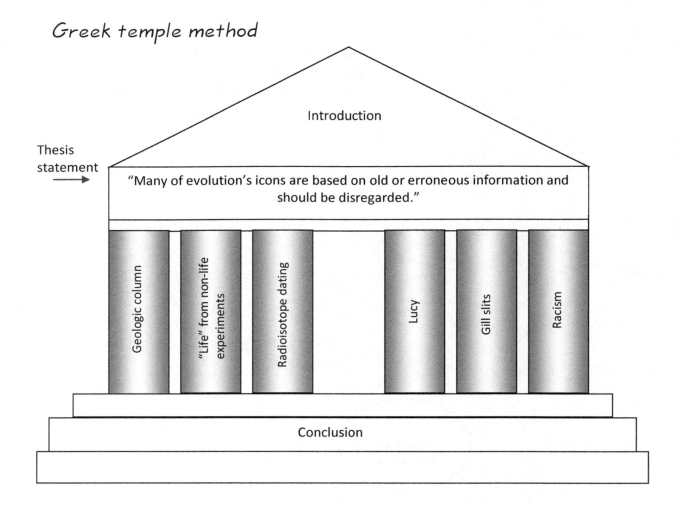

Thesis statement →

Introduction

"Many of evolution's icons are based on old or erroneous information and should be disregarded."

Geologic column

"Life" from non-life experiments

Radioisotope dating

Lucy

Gill slits

Racism

Conclusion

List

Clever intro, thesis statement
Geologic column
- occurs nowhere intact on Earth
- clams in every layer

"Life from non-life" experiments
- created building blocks only
- amino acids are not life
- created left- and right-handed amino acids
- harmful to life when together

Gill slits
- recapitulation proved false over 100 years ago
- scientist debunked
- never develop into breathing structures
- pouches, not slits

Etc.

Outline

I. Introduction and thesis statement
II. Geologic column
  A. Occurs nowhere on Earth in exact form
  B. Clams in every layer
    1. Other "simple" organisms in every layer
    2. In some places, the layers are reversed
III. "Life from non-life" experiments
  A. Created amino acids—only building blocks, not life itself
  B. Created left- and right-handed amino acids—detrimental to life in combo
IV. Gill slits in human embryos
  A. Some high school biology texts still carry this information and illustrations
    1. Proved false over 100 years ago
    2. The scientist who came up with it was debunked
    3. He had tampered with his illustrations
Etc.

Note the small differences between the list and the outline. The list is more casual and can use bullets or dashes. The outline is more formal, with Roman numerals for each larger subject heading, letters for what will eventually become paragraphs, and numbers for supporting statements. If the report is long and there is enough information, even the numbers will indicate separate paragraphs.

If none of these methods of organizing works for you, try the **sticky-note method**. That is, write all your main points and supporting points on sticky notes, one point to each note. Then rearrange them until you are satisfied that you have all the points you need and that your report will flow in a logical direction.

As you develop your paper, you will naturally choose an order into which to put your points. To review these orders, refer to lesson 2 and 3 in chapter 2.

Practice 13.3

Your topic for this exercise is a simple opinion: the animal you love or the animal you love to hate. You can be general ("I love all cats") or specific ("I despise Fluffy").

Brainstorm the reasons why you hold this opinion. Don't hold back. Write down everything you can think of.

Then choose a method of organizing your material: the cluster, Greek temple, list, outline, or sticky note. On a separate piece of paper, organize your reasons and supporting statements, using the method you chose.

You will not be writing this "report."

Lesson 4

The Modern Language Association Strikes Again

Sooner or later, you have to stop brainstorming, researching, and organizing—and you have to start writing. No need to panic, though. Keep telling yourself that a position paper is simply a glorified opinion paper crammed with good thinking and facts.

Follow the handy steps on the next page for your position paper, and you can't go wrong.

- Brainstorm topics.
- Narrow down your topic.
- Think of a temporary thesis statement to guide your research.
- Check your topic and thesis statement with your teacher for approval.
- Begin research; keep notes by topics, on separate pieces of notebook paper.
- Develop a source page and keep all the publishing info there.
- Rethink your thesis statement, as amended by all your research.
- Organize your paragraphs by using a list, outline, Greek temple, cluster, or sticky notes.
- Begin writing your position paper.
- Yes, write the thing.

In a position paper, you may need to define your topic ("human rights") or give some historical background (possible causes of global warming and cooling). Typically this information goes somewhere in the first or second paragraphs.

When you include this information, you may need to move your thesis statement. Will it fit logically at the end of your first paragraph? Or will it fit best at the end of the next paragraphs (after you define your topic or give historical background)?

Play with it a little to find the best place for it.

In the next stupendous sections, you will learn valuable information about how to document your sources and attribute quotations and facts to the right people/books/Internet sources and so forth, using the Modern Language Association (MLA) format. This information is essential to writing any in-depth report, including your position paper.

Read on, O brave one.

> WARNING: You will need your snooze alarm for this material. You may also need pointy pins, random noises, or haphazard jabs to your ribs to keep you awake.

The Modern Language Association (MLA) method of documentation is typically used in English and literature classes but can be used elsewhere. This method of citing your sources uses **in-text citations**, which incorporates source information into the text of your report. You have already used in-text citations in some of your persuasive writing. Every fact, idea, quotation, or illustration that is not yours needs an in-text citation. The only exceptions are facts of common knowledge (the speed of light or an author's year of birth, for example).

An in-text citation in reports uses a **signal phrase** to "signal" that you are borrowing a quotation or fact, and it ends with a **parenthetical citation**. These citations, in turn, refer to the source information on the **works cited page** at the end of your report.

You will review signal phrases in this lesson. Parenthetical citations and the works cited page come in later lessons.

Signal phrases alert the reader that a quotation is coming next or that you are using someone else's fact, idea, or illustration. They look like this:

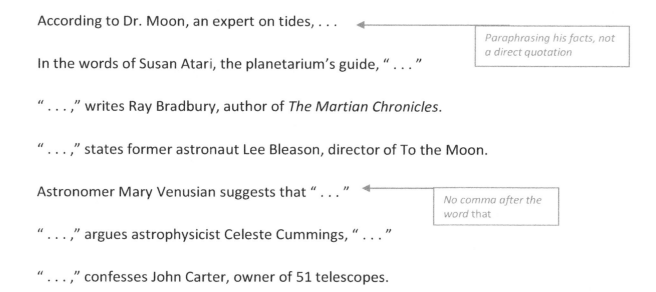

According to Dr. Moon, an expert on tides, . . .

Paraphrasing his facts, not a direct quotation

In the words of Susan Atari, the planetarium's guide, " . . . "

" . . . ," writes Ray Bradbury, author of *The Martian Chronicles.*

" . . . ," states former astronaut Lee Bleason, director of To the Moon.

Astronomer Mary Venusian suggests that " . . . "

No comma after the word that

" . . . ," argues astrophysicist Celeste Cummings, " . . . "

" . . . ," confesses John Carter, owner of 51 telescopes.

Signal phrases can appear before, after, or in the middle of the quotation or fact, and they use **present tense** most often, even if the person is long dead. Occasionally they use **present perfect tense**:

Jules Verne, writer of many science fiction books, <u>has observed</u>, " . . . "

Included in a signal phrase are the person you are quoting or borrowing a fact from and the person's credentials. Readers need to know why they should trust the information. Giving credentials as they relate to your subject tells the reader that the information is reliable ("director of…," "owner of…," "doctor of…," "mother of…," and so forth).

Avoid using long quotations. Yes, it plumps up your word count or page requirement, but it tells your teacher that you relied on other people's work instead of your own. Learn to paraphrase facts, information, ideas, and illustrations. The time to use a quotation is when the original source says it better than you ever could or when the information might be questioned if it were not quoted.

Practice 13.4

On the next page are four goofy quotes/facts, along with the source information. Decide whether to quote, use a partial quote, or paraphrase the information, and then create one in-text citation for each source. There are a number of right ways to do this, so be creative.

Source 1: Mr. Kurtz
Credentials: Runs a trading post in Africa that deals with ivory
Quote: "Severed heads on poles will accomplish much in the way of keeping order and creating respect for authority when one lives in a dark jungle."

Source 2: Henry (Indiana) Jones Jr.
Credentials: an archaeology professor at Marshall College, New Britain, Connecticut, and a world-renown archaeologist
Quote: "Using a whip is not necessary when discovering the buried and hidden past, but it is fun."

Source 3: www.ayankeein.sci
Credentials: a respected time travel Web site
Quote: "Time travel is possible, but only to castles."

Source 4: LOTFlies organization
Credentials: specializes in spear making
Fact: "Six out of ten boys would rather hunt wild boar than go hungry."

Lesson 5

The Long and Winding Quote

When you have a quotation that is at least four typed lines in your report, precede it with an explanatory sentence that ends with a colon. Then set it off by indenting the whole thing ten spaces from the left margin. Finish it by inserting the **parenthetical citation,** a citation in parentheses (see the next page), *after* the end punctuation mark. (Normally, parenthetical citations are *inside* the end punctuation. More on parenthetical citations in the next lessons.)

The sentence before the long quotation will set up the quote in some way by explaining it, writing its context, introducing the author, and so on. Readers need to know why you are using the quote or how the quote fits into your topic.

Your long quotation will look like the one on the next page. "And here arises..." is indented because it is the beginning of a new paragraph in the original source.

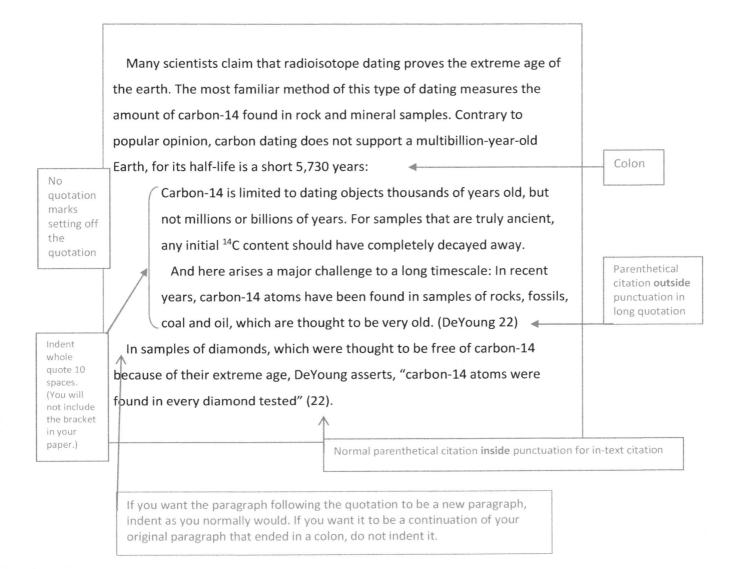

Many scientists claim that radioisotope dating proves the extreme age of the earth. The most familiar method of this type of dating measures the amount of carbon-14 found in rock and mineral samples. Contrary to popular opinion, carbon dating does not support a multibillion-year-old Earth, for its half-life is a short 5,730 years: ← Colon

Carbon-14 is limited to dating objects thousands of years old, but not millions or billions of years. For samples that are truly ancient, any initial ^{14}C content should have completely decayed away.

And here arises a major challenge to a long timescale: In recent years, carbon-14 atoms have been found in samples of rocks, fossils, coal and oil, which are thought to be very old. (DeYoung 22) ← Parenthetical citation **outside** punctuation in long quotation

No quotation marks setting off the quotation

In samples of diamonds, which were thought to be free of carbon-14 because of their extreme age, DeYoung asserts, "carbon-14 atoms were found in every diamond tested" (22).

Indent whole quote 10 spaces. (You will not include the bracket in your paper.)

Normal parenthetical citation **inside** punctuation for in-text citation

If you want the paragraph following the quotation to be a new paragraph, indent as you normally would. If you want it to be a continuation of your original paragraph that ended in a colon, do not indent it.

Sorry about all the nit-picky stuff you've got to learn here! Parenthetical citations finish the in-text citation and often include the last name of the author and the page number. If the author's name is in the signal phrase, it is not needed in the parenthetical citation. The author, DeYoung, will be found on your works cited page, which we'll get to soon.

On the next page you'll find a long quotation that contains some mechanical mistakes. Use the proofreading marks you learned on page 154 to correct the mistakes.

Practice 13.5

In this case, you will note that the writer wants "The Civil War..." to be a continuation of the paragraph beginning "Racism was fueled..." and has not indented it.

Racism was fueled by unfounded beliefs of evolutionists for more than 100 years. Influential evolutionists believed that the black race was closer to our supposed early ancestors (apes) than the white race. They cited skin and hair color, head shape, and brow ridges to prove that Africans were a "lower" race, just a step up from apes. Arthur Conan Doyle, creator of Sherlock Holmes, exhibits this belief in *The Lost World.*

> "They may be undeveloped types, . . . but their deportment in the presence of their superiors might be a lesson to some of our more advanced Europeans. Strange how correct are the instincts of the natural man!" (p. 224)

The Civil War and the popularization of the theory of evolution overlapped. How sad to think that, just when America was freeing slaves, evolution was enslaving them again.

Lesson 6

The MLA Method: Book, Periodical, DVD

This lesson shows how to cite your sources correctly in your position papers, reports, or term papers. You'll see how to insert your sources in your paragraphs and what they'll look like on the works cited page.

Today's focus: parenthetical citations and entries for your works cited page when citing **a book, periodical** (magazine, journal article, or newspaper)**, and video, DVD, or Blu-ray Disc**.

A Web site, the Bible, and an encyclopedia are in the next lesson.

Parenthetical citations come after quotations or borrowed material. This first example uses signal phrases and parenthetical citations when quoting a **book**:

The geologic column is one of the icons of evolution. In this theoretical column, fossils found in the bottom layer are soft-bodied invertebrates or other animals low on the evolutionary tree of life, and the higher layers contain fossils of more evolved and developed animals such as fish, birds, and mammals. However, according to Dr. John Morris and Doug Phillips, authors of *Weapons of our Warfare*, this geologic column is found in its entirety nowhere except "in textbooks. There is no place on Earth where all these layers, with these kinds of fossils, are found *in this sequence*" (22). Though there is a trend that seems to support the column's ages, "clams are found in the bottom layer, the top layer, and every layer in between . . . . The same could be said for corals and jellyfish and many others" (23). Clearly, the geologic column has some problems.

Signal phrase "according to..."

Authors of the book and their credentials

First quotation

Second quotation

Parenthetical citation is page number of original quotation

Page number of second quotation from same source. If you use the same source in the following paragraphs, mention the author or source name again, like this: (Morris and Phillips 23).

If you choose to omit the author's name in the signal phrase, put it in the parenthetical citation:

However, this geologic column does not live up to its advertisement. It does not appear in its complete, illustrated form anywhere on Earth (Morris and Phillips 22).

The parenthetical citation is part of the sentence but not part of the quotation. In other words, it appears after end quotation marks but before the period. There is no comma between the authors' names and the page number.

On your MLA **works cited page**, at the end of your position paper, the **book** used in the above example paragraphs will look like this:

Morris**,** John and Doug Phillips**.** *Weapons of our Warfare***.** El Cajon, CA**:** Institute for Creation

Research**,** 1998**.** Print**.**

Punctuation is exaggerated in this text to highlight it. You will use size-12 font for your works cited page.

Your **book** documentation uses this information:

- name of author (last name first, first name last)
- title of book (italicized)
- city of publication
- publisher
- date of publication
- medium (For a book you hold in your hands, the medium is *Print*.)

Note the hanging indentation in the entry. The first line of each entry on a works cited page begins at the left margin, but the entry's second and following lines begin five spaces in. Learn to do this on your computer. Also take special note of the punctuation and where the periods, colons, and commas go.

When you assemble your works cited page at the end of your paper, arrange the entries **alphabetically** by the authors' last names. If no name is available, alphabetize by the first word in the book's or article's title (other than *the, a,* or *an*).

The following example shows in-text citations using parenthetical citations when quoting from a **magazine, newspaper, or journal article (any periodical):**

Title of article because no author's name was given; otherwise, use author's last name.

Many modern biology textbooks still contain information about an experiment Stanley Miller performed in 1953 ("How Life Began" 54). This iconic "life from non-life" experiment supposedly created amino acids, which are building blocks of life but are not alive. However, what the textbooks omit is that Miller "produced . . . a mixture of left- and right-handed amino acids, which is detrimental to life" (54). Recent experiments of this sort also have failed to produce life (54).

The **magazine article's** information will look like this on your works cited page:

Article's title   *Magazine title*   *Publication date*   *Page number*   *Medium*

"How Life Began – A Textbook Recipe." *Answers* July-Sept. 2006: 54. Print.

This magazine article didn't include an author's name. If it had, the author's name would appear at the beginning:

Arendelle, Elsa. "How I Survived an Iceberg Attack." *North Waters Weekly* 31 Jan. 2016: 180-5. Print.

Magazine, newspaper, and journal articles use this information in their MLA documentation:

- name of author
- title of article (in quotation marks)
- title of magazine (italicized)
- date of publication (abbreviate all months except May, June, and July)
- page range for article
- medium

The in-text citation from a **video, DVD, or Blu-ray Disc** will look like this in your report:

Who hasn't seen Lucy, our hominid ancestress? This evolutionary icon is officially known as Australopithecus *afarensis*, but many call this species Lucy. Statues and illustrations of Lucy show her as having human hands and feet and walking upright. But is this possible, given the fossil evidence? Dr. David Menton, a lecturer and former associate professor of anatomy, asserts it is not. Although the first Lucy fossil was lacking almost all hand and foot bones, Menton reports that other *afarensis* bones have been found—and they possess curved finger and toe bones. While humans have straight finger and toe bones, apes do not. Theirs curve to accommodate a tree-dwelling lifestyle. The curve of the *afarensis* bones is even more pronounced than those of most modern apes or chimpanzees. Menton further points out that Lucy's skull is amazingly primitive (small cranial capacity and sloping face), even for an ape, and her wrist bones lock. Only knuckle walkers have locking wrist bones. Given that so many of her bones resemble those of apes, why do people continue to insist that she was almost human (*Lucy, She's No Lady*)?

Make sure that everything between the signal phrase and the parenthetical citation is from the same source.

A **video, DVD, or Blu-ray Disc** will look like this on your works cited page:

Lucy, She's No Lady. Lecture by David Menton. Answers in Genesis, 2003. DVD.

If the video, DVD, or Blu-ray Disc is a movie, it will look like this on your works cited page:

Weir, Peter, dir. *The Truman Show*. Perf. Jim Carrey, Laura Linney, Noah Emmerich, Ed Harris. Paramount Pictures, 1998. Videocassette.

"Dir." indicates the director, and "Perf." stands for the performers (actors). If the visual source is a documentary, include the narrator's name (after "Narr.").

Videos, DVDs, and Blu-ray Discs (BD) use this information for their MLA documentation:

- name of director
- name of video, movie, DVD, or Blu-ray Disc
- performers
- original year of release (if different from current version)
- company that produced it
- year of VHS, DVD, or BD release
- format (Videocassette, DVD, or Blu-ray Disc)

Practice 13.6

Here and on the next page are "facts" about a book, magazine article, and DVD. You may use this textbook or refer to the Web sites at the end of this practice to create a works cited page. Use a separate piece of paper. Use a hanging indent for each entry.

Take special note of the punctuation. Also note which titles use quotation marks and which ones use italics.

When you assemble your works cited page, arrange the entries **alphabetically** by the authors' last names. If no name is available, alphabetize by the first word in the article's title (other than *the*, *a*, or *an*).

A book:

- Name of author: Q. Modo
- Title of book: *My Life as a Bell Ringer*
- City of publication: Paris
- Publisher: Sanctuary Press
- Date of publication: 1482

A magazine article:

- Name of author: Raymond C. Gallagher
- Title of article: "What Teachers Do When They Are Not Grading Papers "
- Title of magazine: *Vacation Elation*
- Date of publication: September 2012
- Page range for article: 75-100

A DVD:

- Name of video: *Star Wars 10: Death Star Reactivated*
- Director: Giuseppe Lucasano
- Medium: DVD
- Performers: Ewan McGregor, Frank Oz, Harrison Ford II
- Distributor or producer: Jedi Productions
- Year: 2016

Check out these Web sites for more practical information on MLA documentation:

❏ http://www.easybib.com (I hesitate to tell you this because it seems "unteacherly" to do so, but this site will create the citations for you if you have the correct information.)
❏ http://owl.english.purdue.edu (Click either "MLA 2009 Formatting and Style Guide" or "Avoiding Plagiarism.")
❏ http://www.plagiarism.org (Click "How Do I Cite Sources?")

Lesson 7

> MEDICAL ALERT: This section has been known to cause dizziness, gangrene, hiccups, and yawning. Do not take with water.

The MLA Method: Web site, Bible, Encyclopedia

This lesson shows how to document a **Web site (Internet source),** the **Bible,** and **print and online encyclopedias** in your position paper, using the MLA method. And if that isn't thrilling, I don't know what is.

The following example cites a **Web site** source (which often does not have page numbers):

> Another evolutionary icon is the "gill slits" found in human embryos. Formerly, some who supported evolution believed that the embryo exhibited all its former evolutionary stages. Therefore, a human embryo was believed, at different points in its development, to go through a "fish stage" with gill slits and a "bird stage" with a yolk sac. Many biology texts and abortion clinics teach this theory, called recapitulation, even though *all* scientists have long since discredited it. The evidence supports the truth. The gill slits on a fish embryo develop into gills, but "gill slits" in a human embryo are not slits at all. According to researcher and educator George Lindsey, they are pharyngeal pouches that "develop into Eustachian tubes, the thymus, and parathyroid glands" ("Evolution—Useful or Useless?"). ← *Title of article on Web site*

If you use two separate works by the same author, put the author's name in the signal phrase. Then slip the title and page number (if there is one) in the parenthetical citation, like this:

> Josh Alexander, writing student, reveals that he does not organize his material before he writes (*You Can't Make Me* 6).

Or put the author's last name, the title of the work (shortened if necessary), and a page number in the parenthetical citation, like this:

> It is shocking, but students do not always organize their material before they write (Alexander, *Never Again* 19)

A **Web site** on a **works cited page** looks like this:

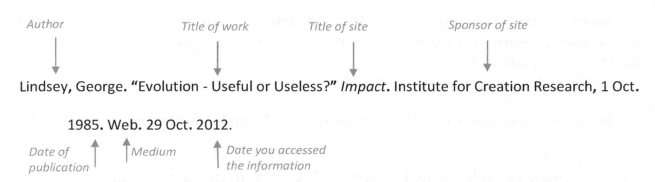

Lindsey, George. "Evolution - Useful or Useless?" *Impact*. Institute for Creation Research, 1 Oct. 1985. Web. 29 Oct. 2012.

Sometimes the title of the site and the sponsor of the site are the same. In that case, you'll have only one name there.

If there were no question mark after the title of the article, there would be a period. If there is no date listed for when the article was posted or the site was last updated, look for a copyright date at the very bottom of the page. If none exists, put this where the date of publication would go: n.d. It means "no date" given.

If your teacher wants you to include the URL, place it in angle brackets at the end of your entry, and then finish with a period, like this:

<http://www.icr.org/article/252/>.

If needed, a URL can be broken after a slash. Don't break it up by using a hyphen.

Your MLA **Web** documentation uses this information:

- name of author (if known)
- title of work (in quotation marks)
- title of site (italicized)
- sponsor of the site (if not already included under author or title of site)
- date of publication, last update, or copyright year (if known)
- medium (Web)
- date you accessed the information
- URL (enclosed in angle brackets), if your teacher requests it

If you do not know the name of the author, begin your entry with the title of the work. You may omit any information the Web site does not include. Remember to **remove the hyperlink** (the underlined blue words) by right clicking on the address. Then click on Remove Hyperlink.

Citing the **Bible** in the MLA method looks like this in your paper:

"Ah, Sovereign Lord, you have made the heavens and the earth by your great power and outstretched arm. Nothing is too hard for you" (NIV, Jeremiah 32.17).

The MLA method uses a period to separate chapter from verse. Most likely, you are used to letting a colon do that job, and you may continue to use a colon in informal writing.

The **Bible** on the works cited page looks like this:

Holy Bible: New Living Translation. Wheaton: Tyndale, 1996. Print.

The **Bible** uses this information for the works cited page:

- name (italicized if other than the title Holy Bible)
- version (if not already included in the name; italicized)
- city of publication
- publisher
- year of publication
- medium

When using an **encyclopedia** or **dictionary** in your paper, cite the word you looked up:

The recapitulation theory, which surmises that the human embryo goes through evolutionary stages, has been thoroughly disproved by all scientists ("Recapitulation").

A print **encyclopedia** or **dictionary** looks like this on your works cited page:

The word you looked up *Organization sponsoring the site* *Year updated* *Medium*

"Recapitulation." *Encyclopedia for Scientists.* 2nd ed. 2001. Print.

An encyclopedia entry on the Web will be treated as a short work from the Web, like this:

Title of Web site

Sponsor of Web site

Date of posting or update

"Recapitulation." *Online Encyclopedia for Scientists.* Scientists for Truth, 2001. Web. 2 Dec. 2012.

Date you accessed the information

Medium

If the encyclopedia entry gives an author's name, put it first, as you would with a book or magazine (last name first).

A **print encyclopedia** includes this information on the works cited page:

- author of the entry, if available
- word you looked up (in quotation marks)
- name of the encyclopedia (italicized)
- edition
- year of publication
- medium (print)

An **online encyclopedia** includes this information on the works cited page:

- author of entry, if available
- word you looked up (in quotation marks)
- name of online encyclopedia (italicized)
- sponsor of site
- year updated
- medium (Web)
- date you accessed the information

Practice 13.7　　Here are the "facts" about a Web site (Internet source), the Bible, and print and online encyclopedias. On a separate piece of paper, alphabetize them for a works cited page and write them according to the MLA method of documentation. Use a hanging indent for each entry. Use required punctuation, quotation marks, and italics. Turn off the hyperlinks.

A Web site:

- Name of author: Roberto Tedioso
- Title of work (page title): "Could This Be Any More Boring?"
- Title of site: *Tone It Down*
- Sponsor of the site: Institute for Duller Education
- Date of publication or last update: February 2, 2012
- Date you accessed the information: March 1, 2016

URL— http://www.dullerthandirt.org

The Bible:

- Name: *The Amplified Bible*
- Version: already given (*The Amplified Bible*)
- City of publication: Grand Rapids
- Publisher: Zondervan Bible Publishers
- Year of publication: 1974
- Bible verse: Jeremiah 32.17

A print encyclopedia:

- Author of the entry: James Hook
- Word you looked up (article title): "Agrizoophobia"
- Name of the encyclopedia: *Encyclopedia for Seafaring Captains*
- Edition: 2nd
- Year of publication: 2001
- Publisher: Barrie&Pan
- City published: London

An online encyclopedia:

- Author of entry: Bradley Manes
- Word you looked up (article title): "Mohawks"
- Name of online encyclopedia: *Encyclopedia of Hair*
- Sponsor of site: Harley-Davidson's College of Beauty
- Year updated: no date given
- Date you accessed the information: November 2, 2015

URL—<http://www.snipsnipheresnipsnipthere.com/mohawk>

Again, you can check out these Web sites for more information on MLA documentation:

❑ www.easybib.com

❑ http://owl.english.purdue.edu

❑ www.plagiarism.org (Click "How Do I Cite Sources?")

Write a Position Paper

Write your position paper on an important, debatable topic. Use at least three reputable sources. See the writing schedule on page 258.

Before you begin writing, check your topic and your thesis statement with your teacher. Review your points with your teacher, too, when you develop them.

Cite your sources using the MLA method: Use in-text citations (signal phrases and parenthetical citations) and then an alphabetized works cited page on a separate page at the end of your report. Use Be Your Own Editor (page 159) to proofread at least three times.

No title page is required for an MLA-documented paper unless your teacher asks for one. Otherwise, simply type your name, the teacher's name, the course title, and the due date (all single-spaced) at the top left of your paper. Then double-space, center your title, and continue typing, double-spacing throughout (even the works cited page). Put page numbers on the top right of each page.

For this assignment, you will submit your official cluster, Greek temple, list, outline, or sticky notes (taped in correct order on a piece of paper) with your paper. Insert it after the works cited page.

Word count for **beginning** writers: at least 1,000 words.

Word count for **intermediate** and **accomplished** writers: at least 1,500 words.

Your name   1
Your teacher's name
Course title
Date due

Snappy Title

   Everything from here on will be double-

spaced, even the works cited page. Make sure

to leave at least 1" margins around your pages.

Each following page will have your name on

the top left and the page number on the top

right. Get going!

Check out your checklist:

- ❑ Is your topic relevant and debatable?
- ❑ Is the title interesting?
- ❑ Is the introduction designed to interest the reader?
- ❑ Is your topic evident in the introduction?
- ❑ Is your opinion evident in the introduction?
- ❑ Is your thesis statement clear?
- ❑ Does your whole paper support your thesis statement?
- ❑ Do you use an appropriate order to arrange your points?
- ❑ Does each point have a fitting topic sentence?
- ❑ Do you adequately support each point?
- ❑ Do you leave the reader with food for thought or a brilliant insight?
- ❑ Do you leave old snacks and dishes in your bedroom?
- ❑ Are you submitting your organizational tool (cluster, outline, etc.)?
- ❑ Do you cite all borrowed facts, ideas, illustrations, and so forth?
- ❑ Do you use signal phrases?
- ❑ Do you correctly use parenthetical citations?
- ❑ Is your works cited page alphabetized?
- ❑ Do you correctly list your sources on the works cited page?
- ❑ In addition to these super-helpful boxes, have you used Be Your Own Editor to help you proofread your paper?

On the next page, you'll find a partial schedule to help you organize your tasks. Fill in the blank days so you can keep a good pace. Check to see if your teacher has a different schedule.

It will be important to give your teacher your topic, points, and thesis statement before you begin writing. In the schedule, these are due on Day 6.

Day 1	Day 2	Day 3	Day 4	Day 5	Day 6
		Topic and temporary thesis statement are due.			Final thesis statement and major points are due.

Day 7	Day 8	Day 9	Day 10	Day 11	Day 12
					Position paper is due, along with your organizational aid.

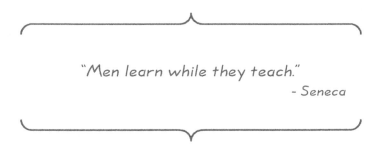

"Men learn while they teach."

- Seneca

Chapter 14: A Devotional

Lesson 1

This chapter about how to write a devotional begins with a special grammar factoid. Anyone writing for almost any publication today knows that they, he/she, she/he, s/he—oh, forget it. Just keep reading.

Gender-neutral Language

If you use certain kinds of correct grammar, are you are sexist (generally, one who believes that men are more important than women)? Today some correct grammar is called *sexist language*. For example,

> <u>Everyone</u> used little scoops and plastic bags while walking <u>his</u> dog in the Bark Park.

That sentence is grammatically correct. Why? Because *everyone* is a singular pronoun—it's true!—and requires a *his*, not a *their*. But because both men <u>and</u> women likely were at the Bark Park, *their* is commonly used today in order to avoid using *he*, which to modern ears excludes all females. Until a few generations ago, women heard words like *he*, *mankind*, and *chairman* and applied them to either sex. This is not the case today; many women like to be included in the language.

What can a writer do? Obviously, using correct grammar does not make a writer sexist. In fact, from now on, let's not use the term *sexist language* but *gender-neutral language*. Much formal writing today demands this type of language.

That doggy sentence can be expressed many ways. Most writers and speakers do it this way:

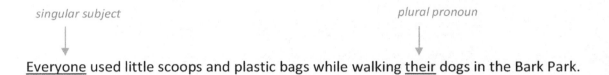

That fixes the gender problem but creates a grammar mistake because the pronoun numbers don't match. The solutions below are cumbersome but used frequently:

<u>Everyone</u> used little scoops and plastic bags while walking <u>his/her</u> dog in the Bark Park.

<u>Everyone</u> used little scoops and plastic bags while walking <u>his or her</u> dog in the Bark Park.

While this fixes the gender and grammar problems, it doesn't make things easy to read. It's as bulky and uncomfortable as a large root on a hiking trail, and reading it aloud is just plain awkward. Also, it often puts the male pronoun before the female one, something that still lacks neutrality.

These two sentences fix *both* the gender and the grammar issues:

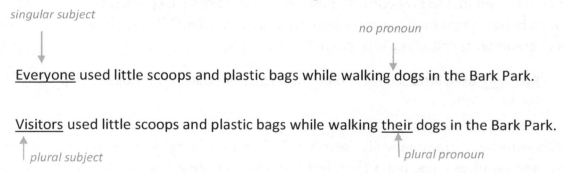

Ah, those are much better. Grammarians and people of both genders now can be happy. The pronoun matches the antecedent to which it refers, and the language is gender neutral.

Gender-neutral language sometimes lacks the punch and individuality of former language usage. The following sentence is <u>not</u> gender neutral, but it is direct and straightforward, and it says something very definite:

No doctor should abandon his compassion.

You may have a picture in your mind of this particular doctor (male?). Using gender-neutral language would change the sentence in these ways:

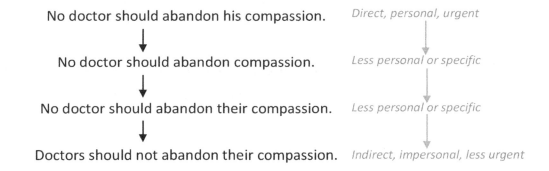

The changes, admittedly, are subtle, but they are there. Work hard to keep your nonfiction writing direct and specific, even while using gender-neutral language.

Some writers choose to use the masculine pronouns in one passage or set of paragraphs and the feminine pronouns in an alternating passage or set of paragraphs. One passage is written as though about a boy; the next, about a girl. This may work well in some situations. Some readers find this confusing while others consider it refreshing. In your own writing, if you maintain male pronouns in one passage and female pronouns in the next, read it out loud to determine whether it makes sense and flows well.

Gender-neutral language also encompasses words such as *mail carrier* instead of *mailman*, and *humanity* instead of *mankind*.

Writers most often have trouble using gender-neutral language when the subject of the sentence is a singular, indefinite pronoun (as in the case with *everyone*). In the sidebar on the next page is the list of indefinite pronouns that are singular. Read the list and see if you find any surprises in it.

Singular Indefinite Pronouns

each
every
either
neither
everyone
someone
anyone
no one
no
one
everybody
somebody
anybody
nobody
everything
something
anything
nothing

All the indefinite pronouns in this list are singular antecedents that deserve singular pronouns later in the sentence (as the doggy-park example shows) and singular verbs.

A word about gender-neutral Bibles is fitting here. When selecting a Bible, you will want to know whether you are buying a translation from the oldest texts or whether you are buying a paraphrase loosely based on original and other texts. No Bible translated from the original texts is gender-neutral. The original language is not gender-neutral. It uses *sons* instead of *children*. It states *When a man*, not *When a person*. Be aware of these differences as you choose your next Bible.

The quotation at the beginning of this chapter is "Men learn while they teach." How can you change that to be gender neutral? Write your ideas here:

Practice 14.1   Below and on the next page are sentences that contain singular indefinite pronouns or singular subjects. First, correct them according to good grammar (using "he" when necessary). Next, rewrite them by using gender-neutral language.

These sentences can be fixed in many correct ways. Use your imagination. And a separate piece of paper.

1. Every child has a right to eat their breakfast before going to school.
2. Each singer wanted to ace their audition.
3. Everybody but Anne did their homework.
4. Neither firefighter could find their boots.
5. Nobody should have to eat their lunch alone.
6. No clown would forget to wear their big, floppy shoes.
7. Either sister will do an excellent job because they are so proficient.
8. Every cheerleader will try on their new uniforms at 3:00 p.m.
9. Anybody who sees a felony being committed can say, "Citizen's arrest," and have their voice count.

10. On Monday, each member of the Spanish Club is to bring their food made from a recipe in a Spanish cookbook.
11. Someone knows the truth about this accident, but they aren't coming forward.
12. Anyone who still believes in phrenology needs to have their head examined.
13. A trapeze artist knows how important it is to be able to trust their partner.
14. For a student to schedule his/her six hours of behind-the-wheel instructions, he/she must have his/her permit from the license branch.

Lesson 2

The Devotional

Someday you may be among the contributors to daily devotionals such as *Our Daily Bread*, published quarterly by RBC Ministries. Most churches and/or denominations also have their own publications. Even some Christian radio stations use short devotionals written exclusively for the air.

Professional Tip

Christian editors often receive submissions with letters that say, "God told me to write this," or, "Don't change a word of this. God told me just how to say it."

This does not bode well for the writer!

Show a willingness to work with editors and meet their guidelines about readership, topics, and word counts.

A devotional is different from a short essay: the introduction is the first half and the spiritual application is the second half. The thesis statement sits between the introduction and the application, tying the two together. It is the transition statement from the first part to the second.

The first half of the devotional contains a story, an interesting fact, or a news item that will later open up the meaning of the verses or spiritual principle. Apostle Paul was aware of the need to tie a concrete life example to an abstract spiritual principle (2 Timothy 2:20-1 NIV):

In a large house there are articles not only of gold and silver, but also of wood and clay; some are for noble purposes and some for ignoble. If a man cleanses himself from the latter, he will be an instrument for noble purposes, made holy, useful to the Master and prepared to do any good work.

Physical truth

Spiritual application

Teaching someone to be a holy container for the Master is easier if you first write about the types of containers found in houses. First the concrete; then the abstract. First the physical; then the spiritual. That's how you will write your devotional, too. Read this example of a short devotional (200 words). It contains a true story although the young man's name is changed:

Josh, a recent high school graduate and a cadet major in the Civil Air Patrol, wanted to attend the elite Pararescuers Orientation Course, a week-long training course run by USAF Pararescue. To be in shape for the grueling survival course in New Mexico, Josh began his personal training a year in advance, long before he knew he was accepted. He pushed himself to run four miles without stopping, walked two miles with a 50-pound pack, often uphill, and he added other conditioning exercises to his routine. He was accepted—an honor awarded to only 60 cadets nationwide.

Godly living is worth training for, too. Living in a way that honors God has value. It is not a meaningless exercise. Being centered on God and his Word instead of absorbing our culture's habits, thought patterns, and lifestyles will help in tough days ahead. Training to react to life's problems and temptations in ways that please God prepares us for life and its difficulties.

And don't forget the life to come. We are training for something we can't even see yet, but the godliness we develop now will benefit us somehow in eternity. Training before we get there—what a novel idea.

Practice 14.2   Answer the following questions:

1. Mark with a star the paragraph(s) that contain the concrete or physical lesson.
2. Put a check mark next to the paragraph(s) that teach the abstract or spiritual application.
3. Underline the thesis statement that connects the physical to the spiritual.
4. Do you agree with the writer of this devotional? Explain.

5. Give this devotional a grade. Explain your grade.

Write a Devotional

Write a devotional. Begin with a story, fact, or news item to illustrate the spiritual principle. Use the thesis statement to transition from the physical to the spiritual.

Write the passage or verse and the reference. However, those words do not count in the devotional's word count.

Use Be Your Own Editor to proofread your work at least three times.

Beginning, intermediate, and **accomplished writers**: Limit yourself to 200 words. Don't go over. Most devotionals are short, short, short.

Check your devotional against this checklist:

- ❑ Did you begin with an interesting fact or story?
- ❑ Does it clearly enhance your exposition of the upcoming spiritual truth from a Bible verse or passage?
- ❑ Is the transition from one topic to the next clear and helpful?
- ❑ Is the spiritual topic clearly related to the concrete topic?
- ❑ Is your devotional concise and pithy?
- ❑ Is it double-spaced?
- ❑ Did you include the passage or verse along with its reference?
- ❑ Did you use gender-neutral language where appropriate?
- ❑ Is the grammar correct?
- ❑ Is the punctuation correct?
- ❑ Is the spelling correct?
- ❑ Do you wish this course were shorter?

"Four hostile newspapers are more to be feared than a thousand bayonets."

- Napoleon

Chapter 15: Newspaper Writing

Lesson 1

Newspapers may be considered old-school now, but writing news articles follows defined formats, whether for a print newspaper, online magazine, or online news source such as Yahoo News or LifeSiteNews.com.

The news and features portions of your newspaper rely on definite patterns in their writing. In fact, if you carefully perused a newspaper, you could probably ferret out the patterns yourself.

But what is news? What events are considered newsworthy? Just in case you don't happen to have a newspaper in front of you . . .

Man Bites Dog

What makes news worthy of being printed? Obviously, when **a large or unusual event happens to a large number of people**, that's news. An earthquake that affects thousands of people fits this category. But there are many other stories that get printed as news, and they are not in this "large event/many people" category. The following formulas will help you identify newsworthy events:

A large or unusual event + a small number of people = News

[tornado, typhoon]

A large or unusual event + an ordinary person = News

[a climber who cuts off his arm in order to get out from under a rockfall; a lottery win; a man bites a dog]

A small event + a large number of people = News

[the theft of an employee's laptop, which happens to contain the personal information of thousands of people]

An ordinary event + a famous person = News

[a prime minister goes on vacation; a celebrity has a child]

Practice 15.1　　Below are the news formulas again. Give one example of each, either from real news stories or from your imagination. Use the spaces below each formula.

A large or unusual event + a small number of people = News

A large or unusual event + an ordinary person = News

A small event + a large number of people = News

An ordinary event + a famous person = News

Lesson 2

Hard News

The idea for a news article begins with an event to cover: a car accident, ballgame, peace summit, trial, flood, terrorist attack, new law, the arrest of a criminal, and so forth. These are events, large and small, that warrant a news article. People want to know about these things.

Hard news—news that deals with an event unemotionally—uses an inverted triangle for its format. This is the order in which hard news typically presents the information:

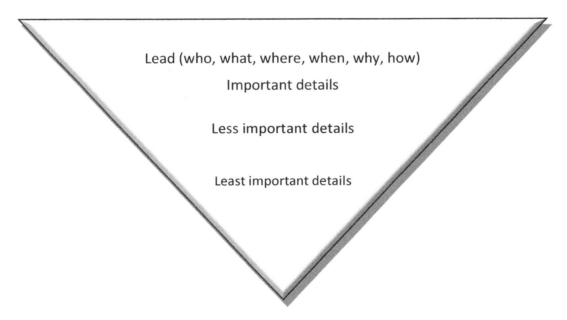

Lead (who, what, where, when, why, how)
Important details

Less important details

Least important details

You will be astute enough to notice that this is one of the emphatic orders you learned way back in chapter 2. It begins with the most important facts and moves to the least important.

In newspaper articles, the five Ws (who, what, where, when, why) and the H (how) go up front. These facts appear in the first sentence or two, which is called the **lead**. Any that don't fit comfortably in the lead follow soon after.

> "What you see is news, what you know is background, what you feel is opinion."
> -Lester Markel, editor

And something else follows, too. Newswoman Katie Couric says this about news reporting: "The biggest job isn't telling people what happened. It's getting them to understand why they should care." Newspaper writers call this the significance (S) of the event. If readers don't know the significance of a news event, why should they care? Why should they continue to read?

Here's a lead with four of the five Ws and the S:

Who ↓   Where ↓

Indianapolis (AP) – An African elephant at the Indianapolis Zoo is expected
What → to deliver a calf in early September. ←——When
The birth will be the second baby elephant born at the zoo in a year.
↑ Significance

How and why don't appear in the lead. They are answered later in the copy when it mentions artificial insemination.

Practice 15.2   Now you try it. Label as many of the five Ws, the H, and the S as appear below and at the top of the next page. Use the space above the lines:

CAIRO – Egyptian and Sudanese troops, backed by European commandos,

swooped down in helicopters Monday to rescue a tour group that had been

kidnapped in Egypt and taken on a 10-day dash across the Sahara.

Freedom for the 11 European tourists and eight Egyptian guides came hours

after Sudanese troops killed six of the abductors and captured two who revealed

where the remaining gunmen were holding their captives.

Do the same thing with the next lead. Label as many of the five Ws, the H, and the S as appear. Use the spaces above the lines.

MEXICO CITY (AP) – Vincente Fox was forced to forego the last state-of-the-

nation address of his presidency Friday after leftist lawmakers stormed the stage

of Congress to protest disputed July 2 elections.

It was the first time in modern Mexican history a president hasn't given the

annual address to Congress.

Please continue with today's lesson.

Specific details follow the leads, beginning with the most important details and ending with the least important. There's a good reason for this format. Reporters are not in control of the article's length as it appears in the paper. Editors are. Editors are the ones who make decisions about what article goes where, based on its importance to the community and the available space. Because a reporter's article (or **copy**) might be shortened, the important information is in the first sentences. Also, if the reporter begins with unimportant information, who would read it?

The rest of the baby elephant copy is below. Notice that the details get less and less important as the copy progresses, moving farther away from the actual event and giving background information:

"Waiting is the hard part," said David Hagan, the curator of the zoo's plains exhibit.
The 7,000-pound elephant, named Ivory, has gained nearly 700 pounds since the 22-month pregnancy began.
Zoo veterinarians have conducted weekly blood tests and given Ivory ultrasound examinations.
Zoo staff members have been taking turns staying with Ivory overnight as her due date draws near. Births can happen several weeks before or after the actual due date.
"It's a huge moment," Hagan said. "We're really geared up and excited."

Ivory's firstborn, Ajani, is 6 years old and weighs just over 4,000 pounds.

Kedar, the zoo's most recent elephant addition, was born in October and weighs 660 pounds.

Ivory's pregnancy follows a decade of work by the zoo to help pioneer artificial insemination techniques, Hagan said.

The delivery will be the fourth calf born at the zoo.

As a reporter, you are expected to gather facts, an important habit to cultivate. Be at the event or scene and take notes. Be an active observer in what is going on around you. What exactly is happening? How are people reacting?

A news article includes at least **two interviews** with witnesses, participants, or other people in the know about the event. From these interviews, cull quotations for your article. For instance, if you cover a car accident, interview people at the scene—emergency workers, police officers, a witness or two, some of the people involved in the accident, and, later, someone in the car insurance industry. If you cover a local chili contest, interview a few participants and one of the major coordinators of the event.

Be an active listener. Ask open-ended questions. Instead of asking, "Were you scared?" ask, "What was it like?" or "Tell me what happened." The first question will only get you a "yes," "no," or "um, maybe" answer. But with the next two questions, you will reap a greater harvest of information, especially if you listen well and take useful notes.

Let people talk. Don't be embarrassed or uncomfortable with awkward pauses. They are simply opportunities for your interviewee to fill in the silence. In fact, these silences will encourage wary subjects to talk. If you listen well, you'll be able to ask good follow-up questions.

Don't assume that your person remembers all the facts. For instance, if an interviewee mentions a date or name, research to make sure the information is correct.

Lesson 3

Attributions

Any news copy relies on quotations for information, clarification, or even reactions. With quotations come **attributions**. When quoting someone, directly or indirectly, you must attribute the quotation to that speaker by identifying the source. The reporter who wrote about the baby elephant used two separate quotations from David Hagan. Who is David Hagan? Write your answer in the margin.

David Hagan's whole name and credentials appear the first time he is quoted, but only Hagan's last name is used the second time he is quoted. You will do the same.

Attributions are simply in-text citations, something you've already learned. So let's review. Below are examples of attributions:

Past tense

"Seventy-five percent of our contestants are underweight," said Wolfgang Hobart, Director of Modern Beauty Pageants.

Who he is (credentials) *Source*

Direct quotation *Source*

"Some acne medicines have adverse side effects," said Suzi MacKenna, a nurse at the local U R Healthy. She also stated that some of her patients have had nervous breakdowns or have developed temporary personality disorders due to sensitivities to the chemicals in these medications.

Indirect quotation or paraphrase

Why we should believe her (her credentials)

Source *Past tense* *Fragment of quotation*

The National Association of Naysayers announced today that "the time has come for action, but we don't expect anyone to really do anything."

[The quotation started, "You might believe the time has come . . .," so only the last half was quoted in the article.]

Paraphrase of fact

Twice as many people invested in pet insurance this year than last, according to the We Luv Our Pets Web site.

Source

Although the above quotations are completely fictional, the way to attribute them to their sources is correct. Most attributions in hard news writing appear after the quotation, and all use the **past tense**.

Facts that are common knowledge do not need to be documented or attributed. For instance, "Earth rotates on its axis every twenty-four hours" needs no attribution. Also, because it is a scientific fact, it is in the present tense, not the past.

Practice 15.3   Below are quotes from a number of strange people. Assemble each quote and its parts correctly for an attribution in newspaper copy. Strange fact: Titles of books and movies are in quotation marks in newspapers, both in print and sometimes online. Use a separate piece of paper.

1. **Quote:** "Singing a sad song with gusto can make you feel happy."
   Source: Neil Tanzanite, from his Web site
   Credentials: He is a singer/songwriter.

2. **Quote:** "It is common for students to fall asleep when reading excessively dull textbooks."
   Include part of this as an indirect quote: "Fifty-eight students each year fall out of their chairs while reading these boring books, and ninety percent of those who have fallen break an arm, wrist, or elbow. Inconsiderate textbook writers are directly responsible for this travesty."
   Source: Ted Zeus, in an interview (by you)
   Credentials: the school nurse at the Learning Should Be Fun High School

3. **Use only a fragment of this quote in your copy:** "Think about the last time you had yams. Was it at Thanksgiving and were they surrounded with brown sugar and those miniature marshmallows? What a waste because yams are a deliciously sweet vegetable that is full of nutrition and can be eaten in any season."
   Source: Samantha Ingraham, from her new book *I Am What I Yam* [Book titles are in quotation marks in newspaper copy.]
   Credentials: the president of the People for the Inspiring Taste of Yams (PITY) organization

Lesson 4

Hard News Guidelines

OUR SCHOOL (Power News Source) – Mia Tarken, a high school senior, fell out of her chair at school and broke her arm earlier this morning.
   "It was just too boring," said the injured Tarken, 17, who attends the Learning Should Be Fun High School. "'The Power in Your Hands' just puts me to sleep. Why do they make us read this stuff?"

Besides writing a fact-filled lead and using attributions, writing hard news follows these guidelines:

1. **Use simple sentence structures.** Simple declarative sentences without extra clauses and phrases work best. Don't get fancy. Keep the subjects and verbs close to each other. Keep the sentences about 20 words or fewer. Each sentence should contain only one idea. Reread the baby elephant copy for examples of concise, simply structured sentences.

2. **Keep paragraphs short.** Each paragraph should be focused on one idea. Pick up a newspaper and notice the short paragraphs. Who wants to read a long, unbroken column? Again, the baby elephant copy is a great example of short paragraphs.

3. **Be objective and factual.** Write the facts, not someone's opinion of the facts. You are not trying to create a mood or a feeling; you are reporting. If you quote someone who supports a new law, also include a quotation from someone who dislikes it.

Unfortunately, even being "factual" can create overtones, depending on which facts you choose to include and in what order. Here's an example: "The president refused to sign the Jimenez Treaty, a treaty many other nations have already signed." Get any vibes from that factual sentence? Also, when reporters insert a positive quotation first for, say, a law, and a negative quotation last, they are subtly stating their bias against the law.

4. **Use the past tense.** Write your copy in the past tense:

When Tony <u>won</u> the regional spelling bee, he <u>said</u>, "Who knew that 'absquatulate' would be such an important word in my life?"

Headlines and captions are in the present tense ("Local student wins spelling bee"), but reporters typically don't write those.

5. **Use simple speaker tags.** "He said" and "she said" are best. "He intimated," "she argued," or "they suggested" are not simple, and they lend shades of meaning reporters are supposed to avoid.

Also, after you have used a person's full name for the first time, use only the last name afterwards. For instance, the first time you mention this name, you might write, "Johannes Gutenberg, famous for his printing press, …," but all other times you refer to the man, you would simply write his last name: "Gutenberg hoped that…."

6. **Add qualifiers.** Words like *allegedly* and *reportedly* are handy when someone is accused of something but hasn't gone to trial yet:

Oscar Triphammer, who allegedly sold his neighbor's Ferrari on eBay,…

Believe it or not, qualifiers can sometimes make the information sound suspicious: "She allegedly had four neighbors at her supposed party" makes her actions sound questionable right away, even if they weren't.

7. **Avoid first and second person.** Personal pronouns such as *I, you,* and *we* have no place in hard news writing. Which leads to the next point . . .

8. **Maintain an objective tone.** Instead of writing, "You would be surprised at the amount of items shoplifted from Diamond Jim's Tourist Emporium each week," write, "The number of items shoplifted from Diamond Jim's Tourist Emporium each week has steadily increased." And then give the facts and statistics.

Another way to maintain an objective tone is to report on what people did ("The crowd clapped their hands and cheered") instead of how they felt ("The crowd was happy"). If you want to report how someone felt, get it in a quote ("I'm so happy they won," said Jim Shortz of Dodge City).

9. **Use the active voice.** Passive constructions add unnecessary words and confusion. Stick to the straightforward active voice. Verbs are important in news writing. Write "Kristyne <u>won</u> the raffle," not "The raffle <u>was won by</u> Kristyne."

10. **Be concise.** "Eight volunteer firefighters chopped through the locked front door, used water from a nearby hydrant to hose down the roof of the burning building and those of neighboring houses, and sent a powerful spray into the interior of the house on 13 Waukazoo Avenue" can be cut down to "Firefighters contained the house fire on 13 Waukazoo Avenue."

Practice 15.4   Although reporters are supposed to be neutral in their writing, this is rarely the case.

Below are sentences that are neutral and some that are slanted (biased). Decide whether each sentence favors the cheerleaders or the chess club members.

Label the sentences that favor the cheerleaders with a CL. Label the sentences that favor the chess club members with a CCM. Label the neutral sentences (which favor neither) with an N.

All sentences concern an incident at a pep rally, as seen from differing viewpoints.

1. Campus security arrested chess club members who protested the cheerleaders' pep rally Saturday.
2. The elitist brainiacs' controversial protest created confusion and dissension at the pep rally.
3. Only the chess club members had the courage to protest the mindless pep rally.
4. The snobbish, clueless cheerleaders engaged in a so-called pep rally, backed by noisy fans. "It is hard to find a quiet place to think," said Hugh Pinkerton III, chess club president. "Did they have permission for their rally?"
5. The issue highlighted in yesterday's heated debate appears to be one of scheduling.

6. Without provocation, chess club members rudely disrupted the cheerleaders' carefully planned routines at the pep rally. "They were devisive," said Ami Tiffany, the cheerleading squad's captain.

Lesson 5

Feature Writing

> OUR SCHOOL (Power News Source) – Mia Tarken, 17, knows firsthand what it is like to be bored in school, and she has the arm cast to prove it.
>
> "Textbooks shouldn't put students to sleep," says Tarken, who fell out of a chair at school Monday and broke her arm. "If teachers had to read these books, they'd tear them up."
>
> Tarken and others like her say they're through being bored. And the experts agree. Exciting textbooks can lead to fewer broken arms, writes Dr. Shirley A. Payne in her new book "Give Me a Break."

While hard news covers an event in a factual, unemotional manner, feature writing focuses on an idea, trend, event, or person that is brimming with human interest. The report of a fatal accident is hard news; writing about the funeral, how people felt about the person, and how much the deceased gave to her community is feature writing. Hard news copy begins with the pertinent facts; features begin with an anecdote or some other sentence or two that will draw the reader into the copy. About half the paragraphs in a feature will be or contain quotations.

Read these differences between hard news and feature writing:

Hard news: Copy about a tsunami.
[Where it hit, when it hit, how many people it displaced or killed, why it developed, how many miles an hour it was going, how high the waves were, and so forth.]

Feature: Copy about the tsunami's effect on people.
[Lead with the story of a person affected by the disaster, use quotations from victims and officials, show what's being done to clean up or help, describe the current needs and living conditions of the victims, and tie the conclusion to the lead.]

Tsunami topic

Cruise ship topic

Hard news: Copy about a cruise ship's accident.
[Where it happened, how it happened, how many people were injured or killed, how people were rescued, and so forth.]

Feature: Copy about the accident's effect on the cruise ship industry.
[Lead with a person who has canceled her family's plans to vacation on a cruise ship because of the accident, use quotations from cruise ship officials about the safety of cruise ships, write about how the cruise ship industry feels the pinch of fewer vacationers, quote experts on the safety of the ships, and so forth.]

Unlike the hard news, a feature creates an emotion or mood. It comes at the news with an angle that allows the reader to get involved. As a feature writer, you will gather facts, research the trend or event, interview people, interview people about the people, interview about the trend or event, and get quotations from people that will tell the story. In other words, make your quotations tell the story as much as possible.

Professional Tip

Professional writers know the trends and hot topics. Periodicals (newspapers, magazines, and e-zines) rely on current trends and events to keep their readership interested.

Pick up a newspaper or magazine and scour their lifestyle sections to learn what's hot. Read the news to stay current with events.

The feature, because it is a human-interest story, puts a human face to the news. It is hard to care about some earthquake that happened halfway across the world in some country you've never heard of before and can't spell. But when you read of a specific person who broke her arm in the quake but can't get the bone set and can't get pain medicine, you become interested. The news becomes real. It has a face.

Feature writers work to find a **face**—a person that will accurately represent the problem and humanize it. Readers are numb to "millions of dollars" or "hundreds of thousands of people." It's too big. It's too impersonal. Your job as a feature writer is to narrow the story down to a small, representative group so readers will think, "Hey, that's awful. Now I understand how important this is."

This copy about the trend of teens not getting enough sleep begins with a real person as an example of this trend:

Constant drowsiness. Inability to focus throughout the day. Unexpected dosing off during work or school. Libby Smallbone, 18, of Vail, Colo., knows these all too well.

"I'm tired a lot," she says. "I want to get more out of my day, so I stay up late and wake up early."

Smallbone, a college freshman, is very active. She snowboards regularly, babysits, hangs out with friends, works part time at an ice rink, and, of course, goes to school. But she often doesn't get the proper amount of sleep.

This feature begins with a student who is trying to be successful but is suffering from lack of sleep. It contains a quotation and uses short paragraphs of only one or two sentences. The writer lists all the things this student is involved in so readers understand this is a real dilemma, not just a lazy student.

Soon after the lead comes the **nut graph**, the paragraph that sums up your main idea in a nutshell. The nut graph in a feature article is the same as a thesis statement in any of your other papers. It focuses the article on the main idea.

A feature article does not use the inverted triangle form. Here's what it looks like (each geometric shape loosely represents a paragraph):

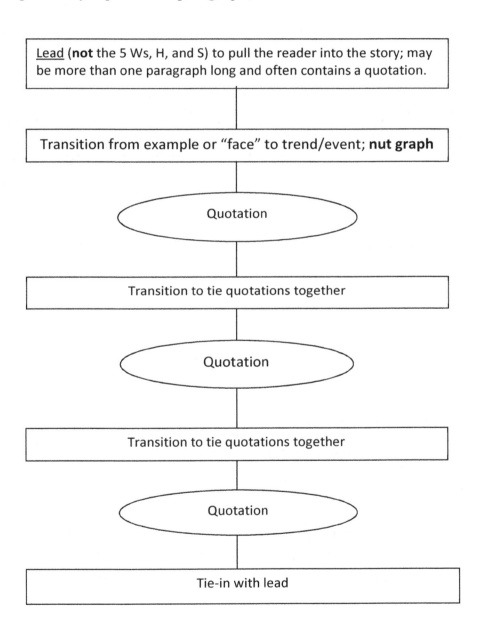

The sleepless student's nut graph? Here it is:

> Lack of sleep is a growing problem for millions of teens today. According to the National Sleep Foundation, only 15 percent of teens are getting enough sleep on school nights. And without the proper amount of sleep, these individuals can and have developed mild to severe disorders and diseases.

Features have a back-and-forth rhythm of transitions and quotations. They also use **short paragraphs** of one to three sentences, a **casual tone** that includes contractions but is still in third person, and the **present tense** in attributions (as opposed to past tense for hard news copy).

Quotations should lead the reader from one point to the next and reveal interesting information. If the quotation contains facts or is rambling, consider restating or paraphrasing it. Then include the attribution after the paraphrase. Notice that the percentage of zombie teens is not in a quotation but is paraphrased from its original source (the National Sleep Foundation—who knew there was one?).

Practice 15.5 Find a feature article in the lifestyle section of your newspaper. Read it through and label its parts: the lead, face, nut graph, quotation with attribution, transition, quotation with attribution, transition, and so on. Check to see if the conclusion ties to the lead.

Lesson 6

Capture Your Reader

> OUR SCHOOL (Power News Source) – Broken arms. Concussions. Sprained eyelids. Think you're on a ball field? Think again. A growing number of students reported these injuries last year as a result of having to read boring textbooks.

Leads are what draw the reader into the rest of the copy, so they had better be interesting. You've already read a **personal experience lead**—finding a representative of the event and using that story (as with the sleep-deprived Libby Smallbone). The following lead begins an article about how some concerned corporations are trying to improve working conditions worldwide:

> The sewing factory in Tepeji del Rio, Mexico, made cute Barbie costumes under a Mattel license, but its workplace allegedly was horrendous.

This is a clever lead because it contrasts *cute* with *horrendous*. (Note the word *allegedly*; the accusations were being investigated). Consider these other types of leads below for your feature writing. All of them are reworked or completely fabricated from the above Barbie lead and facts in the rest of the original copy.

Astonisher lead: That cute Barbie outfit you bought for your daughter might have been the weapon used against women in Mexico to force them to take pregnancy tests, work overtime, and inhale dangerous chemical odors that made them vomit. [An astonisher lead shocks readers with surprising facts or ideas.]

Descriptive lead: Pink, flouncy ruffles bound for Barbie's tutu lay amid the hot, ill-lit confines of the workers sewing the seams. Sounds of vomiting were heard in the next room as other workers reacted to the strong chemical smells in the factory. [Notice the word picture this paints as it describes working conditions. Descriptive leads appeal to the senses; sight, sound, and smell were used in this lead.]

Direct quotation lead: "I never want to go there again," says Lupita Moreno, 29, a worker at Rubie's de Mexico factory that makes Barbie costumes for Mattel. "The conditions are dangerous. But what can I do? I need the money." [An effective direct quotation lead relies on a quotation that will succinctly voice the heart of the issue, trend, or event.]

Question lead: Have you been forced to work overtime? To take a pregnancy test? To smell chemicals that make you vomit? If so, then you might be working at Rubie's de Mexico, a factory that, until January of this year, sewed Barbie costumes for Mattel. [The answers to a question lead are arrows to the nut graph. They are the jumping-off point for the story.]

Suspended interest lead: Tutus. Bikinis. Flight attendant uniforms. Vomiting. Forced pregnancy tests. Overtime. What do these things have in common? The workers at the sewing factory in Tepeji del Rio, Mexico, say they know all too well. [The suspended interest lead keeps the reader guessing—for a very short time—about the topic.]

Recall a recent event, personal or otherwise. Write three separate leads for it, using any three of the above leads. Label the leads. Use a separate piece of paper.

Practice 15.6

Lesson 7

A Kick and a Punch

The conclusion in feature writing is often called the **kicker**. This is it—your last chance to make an impact on your readers. Use it wisely. Be insightful. Be challenging. Use a powerful story. Ask a thought-provoking or shocking question. Look into the future. Reiterate your theme. Pack a punch.

When possible, tie your kicker to your interesting lead. This made-up example uses another quotation to refer to the direct quotation lead in the Barbie feature:

> Despite these alleged infractions, Mattel and other companies say they are committed to making sure their licensed factories worldwide meet rigorous standards. Moreno hopes this is true. "Why treat your workers like animals?" she says. "We need safety regulations."

This kicker mentions the name of the person quoted in the lead, tying the end to the beginning, and it sums up the companies' intentions to make working conditions safer for their employees. You have a variety of tools at your disposal for this full-circle technique:

➤ Repeat a word or phrase from the lead.
➤ Use a synonym or antonym for a word mentioned in the lead.
➤ Refer to something you wrote in the lead.
➤ Finish a story you began in the lead.
➤ Quote someone you quoted in the lead.
➤ Use a similar image you used in the lead.

Practice 15.7   Write a satisfying conclusion to the article on sleep-deprived teens. Use a real quotation from a friend, student, teacher, or some other reliable source that will neatly sum up the main idea of the article. Or write a kicker for the event you wrote about in Practice 15.6. Tie the conclusion to the lead.

Use a separate piece of paper.

Lesson 8

Raising Beef Cattle

This feature article is written by a student (348 words). Part of her assignment was to (1) select a topic of interest to her community, (2) find a face to represent the trend/event, (3) use the feature format, and (4) interview at least two people and include quotes from them in the copy. Read along to learn what she did right and what she could improve.

As twilight settled over the Wolfes' pasture, Liz Wolfe, 16, stood next to the south gate, whip in hand. She'd just had her hair done that afternoon, and the smell of salon products drifted around her face, contrasting with the stench of cow manure. "It was a little strange having salon-perfect hair while standing ankle-deep in poop, but that kind of thing happens a lot around here," says Wolfe.

Good story lead with contrasts in the scents

For the Wolfe family, raising beef cattle has been a bizarre journey.

— Nut graph

Liz's parents, Archie and Regina Wolfe, have been raising hormone-free, grass-fed beef for 18 years. "We started doing beef so I wouldn't have to mow the pasture as often," says Archie.

Since raising their own beef, they have found other advantages.

"Once we got going, I started to see the more philosophical reasons for raising grass-fed beef such as the additives in store-bought meat and the conditions the animals are kept under on a standard commercial farm," says Regina.

Even though there are a lot of good reasons to raise your own beef, there are still disadvantages. The Wolfes don't make a profit from the meat they sell, and it takes a lot of work to raise cattle. Experience and good equipment make the job easier.

Good flow from quotations to transition paragraphs and back again.

"Having the knowledge it takes to properly treat the animals always makes raising them easier," says Regina. She adds that knowing how to handle the cows without hurting them or herself is a big advantage.

"Neutering and vaccinating cows without a head gate is very risky. You basically have to tackle them and keep them lying on their sides," she says. A head gate is a device that closes around the cow's neck without choking it, forcing the animal to stand still.

Adventures? What adventures? Tell us! Readers want to know!

While all the equipment does make their jobs easier, the Wolfe family has still experienced some adventures with their animals. They've chased down escaped cows countless times, and strange medical problems just seem to find their cows.

"At times it feels like we barely keep up with them," says Liz. "But we still enjoy raising—and eating—them."

A quotation ending, quoting the person in the lead

Remember her assignment? How did she do?

1. She selected a topic of interest to her community (natural or organic meat).
2. She found a face to represent the trend.
3. She successfully followed the feature format, putting the nut graph early and moving smoothly from quotations to transition paragraphs.
4. She interviewed three people and included quotes from them in the copy. She could have included how Archie and Regina learned what they needed to know, how many cows they have, who buys the beef, and so forth, to round out the copy.

Additional comments on the student's copy:

- She didn't deliver on her nut graph. Readers expect to learn about "bizarre" happenings. Expanding on the "strange medical problems" would have helped the topic, too.
- It would be wise to include facts, statistics, or quotations from other people who are raising their own beef, quotes from experts and from markets that buy home-raised meat or from government agencies that are either for or against the idea. More information and quotations broaden the reader's awareness of the trend, even if only one family is highlighted. It gives readers a frame in which to understand the featured family.
- The tone is even and light.

Write a Newspaper Article

Choose one style of newspaper writing (hard news or feature) and select an event, idea, issue, or trend to cover.

If you select **hard-news writing**, attend an event, observe a meeting or emergency situation, or follow up on a story you have read or seen in the local news.

Include the five Ws, the H, and the S in your lead.

Use the inverted pyramid format.

If you choose to do a **feature,** brainstorm possible human-interest ideas. You can cover an event or series of events, a group of people, a trend, a game, a concert, an issue, and so forth.

Use one of the feature leads that grabs readers and pulls them into the copy.

Find a face that represents your topic. Begin your copy with this face and quotes from him or her; end with a strong kicker with a tie-in to the lead.

Use the feature format.

For **both types of writing**, interview <u>at least</u> two people so you can include a variety of accurate quotations.

Write your copy in third person (objective tone). Be completely objective in your writing, using facts instead of your opinions.

Use Be Your Own Editor on page 164 to proofread your copy at least three times.

Word count for **beginning** writers: between 350-500 words.

Word count for **intermediate** and **accomplished** writers: between 450-600 words.

Check your work against this assignment's checklist:

- ❏ Is the topic newsworthy?
- ❏ **Hard news:** Does the lead include most of the 5 Ws, the H and the S?
- ❏ **HN:** Is your copy in the inverted triangle format?
- ❏ **HN:** Is the tone objective?
- ❏ **Feature writing:** Does your lead grab the interest of the reader?
- ❏ **FW:** Did you find an appropriate face to represent your topic?
- ❏ **FW:** Does your copy use the feature-writing format?
- ❏ **FW:** Does the nut graph appear early in the copy?
- ❏ **FW:** Does the nut graph show the topic and "thesis" clearly?
- ❏ **FW:** Does the copy support the nut graph?
- ❏ **FW:** Does the copy end with an appropriate quotation or tie-in to the lead?
- ❏ **All writers:** Is the copy interesting?
- ❏ Is it clear and understandable?
- ❏ Is it concise?
- ❏ Which are you more like: Clark Kent or Superman?
- ❏ Are the vocabulary and sentence lengths appropriate for the intended readership?
- ❏ Does the copy quote from at least two interviews?
- ❏ Does the copy adequately cover the event, trend, idea, or person?
- ❏ Is the copy factual?
- ❏ Do you use gender-neutral language where appropriate?
- ❏ Are the facts correctly attributed or cited?

- ❑ Are the quotes correctly attributed?
- ❑ Are the paragraphs one to three sentences long?
- ❑ Are the speaker tags simple?
- ❑ **HN:** Are the copy and speaker tags in past tense?
- ❑ **FW:** Are the speaker tags in present tense?
- ❑ Is the grammar correct?
- ❑ Is the punctuation correct?
- ❑ Is the spelling correct?

Note: If the question does not indicate **HN** (Hard News) or **FW** (feature writing), then it applies to either form of news writing.

Fill in this chart with the necessary tasks to get your article in on time. Or, if you prefer, you can use the chart at the end of chapter 4.

Day 1	Day 2	Day 3	Day 4	Day 5	Day 6

"To be ignorant of the lives of the most celebrated men of antiquity is to continue in a state of childhood all our days."
- Plutarch

Chapter 16: Biographies

Lesson 1

What kind of people do you like to read about? Sports figures? Historical figures? Authors? Scientists? The biography/autobiography section of your library is loaded with stories of the lives of interesting people. Jerry B. Jenkins, co-author of the Left Behind series, likes writing biographies of sports figures: Hank Aaron (baseball), Meadowlark Lemon (Harlem Globetrotters basketball), and Paul Anderson (world's strongest man who, in 1957, lifted 6,270 pounds). Jenkins also wrote biographies of Billy Graham, singer B. J. Thomas, and other luminaries. In many cases, he was able to meet and hang out with the high-profile men he wrote about.

After a short lesson on an interesting writing device, you'll learn some intriguing ways to write biographies. And when you become famous, who will write yours?

I Came, I Saw, I Conquered: Patterns of Three

 People appreciate patterns of three. Threes have a nice rhythm: Stop, drop, and roll; faith, hope, and charity; Flora, Fauna, and Merryweather; and I came, I saw, I conquered. This next one is particularly pleasing because it holds a cumulative pattern of three:

Friends, Romans, countrymen, lend me your ears.

From Shakespeare's *Julius Caesar*, this pattern of three builds upon itself. The first word has one syllable; the second, two; and the third, three. Pause for a few minutes and write in the space below some other patterns or groups of three you find in life, literature (including fairy tales), and the Bible.

Winston Churchill, a former British prime minister, in a speech on the bravery of the British airmen in World War II, used this pattern of three:

Never in the field of human conflict was <u>so much</u> owed by <u>so many</u> to <u>so few</u>.

Apostle Paul knew the power of three when he taught his readers. Examine these threes he packed into 1 Corinthians 13 (KJV):

> Though I speak with the tongues of men and of angels and have not charity, I am become as sounding brass or a tinkling cymbal. *"Though" sentence 1*
> And though I have the gift of prophecy and understand all mysteries and all knowledge, and though I have all faith so that I could remove mountains, and have not charity, I am nothing. *"Though" sentence 2*
> And though I bestow all my goods to feed the poor, and though I give my body to be burned and have not charity, it profiteth me nothing. *"Though" sentence 3*
> . . . whether there be prophecies, they shall fail; whether there be tongues, they shall cease; whether there be knowledge, it shall vanish away.
> When I was a child, I spake as a child, I understood as a child, I thought as a child....
> And now abideth faith, hope, charity, these three; but the greatest of these is charity.

He uses another pattern of three when teaching believers what they were before Jesus reconciled them to God. Fill in the blanks by using the Bible (Romans 5 KJV):

Verse 6: For **when we were yet** _____, in due time Christ died for the ungodly.

Verse 8: . . . while **we were yet** _____, Christ died for us.

Verse 10: For if, **when we were** _____, we were reconciled to God by the death of his Son . . . .

Note the downward progression of "what we were." It adds to the understanding of Paul's nonfiction writing.

Lesson 2

Elegant Threes

Patterns of three (sometimes called the Rule of Three or the Law of Three) are not necessary, but they definitely enhance fiction and nonfiction writing by giving a sort of satisfaction and rhythm to them.

Consider the following excerpt from *Travels with Charley: In Search of America* by John Steinbeck. This nonfiction, on-the-road narrative is filled with patterns of three and patterns within patterns. To fully enjoy the excerpt, please look up the following words now: *calcareous, spate, indigents,* and *warren.*

Steinbeck, author of *The Grapes of Wrath*, was traveling with his dog Charley across the United States in his pickup truck in 1960. We join him as he approaches Seattle, Washington:

The Pacific is my home ocean; I knew it first, grew up on its shore, collected marine animals along the coast. I know its moods, its color, its nature. It was very far inland that I caught the first smell of the Pacific. When one has been long at sea, the smell of land reaches far out to greet one. And the same is true when one has been long inland. I believe I smelled the sea rocks and the kelp and the excitement of churning sea water, the sharpness of iodine and the under odor of washed and ground calcareous shells. Such a far-off and remembered odor comes subtly so that one does not consciously smell it, but rather an electric excitement is released—a kind of boisterous joy. I found myself plunging over the roads of Washington, as dedicated to the sea as any migrating lemming.

I remembered lush and lovely eastern Washington very well and the noble Columbia River, which left its mark on Lewis and Clark. And, while there were dams and power lines I hadn't seen, it was not greatly changed from what I remembered. It was only as I approached Seattle that the unbelievable change became apparent.

Of course, I had been reading about the population explosion on the West Coast, but for West Coast most people substitute California. People swarming in, cities doubling and trebling in numbers of inhabitants, while the fiscal guardians groan over the increasing weight of improvements and the need to care for a large new spate of indigents. It was here in Washington that I saw it first. I remembered Seattle as a town sitting on hills beside a matchless harborage—a little city of space and trees and gardens, its houses matched to such a background. It is no longer so. The tops of hills are shaved off to make level warrens for the rabbits of the present. The highways eight lanes wide cut like glaciers through the uneasy land. This Seattle had no relation to the one I remembered. The traffic rushed with murderous intensity. On the outskirts of this place I once knew well I could not find my way. Along what had been country lanes rich with berries, high wire fences and mile-long factories stretched, and the yellow smoke of progress hung over all, fighting the sea winds' efforts to drive them off.

Underline the patterns of three in the Steinbeck excerpt above. As there are some patterns within patterns, use pens of different colors (or *1s*, *2s*, and *3s*) to show longer and shorter sets of threes. The first two sentences appear below:

Practice 16.1

                                                     1   2

The Pacific is my home ocean; I <u>knew</u> it first, <u>grew up</u> on its shore,

    3   1   2

<u>collected</u> marine animals along the coast. I know <u>its moods</u>, <u>its color</u>, <u>its</u>

   3

<u>nature</u>.

After you have underlined patterns of three, note the geographical progression of Steinbeck's narrative. Even in this, there is a triple pattern. How does he achieve this as he moves from one paragraph to the next? Write your answer below:

Lesson 3

The Biography and the Angle

A well-written biography weaves a narrative of someone's life; it tells a story. (An **autobiography** is the life story of the person writing it; a **biography** is a life story written by someone else.) A biography need not be a dull recital of facts, dates, and places. Who would want to read that?

You learned at the beginning of this course to find the interesting part of the assignment, and that is exactly what you do when you write a biography. Find the **slant** or **angle** that suddenly makes that person come alive for you. For instance, many interesting things happened in Sir James Barrie's life (the creator of the character Peter Pan). But what if, while reading about him, you find that Barrie enjoyed writing miniature notes with tiny writing as though they were from fairies and hid them in clever places like tree trunks for his little friends the Davies boys to find? Now you have a slant or angle from which to write his biography—a man who never grew up.

Every person has so many chapters and facets to his life that, with careful reading and research, you can find something that defines your subject (the person in your biography) for you. For instance, will you put Mark Twain in the context of the young boy who saw all kinds of people while growing up in the river town of Hannibal, Missouri, where he knew the town drunk's son, gamblers, riverboat employees, traveling salesmen and shysters, and pulpit-pounding preachers of questionable repute? Will you write about him as the man who felt he was responsible for the deaths of his brother, his infant son, two of his three daughters, and his wife? Or will you settle on him as the man who brilliantly created lost worlds in order to honor or decry them? Each facet of his life is true; it is up to you to choose the aspect that, to you, defines the man or interests you the most.

A biographical work does not have to cover a person's entire life. It could encompass a politician's term in office, an athlete's retirement years, or a singer's formative years. To write this slice of life, you will briefly mention the years of your subject's life that have little bearing on your slant. This gives your readers a frame of reference (time, place, family, and so on). Then you'll focus on the years or events you feel are important to your paper.

Find someone who interests you and then ferret out an interesting angle.

What happened to simply telling someone's life chronologically? Beginning with the person's birth, mentioning some things she did, and ending with her death may not fit your needs anymore. It's likely that the events surrounding her birth were uneventful. Consider beginning elsewhere.

Use your QSFSQ tools to begin your biography. Hook your reader. Here are some possibilities for how to begin an eye-catching biography:

- **A successful businessman** Begin with the story of one of his failures.
- **A famous singer or actor** Begin with her first time on stage or a story of when she used to don a wig and sing into a hairbrush to mimic someone.
- **A well-known person with a handicap** Begin with life before the difficulty or when she was having a hard time with the handicap.
- **An inventor** Begin with one of his inventions we use every day or an interesting discovery in his laboratory after his death.
- **An explorer** Begin with a story of him lost.
- **A conservationist** Begin with the youthful incident that put him on the path to conservation.

When you write the biography, consider using words and phrases that will highlight your slant and make your paper stick together or be cohesive. You can use synonyms, antonyms, similar imagery, and other devices to pull your paragraphs and essays together.

Below are sentences taken from a student's biography on Milton Hershey—yes, the Hershey chocolate guy. This student highlighted the businessman side of his life while using "sweet" words to make her biography cohesive:

> The road to Milton's success, though, was never as smooth as the creamy chocolates he made.

> Determined to satisfy the public's sweet tooth, Milton refused to let the disappointment of his bankrupt business sour his ambition.

> Selling at a delicious one million dollars, The Caramel Company stepped aside in 1900 to allow room for a new player in the business.

> At the end of 1908, with the support of his wife Catherine, Milton Hershey was able to step back from his business and apply his profits to causes that wouldn't melt in the heat of the sun.

> Milton's passion to enhance Hershey's taste and town shows that success can certainly have sweet satisfaction.

Choose your angle and then figure out how you can highlight it by using words and phrases that support that angle.

Below are the first paragraphs of biographies written by students. Read them and give each a grade in the margin, based on each introduction's ability to capture your attention:

Practice 16.2
Do they make the grade?

1. He is the world's wealthiest man and the chairman of the largest software company, but even before that, William Henry Gates III led an interesting life.

2. Burning, killing, and spreading anarchy. These are some of the things the Ku Klux Klan did in the late 1800s. They tormented the countryside and tortured hundreds, all because a president decided to let Congress do as it wanted. [a biography of President Ulysses S. Grant]

3.   You may look far and wide for an accomplished deaf writer, but there is a language barrier that is many times too hard to break. Laura Redden broke through those walls magnificently. That is what makes her an exemplary woman.

4.   When he was three, he contracted an ear infection that, undetected, resulted in a 75-percent hearing loss. Because the available hearing aids (the body-pack variety) were relatively bulky, clumsy, and primitive, he developed "very defective speech. That was harder to deal with than the hearing loss, because people assumed I was dumb when they heard me talk," he told *People Weekly* in 1981. "I was very introverted and always isolated from my classmates." Lou Ferrigno is now famous for his role in the TV series *The Incredible Hulk*. He has risen out of his near-deaf experience, but the journey hasn't been easy.

But wait! There's more!

How many of those examples begin with the person's birth? Remember your tools. Hook your reader with something interesting.

Avoid hooking your reader with the word *imagine*. When you begin with *imagine,* you are making your reader do the work the writer should be doing. It is the writer's job to paint the picture for the reader. Instead of writing "Imagine how hard it would be to…," try something like this:

Professional Tip
Do **not** begin any writing, either for school or professionally, with *imagine.*

When he cooks, he stirs the food while holding a wooden spoon in his mouth. When he uses his laptop, his fingers are not tapping the keys; his toes are. Brushing his teeth, signing a check, and sticking a fork in his food are all done with the help of his flexible feet. Why? Jay Sanchez was born without any arms.

This writer did the work of a writer. She was specific with her word pictures, descriptions, and actions. This is a much stronger way of writing than telling your reader to imagine something.

Practice 16.3   Walt Disney led a full and interesting life. Any number of people can be added to this interesting list: Mother Teresa, the evangelist Luis Palau, quarterback Tom Brady, Beethoven, Jackie Robinson, Ray Bradbury, Sonya Sotomayor, Queen Elizabeth II, Michael Jordan, and J. R. R. Tolkien. Choose one of those people, learn one interesting fact about his or her life, and write an engaging introduction for a biography. You will not be writing the rest of the biography.

Word count: approximately 100.

Lesson 4

Beyond "He was born. Then he died."

You've already read about possible slants for biographies of Sir James Barrie and Mark Twain. Here are some other ways to slant your biography:

1. **Write about a person you respect.** In this biography, you write about the achievements and character traits you value in this person and how he or she exhibited them.

2. **Write about a person you don't respect.** Choose someone in history or in the public eye, not a friend, neighbor, or family member. Write about your subject's negative qualities and fiascos.

3. **Write about a person who overcame great difficulties.** In this slant, you write about your subject's difficulties and how she overcame them, how she battled on despite them, or what she accomplished in spite of her woes. People who have battled disease, mental illness, discrimination, or troubling childhoods are good candidates for this kind of biography. Highlight the personality trait that got her through the tough times.

4. **Write about a person who invented something interesting.** Who invented the iPod? The BlackBerry? The atom bomb? Velcro? Windshield wipers? How did they get these ideas? What made him interested in inventing or interested in this particular product? Highlight how he invented it and how it has affected his life and the lives of others.

5. **Write about a person from his creation's point of view.** Rudyard Kipling's life might look interesting through Mowgli's eyes. What would the curate in H. G. Wells' *The War of the Worlds* write about his creator? *Reader's Digest* featured "Out of the Hat," an article about the animator Chuck Jones as told from Bugs Bunny's point of view. Not only does it trace the development of Mr. Jones and his interest in cartooning but it also shows his impact on the Bugs Bunny character. Very clever.

6. **Write about a person who was told he would never be successful—and then was.** *Reader's Digest* printed "Yes, I Can," an article that reveals the stories of seven successful people who had been told they would be failures. Included in the stories is a man who did terribly in school but who later, through hard work and tenacity, became a famous filmmaker (Steven Spielberg).

7. **Write about a person from the point of view of a pet,** a close friend or relative, or an inanimate object he used during his life. Robert Lawson does this in *Ben and Me*, a story about the inventive side of Benjamin Franklin as told by a mouse who traveled in Ben's hat or pocket. According to the mouse narrator, all of Franklin's inventions were the mouse's idea. What could Oscar Wilde's jail cell tell us about that famous writer?

8. **Write about a person in a "Who Am I?" manner.** Cram the biography full of interesting things about your subject but don't tell who the person is until near the end of your paper. This keeps the reader guessing and creates an interest in him or her.

9. **Write about a person's spiritual journey.** Trace your subject's spiritual development and how he or she grew to believe something. This method is effective if the person experienced a great change in his or her life or is known for believing one thing but began somewhere else.

Circle any of the above methods that appeal to you.

No doubt you have some good ideas of your own about how to write a biography. Write one or two in the margin.

An important word about research: Use as many reputable sources as you can. The more sources you use, the better and more accurate the information will be. If you read H. G. Wells' autobiography, you will learn many wonderful and interesting things about him, but you will not learn that he had numerous affairs while he was married and even had some children by these women. For some reason, he fails to include this vital information in his autobiography. One wonders why. Get your information from many sources. It will make your biography more complete and truthful—and more interesting.

Practice 16.4
Do they make
the grade?

The student who wrote the following biography (463 words) combined three of the above methods; she wrote about someone she respects who has overcome great difficulties, and she did it from the point of view of the Miss America crown. Read the following biography and then answer the questions at the end:

I am waiting here on this pillow, ready to be placed on Miss America 1996. Miss America 1995 Heather Whitestone and I have endured much this year. But through everything, Heather was a great Miss America. She went through many troubles just to have the chance to wear me. While all of the young ladies who have worn me have worked hard, Heather had to work doubly hard; you see, Heather is deaf.

Heather's mother discovered that her daughter was deaf on a Christmas morning, after Heather had recovered from an almost deadly illness. When some pots fell in the kitchen, Heather's mom, sister, and grandmother were all startled out of their skins, but Heather kept on playing with her new toys. Bringing a pot and a wooden spoon with her, Heather's mom came into the living room and hit the pot as hard as she could with the spoon. Even though it was next to Heather's ear, Heather never flinched. Her mother did the same with the other ear. Again, Heather did not move. Heather's mother was stunned at what had happened in front of her. She hit the pot with the spoon again and again, disbelieving what she saw. Her little girl was deaf. After some hearing tests, she learned that Heather had lost about 95 percent of her hearing.

When Heather was growing up, her mother wanted her to learn how to speak and not use sign language, despite her deafness. While Heather and I spent a whole year together, I learned quite a few stories about her. This one stands out to me. As a young girl, when Heather wanted a drink of water, she signed for it. Her mother said if she wanted something, she needed to ask for it, not sign for it. Again Heather signed for a drink. And again her mother told her she needed to ask. Heather left in a huff. Eventually, she returned and asked for a "dink." Her mother handed her a glass of water. While Heather's pronunciation may not have been correct, her mother was pleased; she had won the battle about speech.

Her mother's determination about speaking paid off when Heather competed in the Miss America Pageant. Heather made it into the top ten, and she was thrilled. When there were just two women standing alone on the stage, Heather was still one of them. She could not hear the announcement that she was Miss America. The first runner-up pointed to her and mouthed the words "You won"; Heather was ecstatic. As Miss America 1994 placed me on Heather's head, the new Miss America looked beautiful.

I'm sad to be leaving Heather tonight. She has been a wonderful companion. Who will spend the next year wearing me as Miss America?

Answer the following questions on a separate piece of paper:

1. Do you find this biography interesting?
2. What facts do you wish she had included?
3. Do you want to learn more about Heather Whitestone?
4. Give this paper a grade. Explain the grade.

The next biography (505 words) combines three methods: the simple chronological, the "he'll be a failure," and the "Who Am I?" Although the subject of this biography has many facets, the writer chose to spotlight only the "crazy" factor, which creates cohesiveness and a central focus. See if you can guess the person before you read his name.

His grandfather was mentally unbalanced and was called feeble minded. His grandmother worked at the lunatic asylum. His father made his crib from the coffin the local count had been laid out in. Into this family about two hundred years ago was born a lad whom we treasure today.

As a young boy, Andy often went to the insane asylum with his grandmother. She was the gardener. There he visited with the inmates and the old, poor women of the village, where they came to do their spinning. Andy often told them about the insides of the human body, drawing crazy pictures in chalk on the doors. They thought him very wise. In return they rewarded him with tales of their own. These must have been very scary, for he soon became afraid to go out at night.

The villagers considered Andy strange. Many times he walked around the village with his eyes shut in order to experience what it was like to be blind. When he was finally able to afford school, he wrote the schoolmaster a poem for the man's birthday. When the other boys found out, they shouted and jeered at him all the way home.

He longed to be an actor and a playwright, so when his mother planned to apprentice him to a tailor, he begged her to let him go to the capital to realize his dream. "People have at first an immense deal of adversity to go through, and then they will be famous," he assured her. He was only fourteen.

At the capital, the manager of the theater said he was too thin to be an actor. "If you will employ me, I will soon get fat!" was his reply. He tried to work for a cabinetmaker, but the boys who worked there ridiculed him. Andy consoled himself with prayer and with this thought: "When everything happens really miserably, then He sends help. I have always read so."

One beautiful spring day he visited the gardens of King Frederick VI. Andy was so overcome, he shouted for joy, threw his arms around a tree, and kissed it. "Is he mad?" he heard behind him. It was a servant of the king.

Mr. Collin, the director of the Theater Royal, paid for Andy to have an education. While at the school, the man he was boarding with told him he would never become a student, that all his poems would grow moldy on the floor of some bookseller's shop, and that he would end his days in the mad house.

But he didn't. This ugly duckling, this man who didn't seem to fit in anywhere, grew to be a wonderful writer of fairy tales. In his lifetime, he gained the respect of poets, playwrights, famous singers, kings, queens, professors, and composers. He became, as one little princess told him, "my fairy tale prince." Author of "The Emperor's New Clothes," "Thumbelina," and "The Little Mermaid," Hans Christian Andersen was not an ugly duckling after all. He was a swan.

Answer the following questions on a separate piece of paper:

1. Mark the place in the biography where you correctly guessed the man's name.
2. Why is this introduction an attention getter?
3. What facts about Andersen do you wish the writer had included?
4. What pattern of three did this writer use?
5. Give this paper a grade. Explain the grade.

Write a Biography

Write a biography.

Choose your subject—anyone in the public eye, living or dead, who can be researched. Do not choose deity, saints, fictional characters, animals, or anyone from the Bible.

Choose a biography method or invent one. Before you write, check your subject and method with your teacher.

While including brief mention of other years and facts, focus on the information that supports your slant or method, just as the biographies of Heather Whitestone and Hans Christian Andersen do.

Include a pattern of three.

Use at least two reputable sources. If you find conflicting information, use a reliable third source to validate your notes.

Check with your teacher about whether to document your source material, and if so, which method to use (in-text citations, a works cited page, etc.).

Use Be Your Own Editor on page 164 to proofread at least three times.

Word count for **beginning** writers: between 400 and 600.

Word count for **intermediate** or **accomplished** writers: between 500-800 words.

Read the next section **after** you write your assignment but **before** you hand it in.

Lesson 5

Transitions

You have brainstormed, researched your person, chosen a slant, arranged the information in a logical order, written the paragraphs of the body, and devised a strong introduction and conclusion. What else could there be?

Linking the thoughts from one paragraph to the next is a good way to keep your reader reading. Certain sentences and phrases serve as those links, and they are called **transitions**.

A transition is the brief link between two paragraphs or thoughts, moving the reader along with the flow of the paper. Whether a complete sentence or just a phrase, transitions guide the reader smoothly along the essay's flow. You learned about transitions when you wrote a how-to essay: *before you hit . . ., after you attach . . ., the next thing . . .,* and so forth.

Please skim Heather Whitestone's biography and underline any transitions now. Then meet me back here.

Some teachers want students to use transitions in every paragraph. If this is the case with your teacher, then do it. Some magazine editors consider transitions, for the most part, unnecessary. How do you know what an editor prefers? It's simple. Pick up a copy of the magazine and skim the paragraphs. Professional writers have to adhere to the editor's or magazine's style preferences. You will, too.

Here are the transitions in the Heather Whitestone biography: *When Heather was growing up* (to transition from an important discovery to life as a young girl), *Her mother's determination about speaking* (to transition from her young life to the Miss America pageant), and *I'm sad to be leaving Heather tonight* (to transition from Heather to the next winner).

Transitions can appear in the first sentence of a paragraph or in the last sentence of the previous paragraph. Or they can be words or phrases such as *Later, Since that day, After she graduated, When he met the Count,* and *As a young boy.*

Practice 16.5   Yes, this is totally and completely unfair to make you do this . . .

> Find **two** places in your biography to include transition sentences or phrases. Rewrite some sentences and make them into transitions. Or simply add transition words or phrases to appropriate sentences.
>
> Then hand in your paper.

Check your biography against this assignment's checklist:

❑ What is your slant or angle? Write it below:

❑ Does your angle show your subject in a most interesting light?
❑ Did you begin the biography with a reader-catching QSFSQ?
❑ If it is not chronological, do you include enough information to show the time period, place, and other facts needed to give your reader a framework for the subject's life?
❑ What important life lesson will your reader learn from this biography? Write it here:

❑ Did you use an appealing pattern of threes?

❑ Did you use at least two transitions?

❑ Is your information from at least two reliable sources?

❑ Did you most often use the active voice?

❑ Did you remember to floss?

❑ Did you use gender-neutral language when appropriate?

❑ Is the paragraphing logical?

❑ Is the grammar correct?

❑ Is the punctuation correct?

❑ Is the spelling correct?

❑ Did you proofread with Be Your Own Editor at least three times?

Fill in this chart or use the one at the end of chapter 4 to help you complete your writing tasks.

Day 1	Day 2	Day 3	Day 4	Day 5	Day 6

"I have been studying the traits and dispositions of the
'lower animals' (so called) and contrasting them
with the traits and dispositions of man.
I find the result humiliating to me."
- Mark Twain

Chapter 17: Compare and Contrast

Lesson 1

Rose Petals and Vikings

You read the book. Then you watched the movie. Automatically you began to compare the two versions of the same story. How were the two similar? Where were they different? How was the movie better or worse than the book? Which did you like better? You've been comparing and contrasting for years; this chapter will help you shape your thoughts into a usable, written form.

Do any of these assignments sound familiar? Compare and contrast . . .

- the process of photosynthesis with the process of cellular respiration.
- one character in a novel with another character.
- one king, emperor, president, or prime minister with another.
- one form of government with another form.
- what the ancient Greeks gave the world versus what the ancient Romans gave the world.

- how women are treated in this country with how they are treated in predominantly Islamic countries.
- organic farming methods and benefits versus traditional farming.

The compare-and-contrast tool isn't just for school. Movie critics use it when they compare two recent movies that feature the same actor or when they contrast one director's work with another's. Remakes are always compared with their originals, and so are sequels.

Historians naturally compare leaders with each other. When discussing a war, historians will review the strengths and weaknesses of two generals or will show the differing effects of two battles. Comparing and contrasting gives meaning to an event.

Comparing and contrasting is already one of your life skills. You are probably making decisions about your future—career, college, or wait and see. This involves examining the advantages and disadvantages of all your choices and the similarities and differences between them (College A has smaller class sizes, College B allows freshmen to have cars on campus, and College C has a more interesting male/female ratio). When you weigh your options, you are comparing and contrasting.

Someday, you may be sitting in a meeting when the boss tells you to get the information on cell-phone plans for company-wide use. You will call cell phone companies; collect data on rates, minutes, features, contracts, and so forth; and put the information on a handy chart or in a report for your boss to examine. You will have done the work of comparing and contrasting so the boss can make an informed decision.

This article uses compare/contrast to explore and celebrate gender differences. Enjoy this humorous look at young men and women, abridged from "Two Kinds of Diners" by Mark K. Atkinson:

> Our daughter, Rebekah, approached us with a request. She and some of her girlfriends from the church youth group wanted to have a Ro---tic dinner.
>
> "What's that?" we asked.
>
> "It's a romantic dinner, without the *man*," she replied.
>
> On the day of the dinner, they set out our best china and water glasses and goblets, and then they carefully folded cloth napkins and placed 50 tea lights throughout the apartment.
>
> Next they sprinkled rose petals on the coffee table and made flower arrangements for each dinner table. They dimmed the lighting and played big band for the dinner music.
>
> By 7 p.m. all the girls had arrived. They retreated to various bedrooms to change into the formal gowns they had carefully chosen for the evening. After the Chinese food was delivered for their no-man dinner, the girls were deliberate about the presentation.

Each dish was transferred to an appropriately fancy serving dish. No sauces were served in a jar, bottle or plastic packaging. Everything was perfect.

Meanwhile . . .

Our oldest, Benjamin, had a dinner invitation that evening—and not by chance. The leader of the senior high youth group, Rick, heard of the girls' dinner for Friday night. So he invited the guys to his home that same Friday for a Viking feast—a primitive meal with no plates or utensils. While the girls dressed up in their evening finest, the guys donned their grubbiest shirts.

For the Viking feast, Rick moved his dining room table to the backyard. At one end, he piled lettuce and a variety of veggies for a tossed salad. The guys would take a bit of lettuce, radishes, mushrooms, etc., stuff them in their mouths, then take a swig from the communal salad dressing curette.

At the other end of the table, Rick dumped a huge batch of spaghetti and meat sauce. This was attacked by hand. For drinks, a variety of sodas were poured into a large pot, and the guys took turns drinking from it, using a ladle. Dessert was gooey, messy chocolate pudding.

The guys ended the night with a food fight.

My wife and I returned to our apartment just as the girls were enjoying their after-dinner tea. The young ladies looked elegant and charming. When Benjamin returned wearing the tomato scars of his Viking feast, we couldn't help but laugh at the contrast.

Both groups had a marvelous time, each in their own unique way. *His thesis*
Yes, God created man in His own image, but male and female He *statement is in*
made them—and that is very different. *his conclusion!*

Which party would you rather have attended?

You have already written a compare and contrast for persuasion. In your persuasive compare and contrast, you chose a side, defended it, and issued a call to action.

But writing an expository compare-and-contrast paper is different from writing one as a persuasive paper. You do not have to choose sides. Instead, you analyze the similarities and the differences of the two people or ideas, and you write about them in order to teach or enlighten the reader. Remember that exposition is meant to teach, inform, explain, and sometimes even to entertain.

In "Two Kinds of Diners," the author does not choose sides or try to persuade his readers to prefer one method of dining to another. He writes about the genders' similarities and differences, and then he draws some conclusions. And so will you. What conclusions (implied and stated) does Atkinson draw about young men and women? Write your answer here:

It is easy to plan a compare-and-contrast paper if you first fill out a chart. If you are preparing a paper on, say, the similarities and differences of World War I and World War II, a chart will be most helpful. On one side of the chart will be facts about the first war, and on the other side will be facts about the second. What facts? You might include some of the following: what incidents built up to the outbreak, what final incident tipped the scale and began it, who began it, where it began, what countries were on what sides, what the war was about, some military tactics and technology used, how long it lasted, how it ended, what the treaty gave and took away, how the boundaries were changed before and after the war, its consequences, and so forth.

After your chart is filled with your research, you easily will be able to write about both wars.

You may want to organize your material by making a list of similarities and a list of differences. Experiment with a chart and the lists to figure out which works best for your topic.

In the next three lessons, you'll discover three methods of writing a compare-and-contrast paper, sometimes called a comparison-and-contrast paper.

Practice 17.1   Compare and contrast two people of your choice. On a separate piece of paper, make a chart based on comparable features: age, gender, personality, beliefs, physical attributes, talents, and so forth. Do not draw any conclusions; simply show similarities and differences by means of your chart.

Or make a list of similarities and a list of differences.

You will not be writing this as an essay.

Lesson 2

Method 1: Block

Armed with charts or with lists of similarities and differences concerning your two topics, what do you do? You carefully weigh your material and thesis statement to determine which method of organizing best fits your essay.

The first method uses "blocks." That is, you write one block of stuff about the first topic and then you write a block about the second topic. The chart below uses examples from the World War I/World War II topics:

Method 1	Example
Section 1: Introduction	**Section 1:** Introduction
Section 2: The first topic	**Section 2:** WW I noteworthy facts
Section 3: The second topic	**Section 3:** WW II noteworthy facts
Section 4: Conclusions	**Section 4:** Conclusions

Use as many paragraphs in each section as are necessary. If your essay is short, a paragraph per section might be sufficient. For a longer essay containing an abundance of facts, any section might need more than one paragraph. In other words, create as many paragraphs as you need for the first topic and then for the second.

In keeping with the war topic, here is a possible **thesis statement**, which would appear at the end of the introduction:

> Despite their differences, the two wars are alarmingly similar.

From this your reader understands that there are two wars and that you are going to highlight the similarities between them.

Moving from section 2 to section 3 (from the first topic to the second) needs a **transition**. The writer of this essay might begin section 3 with this sentence to link the two sections, something like this:

> Although World War II was fought by another generation and on fields farther from the epicenter, it continued to be focused on the original problems from the Great War.

Although is the transition. It cues the reader that the essay is moving from the first topic to the second. The sentence narrows the new topic and gives it a direction.

For each paper, decide whether you are going to highlight similarities **or** differences. If you highlight similarities, you will lightly touch on differences but focus on similarities. If you zero in on differences, you will briefly mention some similarities but focus on differences. Make your decision based on your ideas and how you develop your topic.

The compare-and-contrast paper is not just an empty exercise aimed at keeping students off the streets at night. It is an opportunity to examine topics and draw conclusions based on what you find. So draw them. Be insightful. Be brilliant. In the war example, the writer might sum up what she believes to be the lessons we should have learned from World War I, and she might apply those lessons to today in the hope that we won't experience another world war.

A student used the block method to write this compare-and-contrast paper as a character analysis. His subject matter is the detective in the Pink Panther movie series, but he is lacking an introduction. Read his essay to determine what he is contrasting (269 words), and then answer the questions that follow it:

Practice 17.2

First topic or "block"

Transition from first topic to second topic: "Actually." ————→

Second topic or "block"

Conclusion

Inspector Clouseau, the world-renown French detective, always solves the case and gets his man, and he is proud of it. He will be the first one to brag about how he employed his ingenuity to track down a clever mastermind, using only his wit and skill. He always wins in the end and gains much popularity in the process. Clouseau basks in the spotlight of the public as he tells how he single-handedly apprehended a dangerous criminal by using his instinct—yes, that's what it is—his natural detective instinct.

Actually, Inspector Clouseau is one of the biggest bumbling fools on France's police force or on anyone's police force, for that matter, but he never realizes it. No one can ever tell him so because he never stops boasting about his expertise in the area of the investigative profession. Most of the general public does not realize that he is actually an idiot because he really does always get his man, whether by some inexplicable mistake or wild circumstance. He eventually stumbles across the culprit, with or without realizing it. If it were not for some strange turn of events, he would be shown for the inexperienced, wandering, slow-witted idiot that he actually is. His superiors such as Chief Inspector Dreyfus are driven crazy by the chaos and destruction that follow in Clouseau's wake.

Clouseau believes he is an expert inspector, and the longer he goes bumbling along, the more success he has, which only confirms his claims that he knows his business of detecting and does it well, although this is as far from the truth as possible.

Answer the following questions:

1. What is this student contrasting?

2. Have you seen any of the Pink Panther movies? If so, do you agree with this paper?

3. Write one descriptive word that shows what Clouseau thinks of himself.
4. Write one descriptive word to show what he really is.
5. Give this paper a grade. Explain why you gave that one.

Lesson 3

Method 2: Elements or Features

Instead of writing about your two topics separately (WW I and WW II, for example), this method focuses on elements or features of the items being compared.

Method 2	Example
Section 1: Introduction	**Section 1:** Introduction
Section 2: Element 1	**Section 2:** What the wars were about
Section 3: Element 2	**Section 3:** Where the wars were fought
Section 4: Element 3	**Section 4:** What ended the wars
Section 5: Conclusions	**Section 5:** Conclusions

Elements? Features? What are those? Those are aspects shared by the two topics. If, for example, you were considering which gym shoes to buy and you narrowed it down to buying the Cheetahs or the Roadrunners, you might look at these features: price, sole, composition (leather or canvas), color and/or design, brand name, the coolness factor, which celebrity endorses them, and so on.

For the war topic, you might examine these features or elements: where the wars began, how they began, what was being fought over, which countries were on what sides, the technologies that aided each side, how the wars ended, what the treaties covered, and so forth. These are some of the common elements in almost any war topic.

One student wrote an essay contrasting the differences between modern books children read today versus classic books they read years ago. Here are the elements she wrote about:

- **the characters:** average and wimpy versus brave, strong, and honest
- **the protagonists:** deceive others/no discernible change in character versus being tested for honesty, perseverance, and courage
- **the endings:** "the ends justify the means" versus inspiring readers to greatness

Each section or element begins with the new books and ends with the classics. You can see why a chart will be helpful in keeping track of everything and plotting your strategy.

You will decide whether to highlight the similarities or the differences, based on your research and the conclusions you will draw. And you will write a thesis statement that reveals the two topics you are comparing. Here's the thesis statement for the student's essay on books:

Children's love of reading hasn't changed over the years, but the books they read have.

She's made it very clear what she is comparing and contrasting.

When dealing with features, you may find your job easier if you create a chart instead of two lists. Here's a chart comparing Goliath to David:

Features	Goliath	David
Vocation	Seasoned warrior	Seasoned shepherd, part-time musician for King Saul
Previously killed	Men in battle and other national heroes	A lion and a bear
Weaponry	Bronze helmet, bronze armor weighing 125 lbs., bronze greaves, bronze javelin with a point that weighted 15 lbs., shield	5 smooth stones 1 slingshot
Support	The whole Philistine army	God King Saul, kind of
Enemies	A fearful Israel army	Philistine army His brothers—harassed and belittled him, attributed negative motives to him
Age	Adult	Teen
Size	Giant—over nine feet tall	Teen-sized boy
Motivation	Glory of Philistia Personal glory and plunder Giant-sized ego to uphold	To prove there is a God in Israel To defend God's name

A chart will help you think of ideas and will also help you organize your material.

Practice 17.3   Japan and Jamaica Kingdom are island countries and, because of this, will have elements to compare and contrast. On a separate piece of paper, create a chart and brainstorm some of the elements, features, or aspects of these island nations that a student could write about in a compare-and-contrast paper.

You are not going to write about these two; you are just brainstorming ideas. You also do not have to fill in the complete chart. Simply create the chart and come up with ideas for the "features" column. Then proceed to Practice 17.4.

Practice 17.4   Read this compare-and-contrast essay written by a student (838 words), for which she used a chart to organize her material. Using the feature method, this essay addresses two sources of puppies: pet stores and reputable breeders. Which source does she prefer?

You stop at a pet store window to oooh and aaah at the puppies on display in the front. You notice one in particular; it's so cute but appears sleepy. The puppy lies in a cage with other puppies, its nose on another's back, its paws looking too big for its body. But is that puppy really sleepy, or is it lethargic and fearful? Buying a puppy from a pet store can be questionable, but buying one from a reputable breeder is a definite advantage.

First feature being contrasted

Pet store puppies often come from puppy mills. Puppy mills tend to be in rural areas where they can be hidden. The mother dogs are especially mistreated and are forced to have litter after litter. The adult dogs can be seen crammed into wire cages, stacked so that the dogs' urine and feces can fall through the wire and be deposited on the ground. That forces the dogs on the bottom to sit in the waste. These dogs do not know real ownership or love. They are often sickly and do not receive any healthy exercise. I have visited a small puppy mill, and what I saw horrified me. The dogs were kept in little wire crates all day long in a small shed. Their nails were at least 1.5 inches long. Many of the dogs and puppies were fearful of me. In addition to these poor living conditions, I learned that the pups are taken away from their mothers at only six or seven weeks old and then shipped to pet stores.

Reputable dog breeders, on the other hand, are reliable, and they will want future owners to come to their home to see the setting the dogs are in. These breeders take great responsibility for their dogs' and puppies' health and welfare. The eight-week-old fluff balls will receive their first set of shots and their flea and de-worming medicine. By this time, they are well on their way to healthy socialization. The puppies' parents are friendly, healthy, and well accustomed to children and strangers. Reputable breeders will also be picky about which owners the puppies go with, and being picky is not a bad thing for the dogs. They will go to loving homes.

Puppies from pet stores sell for about $500-$1,000, but these prices are very deceiving. Because the price is high, one might think the puppy is of high quality. But this may not be so. The puppies often do not have their first set of shots or de-worming medicine. They are poorly socialized, especially if they came from a puppy mill, and they might have been mistreated. Their price tag is not a reliable reflection of their history.

Second feature being contrasted

In contrast, puppies from reputable breeders often hold higher price tags but for good reason. They are full-blooded, must always come with registration papers, and have had their first round of shots and medicine. Paying the price for a puppy from a reputable breeder is worth it; the price often includes a six-month, money-back guarantee. In other words, if sometime within that date the puppy becomes ill due to a genetic disease, the puppy may be returned to the breeder with the option to select a replacement puppy. Try getting that from a pet store.

Third feature

Yes, those pet store fuzz balls are cute, but that cuteness is often misleading. They may appear amiable and calm, but if one looks closely at the body language of those pups, one may find fear or timidity as a result of previous mistreatment at the puppy mill. A healthy puppy should be full of energy and curiosity, not lethargically snoozing all the time or fearful of strangers. The puppies at pet stores also can have unseen diseases which are covered up by the clever settings in the store. These illnesses may include eye disorders, parasites, and parvo, an extremely painful and often deadly illness.

Cuteness is more than skin deep in puppies from a reputable breeder. Their physical appeal comes from the benefits of the positive, healthy environment of living in large, safe areas with plenty of room to roughhouse and wrestle with their siblings. The pups will be loaded with energy unless they are napping from a day of hard play. They will be bright eyed and curious, friendly toward strangers and children. When they are finally old enough to be separated from their mothers, at around eight to ten weeks old, they can be given their new homes. Reputable breeders feel the responsibility to give their pups a good head start in life.

Not all puppies in a pet store are from puppy mills, but why take the chance? Whether the frisky puppies are playing with each other or resting after a time of fun, they deserve a healthy, happy environment and life. And you want to know that your puppy will grow into a healthy, well-adjusted dog that will be your friend for years to come.

Answer the questions:

1. What three features does the writer compare and contrast? Write them in the margins next to the essay.
2. This student organized her material so her reader could understand the issue better. In which order does she always address her two topics?
3. Do you agree with her opinions?

Lesson 4

Method 3: Similarities and Differences

This is absolutely the last method you will have to learn for writing your own compare-and-contrast paper. It looks like this:

Method 3   Example
Section 1: Introduction   **Section 1:** Introduction
Section 2: Similarities of the two topics   **Section 2:** Similarities of the wars
Section 3: Differences between the topics   **Section 3:** Differences in the wars
Section 4: Conclusions   **Section 4:** Conclusions

OR

Method 3, still   Example
Section 1: Introduction   **Section 1:** Introduction
Section 2: Differences between the topics   **Section 2:** Differences in the wars
Section 3: Similarities of the two topics   **Section 3:** Similarities of the wars
Section 4: Conclusions   **Section 4:** Conclusions

This method highlights similarities and differences, which I'm sure you figured out by its name. Which will you write about first, the similarities or the differences? That's up to you. If the differences are more important to you, begin with the similarities. If the similarities are more important, begin with the differences so you can end on the important note.

In keeping with the war theme, all the similarities of the two wars will appear in one section, and all the differences will be in the other. Then you will draw your own amazingly thought-provoking conclusions about the wars.

If you have enough information to fill more than one paragraph for each section, use more than one. The next example demonstrates this elasticity. The first paragraph in the body focuses on similarities, and the next two paragraphs discuss the differences. This is still method 3 because the paragraphs are arranged on the basis of first the similarities and then the differences in the topics.

Read this student's compare-and-contrast essay (499 words) about characters in two short stories by the same author. Then answer the questions that follow. Because she wants to highlight the characters' differences, she begins with their similarities, getting them out of the way.

Practice 17.5

In "The Legend of Sleepy Hollow" and "The Devil and Tom Walker," Washington Irving weaves tales of suspense and fright for his readers. Though both stories touch on the supernatural, they have little else in common.

Their women are their one point of commonality. These women both use their men to get what they want, whether by flattery or force. Ichabod, in "The Legend of Sleepy Hollow," is smitten with Katrina Van Tassel, who at first seems like a very sweet girl. However, the sweetness soon melts away to reveal the real Katrina. It becomes clear that she is just using poor

In each paragraph, she organizes her material like this: Information about "The Legend of Sleepy Hollow" comes first, and information about "The Devil and Tom Walker" appears second.

Ichabod to make Brom Bones jealous. Even the narrator laments Ichabod's fate: "Oh these women! These women! Could that girl have been playing off any of her coquettish tricks?" Old Tom's wife in "The Devil and Tom Walker" is also far from sweet. Tom has lived with his wife, who is "fierce of temper, loud of tongue, and strong of arm," for so many years that he no longer fears the devil. For some strange reason, Tom enjoys her argumentative demeanor and forceful attitude. In spite of how their men view them, neither of these women is beneficial to their male counterparts.

Though the women are similar, the protagonists of each story couldn't be more different from each other. Living in Sleepy Hollow, Ichabod Crane is the unfortunate victim of a ghost story come to life. He is a likeable character though obviously not for his looks. Ichabod possesses "narrow shoulders, long arms and legs, hands that dangled a mile out of his sleeves, feet that might have served for shovels, and [a] whole frame most loosely hung together." Clearly, this man needs help, and readers feel empathy toward him. Tom Walker, on the other hand, is not likeable in the least. He is greedy and mean. He squeezed "his customers closer and closer; and then set them out at length, dry as a sponge from his door." Both men differ in how they view the supernatural, too. While Ichabod enjoys scaring himself, Tom is pragmatic and sees no sense in being superstitious.

As in the case of the protagonists, the antagonists also differ from each other. One is a figment of the imagination brought to life by Brom Bones. Bones takes the role of the Headless Horseman and then chases Ichabod down a country lane late at night. The other is the devil, who, going by several names, buys Tom's soul in exchange for great riches. As real now as when "The Devil and Tom Walker" was written, the devil is more than a figment of an excitable imagination prompted by old ghost stories. He is quite real.

Both stories are enjoyable. They have the power to hold the reader's attention and even give some shivers during late-night reading. But because "The Legend of Sleepy Hollow" has a protagonist that is more of an underdog and is likeable, it is the more enjoyable of the two.

Answer the following questions:

1. Underline this student's thesis statement.
2. Next to each paragraph in the body, label briefly what the paragraph is about.
3. What is the topic sentence of paragraph two?
4. Underline the transition statement that moves the paper from the female characters to the male.
5. Underline with a wavy line the transition statement that moves the paper from the protagonists to the antagonists.
6. Explain why the differences are more important in this paper than the similarities.

7. If you have read both stories, do you agree with her conclusion?
8. Give this paper a grade and explain why you chose that one.

Any of these three methods you've learned in this chapter will work for your essays or reports. Experiment with your topics and the methods to determine which one will say best what you want to say in your paper.

A warning about **Ping-Pongs**: Avoid the Ping-Pong Plague in your compare-and-contrast paper. Writing a similarity and then a difference, back and forth, for the whole paper causes readers to get whiplash. It looks something like this:

> Ichabod was nice, but Tom was mean. Ichabod enjoyed being scared, but Tom wasn't the least superstitious. Ichabod was taken advantage of while Tom knew what he was walking into.

Do you feel your head turning from side to side in each sentence? Following the Ping-Pong back and forth is no fun.

To check your paper for the dreaded Ping-Pong Plague, try this: Underline or highlight with a colored pen everything about one topic. Then underline or highlight the other topic with a different pen color. If you find that your sentences continually switch from topic to topic, it's time to rearrange your points into one of the methods in this chapter.

The second paragraph of the Washington Irving paper looks like the following paragraph when the topics are highlighted. This is in grayscale; you will use colors you like:

Their women are their one point of commonality. These women both use their men to get what they want, whether by flattery or force. Ichabod, in "The Legend of Sleepy Hollow," is smitten with Katrina Van Tassel, who at first seems like a very sweet girl. However, the sweetness soon melts away to reveal the real Katrina. It becomes clear that she is just using poor Ichabod to make Brom Bones jealous. Even the narrator laments Ichabod's fate: "Oh these women! These women! Could that girl have been playing off any of her coquettish tricks?" Old Tom's wife in "The Devil and Tom Walker" is also far from sweet. Tom has lived with his wife, who is "fierce of temper, loud of tongue, and strong of arm," for so many years that he no longer fears the devil. For some strange reason, Tom enjoys her argumentative demeanor and forceful attitude. In spite of how their men view them, neither of these women is beneficial to their male counterparts.

Topic sentence to show similarity

Concluding sentence or summation

Here are the three methods again, together at last:

Method 1: Block
Section 1: Introduction
Section 2: The first topic
Section 3: The second topic
Section 4: Conclusions

Example
Section 1: Introduction
Section 2: WW I noteworthy facts
Section 3: WW II noteworthy facts
Section 4: Conclusions

Method 2: Elements or Features
Section 1: Introduction
Section 2: Element 1
Section 3: Element 2
Section 4: Element 3
Section 5: Conclusions

Example
Section 1: Introduction
Section 2: What the wars were about
Section 3: Where the wars were fought
Section 4: What ended the wars
Section 5: Conclusions

Method 3: Similarities and Differences
Section 1: Introduction
Section 2: Similarities of the two topics
Section 3: Differences between the two topics
Section 4: Conclusions

Example
Section 1: Introduction
Section 2: Similarities of the wars
Section 3: Differences in the wars
Section 4: Conclusions

OR

Method 3, still
Section 1: Introduction
Section 2: Differences between the two topics
Section 3: Similarities of the two topics
Section 4: Conclusions

Example
Section 1: Introduction
Section 2: Differences in the wars
Section 3: Similarities of the wars
Section 4: Conclusions

Now that you have learned the methods of comparing and contrasting, turn back to "Two Kinds of Diners" on pages 302-3 and determine which method Atkinson uses. Write it in the margin.

Write an Essay

Write a compare-and-contrast paper. Choose two ideas, people, events, places, books, and so on, that make sense when compared and contrasted. Check your topics with your teacher, who may want your topics to have some weight. In other words, your teacher may prefer that you do not write about something as unimportant as the differences between summer and winter.

Decide on a method.

Before writing, create a chart to compare elements or attributes (as you did with the chart for two people earlier in this chapter). Or make lists to show the similarities and differences of your two topics.

Play around with your thesis statement. Does it fit best at the end of your introduction, in the middle of your two topics, or in the conclusion?

Use Be Your Own Editor on page 164 to proofread your work—three times.

Submit your chart or lists along with your paper. On the back of your paper, write the method you used.

Word count for **beginning** writers: at least 350 words. Word count for **intermediate** or **accomplished** writers: at least 500 words.

Check your compare-and-contrast essay against this checklist:

- ❑ Are you comparing two things that make sense when they are compared?
- ❑ Do your topics have some importance or weight?
- ❑ Does your introduction show the two topics you are comparing or contrasting?
- ❑ Where does your thesis statement fit best? Check one:

  - o At the end of the introduction
  - o Between the two topics
  - o In the conclusion

- ❑ Is there a logical progression from one point to the next?
- ❑ Is it easy to read and easy to understand?
- ❑ Does it deliver what your title, introduction, and thesis statement promise?
- ❑ Do you tie your conclusion to your introduction?
- ❑ Does writing tie your stomach in knots?
- ❑ Do you draw some insightful conclusions about your two topics?
- ❑ Did you submit your list or charts with your paper?
- ❑ Did you write the method on the back of your paper so your teacher can determine if you hit the mark?

Fill in the chart on the next page to help you divide up your writing tasks or use the chart at the end of chapter 4.

Day 1	Day 2	Day 3	Day 4	Day 5	Day 6

"Literature is a luxury: fiction is a necessity."
- G. K. Chesterton

Chapter 18: Literary Analysis

Lesson 1

Reading a book for pleasure is one type of experience, but reading an assigned story for literature class is an entirely different animal. For school, students analyze what they read in order to make discoveries or draw conclusions, and analyzing is an important tool for students who are training themselves to think.

In elementary school and junior high, you wrote a book report; in high school, you write a literary analysis (plural: *analyses*).

Take It Apart

Analyze simply means to take something apart to get a better look at it. In chemistry, when you analyze a molecule, you take apart all the elements—all the parts—and look at each one separately. When you talk about a car, you analyze its parts—the size of the engine, the design of the body, how low or high it sits, the suspension, the ride, the tires, the paint job, the quality of the interior, the audio equipment, and other features. The same is true when you analyze a poem, short story, play, or novel.

Of course, you don't take it apart just to see it strewn across your desk. You determine how it works, just like the kid who takes apart the vacuum cleaner to see what makes it go.

Here are some example assignments literature teachers may give:

➢ How does Jack's rise to power in *Lord of the Flies* compare with Macbeth's rise to power?

➢ Trace Bilbo's development in *The Hobbit*. In your opinion, what is his greatest change? How does it come about?

➢ What are Lord Henry Wotton's views on women in *The Picture of Dorian Gray*? How does the author make these views known? What is their effect on Dorian Gray?

➢ What is the historical significance of *Tom Sawyer*? How was it viewed when it first was published? How has it changed the way we look at novels?

➢ What are the symbols in *Cry, the Beloved Country*? How do they contribute to the theme and the mood?

➢ Explain Julian's character in "Everything that Rises Must Converge." How does the author communicate this? How does Julian differ from his mother?

Fear not. A literary analysis is simply an expository essay in which you support your view. You will write an introduction, a thesis statement, topic sentences, a variety of paragraph types, and an insightful conclusion. If it is a compare-and-contrast analysis, you will use one of the three types of compare-and-contrast models you learned in the previous chapter.

Which thesis statement below is the most appropriate for a literary analysis?

○ *Fahrenheit 451* is long and boring.
○ *Fahrenheit 451* is about firemen who burn things.
○ Guy Montag learns a lot about books in *Fahrenheit 451*.
○ Ray Bradbury's use of imagery in key places in *Fahrenheit 451* enhances his theme of technology versus nature.

The last thesis statement is an opinion you can prove, and it shows that you have been contemplating the book with deliberation and insight.

Along with using short quotations and examples from the story, you will also use short quotations or facts from **secondary sources** in your analysis. The story or novel is a primary source. Secondary sources include . . .

✓ critics' remarks,
✓ what the author has written about the story,
✓ what other authors or experts have written about the story, and
✓ information you find in encyclopedias, biographies, autobiographies, and online about the life and times of the author, and so on.

This chapter differs slightly from others in this course because, to prepare you to write an analysis, it's a short lesson on literature. That way, you'll know what to look for in a novel or short story.

Here's what we'll cover in the next lessons:

- Setting
- Character and characterization
- Conflict
- Plot
- Point of view
- Dialogue
- Voice
- Theme and Symbols
- Digging Deeper: Motif
- Text and context
- You and your interpretation

Near the end of the chapter, you will have a chance to critique a student's literary analysis.

Select a short story or novel with which you are familiar. Write its name below and have the story or book handy so you can answer questions at the end of each section in this incredibly long and possibly even boring chapter.

Practice 18.1

Lesson 2

Setting

Setting is the **place** and the **time** in which the story happens. *The Time Machine* by H. G. Wells happens in England, slightly south of London and close to Wimbledon. It begins in the late 1890s and jumps ahead to around the year 802,000. The true story of Jonah begins in his hometown and moves to the open sea, then the belly of a large fish, and finally to the hated Assyrian capital of Nineveh (near the present-day Mosul, Iraq) around 790 B. C. This was at a time when the Assyrians were constantly raiding Israel and were bent on annihilating it. When you know the setting, the story will make more sense.

Setting may also include **historical events**. Karen Hesse's *Out of the Dust* makes you feel the grit as you read the hardships of a 14-year-old girl growing up in the dry Oklahoma Dust Bowl of the 1930s. And in reading Anne Frank's *The Diary of a Young Girl*, consider both the intimate, inner world of a young teenage girl and the normal landmark events in her life as you read the wrenching evil of the outer world that stole a normal childhood from her.

The **culture** of the story's time period and place are also part of setting. The ancient Greeks observed a strict code of hospitality to friends, strangers, and even enemies. So did the Saxons and the Vikings. Unless readers understand this, the characters in *The Iliad* and *The Odyssey* by Homer or the saga *Beowulf* will be acting in ways that make no sense today. In the day of *Freckles* by Gene Stratton-Porter, draining a swampland (wetland) and felling its trees were considered wise and prudent even though it seems strange in our ecologically minded age.

Setting can include these:
- ✓ Time
- ✓ Place
- ✓ Historical events
- ✓ Culture
- ✓ Weather
- ✓ Time of day
- ✓ Time of year
- ✓ Sci-fi's future
- ✓ Fantasy's new worlds

Have you ever seen a movie that ends on a happy note while storms and icy rains lash the main characters and soak them through? Probably not. The **weather**, the **time of day**, and even the **time of year** can all signal the mood of a story and are part of its setting. "The Fall of the House of Usher" by Edgar Allan Poe begins on a "dull, dark" day "in the autumn of the year" with the clouds hanging "oppressively low." If you think this guy is in for trouble, you will not be disappointed. In contrast, consider the short story "The Lottery" by Shirley Jackson, a shocking but effective look at how harmful some traditions and cultural habits can be. She uses the good weather and a summer's day in a small rural town to fool readers.

Science-fiction writers such as Ray Bradbury, author of *The Martian Chronicles*, and H. G. Wells, author of *The War of the Worlds*, often use the **future** as their setting. Unlike Anne Shirley (from *Anne of Green Gables*), who thinks that tomorrow is always new with no mistakes in it yet, these sci-fi writers assume that the future is troubled, the governments are haywire, and the people are in dire straits. The science-fiction writer uses this troubled but unfamiliar world as a backdrop for his conflict so readers will take a new look at very real and human problems.

Fantasy writers like J. R. R. Tolkien completely invent **new worlds** for their stories. When Tolkien wrote on the back of a student's test paper, "In a hole in the ground there lived a hobbit," he not only had to explain what a hobbit was but also had to create a completely new world (Middle Earth) in which to put his hobbit.

Take note of a story's setting as quickly as possible. Authors are careful to give these clues early so readers will not be lost. Can you imagine reading *A Tale of Two Cities* by Charles Dickens or *The Scarlet Pimpernel* by Baroness Orczy and <u>not</u> knowing they occur during the French Revolution (late 1700s)? It happens all the time to clueless students. Don't let it happen to you.

You already selected a short story, a favorite book, or a familiar novel. *Practice 18.2*
Fill in all the details below about the setting that apply to your story.
Use a separate piece of paper. Then read the questions that follow and
answer questions 3 and 6.

Place:
Time (year, time period, etc.):
Historical events (if they matter to the story):
Culture:
Weather in the beginning:
Time of day the story begins:
Time of year the story begins:
Future:
New world:

Questions to think about when discussing or writing about setting:

1. How does the setting add to or detract from the story?
2. How does it affect or add to the conflict (the main characters' problems)?
3. How does the description of the physical setting enhance the mood of the story?
4. Determine if these story events are happening in the author's lifetime. What effect does this information have on your reading of the text? What effect might it have had on the original readers?
5. Is there anything confusing, unclear, or incorrect about the setting? What could the author have done to fix this?
6. Every story happens in a number of hours, days, or even years. How much time does this story span?

Lesson 3

Characters and Characterization

Characters come in many types. Below are some common labels. Characters can fit into more than one category.

Protagonists: Main characters are often called protagonists. These are generally the good guys. The reader is on their side, cheering them on. We want Pip (*Great Expectations*) to land on his feet when he loses his way more than once. Even though Jean Valjean is an ex-convict in Victor Hugo's *Les Misérables*, and even though he keeps his past hidden, we champion him and his cause while he climbs the social ladder; we applaud his good heart. The protagonist, or main character, isn't always the good guy; Macbeth (*Macbeth*) keeps making wrong choices, but the reader always hopes he will wise up and be an honorable man.

<u>Short Literature Lesson</u>
Setting
Character and characterization
Conflict
Plot
Point of view
Dialogue
Voice
Theme and Symbols
Digging Deeper: Motif
Text and context
You and your interpretation

Antagonists: Antagonists are characters or forces that make life hard for the protagonists; readers generally do not root for their success, though they may be interested in them. Whatever the protagonist wants, the antagonist keeps him from getting it. Although Miss Havisham (*Great Expectations*) appears to be kind to Pip, she is only toying with him and Estella, making life difficult. Jack (*Lord of the Flies*) becomes the leader of the nasty element on the island and is behind much of the violence. Lady Macbeth (*Macbeth*) wants to be powerful at any cost; there is nothing she will not do to accomplish her goal.

Foil: This character exists to make the main character look good by contrast or to use as a sounding board. Dr. Watson is the perfect foil to Sherlock Holmes. The good doctor often says the wrong thing, giving Holmes the right direction in which to go. Foils appear in stories other than mysteries, too. Shakespeare's Horatio (*Hamlet*) is a foil to Hamlet. Horatio's presence there allows Hamlet to speak his thoughts aloud.

In a slightly different way, Elinor and Marianne (Jane Austen's *Sense and Sensibility*) are foils to each other. Elinor represents the mind (*sense*) and Marianne represents the heart or feelings (*sensibility*). Their personalities play off each other throughout the book, highlighting a raging debate of the day: How should we live our lives—by logic or by emotions?

Comic relief: These guys make us laugh; they relieve the tension. Good writers know they can't keep the tension high throughout a story because readers will lose interest. Breaks in tension are necessary. So some writers use characters as comic relief (or clowns). Not every story has a clown or needs one. Shakespeare is a master at this, though. His *Much Ado About Nothing* includes the constable Dogberry, and *Hamlet* uses Two Clowns as gravediggers in the graveyard scene. These characters often use the wrong words or use words that have double meanings, thus giving listeners something to snicker at between tension-filled scenes.

Christ figure: This character sacrifices himself for the good of others, or he is sacrificed through no fault of his own. Billy Budd (*Billy Budd* by Herman Melville), a likeable and kind character, is "crucified" on a ship's mast by a vicious man who hates him, apparently for his goodness. Sydney Carton, in *A Tale of Two Cities* by Charles Dickens, sacrifices himself for the good of the main characters. While you may object to these non-innocent men being called "Christ figures," this is the literary term for characters of this sort.

How does a reader learn what any character is like? Look for these clues:

1. What the character says
2. What the character does
3. What the character wears or looks like
4. What other characters say about the character
5. How other characters respond or react to the character
6. What the author or narrator says about the character

Writers use combinations of these to reveal the inner workings of their characters. You may find a snippet of dialogue here, a piece of an action there; these characterizations are engineered by the author to bring readers three-dimensional characters.

A note on the characters' physical appearances: God may look on the heart, but writers often use externals to give clues about the characters' character or personality. Sir Arthur Conan Doyle's physical description of Professor Challenger in *The Lost World* paints the professor's go-ahead, self-assured personality: broad shoulders, barrel chest, steely eyes, and "a bellowing, roaring, rumbling voice."

How characters react to another character (#5 on the list) has a profound effect on how the reader will react, too. Consider *Lost Horizon* by James Hilton. The passengers on a small plane have just been kidnapped. One of the passengers is Miss Roberta Brinklow, an English missionary. Almost every reaction the main character Conway has toward this woman is negative. He describes her as "tight-lipped and straight-backed" and compares her to "some rather dingy and outmoded idol." He thinks her clothing is ridiculous and that she is not a normal person. Note here that Conway is reacting to how the character looks, dresses, and carries herself.

When Conway considers what the passengers might do to escape their kidnappers, he thinks about Miss Brinklow, the only female on the plane, and determines that he doesn't want to have to give her preferential treatment simply because of her gender. She should fend for herself. About her mission work, he reports, "Miss Brinklow had her work, vocation, or however she might regard it." When the woman says something kind to the group, Conway reacts by saying it was a "typical" statement for a woman of her sort to make.

Why do readers think poorly of Miss Brinklow instead of Conway, who keeps judging her? Because Conway is the protagonist, and, in other things, he has seemed reliable, straightforward, and reasonable. The story is from his perspective; readers are subconsciously on his side. Be an alert reader. Be aware of how the author is manipulating the puppet strings.

Characterization also includes motivation. Why is the character doing what he is doing? Why does he strike out on a quest? Why does he make a certain decision? Careful authors reveal a character's motivation at the right time in the story. For instance, when Roger Chillingworth, Hester Prynne's lawful but presumed-dead husband, visits her in jail (*The Scarlet Letter*), why doesn't he reveal who he is to the townsfolk? Why does he keep his relationship to her a secret? Here is a glimpse of that encounter, in which Chillingworth gives a list of possible reasons:

> "Why not announce thyself openly, and cast me off at once?" [said Hester.]
>
> "It may be," he replied, "because I will not encounter the dishonor that besmirches the husband of a faithless woman. It may be for other reasons. Enough, it is my purpose to live and die unknown. Let, therefore, thy husband be to the world as one already dead, and of whom no tidings ever come. Recognize me not, by word, by sign, by look! Breathe not the secret, above all, to the man thou wottest of. Shouldst thou fail me in this, beware! His fame, his position, his life, will be in my hands. Beware!"

A careful reading of the rest of the story will show that Chillingworth's motivation is his planned vengeance on the father of Hester's baby, which he warns her about here. His name may give you a hint about his heart.

Grab the book you used for evaluating setting and answer the following questions about it: *Practice 18.3*

1. What is the main character's goal or desire? Is it honorable? How is it thwarted? How does he eventually attain it?

2. Write one example from your book of each item below to show how the author reveals the protagonist's inner character:

   ❑ What the character says
   ❑ What the character does
   ❑ What the character wears or looks like

- ❑ What other characters say about the character
- ❑ How other characters respond or react to the character
- ❑ What the author or narrator says about the character

Other questions to consider when discussing or writing about character and characterization:

1. How does the main character change throughout the book? (This is called the *character arc*.) How are you made aware of these changes (dialogue, actions, reactions, and so forth)?
2. How does he or she resolve the major conflict?
3. Which character do you identify with and why?
4. Who or what is the main antagonist?
5. If the antagonist truly is the "bad guy," what makes him bad? (For instance, Lady Macbeth's desire for power made her the "bad guy.")
6. Are the characters believable and/or realistic? If they are not believable today, would they have been when the book was written?
7. In the beginning of their stories, protagonists are often the underdogs. How is this true for your protagonist?
8. How does the author make you empathize with the protagonist?
9. How is the protagonist likeable?
10. Identify a major decision a main character makes. What is his motivation for making this decision? Is the motivation clear and believable?

Lesson 4

Conflict

Conflict is not a happy word. It feels like a knotted-stomach, put-up-your-dukes kind of word. You may be heroic when confronted with a conflict, zipping instantly into fight or flight mode, or you may be more likely to feel your brain slopping out of its pan as it sloshes to the floor, taking your spine with it. Regardless of how you react to conflict in life, it is an integral part of any well-written story. Without it, the monster roller coaster deflates and becomes a speed bump—not exactly what you want to find in a novel. Other words for conflict are these: problems, difficulties, troubles, issues, tension, battles, strife, struggles, pressure, ills, woes, obstacles, or frustrations.

Short Literature Lesson
Setting
Character and characterization
Conflict
Plot
Point of view
Dialogue
Voice
Theme and Symbols
Digging Deeper: Motif
Text and context
You and your interpretation

If the protagonist's problem is small, inconsequential, or easily fixed, we won't care about him. For instance, if he teaches someone how to make and sell soap, so what? But if he teaches someone how to make and sell soap, and it begins to change the culture, and he attracts the attention of a sly wizard and a wicked queen who plot to take his life, and he ends up barricading himself in a cave fortified with explosives—ah! then we care! (You may recognize this as *A Connecticut Yankee in King Arthur's Court* by Mark Twain.)

Authors have to be rotten to their characters and throw troubles at them left and right. It is the character's job to want something and the author's job to make sure he does not get it. At least, not right away or not in the way he originally wanted it.

The greater the conflict, the higher the potential that exists for greatness in the protagonist. In fact, in some stories, the size or ruthlessness of the enemy defines the potential size of the hero: A huge villain makes possible a tremendous hero.

Consider Beowulf, the Anglo-Saxon hero. He has to battle a huge monster—"a malicious foe"—Grendel, who is ripping people limb from limb and eating them. Beowulf later dives into murky waters and fights Grendel's mother, who is bent on vicious revenge, in a bloody battle. Later, as an aging king, the great Beowulf encounters a fire-breathing dragon that he attacks at a critical moment. These villains and how Beowulf fights them define just how brave and worthy Beowulf is. A man who courageously slays giants is himself a giant hero.

Of course, the protagonist may not be fighting monsters and giants. He may be focused on fighting inner demons of doubt, a history of lying to be accepted, or a fear of some sort. How the protagonist overcomes even these inner conflicts can also define his greatness.

The antagonist thwarts the protagonist, keeping the protagonist from getting what he or she desires. Sometimes the antagonist is not another character but a force such as a violent storm, the character flaw of not wanting to appear as a coward, or the deep grief of losing an older brother to a disease. The saying "He is his own worst enemy" is quite true in literature as well as in life. Whether the conflict originates within the character or from outside, the protagonist has hurdles to jump. A short story may focus on one or two; a novel has more room to develop deeper and more varied types of conflicts.

In some stories, the antagonist is not wicked but is simply the agent of change. Who or what are the agents of change in *A Christmas Carol* by Charles Dickens? Write your answer here:

What types of conflicts may assail the luckless protagonist? Read the list below, with explanations to follow:

1. The character against himself or herself
2. The character against another character
3. The character against society
4. The character against nature
5. The character against God/ the gods/fate
6. The character against technology/biotechnology

1. The character against himself or herself. These are personal, inner problems or character flaws the character has to overcome. He could be lazy, jealous, or prideful. Maybe he does not believe he can do anything positive or noteworthy. These inward struggles drive the character and the plot, as in Robinson Crusoe fighting with his rebellious spirit.

The character need not be battling a weakness or flaw. Consider Digory (*The Magician's Nephew*), who carries a terrible burden of grief as his mother is ill and near death. This later becomes an impetus to obey Aslan and is the avenue by which the wicked Jadis tempts the lad.

Consider the true story of Jonah. What are his personal problems? He always takes the easy way out, he lacks compassion for those he is sent to help, and he clings to a comfortable life.

2. The character against another character. One character (or a few) may pursue the protagonist or make life rough for him. It could be a bully, a friend, an evil villain, or, unfortunately in many contemporary books, a parent or authority figure. In Victor Hugo's *Les Misérables*, Inspector Javert is a relentless pursuer of the protagonist Jean Valjean, even after readers know it is unnecessary and that it will harm a good man.

Jonah, on shipboard, reveals that he is the reason for the storm, but the sailors refuse to throw him overboard. This is a problem for Jonah; he knows the truth about the storm yet will not take action because of his innate laziness and passivity. He will not jump overboard himself. He wants the sailors to throw him into the heaving sea, but they balk at the idea. They keep him from achieving his goal of self-punishment. Later he encounters the king of Nineveh, someone who could have killed him on sight. This meeting is tremendously difficult for Jonah; it is most likely one of the reasons he refused to go in the first place.

3. The character against society. In addition to being in conflict with another character, a protagonist may come up against a whole group of characters who have a different way of thinking—a culture with its own set of rules. In Aldous Huxley's *Brave New World*, Bernard yearns for something beyond the life he finds in the skewed utopian society that values only "useful" things. Flowers are seen as meaningless, as is a love of nature, for it "keeps no factories busy." Bernard rebels against this totalitarian society that controls every aspect of life.

What society does Jonah have to battle? Nineveh was the capital of the Assyrian Empire, which had been fighting Israel for decades. They were Israel's major enemy, one that was determined to exterminate them, and years later, they succeeded. Historically, the Assyrian soldiers have been characterized as ruthless and vicious, and it is very likely that they had already killed some of Jonah's friends or relatives.

Nineveh's way of life, too, was repulsive to Jonah because of its violence and immorality.

4. The character against nature. Nature or physical difficulties abound in stories. Tornados (*The Wizard of Oz*), fire (*Lord of the Flies*), ocean currents and storms (*Robinson Crusoe*), and extreme cold ("To Build a Fire" by Jack London) are only a few troubles nature can throw at characters.

What are some of Jonah's struggles with nature? A storm at sea, a giant fish, trying to stay alive in the giant fish for three days, an arduous journey, and the loss of shelter against the beating sun while his skin was still healing from being burned by digestive juices are some of his troubles in this category.

5. The character against God/the gods/fate. Sometimes the protagonist ends up fighting with God or doubting Him for some reason. This conflict does not surface in all stories; however, it is very present in *Silas Marner* by George Eliot, *Robinson Crusoe* by Daniel Defoe, and *Green Mansions* by W. H. Hudson.

"Character against the gods" or "character against fate" occurs often in ancient Greek plays.

When did Jonah fight against God? At almost every turn. In fact, there was nothing on which he did not fight God.

6. **The character against technology/biotechnology**. This is a recent addition to the list of conflicts because of the proliferation of technology. This conflict occurs in many science-fiction (sci-fi or SF) stories and movies, as in *I, Robot* by Isaac Asimov and in the 2004 movie of the same name starring Will Smith. It also raises its head in *Brave New World* by Aldous Huxley, *The Island of Dr. Moreau* by H. G. Wells, and in the 1999 movie *The Matrix*. Now that you've got the idea, you could add at least a dozen more recent movies to this list.

In many of these stories, humankind is struggling to deal with its own inventions or progress.

As you may guess, Jonah did not have to deal with this conflict. He had enough on his plate.

Every novel, short story, play, TV show, movie, and comic book has a conflict. Even many songs contain conflicts. Get your copy of the short story or novel you are using for these exercises. Write down one place in your story where the character struggles with each kind of conflict. Use a separate piece of paper. Then read the questions below.

Practice 18.4

Note: Not every story will contain all the conflicts, especially if the story is short.

The name of the main protagonist is _____.

His/her problems:

1. The character against himself or herself
2. The character against another character
3. The character against society
4. The character against nature
5. The character against God/the gods/fate

6. The character against technology/biotechnology

Questions to consider when discussing or writing about conflict:

1. In a well-written novel, one large conflict (the *story-worthy problem*) carries through from the beginning of the story to the ending. What is the major conflict in your book? Is it as significant and believable today as it was when the story was first written?
2. Smaller conflicts for the protagonist often surface during the story. Are all these smaller problems resolved by the end of the story? Which ones are not? Why do you think the author left them unresolved?
3. How are the conflicts of other characters related to the protagonist's main conflict?
4. Often, the protagonist has a subconscious goal that is at odds with his conscious goal. What is this protagonist's subconscious goal?
5. What good qualities are enhanced, revealed, or developed as a result of the protagonist's troubles?
6. If the protagonist resolves a conflict in a way you disagree with, how did the author make his or her method acceptable in the story?

Lesson 5

Plot

Simply put, plot is the **events** in the book that entangle the character in the conflict. Plot = the *events*, the *action*. It is what the character is *doing* or *what is being done to him*.

Read any *TV Guide* or other publication for TV listings and you'll find plots galore. Each movie listing has one sentence telling viewers what the plot is. A one-sentence plot for *Robinson Crusoe* might be "An adventurer battles loneliness, starvation, sickness, and cannibals when he is abandoned on a deserted island." *Moby Dick*'s might read, "A sea captain seeks revenge on a famous and deadly whale." Would you watch a movie if the plot were "A scientist turns himself into a monster so many times that he can't recover"? If so, you would be watching *The Strange Case of Dr. Jekyll and Mr. Hyde.*

Many plots look like a mountain range with peaks and valleys, each peak taller than the last. Each successive conflict grows worse. The forward movement of the crises indicates that there is more at stake for the protagonist. Examine the illustration on the next page and read the terms that follow, using Jesus' parable "The Prodigal Son" (Luke 15:11-32). Not all plots follow this shape; plots come in many wonderful shapes and configurations. However, we'll review this classic plot structure shown in the figure because it occurs most often.

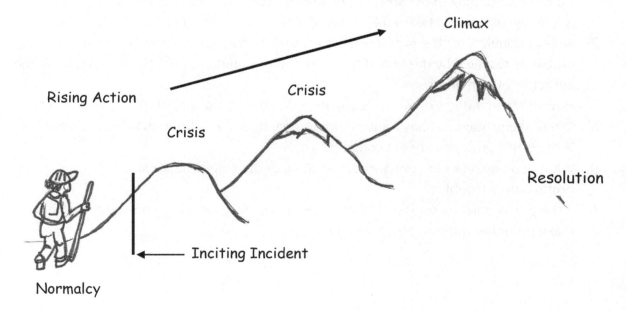

Exposition or **Normalcy:** The author often shows the reader what is normal before introducing the conflicts. That way the conflicts have meaning. Characters are introduced and setting is established. The author can use dialogue, action, or exposition (simply telling as a narrator would). Sometimes the author will begin the story *in medias res* or "in the middle of things." If he does this, however, he eventually has to show the background or find a way to tell the reader what is normal in this character's life. In many older books, this exposition phase can last for many chapters. That is why they seem to move so slowly and finally grab your interest about two thirds through the story. In today's stories, though, this is a fairly short phase—only a few pages, at most.

Jesus' exposition in "The Prodigal Son" is only three sentences long. Right away you know who the main characters are: a father and his two sons. His audience knew that the setting was in their land, for when the younger son left, he went to a "distant land" or a "far country." Jesus set the stage by revealing the characters and quickly introducing the conflict.

Inciting incident: This is the incident that gets the whole ball rolling. In "The Three Little Pigs," it is the appearance of the wolf and his threats. In *A Girl of the Limberlost* by Gene Stratton-Porter, the inciting incident is in the very first sentence, which is dialogue. The protagonist, Elnora, has decided to go to high school (not mandatory in 1909), and her mother is berating her for it. In the movie *Secondhand Lions*, the inciting incident is Walter being dumped on his mother's uncles, two old men who do not want him.

What is the inciting incident in "The Prodigal Son"? The younger son asks for his inheritance, and his father gives it to him.

Rising action or **rising conflict:** Things begin to heat up here. Each event is worse than the one before it and immerses the character deeper into the conflict. This mountain range has turned into a series of crises. If the story is written well, almost everything the protagonist does to regain balance in his life will turn out poorly or will be thwarted. Is this true for the younger brother in "The Prodigal Son"? Absolutely.

Typical Plot Pattern:

Normalcy
Inciting incident
Building crises
Climax
Resolution

First crisis: In his search for happiness, he spends his money freely until it is all gone. Next crisis: the famine. The young man decides to fix the problem by getting a job. Next crisis: It turns out that the employer sends him to tend pigs (unclean and despicable to a Jew at that time). Next crisis: He evidently is not getting paid, for he is not eating. Each crisis is filled with tension as the young man makes decisions and gets into worse trouble.

Climax: The climax is the crisis with the most tension for the protagonist. He must make a decision and break the tension. This is the make-or-break scene of the story. In *The Prince and the Pauper*, the climax occurs when the real prince must prove who he is by remembering where he put the seal of state. If he cannot remember, he will never regain his position as the prince and will be doomed to live the life of a street urchin. The climax in *Peter Pan* is the lad's fight with his old nemesis, Captain Hook. This is the time of greatest tension in the story. Not only does the event have the most meaning for the protagonist but it is also when readers are on the edge of their seats.

What is the climax of "The Prodigal Son"? For the younger son, it is when he approaches his father on the road. He must interact with his father—the person he wronged in the beginning. When the two men meet face to face on the road, readers want to know, along with the son, how the father will react. Will he take him back, or will he throw the smelly guy to the pigs?

Resolution or **Falling action:** This is the time in the story to view the character in his new situation and get used to it with him. If you are sports minded, you can compare this section to the post-game interviews and wrap-up. Most, if not all, the conflicts have been finished, and we read what the new "normal" is for the protagonist and other important characters. The resolution can be as short as a page or as long as a chapter. PLOT SPOILER ALERT! *Lord of the Flies* leaves us on the shore of the island with young Ralph weeping and the rescuing officer looking at the cruiser in the distance, all a few paragraphs long. *The Great Gatsby* ends with a few pages that sum up what happens to Daisy and Tom Buchanan and Jordan Baker, along with some final thoughts about Jay Gatsby and life in general. The resolution in *Les Misérables* takes a few chapters, telling what the antagonist Javert does with himself and how Jean Valjean lives out the rest of his life after he risks everything to reveal his true identity to his new son-in-law.

The resolution to the younger brother's plot of the prodigal story ends with the feast. Interestingly enough, Jesus reveals another conflict there that involves the older brother. He ends the story while the older brother is still angry and before the two brothers meet face to face. Much in this story is unresolved.

Stories can have an **up ending** in which everything gets resolved to the protagonist's satisfaction. They can have a **down ending** where the protagonist fails to gain his major goals, making the reader want to throw the book across the room and wonder why he wasted his time reading it. Or they can have an **ironic ending**, a combination of up and down for the protagonist. In this sort of ending, the protagonist may not have attained his goal (getting filthy rich, for example), but he finds something even better (true happiness).

What type of ending does "The Prodigal Son" have? Write your answer here:

Draw an illustration of your story's plot. Label the inciting incident, the crises, the climax, and the resolution by telling what each major event is in the story. Then answer the first two questions.

Practice 18.5

❑ What sort of ending does this story have: up, down, or ironic? If the ending had been different, how would that change the meaning of the story? Do you like the ending? Explain.

❑ In 50 words or less, write the plot. Focus on the main action of the story, not the conflicts.

Other questions to consider when discussing or writing about plot:

1. How does the protagonist resolve the climax at the ending? Is it honorable? Does he cheat, lie, or "break a few rules"? How would you have done it differently?
2. The author has engineered the climax so that the protagonist has only the choices the author wants him to have. Brainstorm other choices.
3. Are there any subplots (other characters working toward their own goals)? For instance, even though Elizabeth Bennet is the main character in Jane Austen's *Pride and Prejudice*, sisters and parents have separate subplots related to the main plot, often with character goals that conflict with other character goals.
4. What has the main character learned during the story that helps him or her during the story's climax?
5. What part of the book would you like to delete? Be specific.

Lesson 6

Point of View

Someone is telling the story. Someone is revealing inner secrets, guiding or misguiding the reader, dishing dirt. You may think you are receiving information directly from the author (and in a way, you are), but she is only standing behind her characters, making them tell the story.

You will find clues to the point of view (POV) by reading the **narrative portions** of your book, not the dialogue. If the narrative portions contain personal pronouns such as *I, my, we,* and *us*, chances are you are reading a book in first person. The exception, of course, is if the author intrudes himself. But careful reading will determine this.

Short Literature Lesson

Setting
Character and characterization
Conflict
Plot
Point of view
Dialogue
Voice
Theme and Symbols
Digging Deeper: Motif
Text and context
You and your interpretation

Although an author or narrator will sometimes intrude himself, speaking directly to the audience as James Barrie does in *Peter Pan* ("I suppose it was all especially entrancing to Wendy" and "The cooking, I can tell you, kept her nose to the pot"), many choose not to.

Read the following list to determine what POV your story is written in. These are the most common points of view.

First person: Information comes through one person's eyes, and he becomes our narrator or guide. He is telling the story. Robinson Crusoe is the main character *and* the viewpoint character ("I was now in my twenty-third year of residence in this island"), as is Bertie Wooster in *How Right You Are, Jeeves* ("The first thing I noticed about their demeanor was the strange absence of gloom, despondency and what not"). You get first-hand information from the source. You know what the narrator or protagonist is thinking and feeling. Everyone and everything else is viewed through his—or her—eyes.

Sometimes the first-person narrator is not the main character. *Heart of Darkness* (Joseph Conrad) and *The Great Gatsby* (F. Scott Fitzgerald) use a secondary character through which to view the events in first person: "When I looked once more for Gatsby he had vanished, and I was alone again in the unquiet darkness." In this case, you know what the personal narrator thinks and feels, and you know what the narrator makes of Gatsby. But you do not know about the main character Jay Gatsby from any original sources other than from his actions, which are interpreted through the narrator's eyes. This is called *first-person peripheral* (a character is standing on the periphery, the edge, looking in on the story).

Second person: This POV is used infrequently. In second person, the information comes through one viewpoint character, but instead of his saying, "I nailed my thumb to the board with a nail gun," he says, "You nail your thumb to the board with a nail gun and you scream. You stand there helpless, fighting the nail and making the hole in your thumb bigger. Maybe you think of the doctor's cruise to Tahiti that you are helping to fund, and maybe you don't."

In second person, *you* often stands in for *I*. At least, it has that effect on the reader.

Second person always brings with it a tone all its own, and it frequently works in tandem with the present tense.

Third person omniscient: Information is given through the narrator's all-knowing pen. He sees everything and knows everything. The narrator, even if you are unaware of him and he is invisible, reveals the secrets of many characters' hearts and their inner thoughts and feelings as he looks over their shoulders. This POV is in disfavor now, but writers often used it in the 1700s and 1800s. It can lack cohesiveness and feel scattered to modern readers, who want to know only one or two characters, not a whole slew of them.

All third-person POVs use pronouns like *he, his, she, her,* and *they* in the narrative portions of the book. Example of third person: "At <u>his</u> arrival in the market-place, and some time before <u>she</u> saw <u>him</u>, the stranger had bent <u>his</u> eyes on Hester Prynne" (*The Scarlet Letter* by Nathaniel Hawthorne, underlines added).

POV summation

First person: I love riding this Ferris wheel.

Second person: You love riding the Ferris wheel, but you threw up last time.

Third-person omniscient: Cecily loved riding the Ferris wheel. Nigel hated it.

Third-person limited: Cecily felt her stomach turn as the Ferris wheel made its downswing. It made her so giddy that she laughed. She could do this for hours. She looked over at Nigel and noticed his hands wrapped around the bar like a boa constrictor around a baby boar. What was his problem, she wondered.

Third-person objective: Cecily kicked her feet and made the bench swing. This was the seventh time she had gone around. She laughed. Nigel's face turned green, and he clapped his hand over his mouth.

Third person limited (or third person single vision): Information is given by the narrator through one character, most likely the one whose goals matter to the story. You know what this character is thinking and feeling as you look over her shoulder or as you inhabit her experiences. This focuses the events and adds to the tension. You feel her conflict as you view the story through her eyes or experience the story in her skin, even though it is not first-hand information. For example:

> A drop of bleach splattered on the floor and landed in Erin's eye. She shot up and dropped the brush. She grabbed for her eye. It burned. She felt tears spurting into her eye to wash away the sting, but it still burned. The room fell away. Nothing mattered but her eye and that drop of bleach in it.

None of that information is first-hand, but you still know what she is thinking and feeling. Erin is the *viewpoint character* (the character through which you view the action).

Third person objective: The information comes to you as though a reporter were writing it in an objective tone. You do not see into any characters' minds. There are no paragraphs of ruminating or pondering. Everything is revealed through dialogue and action. This is especially effective if the author has a surprise ending, as happens in "The Lottery" by Shirley Jackson.

Practice 18.6   By now you know the drill. Get your story or novel and answer the first set of questions.

1. In what POV is your story written?
2. If your story is written in third-person limited, write the name of the viewpoint character.
3. Is the POV narrator in your story a reliable storyteller? In other words, do you believe him? Are there any places in the story where the narrator's information is incorrect or suspect?

Other questions to consider when discussing or writing about point of view:

1. Authors make a conscious decision about what POV to use. In your opinion, does this particular POV enliven or detract from the story? Explain.
2. How does this POV add to the total effect of the story? If you are unsure how to answer this, choose a paragraph from the story and rewrite it in a POV other than the one the author used. Then compare your results with the original paragraph. How does this new POV change how the story feels?
3. If your story is written in third-person omniscient, narrow down the field and select a character or two to be the viewpoint characters. Which characters did you choose? Which POV fits them and the story best?

Lesson 7

Dialogue or, if You Prefer, Dialog

Dialogue is not conversation. How boring would it be to read the following dialogue?

"Did not!" he said.

"Did too!" she said.

"Did not!"

"Did too!"

"Did not!"

"Did too!"

Yet how many times in real life have you heard (or been in) a conversation like that?

Dialogue is the *illusion* of conversation. It takes out all the boring stuff (one hopes) and includes only what will . . .

- ✓ advance the plot,
- ✓ reveal character, or
- ✓ create tension.

Take note of what the characters are doing when they speak. Their physical actions, called *narrative actions*, can sometimes be a clue to what is really going on in that scene.

A fun example comes from Jane Austen's *Pride and Prejudice*. In the following scene, Elizabeth Bennet and Mr. Darcy are dancing a complicated and measured dance. Every dancer works together in harmony for the full effect of the steps and the motions, like modern square dances but more sedate. In contrast to this, Elizabeth and Mr. Darcy are not in harmony at all; they are sniping at each other:

> He replied, and was again silent. After a pause of some minutes, she addressed him a second time with—"It is *your* turn to say something now, Mr. Darcy. *I* talked about the dance, and *you* ought to make some kind of remark on the size of the room, or the number of couples."
>
> He smiled, and assured her that whatever she wished him to say should be said.
>
> "Very well. That reply will do for the present. Perhaps by and by I may observe that private balls are much pleasanter than public ones. But *now* we may be silent."
>
> "Do you talk by rule, then, while you are dancing?"
>
> "Sometimes. One must speak a little, you know. It would look odd to be entirely silent for half an hour together; and yet for the advantage of *some*, conversation ought to be so arranged, as that they may have the trouble of saying as little as possible."
>
> "Are you consulting your own feelings in the present case, or do you imagine that you are gratifying mine?"
>
> "Both," replied Elizabeth, archly . . . .
>
> He made no answer, and they were again silent till they had gone down the dance.

This is a humorous scene because of the contrast between what the two characters are *saying* and what they are *doing*. And it is good dialogue because it heightens the tension.

Voice

How a narrator tells the story establishes his **voice**. Voice means how the narrator sounds in the reader's ear. An example of an informal, conversational voice comes from Ring Lardner's *You Know Me Al*, an epistolary novel (the novel is a series of letters). This ungrammatical letter writer with the terrible spelling skills, a minor-league baseball player, sounds uneducated and self-important. Note: "De Lukes" means "deluxe."

Old Pal Al: Well Al we been in this little berg now a couple of days and its bright and warm all the time just like June. Seems funny to have it so warm this early in March but I guess this California climate is all they said about it and then some.

It would take me a week to tell you about our trip out here. We came on a Special Train De Lukes and it was some train. Every place we stopped there was crowds down to the station to see us go through and all the people looked me over like I was a actor or something. I guess my hight and shoulders attracted their attention. Well Al we finally got to Oakland which is across part of the ocean from Frisco. We will be back there later on for practice games.

This next narrator uses an informal, conversational voice, too, but it sounds different from the letter writer's. Max, who tells his story in *Freak the Mighty* by Rodman Philbrick, manages to sound irked and world-weary:

That summer, let's see, I'm still living in the basement, my own private down under, in the little room Grim built for me there. Glued up this cheap paneling, right? It sort of buckles away from the concrete cellar walls, a regular ripple effect, but do I complain about the crummy paneling, or the rug that smells like low tide? I do not.

How does this narrator from Patrice Kindl's *Goose Chase* sound to you?

The King killed my canary today.

Now, I know full well that the customary way to begin such a tale as mine is: "Once upon a time, when wishes still came true, there lived a poor orphan Goose Girl," or some such fiddle-faddle. But what do I care for custom?

Scout, the narrator of *To Kill a Mockingbird* by Harper Lee, uses a more formal voice to tell her story. In fact, it is this formality that lets readers know that she is writing it from her adulthood years, looking back:

The Radley Place fascinated Dill. In spite of our warnings and explanations it drew him as the moon draws water, but drew him no nearer than the light-pole on the corner, a safe distance from the Radley gate. There he would stand, his arm around the fat pole, staring and wondering.

All these examples of voice have been in first person, but even a third person narrator has a voice. Consider these sentences from *Uncle Tom's Cabin* by Harriet Beecher Stowe from a formal third-person narrative:

> The subject appeared to interest the gentleman deeply; for while Mr. Shelby was thoughtfully peeling an orange, Haley broke out afresh, with becoming diffidence, but as if actually driven by the force of truth to say a few words more.

How do authors give their narrators such varied voices? By means of word choice, vocabulary, sentence length, sentence structure, dialect, slang, phrasing, figurative language, and so on. The informal voices above use contractions, but the formal voice does not. Notice the difference in the vocabularies of the informal and the formal. Even in the two informal examples, the narrators have widely different vocabularies and word usage patterns.

Answer the first two questions.   *Practice 18.7*

❑ Select a portion of dialogue that is important to the story. How does it reveal character, advance the plot, or create tension?

❑ What voice is the narrator using to tell his or her story? You may use words like *witty*, *engaging*, *lighthearted*, *vulnerable*, *sassy*, *jaded*, *street-smart*, *cynical*, *polite*, *formal*, *educated*, *ironic*, and so forth.

Consider these additional questions when discussing or writing about voice:

1. Does the dialogue seem realistic and do each character's words seem to fit him or her?
2. Do the characters speak with a dialect, as does Huckleberry Finn in *The Adventures of Huckleberry Finn* by Mark Twain? If so, how does it enhance or detract from the story?
3. Select a dialogue passage that uses narrative actions to deepen the meaning of the spoken word (as in the *Pride and Prejudice* excerpt). How do the actions change the meaning of the words?
4. How does the narrator's voice add to the overall meaning of the story?
5. What does the author use to create the narrator's voice?

Lesson 8

Theme and Symbols

"But what's the book *about*?"

Isn't it enough that you've actually read the book without having to come up with an answer to that annoying question?

We read fiction for enjoyment, not to grab a story by the throat and demand that it coughs up its secrets. We want the story to take us somewhere, to involve us with characters we like and some we like to despise. But the question is unavoidable, and you must answer it, at least in school.

A short story or poem often has only one theme. It is too short to allow for a fuller development. But a novel is a cavernous house in which there is plenty of room for a variety of pictures (themes) to be hung.

A story's **theme** is like the thesis statement of your papers: What is the main idea or emphasis of the story? What is the controlling idea? In *The Count of Monte Cristo* by Alexander Dumas, the theme may be stated in one word (*revenge*) or in a sentence: "Revenge only ends up hurting you and the people you love." *The Hobbit* by J. R. R. Tolkien may support a one-word theme (*bravery*) or a sentence: "Adventures are better when shared."

Do you disagree? Was Tolkien saying something entirely different? Good! Let the discussion begin! That's part of the fun of exploring a novel's theme—each reader might see it differently based on the clues the author has left and the experiences that you've lived through.

Authors may intentionally write to support a theme, but sometimes it happens subconsciously because of their worldview or outlook on life. And what is even more confusing is that one reader can identify one theme while another reader can be equally correct in finding another theme in the same story. What you bring to the story—your thoughts, experiences, and background—sometimes colors what you see in it. And that is quite all right. A story involves two people: the writer and the reader. Your interpretation is just as valid as someone else's, as long as you can support it with examples from the book and from the life of the author.

To find a theme, note what happens to the characters, how they react to the conflicts, and how they change. Also look for direct statements that have meaning. In *A Christmas Carol*, Marley's ghost says this in his warning to Scrooge:

> "Mankind was my business. The common welfare was my business . . . . The dealings of my trade were but a drop of water in the comprehensive ocean of my business!"

This passage contrasts the idea of *trade* versus *business* and amplifies the importance of Scrooge's character flaw.

Be a sleuth. The theme might not be stated outright. It might be implied by what happens to the characters.

Or perhaps the author uses symbols.

What are symbols?

A **symbol** is something that has a meaning on its own, but, when used artfully in a story, can take on another, fuller meaning. In other words, it is something concrete used to show something abstract.

For example, in "Young Goodman Brown," author Nathaniel Hawthorne gives the protagonist's wife a hair ribbon of pink. So what? Pink is pink. Unless you use it to also mean innocence. Unless it stands for having faith in what is good, in the ones you love. It is no coincidence that Brown's last name is *brown*, a subtle contrast to the color pink. It is also no coincidence that when Brown is in the woods, viewing what he believes to be the devil's gathering, colors like black, red, and sable are used to describe objects. A far cry from the hair ribbon's delicate pink.

Do any of these serve as your story's symbols?

- Colors
- Names
- Objects
- Events
- Shapes
- Senses
- Actions
- Contrasts

Names can also be used for symbols or have double meanings. Goodman Brown's wife's name is Faith. By the end of the story, Brown has lost his faith in his fellow man, in God, and in his wife. In fact, at one point, he cries, "My Faith is gone!" and "There is no good on earth."

A conch shell becomes a symbol of authority in *Lord of the Flies* by William Golding. Each plane-wrecked boy holds it when he speaks during their beachside assemblies until the rougher group of boys gathers strength and finally despises the ritual. Watching what happens to the conch shell will give you some insights into the novel's theme.

If you find that a particular color, image, event, object, or sense (smell, touch, sound, etc.) keeps cropping up in the story, chances are the author is using it as a symbol. Something as simple as a hat can be used to stand in for or symbolize a character's self-perception ("Everything that Rises Must Converge" by Flannery O'Connor).

If you are a **beginning** writer, skip the next lesson and join the text at Practice 18.8.

If you are an **intermediate** or **accomplished** writer, complete lesson 9.

Lesson 9

Digging Deeper: Motif

What if you find a particular image, situation, or character type recurring in many books you read? Chances are, you have found a **motif** (mo TEEF), and literature is full of them. Through the years and in many stories, a dark forest symbolizes mental confusion or testing. *Snow White*, *The Hobbit*, and "Young Goodman Brown" all use a patch of dark woods in their stories to mean mental confusion for the hapless characters who have wandered into these troubling places. Can you think of another story that incorporates dark woods? In that story, does it mean confusion or testing? Because dark woods are so full of meaning and have been used for so long in literature, they can graduate from *symbol* to *motif*.

The duality of human nature may also serve as a motif. Consider Romulus and Remus (mythic co-founders of Rome), the two-headed Roman god Janus, the twins and doubles found in *The Prince and the Pauper* and *Pudd'nhead Wilson* by Mark Twain, the two-in-one personalities found in *The Strange Case of Dr. Jekyll and Mr. Hyde* by Robert Louis Stevenson, and the town and country versions of John Worthing in *The Importance of Being Earnest* by Oscar Wilde. And don't forget the dual personalities of many major comic-book heroes: Iron Man/Tony Stark, Spider-Man/Peter Parker, Batman/Bruce Wayne, and so on.

The story line of a character going on a quest or the type of character that is the "wise fool" is also considered a motif, as is the magic mirror of many fairy tales and in *The Picture of Dorian Gray* by Oscar Wilde.

A motif brings with it all the meaning that has clung to it through the ages plus the special meaning the author of your book brings to it. Why is your author using a particular motif, and what is she saying about it as she uses it in her story?

Practice 18.8

Answer the following questions:

❑ Other than wanting to eat and pay the rent, why do you think the author wrote the book you've been examining in this chapter?

❑ The author is standing in front of you and is saying, "I wanted you to understand *this* about life." What would "this" be, in your opinion?

Consider these additional questions when discussing and writing about theme, symbol, and motif:

1. What does the story seem to say about the human condition? Do you agree?

2. How does this author view the world? (Negatively, positively, cautiously, boldly, humorously, ironically, etc.)

3. Is the theme stated outright (as in *A Christmas Carol*), or is it implied?

4. What symbols has the author used to deepen the meaning of the theme? How has he or she used the symbol? For instance, when Ethan Frome (*Ethan Frome* by Edith Wharton) sees Mattie Silver with a red scarf, he is entranced by her. Later, when the two of them break an important dish that is red, readers guess that nothing good is going to follow.

5. Have you unearthed any motifs common in literature, myths, or fairy tales? If so, how does your author use it to shed light on the theme or life in general? How does she put a unique spin on it to add depth to its meaning?

Lesson 10

Text and Context

> BIG FAT *SO WHAT!!* In case you forgot, you are reading so you can analyze a story. There really is a reason for all this reading! It may not be a good one, but there is a reason.

When you read a novel, short story, poem, or play, you are reading the primary source or what is called the **text**. The word *text* simply refers to the story you are reading.

The **context** is all the stuff outside the story that may color it and put it in a different light: the author's upbringing; events that were shaping the author and the world at the time; the moral, spiritual, or ethical temperature of those first readers; and so forth. In the figure on the next page, the story or novel is the *text*, and the squares are the *context* through which it is viewed.

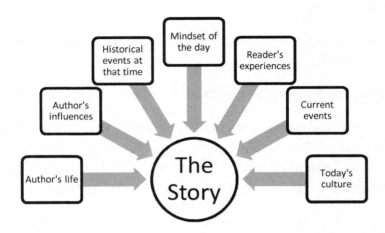

Text and context figure

Here are two examples of how the context can change how we view a story today. This first example concerns the **mindset of the day**. When *A Girl of the Limberlost* by Gene Stratton-Porter was published in the early 1900s, it was common practice to drain wetlands to make them useful for some other purpose. Cutting down old-growth trees also was common. Though there is some sadness on the part of some of the characters concerning the loss of the beautiful wetlands (the author was a naturalist), none of them lead a crusade to stop it. They simply accept it as normal; in fact, one is guarding the marshy forest until it can be cut down. The conflicts are elsewhere. The mindset of that earlier time period concerning conservation is foreign to our thinking today, and if we interpret the story based on our modern ideas, we will have completely missed the personal, human point of the story.

This second example pertains to the **reader's experiences** and comes from Laura Ingalls Wilder's Little House series. Some readers view Pa as a brave adventurer, always moving to new locations to best provide for his family. Others may view him as reckless or unfeeling, especially if those readers have had to move often in their own lives and have known the hardships of losing friends and starting over again with every move. Readers' experiences can color how they view the story and its characters.

Books do not simply spring to life. They have a parent (the author), a family tree (its kind or *genre*), and a family history (where it fits in literary history). A careful reading of the text is important, but so is the book's context. Here are some questions to help you place your story in its proper context:

- What historical or political events were occurring when the author wrote this book?
- What historical or political events, that may or may not have been mentioned, were occurring during the story's setting?

- When was the book first published?
- How did readers and critics view the book when it first came out?
- Is it the first book of its kind? In what way?
- Did this author try something that had never been tried in a story before or was considered questionable at the time?
- Is there anything notable or unusual in the text: use of the present tense, use of second-person POV, the shape of the plot, and so forth?
- Consider the author's life. How is the author's life reflected in her novel?
- Consider the author's times. How might these have shaped the author's views, beliefs, or subject matter?
- Charles Lutwidge Dodgson, author of *Alice's Adventures in Wonderland*, used the **nom de plume** (pen name) Lewis Carroll. Does your author use a nom de plume? If so, why?
- Who were the author's influences?
- To what genre does your story belong (adventure, mystery, historical fiction, literary, and so forth)?
- **Style** is the way a writer writes; this includes her choice of words, sentence length and structure, use of figurative language, etc. Ernest Hemingway's style might be considered spare or terse while Dylan Thomas's might be lyrical and flowing. Is your author's writing style spare, choppy, effusive, lyrical, or otherwise noteworthy?

Secondary Sources

Secondary sources are books, articles, and online articles written about your story and written by critics, experts, and even the author of the story. Biographies of your author and autobiographies are also considered secondary sources. You are looking for experts in the field of literature; a friend's opinion or most blogs are not considered a reliable secondary source.

To truly understand the story and its context, secondary sources are helpful and even necessary.

A warning about secondary sources: Study more than one. Why? Some critics and other experts view the story only through their lens and cannot see the broader picture. They limit their interpretation of the story based on their own worldview, political leanings, and so forth. Which leads to the next warning . . .

Resist the urge to analyze or interpret every story only in the light of politics, gender studies, economic warfare and inequities, the stratification of society into classes, and so on. Yes, your story may address these issues and other important social issues of its day, but if it doesn't touch a human chord somewhere, if it doesn't say something elemental and important about relationships and life as humans, it has ceased to be a story and is merely a social sermon or propaganda. So find the human element in your story; dig for the exquisitely beautiful or depressingly tawdry thing the author communicates about life.

Limit your quotes and information from secondary sources. Avoid padding your word count. Secondary sources are important, but, after all, this is not their essay. It is yours.

You and Your Interpretation

Your reaction to and interpretation of the story can be an important part of your literary analysis. Ask these questions to help you solidify your views and to prepare you to write your analysis:

- Did I react to something in the story (a character, event, attitude, and so forth)? Why?
- Why do I think others react to this book?
- What do I like about this story?
- What do I not like?
- If I have read other books by this author, how does this one compare?
- Other than trying to bore or punish students, why do I think teachers assign the novel?
- What are the ages and genders of the main characters? Does this influence how I feel about the book?
- If I believe something to be a symbol or motif, have I gathered enough evidence to prove it?
- What material from the story will I select to support my views and thesis statement?
- Have I used short, fitting quotations from the book and from secondary sources to support my conclusions and remarks?
- Have I cited my secondary sources correctly?
- Do I give enough summary or information about the story's content to let the reader know what I am talking about?

A Teeny-Tiny, Minuscule Punctuation Lesson

Titles of books, plays, and long poems are italicized:

The Martian Chronicles
Our Town
Paradise Lost

When you write those titles out by hand, you will underline them. When you type them, remove the underlining and italicize them.

Titles of short stories and other poems are set off in quotation marks:

"A Good Man Is Hard to Find"
"Stopping by Woods on a Snowy Evening"

Commas and periods go *inside* the <u>last</u> quotation marks, like this:

The first story Mark Twain ever sold, "The Jumping Frog of Calaveras County," was an instant success.

My favorite poem is Robert Service's "The Cremation of Sam McGee."

Colons and semicolons go *outside* the <u>last</u> quotation marks, like this:

This afternoon I read "The Pit and the Pendulum"; now I can't get to sleep.

I had to look these words up from the poem "The Bells": *tintinnabulation, euphony,* and *expostulation.*

"The Lottery" by Shirley Jackson is a popular story to read in high school. If you read it, be careful not to read ahead because that will spoil the ending. Just read along and go with the flow of the story. Also, if you are going to read it, plan to do so before you read this next student's paper because he will give away important plot points and ruin the story for you.

Practice 18.9
Does he make the grade?

Please be aware that Jackson is not advising that readers imitate the characters in this story. If you read it literally, you will have missed her point. Find the broader, figurative meaning.

You can access this short story on the Internet by searching "The Lottery" by Shirley Jackson. Please take a few minutes to read it now.

Below is a literary analysis written by a student (703 words). His assignment was this:

How does Jackson achieve her surprise ending? In other words, analyze the elements that contribute to the surprise ending.

Read his paper to see how he did.

CAUTION: Plot Spoilers Ahead!

Title and author mentioned in first paragraph

Present tense is used in literary analyses—even if the author is long dead.

After first mention of author's full name, author is referred to by last name.

As a spider draws a fly into its web, so does Shirley Jackson draw us into a web of deceitful cheerfulness in "The Lottery," and we, the unsuspecting flies, are led to believe a tale of happiness, only to be astounded by the simple, brutal truth sitting in the center of the web. But how does she do it?

As any master spider knows, camouflage is pivotal to a successful catch. And Jackson is no novice. She paints subconscious pictures of cheeriness into the story while deftly weaving the story around them so as not to raise suspicion.

The first move Jackson makes to cover up her web is one usually not thought of: the title. The name "The Lottery" has a positive connotation. Readers expect the story to be about a person winning money at the lottery and being overjoyed. Little do they expect the name to mean the process of choosing a person to be stoned.

If the title doesn't subconsciously deceive, then the setting probably will. Jackson paints the weather as being magnificent. In the "fresh warmth . . . flowers were blossoming . . . and grass was richly green." This puts in mind a bright setting that adds to the deceit. The physical setting is a very powerful guise, and Jackson uses it to its utmost value.

Jackson weaves hints of the maliciousness of the tale throughout the story. The first subtle clue is the children gathering stones. Readers attach no significance to this action, though, because any shadow of suspicion is immediately doused by the relatively inherent innocence of young children.

Another, more obvious clue that pulls away a corner of the web's camouflage is the fact that everyone in the gathering is fairly somber. If it were a monetary lottery, everyone would be nervous but excited and fairly cheerful. Not so with this doleful crowd. At this point, observant readers may begin to doubt the pleasant atmosphere of the story.

Then Mr. Summers, a "round-faced, jovial man," asks Clyde Dunbar's wife if she doesn't have a grown boy to draw for her. Why would she need a grown boy to draw for her if it were just a lottery?

Mr. Warner quotes an old proverb: "Lottery in June, corn be heavy soon." Superstitions do abound in isolated places, but that is an odd superstition. He also states that another town is inviting trouble by stopping the lottery. Why would that invite trouble? Old Man Warner reveals that he is surprised at being in the lottery for 77 years. The age is impressive, but what would be the significance of mentioning his age in reference to the lottery? Jackson has given us another peak at the foreboding truth.

The next clue is less subtle. When Bill Hutchinson's family is chosen to draw papers from the box, he is far from ecstatic. In fact, he is "standing quiet, staring at the paper in his hand." Then his wife Tessie starts shouting, "It wasn't fair!" If Bill was chosen, then why is it something undesirable, even to the point of being unfair?

Finally, during the drawing, someone in the crowd whispers nervously, "I hope it's not Nancy." Logically, this should blow the whole ruse. But there are still shreds of the happy tale that was promised in the beginning. Readers might suspect an embarrassing or tiring chore.

Of course, none of these clues alone is enough for someone to decipher the end, but together . . .

Jackson weaves her web so carefully that none of the clues seem anything more than background, so readers ignore them. At the ending, readers are left speechless at their own incredible ignorance and naïveté.

Overall, Jackson is the master spider, and readers are her guests that, though entirely tricked by her web, are enticingly amused and entertained at her craftiness at ensnaring them. After all, readers know that they are safe from the harmful traditions like the one that happens in the story.

Or are they?

Answer the following questions on a separate piece of paper:

1. Write this student's thesis statement.
2. Which story elements does this student mention? (setting, characters, and so on)
3. Do you agree with his analysis of how Jackson achieved her surprise ending? Explain.
4. What is the extended metaphor he uses throughout his paper?
5. Write three of his transition statements that help to move the paper along.
6. Why is the last sentence effective?
7. Give this paper a grade and explain it.

Write a Literary Analysis

Choose **one** of the following assignments:

1. Write a literary analysis of "The Lottery" by answering this question:

In your opinion, will the town ever abandon the lottery? Support your opinion with (1) elements you have scrutinized from the story and (2) your research of Shirley Jackson and the context in which she wrote the story.

➤ Use quotations and examples from the story.
➤ Use at least one secondary source and cite it with an in-text citation.
➤ In addition, use one paragraph to discuss another tradition/habit that today might seem beneficial but is really harmful.

The format for this paper is on the next page.

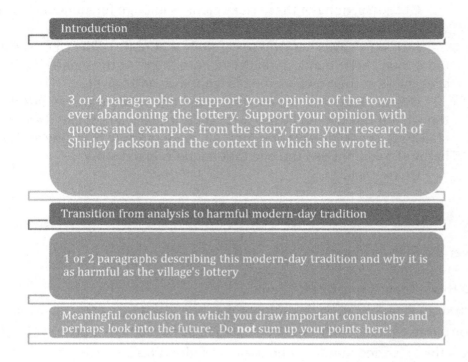

Introduction

3 or 4 paragraphs to support your opinion of the town ever abandoning the lottery. Support your opinion with quotes and examples from the story, from your research of Shirley Jackson and the context in which she wrote it.

Transition from analysis to harmful modern-day tradition

1 or 2 paragraphs describing this modern-day tradition and why it is as harmful as the village's lottery

Meaningful conclusion in which you draw important conclusions and perhaps look into the future. Do **not** sum up your points here!

2. The book or short story you read for English or literature class is likely a classic—something that has been around for many years and has redeeming qualities. In light of this, here is the question for your analysis:

> What are the elements and features that have contributed to making your assigned novel or short story a classic? In other words, why do people *not* forced to read it still read it? In your paper, identify and analyze the elements that have made this a classic.

➢ Use the elements mentioned in this chapter and add others you have learned in literature classes.

➢ Include short quotations or examples from the book or short story to support your opinion.

➢ Use brief quotations from secondary sources. Cite your sources with in-text citations.

Use Be Your Own Editor on page 164 to proofread.

Word count for **beginning** writers: at least 400 words.

Word count for **intermediate** and **accomplished** writers: at least 600.

Day 1	Day 2	Day 3	Day 4	Day 5	Day 6

Fill in this chart to schedule your writing tasks or adapt the chart at the end of chapter 4.

Check this list against your analysis:

- ❑ If your teacher gave you the freedom to choose your own novel or short story, did you choose a classic?
- ❑ Did you read it?
- ❑ No, really. Did you read it?
- ❑ Does your introduction grab the reader with an interesting QSFSQ?
- ❑ Are the topic, story's title, and author mentioned in the introduction?
- ❑ Is your thesis statement near the end of the introduction?
- ❑ Is it something you can defend and support?
- ❑ Did you choose "yes" or "no" as the answer to the townsfolk ever abandoning the lottery, and do you adequately defend your view?
- ❑ **OR** Do you clearly identify the elements and features that, in your opinion, have made your selected book a classic?
- ❑ Do you sufficiently analyze the elements you discuss?
- ❑ Have you adequately supported your views?
- ❑ Do you use short quotations from the book or short story to illustrate your points?
- ❑ Have you quoted at least one secondary source?
- ❑ Have you cited it (them) correctly?
- ❑ Do you use the present tense?
- ❑ Does it all hang together in one thrillingly cohesive unit?
- ❑ Do you use strong verbs instead of turning them into nouns?
- ❑ Do you tie your conclusion to your introduction?
- ❑ Do you leave your reader with brilliant insights into this book and maybe even life in general?

"My definition of an intellectual is someone who can listen to the 'William Tell Overture' without thinking about the Lone Ranger."
- Billy Connolly

Chapter 19: The Definition Essay

Lesson 1

Happiness Is . . .

Occasionally you will have to write a definition essay, and you will wonder why you can't just look up the word, copy out the definition, and be done with it.

Professionals and organizations have to define important terms. For example, doctors and hospital ethics committees have to define the words *dead* and *death* so they know when someone really is. Legal systems have to define *sanity* and *insanity*, and their definitions might vary slightly from the psychiatric community's definitions. How a court defines *competent* will differ from a plumber's definition, which will differ from a parent's. Who knew words could be so complicated?

The expectation for a definition essay is that you explain what something means, using your keen insights and plenty of examples and illustrations. The word you define may be a concept, something like *freedom* or *courage*, or it might be concrete, like *reality TV*, *onomatopoeia*, or *bull market*.

Defining a concept or term is the act of narrowing it down, making it very specific. For instance, if you were to write a definition essay on the word *boring*, your definition might be similar to another student's definition, but your illustrations and examples might vary widely from another's. Perhaps to you it is the height of boredom to be stuck in a library with hours of research ahead of you while to someone else it would be long, slow, tedious boredom to watch Saturday morning cartoons for six hours.

In an essay defining *beauty*, one student might write about mountain ranges topped with snow, edged with evergreens, and hemmed with a pure, fresh stream. Another might define *beauty* as an over-the-shoulder touchdown reception of a thirty-yard pass capping off a fourth-quarter drive with less than two minutes remaining. Two very different illustrations, indeed.

Your essay will go beyond the simple dictionary denotation. It will illuminate the reader with your stunning take on the word's connotation—the underlying implications and what the word implies to you. And, of course, you will draw some interesting conclusions, leaving the reader with something to think about.

Most likely, your thesis statement will be your definition.

Practice 19.1　　　Write a one-paragraph definition of the word *happiness*. Do not use a dictionary. Begin with a one-sentence definition and then, by examples and illustrations, explain what the word means *to you*. Be specific. Use a separate piece of paper.

If you write "Happiness is the state of being happy," give yourself a dope slap and start your paragraph over again.

When you complete your assignment, trade papers with someone who has also written to define happiness. You may be surprised at the individuality this assignment displays.

Word count: approximately 100 words.

Lesson 2

Beyond the Dictionary

Henry Ward Beecher was a minister in the 1800s and the brother of Harriet Beecher Stowe (*Uncle Tom's Cabin*). In 1843-4, Beecher delivered a series of lectures that he put into a book titled *Seven Lectures to Young Men, on Various Important Subjects*. One lecture he titled "Portrait Gallery," in which he warned young men against certain types of people and about becoming those people. The cynic was one type he warned against. Below is an excerpt from his speech, modernized for punctuation and paragraphs. See if you agree with his definition of a cynic:

The cynic is one who never sees a good quality in a man and never fails to see a bad one. He is the human owl, vigilant in darkness and blind to light, mousing for vermin and never seeing noble game.

Definition and a comparison

The cynic puts all human actions into only two classes—*openly* bad and *secretly* bad. All virtue and generosity and disinterestedness are merely the *appearance* of good, but selfish at the bottom. He holds that no man does a good thing except for profit. The effect of his conversation upon your feelings is to chill and sear them, to send you away sore and morose.

Describing a cynic's effect on others

His criticisms and innuendoes fall indiscriminately upon every lovely thing, like frost upon flowers. If a man is said to be pure and chaste, the cynic will answer: *Yes, in the daytime.* If a woman is pronounced virtuous, he will reply: *Yes, as yet.* Mr. A is a religious man: *Yes, on Sundays.* Mr. B has just joined the church: *Certainly, the elections are coming on.* The minister of the gospel is called an example of diligence: *It is his trade.* Such a man is generous: *Of other men's money.* That man is obliging: *To lull suspicion and cheat you.* This man is upright: *Because he is green.*

Defining through illustrations

Thus his eye strains out every good quality and takes in only the bad—as the vulture, when in the highest heaven, will sail by living flocks and herds but comes like an arrow down upon the smallest carcass. To him religion is hypocrisy, honesty a preparation for fraud, virtue only a want of opportunity, and undeniable purity, asceticism. The livelong day he will coolly sit with sneering lip, uttering sharp speeches in the quietest manner and in polished phrase, transfixing every character that is presented: "His words are softer than oil, yet they are drawn swords" (Psalm 55:21).

Adding figurative language, cynic's negative definitions of positive words, and physical description to definition

It is impossible to indulge in such habitual severity of opinion upon our fellow men without injuring the tenderness and delicacy of our own feelings.

Effect of cynicism on the cynic

A man will *be* what his most cherished feelings are. If he encourage appetites, he will not be far from beastly; if he encourage a noble generosity, such will he be; if he nurse bitter and envenomed thoughts, his own spirit will absorb the poison, and he will crawl among men as a burnished adder whose life is mischief and whose errand is death.

He who hunts for flowers will find flowers; but he who hunts for vermin will find vermin; and he who loves weeds may find weeds.

Further effects of cynicism and a warning

Let it be remembered that no man, who is not himself mortally diseased, will have a relish for disease in others. A swollen wretch, blotched all over with leprosy, may grin hideously at every wart or excrescence upon beauty. A wholesome man will be pained at it and seek not to notice it. Reject, then, the morbid ambition of the cynic, or cease to call yourself a man!

Practice 19.2   Answer the following questions on a separate piece of paper:

1. Do you agree with Beecher's definition of a cynic?
2. Do you know anyone like this?
3. Which paragraphs are his examples?
4. Write out a metaphor Beecher uses to sharpen his definition.
5. Write out one of his similes.
6. What physical attribute does he give the cynic?
7. Beecher is specific with his illustrations of a cynic. Give two examples.
8. What is the conclusion to which Beecher comes?
9. What is his warning?
10. Write your own one-sentence definition of a cynic.

Lesson 3

Tools for Definitions

 **Being specific** with your examples and illustrations is the cornerstone to writing a definition essay. Beecher could have written that a cynic makes trouble for everyone, pits people against each other, and is a miserable creature. But those things aren't specific for the cynic. They could be said of people who lie, gossip, are practical jokers, argue, are hypocritical, have to win no matter what, are manipulative, and so on. Reread his third paragraph and note the things the cynic says. They are not general musings that any nasty person might say; they are particular to cynics. In your writing, give specific examples. Be specific.

Below is a paragraph from a definition essay about a pest. The writer is not specific about what a pest is; he does not identify a pest and his irritating habits:

Everyone knows a pest but nobody wants to be around him. He's hard to like, even if you try. He doesn't have many friends. A pest is an irritation I like to avoid.

Try this: Insert these words, one by one, into the above paragraph where the word *pest* occurs—*troublemaker, loudmouth, bully.* My guess is that any of those words can fit just as neatly into the paragraph as the word *pest* does. This is not a good thing.

Write so that if you substitute your main word with another, your essay will not make sense.

These two sentence formats may help you when thinking about your own examples:

- A person is ugly when . . .
- Utopia occurs when . . .

Mention briefly other views of the word you are to define. Take into account how experts define the word and what they say about it. For example, if your word is *intelligence*, you may bring into your essay the views of educators, scientists, authors, or other cultures, all the while using their definitions to shape yours or to contrast theirs with yours. You may also include examples from life and literature to support your definition. You will be specific about what defines intelligence to you, and you will astound the reader with your deep and witty insights.

Use a negative definition. At times, it might be helpful to add an example or definition of what your word is *not*. For instance,

A cynic is not someone who sees the "real" world.

Defining something negatively ("A cynic is not . . .") eliminates extraneous definitions and narrows the field. It adjusts your definition by crossing off other possible definitions.

Use a negative comparison. It might look like this:

Some may say that a cynic is the only rational person in the room. After all, he has the ability to take the rose-colored glasses from his eyes and see life as it really is. But this is far from true.

This has the effect of getting rid of definitions you think are erroneous, and it allows you to show your readers why they can ignore those definitions.

Avoid using a form of the word to define your word. Below is an example of how not to write. This student is trying to define the word *success*—and he isn't very successful:

Success is a personal thing that everyone strives toward; everyone wants to succeed in something in his or her lifetime.

Practice 19.3   Look up one of the following words in a dictionary *and* a thesaurus. When you clearly have a definition in mind, write three negative definitions for your word ("Chutzpah is not . . .") and one negative comparison ("Chutzpah may seem like fearlessness, but . . .").

flattery	education	music	marriage
an expert	angst	wealth	euphemism
spontaneity	graduation	grits	employment
piety	Christmas	prayer	homeopathy

Practice 19.4
Does he make the grade?

Below is a definition essay (301 words) written by a student defining the word *pest*. As you read it, see if you know anyone like this:

A pest is a real nuisance. He comes when I am working, doing my school or relaxing. I want him to get off my case and find somebody else to nag and annoy.

He gets on my nerves and just never stops. This person you may call a pest is more than just that; he is a lifetime pain in the neck. It is one thing to be bugged occasionally, but when the bugging never stops, he is really being a pest.

The pest is very recklessly loud. He uses noise to block out all of my thoughts. I often have an exhausting time accomplishing my homework because the pest is nearby. How can I work on anything with the pest around? He gets near my ear and yells. He sings a little bit of a song over and over again. This pest has enormous vocal force. Oh, he drives me up the wall! When he sets the alarm clock to three o'clock in the morning, it really gets on my nerves.

When the pest gets in my face and is loud, I tell him to leave; he does not. When I tell him to leave so I can get some work done, he does not listen. The pest never does what I tell him. The pest reads over my shoulder out loud everything I am trying to read. The pest wakes me up at a time when I do not wish to get up.

A pest can be anyone. It can be parents, a sibling, an acquaintance or a close friend. Basically, it is anyone who is on my nerves. How many days has he bugged me? How many nights have I lost sleep because of that person who enjoys bugging me? How will I be free from this pest?

Answer the questions:

1. Underline this student's definition of the word *pest*.

2. Can you feel this writer's frustration at this pestiferous person? Write the specific actions this pest does to make himself so annoying.

3. Add some things of your own to his list. In other words, when someone is being pesky around you, what is he or she doing?

4. Underline the words *the pest* each time they occur in paragraph four. Using the same words so many times is being redundant unless you are giving a speech in which you are going to pause for applause at the end of each sentence. Rewrite one of his sentences from that paragraph. Do not include the words *the pest*.

5. This student forgot to include an introduction and conclusion. Write an appropriate intro or conclusion for this pestilential problem.

6. Give this essay a grade. Explain why it earned that particular one.

Write an Essay

Write a definition essay. Carefully select **one** of the following words for the topic of your essay:

Responsibility	Weakness
Tolerance	Communication
Utopia	Rudeness
Ugliness	A hero
Bravery	Confidence
Strength	A hypocrite (or hypocrisy)
Mother wit	Success
A bully	Forgiveness
Conservation	Art

Do NOT quote or refer to a dictionary definition. You may use a quote from an expert only if it will sharpen your definition or be a contrast to yours.

Include a clear, concise, yet interesting definition, as Reverend Beecher does with the cynic.

Use a metaphor, simile, analogy, or other figurative language at least once. Make use of a negative definition or negative comparison, if appropriate.

Proofread with Be Your Own Editor on page 164.

Word count for **beginning** writers: at least 300 words.

Word count for **intermediate** and **accomplished** writers: at least 400 words.

Check your definition essay against this checklist:

- ❑ Is the title appropriate and interesting?
- ❑ Is your definition clear and near the beginning, as in Reverend Beecher's definition?

❑ Is the topic clearly expressed in your introduction?

❑ Are your examples and illustrations specific?

❑ Have you used any figurative language to paint vivid word pictures of the word you chose?

❑ Can another word be substituted for your original word? (Let's hope not.)

❑ Have you used a negative definition or negative comparison where needed?

❑ Is there a logical progression from one point to the next?

❑ Is your definition easy to read and easy to understand?

❑ Does your essay deliver what your title, introduction, and thesis statement promise?

❑ Have you brought understanding and clarity to your word and what it means to you?

❑ Do you avoid redundancy?

❑ Are you wondering what *kokum* means?

❑ Do you leave your reader with an insightful conclusion?

❑ Did you proofread with Be Your Own Editor?

Fill in this chart out help you finish your writing tasks on time or adapt the chart at the end of chapter 4.

Day 1	Day 2	Day 3	Day 4	Day 5	Day 6

Part 5: Description

> *"The greatest writers are effective largely because they deal in particulars and report the details that matter."*
>
> *- William H. Strunk*

Chapter 20: Descriptive Essays

Lesson 1

When you ate your breakfast this morning, did you read the cereal box? Most likely, you found words like *beneficial, whole-grain, healthy, lightly sweetened,* and *great tasting.* Or maybe *chocolate-coated* and *sugar-soaked.* Whatever the case, someone wrote the material on the back of that box. Someone was paid to write descriptively.

Descriptive writing is used for more than just advertising purposes, though. An article for *Popular Mechanics* on the latest stealth plane will include a description of the plane. A newspaper article on a new artificial heart will, among other things, tell readers what the invention looks like. Description is an important tool to have in your tool box, whether you use it for professional writing or for school.

In this chapter, you are going to learn how to describe three things: an object, a place, and a person. So buckle up and hang on.

An Object

In chapter 2, you learned a method of organization called spatial. A **spatial order** uses direction to organize material. For example:

> ➤ Left to right
> ➤ Top to bottom
> ➤ Inside to outside

Description Tools

Spatial order
Specific details
Dominant impression
Sensory imagery
Compare and contrast
Vantage point
Figurative language

The spatial order comes in handy when you write descriptively. It helps you organize, and it helps your reader visualize. As you read the following description of a fish, determine which direction this student used:

> Its tail was an enormous specimen. With one swipe it could dispatch any bothersome thing that would dare come near it. Its scales were as gray as an overcast day, and it must have seen many of these because it was very, very old. Its body was as long as a large van, about fifteen feet, and it was two feet tall and a foot and a half wide. It boggles the mind that a fish of this size could live in fresh water. Anyone trying to catch it would be in for the fight of the century. It possessed strong and powerful fins, but the most remarkable thing about this fish was its head. The eyes were as black as the ocean depths where no light ever ventures. A majestic supremacy shone from them. The way that it commanded its surroundings proved that it was the top fish for miles around. Its mouth was very long and was literally stuffed to the gills with razor-sharp, pointed teeth. This magnificent creature could eat anything that came its way. It truly was the old king of the river.

Write in the margin the spatial direction he used for his fish.

So who cares? It's long, silver, scaly, and wet. A description is just the snooze part of a book that you most likely skim or skip anyway. Right?

Well, you do not have to be one of those writers who bores readers.

Choose **specific details** for your description. Writing about a tree isn't very specific; the word *evergreen* narrows it down a bit. *A feathery white pine* is more specific and puts a particular image in the reader's mind. Choose your details well and make them specific.

Description Tools

Spatial order
Specific details
Dominant impression
Sensory imagery
Compare and contrast
Vantage point
Figurative language

Choose specific details that show how you *feel* about the object. Write three words in the margin that indicate how the fishy writer feels about the fish.

What if the student had negative feelings about the fish? What if he wrote a description of a fish that grossed him out? In the margin, write a few specific details to include in a description of a gross or creepy fish.

Here is a humorous example from *She Got Up Off the Couch* by Haven Kimmel that uses specific details to convey a feeling about an object. How does she feel about the couch?

> The couch in the den was the color the crayon people called Flesh even though it resembled no human or animal flesh on Planet Earth, and the couch fabric was nubbled in a pattern of diamonds. It was best to prevent the nubbles from coming into direct contact with one's real Flesh, so there was usually a blanket or a towel or clothing spread out as a buffer.

Practice 20.1

Think of an object for which you have some positive or negative feelings. Your object could be a guitar, basketball, trophy, special collection, work of art, musical instrument, dirt bike, and so on. As you already know, it is easier to write about something you like or dislike, not something about which you feel neutral.

Write a description of this object and use a spatial direction.

Choose specific details that reveal how you feel (positive or negative) about the object.

Word count: about 100.

Lesson 2

A Place

The spatial order and specific details you learned about in the last lesson also apply to describing a place. And now, on to the next tools . . .

Every detail of the fish in the last lesson was meant to create just one impression of that fish. Write in the margin a trait or impression the student was aiming for.

A **dominant impression** makes a description hang together. It gives it focus. You create a dominant impression by selecting specific details. You also use these other ingredients (we'll get to each of these soon) for a stupendous description: sensory imagery, compare and contrast, a vantage point, figurative language, anecdotes, and reaction.

Description Tools
Spatial order
Specific details
Dominant impression
Sensory imagery
Compare and contrast
Vantage point
Figurative language

You are not writing a description only to describe something. No, that would be too easy! You are writing to convey—to communicate—something to your reader.

Melba Pattillo Beals, one of the Little Rock Nine who first integrated a white high school in Little Rock, Arkansas, in the 1950s, writes about the high school *before* she attended that fateful year: to her, it looked "so tall, so majestic, like a European castle I'd seen in history books."

After she suffered a year of physical and emotional abuse from students, teachers, and local parents, she called the high school "a hellish torture chamber" and "a furnace that consumed our youth."

Due to your experiences, your perspective of a certain place can change greatly.

Below is a set of paragraphs written by a student. Sometimes she likes her room; sometimes she does not. Read these and fill in the blanks with your conjectures of how she feels about her room:

Decorated in a multitude of colors, my room gives the appearance of a happy kaleidoscope. Colorful art work and beautiful photographs grace the cheerful pink walls, and between the pictures, I have hung my worn-out pointe shoes. All the pictures, shoes, and other objects are familiar, and everywhere I look, there is something to interest me. These things feel like they belong here. And to me. A large window over the desk allows sunlight to stream into the room at any time of day. Usually my cat curls up on the softly colored quilt on my bed. Her presence gives a sense of peace to the room. A place where I can do what I like and be myself, my room is my

_____.

■■■■■■■■■■■■■■■■■■■

The Pepto-Bismol pink walls are pressing in. The color seems to laugh at me. Pictures everywhere are driving me to dizzy distraction. To focus on just one thing takes all my concentration. Sitting at my desk trying to type a paper, I almost can't take it. The sun is blinding and makes it difficult to see the computer screen, not that I can see much of it anyway because my cat insists on rubbing the corner of it, which causes it to wiggle. She also takes a wicked pleasure in walking on the keyboard. I just want to get out of this room and do something else. At times like this, my room feels like a

_____.

This student's specific details help create two dominant impressions of the same room.

Sensory imagery will make your descriptions come alive for your readers. It will also help you forge a dominant impression.

What is sensory imagery? Take a look at the list of senses below, with examples of each:

Description Tools
Spatial order
Specific details
Dominant impression
Sensory imagery
Compare and contrast
Vantage point
Figurative language

- ○ Visual imagery (sight)—black and red licorice
- ○ Auditory imagery (sound)—the squish of a shoe in mud
- ○ Gustatory imagery (taste)—a tart apple
- ○ Olfactory imagery (smell)—the acrid, rotting scent of two-day old garbage
- ○ Tactile imagery (feel, touch)—the rough, cold texture of a cinder block
- ○ Kinetic imagery (movement, motion)—a curtain fluttering in the breeze

On the next page are, again, two versions of one place. This time, the descriptions are written from two perspectives—a kid enjoying a pizza place, and an older brother barely surviving the same place.

As you read these versions, watch for a spatial flow or direction that creates movement (kinetic imagery). Also watch for specific details and sensory information that, together, create two very different dominant impressions. These were written by a student.

The first one (193 words) is written from the kid's perspective:

> On top of my favorite restaurant was the mouse, Chucky Cheese himself, with his gleaming eye and a smile that made me smile back.
>
> I went into the building with my brothers and, right away, a friendly worker gave all of us a free hand stamp of a blue Chucky Cheese face! I won't wash my hand for a long time. This is too cool to wash off!
>
> I walked around at first, just listening to the rumble and pings of the Skeet-Ball machines and the whack, whack, whack of someone trying to hit a gopher. It was noisy in there with everyone laughing and shouting. Awesome. It made me feel like jumping inside.
>
> There was only one booth left, so my brothers and I took it. I didn't notice the sticky candy on the seat until I put my hand on it. Everyone laughed. Me, too. Then I licked it off. It tasted like strawberry. My brothers saw me do that and made gagging noises.
>
> We looked at our menus, and all we saw was pizza. Perfect! That's my favorite food. I couldn't wait to order. The day was going too fast!

What is the dominant impression this kid gives you of the pizza place? Write your answer here:

This version (285 words) is written from the older brother's perspective, using second-person point of view. Can you guess what his word *verminophobes* means to him?

> A snide-looking, gray, worn, giant cartoon mouse head plasters the front of the local Chucky Cheese, a restaurant and entertainment emporium for younger kids. It is the face that incites fear in verminophobes everywhere, yet it is supposed to come off as a happy symbol here.
>
> You walk into the entrance with your younger siblings only to have your hand abducted by an overly friendly greeter who presses a putrid-smelling blue stamp on the back of your hand. You can only imagine how many other hands that has touched, how much germy mess is hidden in that blue-colored sponge. Trying not to think about it, you walk into the fray.
>
> Everywhere you look, kids of every age are yelling, screaming, jumping, and running back and forth. Kids bump into you on their way to making more noise. Insanity is too kind a word for this place.
>
> You try to find a quiet booth but soon give up and plop down in the nearest one, landing right in some sticky candy goo. Something sour comes up from your stomach and spreads out in your mouth. You swallow hard. Then you move to the other side of the booth and survey the area.
>
> The floors are covered with the ground-in waste of messy little children. The tables are filthy from half-eaten pizza, spilled drinks, and chunks of breadsticks. The walls pulse from lights suspended from the ceiling, and speakers embedded in the ceiling are churning out throbbing popular music. Your head begins to ache.
>
> You pick up a greasy menu to see what this place has to offer that might help calm your raging stomach. You see only pizza. It's going to be a long day.

What is the dominant impression this older brother gives you of the pizza place? Write your answer here:

Practice 20.2   Using the material in the two pizza-restaurant descriptive essays, identify specific examples of the sensory imagery that feed the dominant impressions:

❑ Visual imagery (sight) -
❑ Auditory imagery (sound) -
❑ Gustatory imagery (taste) -
❑ Olfactory imagery (smell) -
❑ Tactile imagery (feel, touch) -
❑ Kinetic imagery (movement, motion) –

Lesson 3

A Place, part 2

To spatial order, specific details, dominant impression, and sensory imagery, add the familiar tool of **compare and contrast**.

From Rachel Dickinson's *Falconer on the Edge: A Man, His Birds, and the Vanishing Landscape of the American West,* you can see the hunter and the falcons in search of sage grouse in southwestern Wyoming:

Description Tools
Spatial order
Specific details
Dominant impression
Sensory imagery
Compare and contrast
Vantage point
Figurative language

> The sun is just peeking above the horizon, illuminating the desert floor with sharp rays of light like knife points, piercing the woody branches of the low-slung sagebrush at oblique angles. Miles and miles of sagebrush, more gray than green, surround the Toyota holding the falcons, the dogs, and the hunter. In the predawn light, the desert vegetation had looked soft, as if, if you could reach out and stroke it, it might tickle your hand. But the light shards of dawn show the plants for what they really are: Prickly. Sharp. A million hiding places for a chicken-sized bird.

What is being contrasted? How does the contrast give a clearer picture of the desert? Write your answers here:

The **vantage point**, the perspective from which you view the action or narrative, is either moving or stationary. The vantage point in the above pizza-restaurant descriptions is moving: from the outside the restaurant to the entrance to the game room to the dining room. Below is an example of a stationary, or unmoving, vantage point:

Description Tools
Spatial order
Specific details
Dominant impression
Sensory imagery
Compare and contrast
Vantage point
Figurative language

> Sitting here on the roof of my house, I hear the trees shaking their leaves like a wet dog after a romp in the rain, the wind blowing the last of the rogue leaves from the gutters, and the rushing sound of traffic from a nearby road. A few lone birds fly by on their way to the neighbor's feeder. The sun warms the tan shingles, and suddenly I am sitting on a warm, sandy beach.

Even though there is a sense of movement (kinetic imagery) here in the leaves shaking, the wind blowing, the traffic rushing, and the birds flying, the vantage point of the narrator up on the roof never changes. He is sitting still on the warm, tan shingles.

Description Tools
Spatial order
Specific details
Dominant impression
Sensory imagery
Compare and contrast
Vantage point
Figurative language

Figurative language can give depth and meaning to your description. You've already studied similes, metaphors, personification, hyperbole, and analogies in this course. What word picture does Isak Dinesen paint of the arid African highlands in this analogy?

The early morning air of the African highlands is of such a tangible coldness and freshness that time after time the same fancy there comes back to you: you are not on earth but in dark deep waters, going ahead along the bottom of the sea. It is not even certain that you are moving at all, the flows of chilliness against your face may be the deep-sea currents, and your car, like some sluggish electric fish, may be sitting steadily upon the bottom of the Sea, staring in front of her with the glaring eyes of her lamps, and letting the submarine life pass by her.

Practice 20.3   Write a description of a real place, a place you have been to and seen. Brainstorm details before you begin to write.

Create a positive dominant impression of it by clever use of a combination of any of these tools: spatial orientation, specific details, sensory imagery, compare and contrast, a vantage point, and figurative language.

A word of caution: Choose a place. Choose an impression. Choose a vantage point. Then just write. After you have written your first draft, you can add the spatial orientation, specific details, and so forth. Avoid writing _and_ adding at the same time.

Word count for **all** writers: 100-250.

After you have written your descriptive paragraphs of a place, write another one of the _same place_ (same word count). This time, create a **negative** dominant impression of it. Hand in both essays.

Lesson 4

Describing a Person

Normally each chapter ends after you write something. It is my sad duty to inform you that, unfortunately, that is not the case with this chapter. You've written, but we need to plow on. Next up: describing a person.

Let's begin with you. Yes, it's time to describe yourself. On a separate piece of paper, write a few sentences to describe yourself as you would in a letter to an exchange student your family soon will be hosting. No, you cannot simply send a picture.

Practice 20.4

After you finish that first description, describe yourself again. This time, the exchange student is traveling by airplane to meet you. He or she is sight impaired and will not be able to identify you by visual inspection. Describe yourself so your new pal will know it is you when you bump into each other in the airport. What sensory details, other than sight, will you use? You are not allowed to identify yourself by singing a song or muttering a spy phrase such as "The duck flies at midnight."

For the third and last time, describe yourself again. This time, you are interviewing for a job you really want. How will you describe yourself to your prospective employer?

Notice how you described yourself differently as each occasion called for it. This is like the slant or angle you used when writing a biography. You did not tell everything, but you selected details that were consistent with the purpose of the essay, giving you a focus. This helps your writing feel clearer and less scattered.

Not through yet.

Do you know anyone like this dance student?

Samantha is tall and willowy. Each movement is as precise and delicate as a paper birch in a light breeze. If Narnia is missing a dryad, I know where you can find her.

Description Tools

Spatial order
Specific details
Dominant impression
Sensory imagery
Compare and contrast
Vantage point
Figurative language

Let's use this short paragraph to revisit the topic of **figurative language** because everything you've already learned in the list on the left, from spatial order to figurative language, also can be used when you describe people.

You likely have a very distinct image of the dancer. The writer selected specific details and used figurative language to compare this young woman, whom you have not seen, with objects you have seen. She used a simile ("as precise and delicate as a paper birch"), a metaphor ("willowy"), and an allusion (a dryad, in Greek mythology, is a wood nymph; Narnia is the land C. S. Lewis created, in which you will find dryads).

Using figurative language will make your descriptions clearer and more enjoyable (translation: *less boring*).

Practice 20.5   Select a friend, classmate, neighbor, or family member to describe. Brainstorm this person's attributes you could write about and then select one. Make a list of specific details to reveal this attribute to readers.

Write one paragraph of no more than 100 words to describe this person. Use specific details and figurative language to show the attribute you selected. Use a separate piece of paper.

Lesson 5

Describing a Person, part 2

Describing a person uses all the writing tools you have learned in this chapter. It also uses skills you have learned earlier in this course: brainstorming ideas, choosing facts and examples to illustrate your points, organizing your material in a logical order, developing a flexible thesis statement, and drawing some stunning conclusions. That list contains nothing new.

Below, however, are a few new things.

When describing a person, consider asking yourself a few questions before you write:

- ✓ What is the trait, attribute, or dominant impression I want to convey to my reader?
- ✓ What specific details can I include that will contribute to the dominant impression?
- ✓ What anecdotes can I include?
- ✓ What recurring activities can I include?
- ✓ What don't I want to leave out when I write about this person?
- ✓ What conclusions can I draw that are centered on this person or on what I've learned from this person, not on what others should do.

An **anecdote** is a true story, usually complete with dialogue and **narrative action**. Narrative action simply means the movements or gestures a person performs when in the story. "He flopped down on the couch and shoveled in popcorn with his grimy fists" gives a clearer picture to the reader than "He sat on the couch and ate popcorn." What anecdotes and narrative actions will best portray your person to the reader?

Here's an anecdote taken from a student's essay about her ninety-year-old dance teacher, in which is conveyed a forceful personality:

> Miss Dottie didn't stand for things she didn't like. During the hours that she reigned each evening, everything went Miss Dottie's way. Everything.
>
> Miss Dottie's home and basement studio were in the city and right in front of a busy intersection. One evening during class, a car waiting at the stoplight was blaring very loud music. It was interfering with Miss Dottie's music, and she wasn't about to stand for it. Before we students could even scurry to the window, Miss Dottie had made it up the stairs and out the front door all while muttering about today's crazy kids and their impolite music. In less than a minute, we heard the music cease. The front door slammed, and Miss Dottie, still mumbling about giving the driver a piece of her mind, appeared in front of us. I almost felt sorry for the driver and wondered if he would ever play music within a block of Miss Dottie's domain again.

A **recurring activity** is something repeated over a period of time—a hog-tying contest every Saturday night or a yearly visit to a museum, for instance. Which recurring activities will underline your person's trait or significance?

It looks as though speeding is a recurring activity in the next example; this student encounters it more than once when riding with his nineteen-year-old friend:

> I will never forget the time when Jamie almost got us killed. He was driving, taking my brother and me home from a movie, when it started raining. I thought nothing of it, and obviously neither did Jamie. He was speeding and changing lanes when the light changed to red. He slammed on the brakes. The car fishtailed. I jammed my foot to the floor, a desperate lunge for brakes, and grabbed the door handle. Praying might have occurred. I was sure we were going to hit the cars around us. Where are the police when you need them, I thought. This guy needs a ticket!
> Another time he and I were driving back home from a War of 1812 reenactment when a police officer pulled Jamie over for speeding.

Description Tools

Spatial order
Specific details
Dominant impression
Sensory imagery
Compare and contrast
Vantage point
Figurative language
Anecdote
Recurring activity
Reactions

Trait

Anecdote to prove the trait

Narrative actions of scurrying, slamming a door, and mumbling

Reaction of student to event

Description Tools

Spatial order
Specific details
Dominant impression
Sensory imagery
Compare and contrast
Vantage point
Figurative language
Anecdote
Recurring activity
Reactions

First mention of recurring activity

Second mention of recurring activity—with a different outcome

Yes! Finally a ticket!

She gave him a warning, which makes two now, and let him go.

"Because you were honest, I'm only going to give you a warning," she said.

I wanted to lean over and shout to her, "No! Give him the ticket!"

"Thank you so much, Officer," sighed Jamie. He had been honest with the police officer, but he wasn't even close to sorry. This brush with the law would scare most people into driving slower, but within ten minutes, Jamie was speeding again. I jabbed my finger at the speedometer, but he ignored me.

The first time Jamie speeds, his friend wishes the police were around to give him a ticket for unsafe driving. When one finally enters the second occurrence, she gives him only a warning. This warning, coupled with the earlier rainy-night incident, creates a higher frustration in the student's mind and maybe in the reader's, too. Telling the story of a recurring activity—and including a time when the activity or the results were different—can make your description of the person's trait stronger.

Description Tools

Spatial order
Specific details
Dominant impression
Sensory imagery
Compare and contrast
Vantage point
Figurative language
Anecdote
Recurring activity
Reactions

Include your **reactions**, thoughts, and feelings to events in your description. TV and movie directors rely on a reaction shot to show how a character reacts to an event, another character, or a bit of dialogue. When you view the show or movie, you see the event or hear the dialogue and, in the very next frames, you see a character's reaction. Why?

How the character reacts to an event influences how viewers interpret it. The character's reaction forms your opinion and gives you an idea of how important the event is. These reactions help interpret the event for you.

Learn to do this in your narrative writing. An event becomes significant to the reader when you include your thoughts, feelings, and reactions. If you do not show the event's importance in this way, the reader will think it is unimportant.

The student feeling sorry for the driver playing loud music tells readers that Miss Dottie can take care of herself. The student's reactions of jamming his foot on an imaginary brake, thinking they were going to die, and then wanting to tell the officer to give Jamie a ticket all show that Jamie's speeding habit is a serious problem, not one to joke about.

Below is a descriptive essay written by a student (549 words). In it, he describes his older brother and tells an anecdote to support his brother's trait of competitive cruelty.

Practice 20.6
Does he make
the grade?

Read it through once for the content. Then read it through a second time to find the answers to the questions that follow the essay.

Whether it was wrestling on the floor or quarreling, Adam always had to win. He constantly stirred up some kind of trouble between us. At one point we would be brothers, and the next thing you know, we would be mortal enemies in a duel to the pain, using both wits and brawn. Teasing me was his pastime, and laughing at the results of his teasing was his pleasure. Was it his flaming red hair? Was it just an older-brother syndrome that made him mean to me? I do not know. But like a hyena preys on smaller animals, so would Adam prey on his little brother—me. This seemed to be especially true one time in particular.

On a normal summer's day just like any other, Adam and I were in the house alone. Only this time was destined to be different.

I had just opened a bag of ready-made Caesar salad for my lunch. I appreciated the convenience of having an instant meal, and I most thoroughly enjoyed the many flavors in the Caesar salad. But apparently Adam had been eyeing the single serving, too, but had not let me know his intentions.

As I sat at the counter digging into my lunch, Adam stormed up to me and got in my face.

"What do you think you're doing?" he demanded. His green eyed drilled into my soul. I shifted on my seat.

"Well, obviously, I'm eating lunch," I replied, ready to run at the first sign of danger.

Adam looked me over as if evaluating a slug. His freckle-covered face and round cheeks tensed. "That was my salad!"

Instantly he thrust his big, clammy, pale hands toward me, but I was already up and away, running as if my life depended on it.

I did not stop to see what Adam would do to me, for I was sure it would be most unpleasant. I heard his powerful legs crashing across the floor behind me. I kept running until I came to a sharp turn into another room. I quickly attempted to dig my toes into the slick hardwood floor but to no avail. My foot smacked the corner of the door frame, breaking my big toe.

Pain shot up through my foot and leg as I hit the ground and curled into a fetal position. Tears welled up in my eyes from the fire in my toe lighting up my nerves. I was almost certain at the time that it would never heal and that I would be cursed with a misshapen toe forever.

I sat up and cupped my injured toe in my hands. Adam walked up to me and laughed.

"Come on. Get up and get over yourself. It's not that bad," he said. "And, see, if you hadn't run from me, you wouldn't have hurt yourself, now would you?

Adam looked me over and then walked away, leaving me to my throbbing toe.

The teasing and the meanness continued every day until he moved out of the house. Only then did the teasing stop. After all the experiences that I had with Adam, I learned to be kind to my younger siblings. I really don't want to treat them like Adam treated me. Even from unpleasant people I can learn important things.

Answer the following questions:

1. Do you know anyone like Adam? Do you know anyone in the younger brother's situation?
2. This student distributed throughout the essay the physical description of his brother. Underline those descriptions.
3. Put an arrow next to a narrative action of either Adam or the younger brother.
4. Put a star next to a reaction. (A narrative action can be a reaction.)
5. This student turned the negative influence his brother had on him into a positive resolution. What is his resolution?
6. If you were in this situation, what would your resolution or conclusion be? Write it in the margins.

Write an Essay

Write a descriptive essay about a person who has had an influence in your life, whether negative or positive. This person must be someone you know personally, not a hero, saint, celebrity, animal, or deity.

Before you write, reflect on the person and how he or she has influenced you. Make lists of events, anecdotes, and other examples you might include to bolster the dominant impression you want to convey.

Include a short physical description, whether in one paragraph or cleverly scattered throughout your narrative in the form of narrative actions, or, more likely, a combination of the two.

After you have written your first draft, go back and include the tools you've learned in this chapter: a spatial order, specific details, dominant impression, sensory imagery, and so on.

If you are a **beginning** writer, your word count is 400.

If you are an **intermediate** or **accomplished** writer, your word count is 600.

Fill in this chart to help you finish your writing tasks on time or adapt the chart at the end of chapter 4.

Day 1	Day 2	Day 3	Day 4	Day 5	Day 6

Here's your describe-an-influential-person checklist:

Did you . . .

- ❑ Choose a person who has influenced you, someone you know personally?
- ❑ Give a short physical description of this person?
- ❑ Include an anecdote or two about the person?
- ❑ Include a recurring activity that highlights the trait you want readers get?
- ❑ Use a spatial description (a direction) where appropriate?
- ❑ Use specific details, including powerful verbs?
- ❑ Use sensory imagery?
- ❑ Use figurative language?
- ❑ Include narrative actions with the conversations?
- ❑ Punctuate the conversations correctly? (See lesson 5 in chapter 10.)
- ❑ Include your reactions or your person's reactions to events?
- ❑ Reflect on how the person has influenced you?

Does all of the above contribute to the dominant impression? Circle one: No   Somewhat   Yes

What dominant impression do you want to convey to your reader? Write it here by finishing the sentence: I want to show the reader . . .

Part 6: Narration

> *"The only end of writing is*
> *to enable the reader better to enjoy life,*
> *or better to endure it"*
> *- Samuel Johnson*

Chapter 21: Personal Testimony or Spiritual Journey

Lesson 1

Narration? What's narration doing in a book on nonfiction?

Narration can be either fiction or nonfiction. In fiction writing, it means telling made-up stories, but in nonfiction writing, it means writing true stories about real people.

In the following chapters, you will adapt an interview into a narrative style and write a personal narrative from your own experience.

In this chapter, however, you will write your own personal testimony. But you will not call it a testimony because *testimony* used in this sense is Christian jargon. And you will remember from previous chapters that you are to avoid jargon for audiences that don't speak your language. Instead of *testimony*, which may conjure up images of courtrooms, judges, and lawyers, we'll use the phrase *spiritual journey*.

No Christianese

Christianese is a term for language that works well in your church but only confuses people who are unfamiliar with the words. The hymn "There Is a Fountain Filled with Blood" may be comforting to some, but others may think of weird and ghastly Halloween rituals. Writers can become used to certain jargon or technical terms and forget that others do not understand what they mean.

Here's an example of how using Christian jargon can confuse people:

> When I was a young girl, I attended a yearly church camp. We had morning and evening meetings in a *tabernacle* and people *went forward* to *pray through* at an *altar,* all jargon I completely understood. One year, the altar needed repairs, so some of the women of the camp volunteered to fix it. They went to a local hardware store and talked to one of the employees.
>
> "We need some planks," the women said.
>
> "What for?" the fellow asked.
>
> "We need it for our altar. We need it for people to pray through on."
>
> "Well, if people pray *through* it, don't you need a pipe?"
>
> No kidding. This is the conversation as reported back to us by the women. And who can blame the hardware store employee? He was not making a joke; he just didn't speak our language.

Even the word *Christian* has so many meanings today in various parts of the world that the term needs to be defined before a serious conversation on the subject can even occur. Write your own definition of *Christian* in the margin. Then ask at least two other people how they define the word and compare notes.

Each religion and denomination has its own set of religious terms that might be hard for those on the outside to understand. Your jargon may not be the same as a friend's.

Don't misunderstand. It is perfectly all right to use these words—when you are with others who understand the language. For other people, however, try to adapt your words to fit their ears. You will not change the meaning of the words; you will simply use synonyms.

Practice 21.1   On the next page are some religious words that Christians from varying backgrounds use but that others might not understand. In fact, you may not understand all of them. Put the ones you recognize into a language that a friend not familiar with church language will understand. In this way, you are writing for a specific audience. For instance, for the word *pray*, you might write *talk to God*. Use a separate piece of paper.

Share your definitions with others in your class or group.

1. having devotions
2. an altar call
3. Bible
4. prayer of salvation/sinner's prayer
5. communion
6. excommunication
7. serve God
8. immutability
9. redemption
10. immaculate conception
11. felt conviction
12. God

Continuing on . . .

You Can't Say That Name Here!

Many countries, provinces, and states are passing laws in which ministers who open governmental sessions are not allowed to mention any religion in their prayers. More specifically, ministers are not allowed to mention the words *Jesus, Savior, Son of God,* or any other words that would indicate a preference for Christianity. The word *God* is generic enough to be permissible in public prayers, though.

Write three separate prayers as though you are a minister opening the legislative session for your country that does not allow you to mention words referring to the God of Christianity. *Practice 21.2*

In the **first** prayer, use generic religious words that will not ruffle any feathers.

In the **second** prayer, use veiled references to the God of Christianity and his son Jesus. Find ways to insert Him without actually using his name.

In the **third** prayer, use any words at all that will definitely refer to the fact that you are praying to the God who created us and/or to his son Jesus.

Use a separate piece of paper.

Lesson 2

Your Story

What's your story? Whether or not you are a Christian, you have thought about spiritual things and have come to some conclusions. You might also have had some religious or Christian experiences.

Josh McDowell, a famous writer, speaker, and Christian apologist, begins his testimony—oops! his spiritual journey—this way in *Evidence That Demands a Verdict*:

> Several years ago my life was described by Thomas Aquinas when he said that within every soul there is a restless thirst for happiness. I wanted to be happy. Who doesn't want to be happy?
>
> . . . First I thought that the answer might be religion, so I went to church. But I never found anything that changed my life. I've always been a very practical person, and if something doesn't work, I chuck it. So I chucked religion.

He goes on to describe his search for happiness and meaning and how he found it in the religion he had originally rejected (Christianity).

C. S. Lewis, famous for his Chronicles of Narnia series, writes this about his spiritual journey in *Surprised by Joy*. A *Theist* is one who believes that there is a God or a god.

> As soon as I became a Theist I started attending my parish church on Sundays and my college chapel on weekdays; not because I believed in Christianity, nor because I thought the difference between it and simple Theism a small one, but because I thought one ought to "fly one's flag" by some unmistakable overt sign . . . . [T]he fussy, time-wasting botheration of it all! the bells, the crowds, the umbrellas, the notices, the bustle, the perpetual arranging and organizing. Hymns were (and are) extremely disagreeable to me. Of all musical instruments I liked (and like) the organ the least. I have, too, a sort of spiritual *gaucherie* which makes me unapt to participate in any rite.

The whole book is a map of his spiritual journey to the God of Christianity. You may not be as famous—yet—but you do have a spiritual story to tell, even if you do not consider yourself to have arrived at your final destination.

The important thing to remember in writing your spiritual journey is to keep it as narration, that is, as your personal story. Avoid the temptation to preach or to say what others should do with the information or facts that changed your life.

This is not a devotional or a sermon. This is not exposition (teaching or explaining). It is narration—telling a story. Let your life story speak for itself.

A student wrote a slice of her spiritual journey as she faced many changes in her life (370 words). Can you identify with what she is experiencing?

Practice 21.3
Does she make the grade?

> I am standing at a crossroads, making some of the most important decisions of my life. I have learned a lot, yet there are many things I don't know. The entire world is open for me if I want it. Yet I am unsure. At a time when I am supposed to have it all figured out, I am not certain of anything. I can have the world, but I am afraid.
>
> Maybe I am a little afraid of getting older. Maybe I am a little worried that I'll become a loser or that people will think I'm a loser. Maybe I am a little concerned that in the process of making monumental decisions or just getting through everyday life, I'll lose sight of what is really important to me.
>
> True to my nature, I revert to my eight-year-old self. I remember being eight. I was afraid that something would reach out from under the bed and drag me under. I hated the thought so much that I would get a running start and jump into bed. If all else failed, I could always yell and scream for my parents.
>
> But it is getting harder to scream for help. I stand next to my bed and realize that I have to grow up now. I am no longer eight. But the fear that lurks in the back of my mind is stronger than the idea of monsters. It takes more than a flashlight to drive it away. I am at a crossroads.
>
> I didn't mean to find it. I don't even remember picking up my Bible. But there it was in my hand. It opened up to Mark 4:40: "Why are you so afraid? Do you still have no faith?"
>
> Here I am—that girl who is unsure of everything and so very afraid of moving forward. There God is, telling me that I'm being silly and that there is nothing to be afraid of.
>
> Though it's scary, I'm more than ready to push the limits of my faith and move on. Maybe tonight my jump from the monster will be smaller. Maybe tomorrow I'll make it even smaller. Maybe, eventually, I won't even remember what made me so afraid.

Answer the questions on a separate piece of paper:

1. Do you identify with this young woman who is making major life decisions?
2. What do you do when you are afraid or unsure of yourself?
3. Does she write anything that is helpful to you?
4. Does she use any Christianese?
5. Give this paper a grade and explain it.

Write a Narrative

Write your spiritual journey (personal testimony). This is not a sermon or a theological discussion. It is not your life story. It is only a sliver or snippet of it.

Keep your narration centered on *your* story, not on what others should do. In other words, simply tell your story or some part of it.

Avoid Christianese. Assume your audience is unfamiliar with church or religious lingo.

You need not write about a conversion experience. Perhaps you learned something valuable in your spiritual journey. Did God answer a specific prayer? Have you had a moving experience that pointed you to God? Any of these stories will have value as a spiritual journey story. Work hard at expressing your story in plain words that anyone can understand.

Proofread with Be Your Own Editor on page 164.

Word count for **beginning** writers: at least 350 words. Word count for **intermediate** and **accomplished** writers: at least 500.

Check out this check list for your spiritual-journey narrative:

- ❑ Did you write about an important time in your life when you learned something?
- ❑ Did you include what you learned?
- ❑ Did you avoid Christianese?
- ❑ Did you avoid preaching or teaching?
- ❑ Did you tell your tale in a clear, concise, and chronological manner?
- ❑ Have you checked under your bed lately?

Fill in this chart to help you schedule your writing tasks or adapt the chart at the end of chapter 4 to your needs.

Day 1	Day 2	Day 3	Day 4	Day 5	Day 6

"Talent is helpful in writing, but guts are absolutely necessary. Without the guts to try, the talent may never be discovered."

- Jessamyn West

Chapter 22: Interview into Narrative

Lesson 1

Do you know someone who was a prisoner of war? Does your neighbor tutor adults in reading? Does that man in your church train dogs to work with police? Did a parent live through a frightening event?

The 96-year-old woman who lives in your neighborhood has lived nearly a century, and she has seen a lot of changes. Readers may be interested reading about a time when a toothbrush and a wicker clothesbasket were considered nice birthday presents and when women did not go on trips unless accompanied by a chaperone.

Some people feel too shy to conduct interviews. But shy people can be the best interviewers because they listen well; the attention is not focused on them. Shy or outgoing, all interviewers follow the same guidelines.

The Interview

Here's a list of general guidelines to follow when working with an interviewee:

Before the Interview

1. **Make an appointment** ahead of time.
2. **Do your research** before you go. If your subject has written a book, read it. If she is involved in an organization, find out about it. If she is a cancer survivor, read up on that cancer.
3. **Prepare a list of questions.**

During the Interview

1. **Arrive on time**.
2. If you have to be late, **call ahead**. If you can't call, apologize profusely when you arrive. Work extra hard to overcome your social gaff and have a successful interview.
3. Bring a pencil or pen**,** a notebook, and a device with which to **record the interview**.
4. Ask your subject if you can record **the interview**, but also take notes.
5. **Warn your subject** ahead of time that if she wants something "off the record," she has to say so before she divulges the information. That way, you will stop recording, stop taking notes, and just listen; you will not add this information to your assignment unless you can find it from another source. In journalistic circles, if the subject says she wants to say something "off the record," but she says so *after* she dishes, it is too late. However, you will be conducting a friendly interview, not a journalistic one.
6. Engage in a little **chitchat** before the interview. This will relax your subject. And maybe you.
7. **Be flexible** with your list of questions. The interview may take an interesting turn.
8. **Ask open-ended questions**. These are questions that require more than a yes or no answer. Don't ask, "Did you like being a trapeze artist with the traveling circus?" but "Tell me about your days as a trapeze artist with the traveling circus."
9. **Listen actively**. People who perceive that they are being listened to will talk more openly. Also, being attentive will enable you to ask effective follow-up questions.
10. Do not be afraid of **pauses in the conversation**. Many times this is just the time when your interviewee will become uncomfortable and fill in the silence with something interesting. Assume that a conversational gap is simply an opportunity.
11. **Follow tangents**, but only if they take you somewhere interesting. If you learn that your trapeze artist lost a partner due to a fall, ask more about it. But if you find that the tangent is only wasting time and that your readers will not be interested in the information, politely move on.
12. **Ask your interviewee** if there is something else she would like to say. Often the informality of the question elicits an interesting response.

After the Interview

1. **Thank your interviewee** for her time. When you get home, send a thank-you note.
2. Offer to send a **copy of the write-up** to your interviewee. Journalists are not required to do this and, in fact, usually avoid offering to send a copy unless it is in the original contract with the interviewee. But as a friend, neighbor, or family member, this is polite and often can be useful in double-checking facts.
3. **Double-check your facts** before submitting your paper. Sometimes your subject will not properly remember names, dates, organizations, and so forth. You may have to do a little digging to make sure your facts are accurate.

Practice 22.1

You are going to interview someone famous. Choose your person and write his or her name below. Then brainstorm a list of questions to ask your subject. Be mindful of what readers will want to know. (Often what you are curious about, readers are, too.)

Famous person:

Questions:

Lesson 2

The Narrative

You've got your notes. You've got your recorded session. You've got your assignment glaring up at you. How do you develop this question-and-answer interview into a story readers will be interested in?

Find an interesting anecdote for a beginning and remember the QSFSQ tools you learned long ago in this course: question, statement, fact, story, or quotation. What stands out in the interview that might catch the attention of your readers? Is there an interesting disparity between her age and what she has accomplished? Between her humble beginnings and her present success? Did she learn to do something readers might find interesting? Find the hook and begin there.

Your paper will **not** look like a question-and-answer interview:

Student on Assignment: Tell me about your life as a trapeze artist.

Interesting Interviewee: My mother was a trapeze artist, and I grew up watching her graceful figure fly across the tent. I thought, "If I can be as good as her, I'll be successful."

SA: And you certainly have been. What circus did you begin with?

II: The first one I worked with was the one I grew up in—the Karloff Flying Circus. Any of the children of the performers who wanted a spot anywhere in the circus were offered one, as long as they were good enough. There were some who never could learn the acts. They became the managers.

Your write-up will take a different form. You are going to weave a narrative, a story based on what your person has told you, and you will choose a feature or time period in your subject's life and write about it.

In the monthly column on heroes, *Reader's Digest* writers do just that. Gail Cameron Wescott interviewed Ednei Lima, a man who jumped off a bridge to save another man who was trying to commit suicide. Here's part of Wescott's narrative, titled "Into the Still River":

> On their way home, Lima and his girlfriend, Adriana Pelegrini, saw a man through their rain-spattered windshield. He was walking near the center of the Casper Street bridge.
>
> To the couple's horror, the man climbed up onto one of the cement barriers and, right before their eyes, jumped off, plunging into the swirling waters of the Still River some 20 feet below.

Wescott describes the couple as horrified. Did one of them say in the interview, "We were horrified"? Maybe. Maybe not. But Wescott describes for her readers the reaction Ednei and Adriana had as they watched someone jump off a bridge. Did anyone say the waters were swirling? Who knows? But that evening there had been a "violent storm," and because Wescott did her homework, she found that the date of the storm matched the date of the rescue, and she also learned the conditions of the storm-laden Still River by asking the victim, the rescuer, and residents.

Wescott did not *report*; she used her skills as a *storyteller*.

What does your interviewee look like? Include a brief description, with an age, so readers can "see" your subject. Use the descriptive techniques you learned in chapter 20.

One useful form for writing your narrative is to begin with an interesting story but leave it hanging in the middle. Then backtrack some and give readers a little background, some context in which to view the interrupted story. When you catch up to the story chronologically, end your narrative with the rest of the interesting story and a quote from your subject to sum up the experience or what she learned from it.

Wescott tells a story about a rescue. You will tell a story, too. Whose will you tell?

This student interviewed her grandmother (343 words). She chose not an event but a feature of her grandmother's life. The names and places have been changed. Read this interview-into-narrative and be ready to answer questions.

Practice 22.2
Do they make the grade?

Though just married, Billi Jo and Gordon Benson were not eating wedding cake but hamburgers. The couple had had a simple ceremony at the parsonage with two friends present and no reception afterwards. The year? 1947.

Growing up as a farmer's daughter, Billi Jo had experienced a content childhood with very few material things. Even something as common as a bicycle was an amazing gift for her as a young girl. Her uncle once offered her a new bike if she would take care of a sickly aunt for the summer.

"He told me if I came and stayed with her the whole summer, he'd give me a bicycle. That to me was like somebody telling' me they'd buy me a new car."

Although her family was very poor and she had just a few dresses, Billi Jo never went hungry. "We always had plenty to eat because Daddy was a farmer." She added, "Mother made most of my clothes. Out of flour sacks, uh-huh. One of the prettiest dresses I ever owned was made out of a blue and white—a white background with blue flowers. It had a square neck and puffed sleeves. Oh, it was so pretty. It was just a cotton fabric."

Before marrying Billi Jo, Gordon had been drafted for World War II at only 18 years of age. During his stationing, Billi Jo and Gordon could never call each other; therefore, Billi Jo wrote letters nearly every day while anxiously awaiting her loved one to return from England. While Gordon was in England, Billi Jo worked in a factory making gas masks for the service men. Gordon returned home in 1946. They were married the next year.

Gordon died suddenly of a heart attack in 1986, at the age of sixty-two. "Life just hasn't been the same since," says Billi Jo.

My grandma, Billi Jo Benson, is now in her eighties. She has a good life with four loving children and many grandchildren but admits, "We didn't have as much then, but I think times were better."

Answer these questions on a separate piece of paper:

1. Does this student begin her story with an interesting first paragraph?
2. Is her ending effective?
3. What else do you want to know about Billi Jo?
4. What aspect or feature of her grandmother's life does this student highlight?
5. How does her use of her grandmother's dialect and speech patterns enrich the narrative or distract from it?
6. Give this paper a grade and explain it.

Another student wrote this narrative from an interview she had with her dad (297 words). The topic? The father-son relationship. Read it and be ready to answer questions.

Jack Higgins, my dad, was only 15 years old in 1976. It was a tough time for my dad and his dad. They were alike in so many ways and both stubborn. And they were having a hard time getting along because my dad was being rebellious.

Jacques, my grandfather, asked the Lord to help him build a stronger relationship with his son, and he talked with his pastor about what he should do.

"When people work together, it helps bring them closer together. Build a hotrod or fix up an old car," replied his pastor.

My grandfather didn't much care about cars, but he did know a lot about airplanes. After praying and talking to his wife, they unanimously agreed to make the sacrifices that it would take to build this airplane.

Many interesting things happened. In late 1977, my dad and his cousin drove from Chicago to St. Louis to pick up a fuselage kit. On their way home, they were stuck in some little town because of an ice storm.

Building the aircraft took a long time. The wings, 17 feet each, were assembled on top of the pool table in the living room. They did a lot of the welding in the garage.

Two and a half years after they began building the plane, it was time for a test flight. In July 1980, a local pilot took the plane, dubbed "The Cubby," on its first ride through the sky. The J-3 Cub performed without a hitch.

My dad said, "This was the neatest thing in my life." He enjoyed working with his dad as they built a great relationship. They have done numerous projects since then, right up until my grandpa died two years ago. No project, however, ever matched that plane.

Answer the questions on a separate piece of paper:

1. Does she begin with an interesting hook?
2. Is her ending effective? Explain.
3. Do you find the rest of the narrative interesting?
4. What do you wish she had included in her narrative?
5. Where could she have expanded her narrative?
6. Give this paper a grade and explain it.

Write a Narrative

Interview someone. Then write the interview in narrative form (a story).

Proofread with Be Your Own Editor on page 164.

Word count for **beginning** writers: at least 400 words.

Word count for **intermediate** and **accomplished** writers: at least 600.

Check this out for your narrative derived from an interview:

- ❑ Did you conduct an interview?
- ❑ Is the title interesting?
- ❑ Is your article double-spaced?
- ❑ Does the opening sentence or paragraph grab your reader's attention by using an intriguing QSFSQ?
- ❑ Did you turn the interview into a true story of interest?
- ❑ Did you know that according to dumbwarnings.com, ironing your clothing can be dangerous? The Rowenta iron includes this warning: "Never iron clothes on the body." Well, I won't do that again.
- ❑ Did you quickly describe your interviewee so readers can see him or her? ("He is a tall, quiet man" or "Petite, with blonde hair, she appears fragile. But wait until you see her handle a horse that is head and shoulders taller than she is.")
- ❑ Did you add narrative action along the way that adds to the description? (For example: Nina wept as she recalled her partner's fall from the trapeze. She put up one gnarled hand. "I wouldn't be able to catch him today, either," she said.)
- ❑ Which form did you choose? Check one:

    ○ A feature of the person's life
    ○ An interesting slice of the person's life

❑ Did you pepper your narrative with quotations from your subject that help move the story along?

❑ Have you anticipated questions from your readers and included the answers in the narrative?

❑ Did you enjoy the interview process?

Fill in the chart with writing tasks to help you finish on time. If you wish, you may adapt the chart at the end of chapter 4 to your current needs.

Day 1	Day 2	Day 3	Day 4	Day 5	Day 6

> "The fact is that anybody who has survived his childhood has enough information about life to last him the rest of his days."
> - Flannery O'Connor

Chapter 23: Personal Narrative

Lesson 1

What's Your Story?

You have a story to tell. Things have happened to you, you have done things, and you have learned things.

Whether you consider your life to be boring or exciting, you have a story that most likely will interest other people.

Writing a personal narrative is simply telling a story of something that happened to you. Did you have an interesting experience at camp or on vacation? Do you remember how traumatic it was to learn how to ride a bike? Did you help your team win an important game? Does your family have any quirky habits that would be worth a story?

Check out the prompts on the next page to get you thinking about writing your own personal story.

- What's the craziest thing you did as a kid?
- Write about finding something you lost.
- Write about a time when you were stuck somewhere.
- What is your first childhood memory?

- Write about a time when you received a warning but ignored it.
- What's the most painful thing you've endured?
- Do you hate it when your family has to move?
- Do you have a collection? What started it, how did you get it, and who gave it to you?
- "The last time I was really happy was when . . ."
- Write about a time you were brave . . . or wish you had been.
- Have you been through a natural disaster?
- Write about a time when you met someone famous.
- "I knew it was the wrong thing to do, but . . ."
- Do you know how to water-ski? Mountain climb? Juggle? How did you learn? What experiences have you had with this ability?
- Do you know how to drive? Who taught you? What was it like to drive alone for the first time?
- Write about how you are battling a disease.
- Write about a strange coincidence that occurred to you.
- Have you ever had a hunch? Did you follow it?
- What are you secretly proud of accomplishing?
- What's the weirdest thing you've eaten?
- What have you survived?

You have plenty of options from which to choose. In fact, you probably can think of some other interesting prompts. If so, write them in the margin.

Here are some things to keep in mind when writing your story:

- ✓ Let readers know the **setting** (time and place) or your story early on.
- ✓ Create a **mood** by use of specific words and images. (Examples: *crackling air, oppressive weight of the air on my skin*, and so on.)
- ✓ If you move in time or place, write **transitions** to let your reader keep up with you. (Examples: *later that evening, the next day during the storm, after the lightning strike, in the hospital, back at home*, and so forth)
- ✓ Tell your story **chronologically**.
- ✓ After each important event, write your **thoughts**, **feelings**, and/or physical **reactions** or responses to it. (Examples: "The hairs on my arm stood up," "I felt jolts of electricity slam into me. How could I have been so stupid?" "Would I live long enough to play in the big Monopoly match? Would I even know how to play it anymore? I felt confused and lightheaded," and so on.)
- ✓ Conclude with the **lessons** you have learned from the event or with the **significance** of the story now that you are older and see it from a different perspective.

Avoid making your conclusion into a lesson for the reader. This tendency to teach in your narrative makes the reader feel snookered; he thought he was reading an interesting story, but, instead, he found a lecture. Keep your "lessons learned" or "significance" paragraph focused on you and what you learned, not on what others should get from your story. Your readers will learn something from you. Let it come naturally.

This student wrote about baseball and his participation on a team (333 words). Read his personal narrative and be prepared to answer questions.

Practice 23.1

As I approach the field with my bat on my shoulder and my glove in my hand, I start to sweat already from the hot afternoon sun beating down relentlessly. I spot a few of my teammates warming up in front of the first-base dugout, and I know that it is a great day for baseball.

Setting, mood, physical reaction (sweat), thoughts (I know that it is a great day…)

One at a time, the rest of my teammates arrive, and soon we are all out in the field, looking pretty snazzy in our colorful, matching uniforms, snapping the ball back and forth, yelling and joking, and trying to psyche the other team out. Then we all trot into the dugout, anxiously checking the lineup, and chat on the bench about how good the other team's pitcher is and who the best guy might be to hit a pop fly to. I remember that for every game so far, Rogers has hit at least a double or a triple, but he is nonchalant when we ask if he is planning on hitting one again.

Transition

After each inning, we all return to the dugout a little slower because the midsummer heat is taking its toll. But we are sure giving the other team a run for their money.

Transition

Finally, we're triumphant in the seventh inning, and we go out single file to shake hands with our opponents. I ponder my teammates: we are all from different backgrounds and possess different skills, but we have come together to form a perfect union—a baseball team.

Significance of the event and what it means to him

Baseball, for the last century, has been a common bonding link for American boys, the never-failing institution that makes them want to pick up a bat and wave it defiantly at all opposition. Does baseball still hold the same magic? For some, yes; they can still steal second base with an innocent smirk, or stare down the pitcher good-naturedly with a 3-and-2 count. I am honored to have had the chance to participate in the grand old tradition of baseball.

Personal musings, reactions to baseball

Answer the questions:

1. Do you like this young man's personal narrative? Explain.

2. Underline the verbs in the second paragraph that give motion to his narrative.

3. In what tense does he write his story?

4. Sum up in 20 words or less what his experience meant to him.

5. Give this paper a grade and explain it.

Lesson 2

Sensory Info and Reactions Again?

Include **sensory information** in your narrative. What did that old shoe smell like? How did the wind feel on your face? Just how cold were you? Readers enter stories through their senses, so be sure to include enough to put your readers in the scene.

Include **reactions to events** in your narrative. How did you react when you saw you had your shirt on inside out? Then what did you do? What did your gut do when you put your foot on the brakes and nothing happened? When you write about an event but don't show a reaction, readers will not think the event is important. They will not care about it. Or they simply will not know how to interpret the event. Appeal to their empathy and interest by adding sensory information and reactions in your story.

Practice 23.2 Do they make the grade?

A student wrote this personal narrative (764 words) about a backyard game. While the tone of the baseball narrative is reflective, this one is action packed and energetic. Check out his sensory information and reactions to events.

It was a gorgeous winter afternoon with the once lush, green yard covered in two feet of snow. The last leaf had fallen months ago, and the last chirping summer bird was all but forgotten. Snowplows and salt trucks were kings of the road.

Dressed like a special op in alpine gear, I cautiously stuck my head out the rear deck door and prepared for sudden ambush. Frosty air hit my face and shocked my lungs. Not to worry. I was armed with every plastic gun and Nerf weapon known to man. But even with all the destructive weaponry that a twelve-year-old would give his retainer for, I shivered with anticipation to what lay ahead of me in my snow-covered backyard. This yard is a Nerf sniper's wonderland filled with pine trees, bushes, and a large open area in the center. As soon as my foot mushed the slushy snow under my boot, I hightailed it for cover in the frozen tomato garden. As I lay there in the snow, assessing the situation, I switched on my mobile headset walkie-talkie for a brief recon report of the field from my comrade Pete. He was warming himself in our neatly dug snow fort, complete with its vast arsenal of snowballs.

Wounded from the shrapnel of many icy snowballs, I began the tedious jog through the snow to camp and returned victoriously to our base camp. As I crouched behind our snow fort's impenetrable wall, I smoked a victory icicle and reminisced with Lieutenant Pete over our decisive victory against our brothers, Gabe and Sandy. Pete was still armed to the teeth with hidden snow grenades and plastic guns. He described to me how he had sneaked up on his brother while Sandy was distracted, beaning him with a perfectly placed snow grenade. I recounted to Pete how I had impaled my brother with a Nerf arrow and had sent him into a snow pile. Ah, what great war victories we had achieved against our kid brothers. Little did we know that the enemy was preparing their most devastating weapon yet. The ASB, otherwise known as the Atomic Snow Bomb, was about to be unleashed.

Just to play it safe, we fabricated plans for a final spy mission into enemy territory. I nominated Pete. So Pete, being the courageous soldier he pretended to be, began the dangerous walk to the enemy's camp. He carried binoculars and remained in close radio contact with me at camp.

Some time passed, and the winter sun began its quick descent into the knee-deep snow. I nestled into a cramped, quiet snow tunnel and breathed out a sigh that immediately turned into steam. Pete's voice finally crackled over the black two-way radio, relaying his position. He reported that he had penetrated the enemy's construction facility and was now deep inside the bowels of the enemy fortress with no sign of a guard in sight.

I found that to be a little odd. Why would the enemy abandon their fort? Then it hit me. Pete's voice screeched over the radio, sending me flying into the cave wall of snow, crashing the tunnel in on me.

"It's a trap!" I screamed over and over, jamming the button down on the walkie-talkie. It was too late. The enemy had overtaken Pete with an ASB. Pete immediately disintegrated into a mushy, icy pulp.

I grabbed my binoculars and spied from my vantage point the icy forms of Nerf crossbows and an ASB. The enemy was creeping closer and closer to my location. I hightailed it to the garage, slid on the icy patio, and lost my balance, landing right at the feet of the man with the ASB.

"Surrender!" he shouted.

"Never!" I screamed back as I executed a powerful flip and slid under cover of the parked van. After what seemed like an eternity, Sandy and I charged at each other, he brandishing five huge snow grenades and I with my plastic gun.

We met, slipped, and sprawled out on the snow, where we lay making snow angels.

From this and many other friendly snow wars, I have learned three valuable lessons. Lesson number one I learned the hard way: Never trust a brother with a snowball in his hand, even if he is grinning. Lesson number two I learned the frustrating way: Brother versus brother doesn't work. Someone gets hurt, and then someone gets mad. But the most valuable lesson is lesson number three: Good friends who know how to wage an incredibly fun and nasty snow war are extremely difficult to find.

Answer the questions:

1. Do you like this young man's personal narrative? Explain.

2. What extended metaphor does he use for the afternoon snowball fight?

3. How does the metaphor add to the enjoyment of the narrative?

4. Underline one of his reactions. Underline twice one sensory impression.
5. In the last paragraph, is he telling you what you should have learned from his narrative, or is he recounting what he learned?
6. Give this paper a grade and explain it.

One more student narrative (409 words). This gal and her sisters are watching a movie—or trying to. Her narrative is not about the movie but about the reactions to it. What would your reaction be?

The house is dark except for the glow of the TV, silent except for the hushed dialogue of the movie, and still except for an occasional movement of my sisters on the couch. The salty, buttery aroma of popcorn drifts about the room. Everything is peaceful.

It's 12:30 at night. Just we three sisters are awake. Mom and Dad went to bed over an hour ago. *Pride and Prejudice*, our movie of choice, is almost over.

"This is sappy," says Deena, our youngest sister. "Why can't someone die or something?"

"Shhh," says Amanda, the oldest.

A romantic melody floats out of the speakers. Amanda sighs while Deena fidgets. I sit in a squeaky rocking chair, watching my sisters and the movie while I crochet absentmindedly. Soft yarn slides over my fingers without effort.

The relative silence is soon broken. Deena covers her eyes with her hands; her face is twisted in an offended grimace.

"Gross!" she says, moaning loudly. Evidently her hands are not sufficient protection from the mushy scene, so she reaches for a pillow and mashes it into her face with a groan. This draws a response from Amanda.

"Go to bed if it bothers you," she says. Her aggravation mounts as she tries to watch the end of the movie and block out Deena, but soon Amanda becomes more engrossed in it and grows quiet. Her eyes are focused on the television screen. *Mr. Darcy leans forward to kiss Lizzy and . . .*

"Eww! What's this movie rated?" says Deena.

She breaks our concentration. We sit back. The effect of the scene is ruined by her outburst.

"It should be rated *R*!" Of course she had removed the pillow from her face at the critical time in the movie.

"Can't you just be quiet?" says Amanda.

"But that's disgusting!" She points to the TV and stares at Amanda, eyes wide, a look of disbelief on her face. Ignoring her, Amanda watches as the credits roll by. I lay my crochet hook aside, click on the lamp, and begin to take dishes into the kitchen.

"What a stupid ending! He marries her!" Deena says. Appalled that the movie had a happily-ever-after ending, she tromps up the stairs to bed.

"Why aren't there any real guys like Mr. Darcy?" Amanda asks. She has taken care of her things and is getting ready to head upstairs, too.

"Don't know," I say. Click. The house goes completely dark.

Write a Personal Narrative

Write a personal narrative—a story about something that happened to you. Use the prompts in the beginning of this chapter if you get stuck for subject matter.

Include your physical and mental reactions to the events in your narrative. Also include sensory information. Bring the readers along with you.

Write a conclusion about the lessons you learned from your experience or what its significance is to you.

This is the last assignment of this course (yay!). Consider reading your narrative aloud to your family or class as a parting gift to them.

Proofread with Be Your Own Editor on page 164 and 395.

Word count for **beginning** writers: at least 400 words. Word count for **intermediate** and **accomplished** writers: at least 500.

For one last, weary time, check out this checklist:

- ❏ Did you tell your story chronologically?
- ❏ Did you make it interesting by use of a device such as an extended metaphor, present tense, humor, word choice, and so on?
- ❏ Did you include how you reacted to events in your narrative (thoughts, feelings, physical reactions, and so forth)?
- ❏ Did you include sensory information?
- ❏ Does your conclusion focus on the meaning of *your* experience?
- ❏ This is your last assignment in this course. Are you doing a happy dance?

Day 1	Day 2	Day 3	Day 4	Day 5	Day 6

THIS IS THE END OF THE COURSE!!! YOU MADE IT TO THE END!!!
SHOULDN'T THERE BE A PARTY OR SOMETHING?

Part 7: Reference

Your Toolbox

Be Your Own Editor

"Write down the revelation and make it plain…." (Habakkuk 2:2)

1. **Reread** your paper:
   - Does it have an interesting title?
   - Is it double-spaced?
   - Does the opening sentence or paragraph grab the reader's attention by using an intriguing question, statement, fact, story, or quotation?
   - Is the thesis statement near the end of the introduction?
   - Does your paper support the thesis statement?
   - Does your paper get to the point quickly? Does it stick to the point?
   - Are the topic sentences clear and fitting for each paragraph?
   - Is there a logical progression from one point to the next?
   - Is it easy to read and easy to understand?
   - Does it deliver what your title, introduction, and thesis statement promise?
   - Did you follow the assignment directions?
2. Read your paper **aloud**. Are words missing? Are you too wordy? Are you redundant? Are you really saying what you want to say? Are you using cliché's?
3. **Streamline** your writing for more impact. Do you use strong verbs instead of turning them into nouns? Do you most often use the active voice? Do you write with a specific audience in mind? Do you vary your sentence lengths and structures? Are you careful with your word order?
4. Check the **spelling**. Even a computer won't catch *there, their,* or *they're* mistakes.
5. Check the **punctuation**.
6. Check the **grammar**. Don't rely entirely on your computer. Use your head and a good reference book.
7. Use these **tricks** to catch more mistakes:
   - Proofread from a printed copy of your paper, not the screen.
   - Resize the font or choose another font to aid in your editing. This moves the words into new positions, making it easier to catch mistakes you normally would read over.
   - Read your paper aloud. Your ears will catch some mistakes for you.

Point Orders

Importance or emphatic orders:
- Inverted triangle
- Psychological order
- Climactic order

Chronological order
Spatial order
Effect-size order
Specific-to-general order
General-to-specific order

Introductory Paragraph Tools

- **Q:** An intriguing **question**
- **S:** A thought-provoking **statement**
- **F:** A shocking, tantalizing, or to-the-point **fact**
- **S:** An engaging **story**
- **Q:** A clever **quotation**

Paragraph Types

Direct: Topic sentence is the first sentence and is a declarative statement

Climactic: Topic sentence is the last sentence

Interrogative: Topic sentence is a question

Transitional: Moves essay from one topic to the next

Turnabout: Begins with opposing view and then refutes it

Effect to cause: Topic sentence is the effect; the rest of the paragraph explores what caused it

Enumerative: Topic sentence shows parts; rest of the paragraph lists the parts

Comparison and contrast: Paragraph compares and/or contrasts an element; topic sentence may appear at the beginning or at the transition of the two topics

Problem to solution: Topic sentence states a problem; rest of the paragraph seeks to solve the problem

Paragraph Essentials

Unity: Everything in the paragraph belongs there and supports the topic sentence.

Completeness: The topic is adequately covered in the paragraph.

Cohesion: The paragraph sticks together by use of writing devices such as synonyms, antonyms, parallel sentence structures, sets of contrasting words, repetition of key words, and so forth.

Don't List for Persuasion

1. Don't insult a person or an entire group of people.
2. Don't wander off your subject.
3. Don't go on and on.
4. Don't contradict yourself.
5. Don't rant and rave.
6. Don't write without evidence; don't exclude facts.
7. Don't threaten your audience.
8. Don't be vague.
9. Don't forget your audience.
10. Don't use jargon, lingo, slang, or technical words unless you define them right away.
11. Don't be illogical; that is, don't draw wrong conclusions, make sweeping generalizations, present false dilemmas, and so forth.
12. Don't use "I believe...," "I think...," "It is my opinion that...," "I choose to believe...," or "I feel that...."
13. Don't announce what you are going to write. Just write it.

Do List for Persuasion

1. Know your audience.
2. Define your terms.
3. Indicate your topic early.
4. Treat your reader intelligently.
5. Write about an opposing view fairly. Know the argument.
6. Be concise. Stay focused on your objective.
7. Be logical and orderly.
8. Identify yourself with regard to your topic (only if it adds weight to what you write).
9. Quote people, experts, or the Bible.*
10. Tell a relevant story.*
11. Use humor if the situation calls for it, but use it sparingly.*
12. Be positive. Have a "we can fix this" attitude.
13. Issue a specific call to action.
14. Maintain an objective tone, if appropriate.

* optional tools

Logical Persuasion List

1. Use reliable evidence.
2. Use logical thinking to build your case.
3. Avoid logical fallacies.
4. Know the argument. State an opposing view fairly and then refute it.
5. Use quotations from knowledgeable people in the field about which you are writing, especially when disproving an opposing view.
6. Cite your sources correctly.

Moral/ethical persuasive essay (or speech)

1. In the first paragraph or two, give your readers a little bit of **background** so they know what the issue is and what has been done about it in the past. This gives a historical perspective and puts the issue in a "frame" for your audience. Keep this section short and interesting; you don't want to lose your readers.

2. In the next paragraphs, write about the **moral or ethical line** that shouldn't be crossed. Include facts and quotations. State why crossing the line is wrong. Mention alternatives, if there are any.

3. In the conclusion, **encourage** readers to seek positive moral solutions and to avoid crossing that line.

Moral/ethical letter

1. In the first paragraph, write something **positive** about the company, politician, or celebrity. Be genuine about it.

2. In the following paragraphs, write about the **moral or ethical line** they shouldn't cross (or shouldn't have crossed, if they already have). Explain why.

3. In the last paragraph, **encourage** them to do the right thing.

Emotional Appeal Strategies

1. Do it "for the children."
2. Know when to use loaded words and phrases and when to use neutral ones.
3. Include shared cultural experiences that create a response or remind readers of an emotion.
4. Allude, even obliquely, to other writings (hymns, historical or patriotic documents, Bible verses or characters, Shakespeare, Greek or Roman myths, and so forth).
5. Use repetition. Repeat a key word or phrase for emphasis.
6. Use figurative language.
7. Relate a specific and loaded story to illustrate your point.
8. Use religious or patriotic words in ways different from their original meaning.
9. Use flattery.
10. Use ridicule.

The questionable tactics

Methods of Persuasion Compared

Logical   Two or three premises on the nutritional value—protein, dairy, fiber content—of hamburgers will lead to the logical conclusion that your readers should eat more hamburgers. You can cite facts from experts on how many burgers people eat daily around the world, how nutritional they are, how the industry ensures the meat to be healthy, and so forth. You also can set up an opposing argument to be refuted by a quotation from a McDonald's executive or a government employee who works in the cattle industry stating how safe, healthful, and economically sound eating burgers is. Key sentence: "I'll prove it!"

Compare and Contrast   You can choose similar burgers from two fast-food restaurants and show the readers the similarities and differences of all the features, with an eye toward nudging the readers to choose one of the burgers over the other. Or you might select a burger and a chicken sandwich from the same restaurant and compare the features, taste, and nutritional values of both, guiding the reader to choose one. Key sentence: "*That* is bad, but *this* is worse" (or some variation: "*That* is tasty, but *this* is tastier").

Moral/Ethical   This method can be effective when writing about animal rights, humane treatment of the animals from which the burgers are made, or the ethics of a fast-food joint on every corner. Because this is a persuasive essay, you will convince readers to frequent burger joints more often, boycott them because of questionable practices, or join an animal rights' group that works for more humane treatment of animals tagged for slaughter. Key sentence: "You've crossed the line" or "Here is the line. Don't cross it."

Emotional Appeal   You might appeal to your readers' sense of hunger in this method. In other words, make them feel hungry! Write about the juicy, steamy, sizzling burger, the cheese that melts before your eyes, and the crisp lettuce wedged between the bun and the burger. Then you might describe taking large bites to taste the soft coolness of the bun against the hot saltiness of the burger. Your readers will salivate. Their stomachs will growl. They'll buy the burger. Key sentence: "Use an emotion to plant the notion."

How to Write a How-to

1. **Write an introduction** to set the mood and tell readers what you are going to teach them.
2. **List items** or ingredients the readers will need.
3. Go **step by step** chronologically.
4. **Be clear** in your instructions.
5. **Use transition words** and phrases between the steps.
6. Include **charts or pictures**, if necessary.
7. **Define** any jargon.
8. **Write a conclusion** to tell readers what to do once they're finished.

Biography Slants

1. **Write about a person you respect.** In this biography, you write about the achievements and character traits you value in this person and how he or she exhibited them.

2. **Write about a person you don't respect.** Choose someone in history or in the public eye, not a friend, neighbor, or family member. Write about your subject's negative qualities and fiascos.

3. **Write about a person who overcame great difficulties.** In this slant, you write about your subject's difficulties and how she overcame them, how she battled on despite them, or what she accomplished in spite of her woes. People who have battled disease, mental illness, discrimination, or troubling childhoods are good candidates for this kind of biography. Highlight the personality trait that got her through the tough times.

4. **Write about a person who invented something interesting.** Who invented the iPod? The BlackBerry? The atom bomb? Velcro? Windshield wipers? How did they get these ideas? What made him interested in inventing or in this particular product? Highlight how he invented it and how it has affected his life and the lives of others.

5. **Write about a person from his creation's point of view.** Rudyard Kipling's life might look interesting through Mowgli's eyes. What would the curate in H. G. Wells' *The War of the Worlds* write about his creator? The September 2005 *Reader's Digest* features "Out of the Hat," an article about the animator Chuck Jones as told from Bugs Bunny's point of view. Not only does it trace the development of Mr. Jones and his interest in cartooning but it also shows his impact on the Bugs Bunny character. Very clever.

6. **Write about a person who was told he would never be successful—and then was.** *Reader's Digest* printed "Yes, I Can," an article that reveals the stories of seven successful people who had been told they would be failures. Included in the stories is a man who did terribly in school but who later, through hard work and tenacity, became a famous filmmaker (Steven Spielberg).

7. **Write about a person from the point of view of a pet,** a close friend or relative, or an inanimate object he used during his life. Robert Lawson does this in *Ben and Me*, a story about the inventive side of Benjamin Franklin as told by a mouse who traveled in Ben's hat or pocket. According to the mouse narrator, all of Franklin's inventions were the mouse's idea. What could Oscar Wilde's jail cell tell us about that famous writer?

8. **Write about a person in a "Who Am I?" manner.** Cram the biography full of interesting things about your subject but don't tell who the person is until near the end of your paper. This keeps the reader guessing and creates an interest in him or her.

9. **Write about a person's spiritual journey.** Trace your subject's spiritual development and how he or she grew to believe something. This method is effective if the person experienced a great change in his or her life or is known for believing one thing but began somewhere else.

Compare and Contrast—Three Methods

Method 1: Block
Section 1: Introduction
Section 2: The first topic
Section 3: The second topic
Section 4: Conclusions

Example
Section 1: Introduction
Section 2: WW I noteworthy facts
Section 3: WW II noteworthy facts
Section 4: Conclusions

Method 2: Elements or Features
Section 1: Introduction
Section 2: Element 1
Section 3: Element 2
Section 4: Element 3
Section 5: Conclusions

Example
Section 1: Introduction
Section 2: What the wars were about
Section 3: Where the wars were fought
Section 4: What ended the wars
Section 5: Conclusions

Method 3: Similarities and Differences
Section 1: Introduction
Section 2: Similarities of the two topics
Section 3: Differences between the two topics
Section 4: Conclusions

Example
Section 1: Introduction
Section 2: Similarities of the wars
Section 3: Differences in the wars
Section 4: Conclusions

OR

Method 3, still
Section 1: Introduction
Section 2: Differences between the two topics
Section 3: Similarities of the two topics
Section 4: Conclusions

Example
Section 1: Introduction
Section 2: Differences in the wars
Section 3: Similarities of the wars
Section 4: Conclusions

Acknowledgments

(in order of appearance)

Chapter 4

Visser, Sonia. Letter. *Kokomo Tribune* 14 Apr. 2007. Print.

Letter. *Kokomo Tribune* 18 Oct. 2000. Print.

Vasicek, Edward. "How to raise a bratty child." *Kokomo Tribune* 22 Sept. 2005. Print.

Deyoe, Alexandra. Letter. *Kokomo Tribune* 23 Dec. 2005. Print.

York, Barry J. Letter. *Kokomo Tribune* 1 Oct. 2002. Print.

Kerry, John. Letter. Dear Abby. *Kokomo Tribune* 20 May 2004. Print.

Chapter 5

Way, Tom. "Dihydrogen Monoxide FAQ." *Dihydrogen Monoxide Research Division*. Tom Way, n.d. Web. 10 May 2012.

Mikkelson, Barbara and David. "The Ten-percent Myth." *Urban Legends Reference Pages*. Snopes, 21 July 2007. Web. 10 May 2012.

Chudler, Eric, Ph.D. "Myths about the Brain: 10 Percent and Counting." *Brain Connection*. Posit Science, n.d. Web. 10 May 2012.

Dawkins, Richard. Review of *Blueprints: Solving the Mystery of Evolution*, by Maitland A. Edey and Donald C. Johanson. *New York Times* 9 Apr. 1989:7, 34. Print.

Levitt, Arnie. Letter. *USA TODAY* 28 June 2007. Print.

Ertelt, Steven. Letter. *The Spencer Evening World*. Print.

Chapter 6

Cinergy Public Safety. Advertisement. WFMS, Indianapolis, Indiana, 1 Oct. 2004. Radio. Used with permission of Cinergy Services, Inc.

Rickel, Tim. Letter. *Kokomo Tribune* 2 July 2004: A. Print.

Goldberg, Jonah. "The Evolution of Religious Bigotry." *Town Hall*. Townhall.com, 2 Apr. 2008. Web. 10 May 2012. © Tribune Content Agency, LLC. All Rights Reserved. Reprinted with permission.

Chapter 7

Earley, Mark. "Writing Love on Their Arms," *BreakPoint*. Prison Fellowship, 9 May 2008. Web. 10 May 2012. From *BreakPoint*, May 9, 2008, reprinted with permission of Prison Fellowship, www.breakpoint.org.

Nathanson, Bernard. "Confessions of an Ex-Abortionist." Catholic Education Resource Center, 1997. Web. 10 May 2012.

Chapter 8

Edwards, Jonathan. *Sinners in the Hands of an Angry God*. New Kensington, PA: Whitaker House, 1997. Print.

Milton, John. *Paradise Lost*. New York: Barnes & Noble Classics, 2004. Print.

Ham, Ken. Letter to *Answers in Genesis* subscribers. Aug. 2005. Print.

Mooney, Michael G. "Valley air hits children hardest." *The Modesto Bee* 28 Apr. 2005: A1. Print.

"Undercurrents." *Numb3rs*. CBS. 12 May 2006. Television.

"November: There's never been a better time to own a TV." *TV Guide* 23-31 Oct. 1997: back cover. Print.

The Holy Bible: The New International Version. Grand Rapids, Mich.: Zondervan Bible Publishers, 1978.
    Print.

Chapter 11

Paine, Albert Bigelow, ed. *Mark Twain's Letters, Vol. II*. New York: Harper & Brothers Publishers, 1917.
    Print.

Keillor, Garrison. *We Are Still Married*. New York: Viking, 1989. Print.

Derbyshire, John. "The Paomnnehal Pweor of the Hmuan Mnid." *The Corner*. National Review Online, 7
    May 2004. Web. 25 May 2012.

Chapter 12

Cairns, William B., ed. *Benjamin Franklin's Autobiography*. New York: Longmans, Green and Company,
    1909. Print.

Stiller, Gary. "Fear of Flying Can Cripple Workers." *USA TODAY* 21 March 2006: A1. Print.

Twain, Mark. *A Connecticut Yankee in King Arthur's Court*. New York: Tom Doherty Associates, 1991.
    Print.

Nickens, T. Edward. "50 Skills: Hunt Better, Fish Smarter, and Master the Outdoors." *Field and Stream*
    May 2008. Print.

Anchell, Steve. "Sharpening Strategies: There's More than One Way to Get it Done." *Digital Photography
    How-To Guide* 2008: 50-3. Print.

Wilder, Laura Ingalls (Mrs. A. J.). "The Great Woods Have Been Destroyed." *Fact and Fiction of Laura
    Ingalls Wilder*. Pioneer Girl, 9 Dec. 2009. Web. 1 Aug. 2011.

Chapter 13

Kennedy, D. James and Jerry Newcombe. *What if Jesus Had Never Been Born?* Nashville: Thomas Nelson
    Publishers, 1994. Print.

Chapter 14

The Holy Bible: The New International Version. Grand Rapids, Mich.: Zondervan Bible Publishers, 1978.
    Print.

Chapter 15

Mitchard, Jacquelyn. "The Woman Behind the Smile." *Parade* 13 Aug. 2006. Print.

"Zoo awaits birth of baby elephant." *Kokomo Tribune* 13 Aug. 2006: A. Print.

"Tourists rescued from kidnappers." *USA TODAY* 30 Sept. 2008: A. Print.

"Protests prevent Mexican leader from giving address." *The Holland* (Michigan) *Sentinel*
    2 Sept. 2006: A. Print.

Iwata, Edward. "How Barbie is making business a little better." *USA TODAY* 27 March
    2006: B. Print.

Chapter 16

Steinbeck, John. From TRAVELS WITH CHARLEY: IN SEARCH OF AMERICA by John Steinbeck, copyright ©
    1961, 1962 by The Curtis Publishing Co.; © 1962 by John Steinbeck; copyright renewed © 1989,

1990 by Elaine Steinbeck, Thom Steinbeck, and John Steinbeck IV. Used by permission of Viking Books, an imprint of Penguin Publishing Group, a division of Penguin Random House LLC.
Kanfer, Stefan. "Out of the Hat." *Reader's Digest* September 2005. Print.
"Yes, I Can." *Reader's Digest* July 2005. Print.

Chapter 17
Atkinson, Mark D. "Two Kinds of Diners." *Focus on the Family* October 2006. Print. Used by permission.

Chapter 18
Hawthorne, Nathaniel. *The Scarlet Letter.* New York: Dover Publications, 1994. Print.
Austen, Jane. *Pride and Prejudice.* New York: The Book League of America, 1940. Print.
Lardner, Ring. *You Know Me Al.* New York: Dover Publications, 1995. Print.
Philbrick, Rodman. *Freak the Mighty.* New York: Scholastic Inc., 1993. Print.
Kindl, Patrice, *Goose Chase.* New York: Scholastic Inc., 2001. Print.
Lee, Harper. *To Kill a Mockingbird.* New York: Perennial, 2002. Print.

Chapter 19
Beecher, Henry Ward. *Seven Lectures to Young Men, on Various Important Subjects.* Indianapolis: Thomas B. Cutler, 1844. Print.

Chapter 20
Kimmel, Haven. *She Got Up Off the Couch.* New York: Free Press, 2004. Print.
Beals, Melba Pattillo. *Warriors Don't Cry.* New York: Washington Square Press, 1994. Print.
Dickinson, Rachel. *Falconer on the Edge: A Man, His Birds, and the Vanishing Landscape of the American West.* New York: Houghton Mifflin Harcourt, 2009. Print.
Dinesen, Isak. *Out of Africa.* New York: Vintage Books, 1985. Print.

Chapter 21
McDowell, Josh. *Evidence that Demands a Verdict.* N.p.: Campus Crusade for Christ, 1972. Print.
Surprised by Joy in *The Inspirational Writings of C. S. Lewis.* New York: Inspirational Press, 1994. Print.

Chapter 22
Westcott, Gail Cameron. "Into the Still River." *Reader's Digest* November 2005. Print.

Index

Made in the USA
Coppell, TX
08 May 2024

32170431R00236